To Howard

A Dear Friend
And A
Great Dentist

The Best Always

Larry Hart

JOURNEY WITH GRANDCHILDREN
A LIFE STORY

Journey with Grandchildren

A Life Story

Lawrence S. Harte

Cover illustration by David McCoy, www.davetoons.com
Cover and interior design by Lynne Adams
Manufactured in the United States
First edition. First printing

ISBN: 978-0-9834752-1-7
Library of Congress Control Number: 2011926433
Publisher's Cataloging-in-Publication Data:
Harte, Lawrence S.
Journey with grandchildren : a life story / Lawrence S. Harte.
p. cm.
ISBN: 978-0-9834752-1-7
1. Brooklyn (New York, N.Y.)—Biography. 2. Brooklyn
(New York, N.Y.) —Social life and customs—20th century.   I. Title.
F129.B7 .H37 2011
974.747—dc22
2011926433

WHITE POPPY PRESS
34 Main Street #9
Amherst, Massachusetts 01002
www.whitepoppypress.com
413-253-2353
White Poppy Press is an imprint of Modern Memoirs, Inc.

To Alexander, Haleigh, Rebecca, and
all of the grandchildren of the world—
may you live life and enjoy it!

Life is like a balloon:

You get a great deal of built-up air in a balloon, and unless you do something, the balloon will burst. It is important that when you have a balloon, you have ways of letting out air from time to time and maintaining the balloon so it can fly in the sky.

It is the same with life! Enjoy!

—*Lawrence S. Harte*

Contents

ACKNOWLEDGMENTS

I would like to sincerely thank those who have been an intricate part of my life and its journey; you are the substance of my soul. This memoir is a result of many years of initiative and constant motivation.

I want to thank my loving children, Douglas, Jonathan, and Helaine. At times, I acted like the person in the movie *The Bicycle Thief*, incapable of truly expressing my feelings and of letting myself go to show vulnerability. Each day when my ankle hurts, my knee squeaks, or my neck stiffens, these all go away through the elixir of feeling that I am so proud of each of you.

Douglas, my Taipan, as the oldest you were stuck with the guilt of "Head of The House of Harte." If anybody else goofed up, it was your fault and you had to take care of the situation. I was so pleased that you came with me to temple and that you became my partner in our practice.

Jonathan, my extra adventurer, I tried to show you the sport of adventure into places unknown and uninhabitable. You have surpassed my reality and my dream by traveling life your way.

Helaine, so many of my dreams you fulfilled. In some way, I vicariously lived my life through your actions (although some of them drove me crazy). I was tougher on you, but I felt that you could handle it.

My thanks to Judi, their mother, the very best mom, who took care of their bloody noses, schoolwork, and everyday activities, which allowed me to pursue my career.

The publication of this book could not have been possible without the efforts and contributions of so many people. Sandy Wills and Marigene Kowalski, my secretaries, who stayed up nights to decipher my handwriting and the slurriness of my tape recorder. Many thanks to my editor, Doryann Carregal, who listened with an attentive ear, transcribed the text from Brooklyn-ese to English, and gave graciously of her feelings. She let me lead the way, but prodded me when I wanted to stray from a sensible path. I also received inspiration and encouragement from a special person, Kathy Phillips, who initially put forth the idea of writing this book.

Finally, to the thousands of people that I have had the good fortune to be touched by—each of you, in your own way, has given me a little piece of your wisdom, your heart, your experience, and your love. From all of me to all of you, I am eternally grateful.

INTRODUCTION

My son Douglas once asked me a question. I told him the answer was in my head. He said, "Dad, get it out of your head and put it on paper or the computer." I soon began to realize that what was once in my head was beginning to fade into distant memories. As my son Jonathan said, "A definition of a memoir is what one remembers or chooses to remember about one's past." My daughter, Helaine, asks me questions these days; it takes me so long to answer that she answers them herself.

Any interpretation of memories is a form of selective hearing and selective amnesia. So, the adventure begins. I have arranged the book into various chapters, each with individual subjects and photos. It was written with the hope that our family, like any other family, will be able to connect with memories of the past, see how life affects us today, and envision our dreams of tomorrow. As the pages of the book come to an end (thank golly), please remember, my children, that as usual, you all will be getting an open-book test. As usual, 100 passes!

This book is a memory of my life. What made me do what I did. How I walked around the streets and looked at people. How I smelled the air, touched and felt everything around me. What brought me from my childhood to who and what I am today. These memories, I think, are the greatest gift to people reading about my love of life and how it affects me, my family, and the world.

When we were kids, we all had dreams, but we were optimists. As bad or as good as the world was, we felt that whatever was given to us, we could make it better. We knew we would be better financially than our parents. We knew that we would be in higher positions than our parents. We hoped that we could give the same love to our children that our parents had tried to give to us.

When I was young, I didn't have any brothers and sisters, and so my life in some ways was lonely, in that I didn't have anybody to shove around or someone to shove me around. That's why I had so many hobbies and became so involved with other people—because they, in turn, became my family. As a youngster, I had a dream, and one of my dreams was, when I got married, to have children. To have a family and try and give my children the love that I possibly never received. This love would not be just material love, but spiritual love. A love that transcends generations. This is what life is truly about.

Life is about dreams and family. My dream came true. My son Doug and his wife, Ronni, have two children, Alex and Haleigh. Alex has brown eyes and hair, is very serious and lovable, and is excellent in golf, chess, and skiing. He is quiet, very articulate, and, in many ways, grown up for his age. Haleigh has bluish-green eyes and strawberry-blond hair. She is rambunctious and independent, loves to dance, follows her brother, Alex, around, and wants everything her way. She is so lovable and always gives me kisses and hugs.

My daughter, Helaine, and her husband, David, have a daughter, Rebecca. She reminds me of Helaine in so many ways. She is pretty and very independent. She wants to do everything herself, and she's a chatterbox. When Helaine was young, I said to her, "I wish a daughter upon you like you were wished upon us!" And I must laugh because it's coming true.

My son Jon and his wife, Belynda, have a 60-pound Labrador retriever, Mesa, their child. He has a very light yellow, kind of blonde fur and dark brown eyes.

Another part of my life is Kathy Phillips, along with her family and her grandson, Nicholas, who is twelve years of age. He has an awesome voice and I sincerely hope that he follows his pursuits in art and music.

In addition, I have made a "family" with those I've met in life along the way.

A memoir is a series of data that I think (or hope) happened in the past. It is my hope that these memories will stimulate future generations to remember the past, actively participate in the present, and dream of the future.

A future in which our country will continue to re-examine itself as a guiding light for the whole world, in which we all will continuously work toward living in peace with freedom and prosperity, and in which we will give our children a little bit more than was given to us. A future in which we have the opportunity of getting on the trains of life, rather than letting the trains go by.

A future in which we can climb mountains, skin our knees, bloody our noses, but say we tried. A future in which to grow older, hopefully remaining healthy, to sit back in the rocking chair under a vibrant, setting sun that hovers over the water without movement, and say, with a twinkle in the eye, "I tried." And not have to say, "If only...."

At times Don Quixote and Sancho Panza, in a mythical way, attempted to make this world a better place, to reach the impossible dream. We—the past, present, and future generations—can achieve the dream.

The Smell of the Roses

Oh give me the song of the open road
And a chance to smell the rose, too

Climb every mountain, act every dream
Fly with ghosts through the air with a view

Stop time to saddle the horses on trails
Hike the roads to test my mettle

Sail my boat over waves of promise and hope
Smell the roses while the bloom is in the petal

Take my pen to paper
My tongue to the ear

My swirling feet to the floor
My reaching hand for a cheer

Fly me to the land of regal souls
Lead me to the hearts of people true

Drive me to the countryside to picnic by the streams
And have the chance to let all I touch
Smell the roses, too

Lawrence S. Harte
March 1989

JOURNEY WITH GRANDCHILDREN
A LIFE STORY

A Walk in the Park

As a kid, every day was forever.
—*Lawrence S. Harte*

The warmth of the sun surrounds us and the first blooms of spring are everywhere. It's a beautiful day for a walk in the park with my dear grandchildren—Alex, Haleigh, and Rebecca, and my grand-dog, Mesa!

As we begin our journey, Mesa sniffs the ground around the trunk of a maple tree and discovers a tiny bird. She gently picks up the robin, fallen from its nest, and brings it to us. Taking the chirping robin into my hands, I have a surge of memories. I think of my son Jonathan, who, as a child, picked up everything he could find off the street.

"Can you guess what this baby robin reminds me of?" I ask.

"I think it reminds you of us!" says Haleigh, taking my hand lightly for a closer look. She is inquisitive, like her dad, Douglas.

"Yes, Haleigh, it reminds me of you all. It also reminds me of my days as a child. This baby robin is trying to fly away from the nest. It tries to fly even though it may fall. It will try and try again until it finally flies away."

"What do you mean, Papa Larry?" Rebecca inquired, looking at the robin.

"All of you want to try things your own way even if you goof up in the beginning. That's how you learn to be independent." I explain.

Alex adds, "I think it reminds you of when you were a Boy Scout, Grandpa!"

I had to laugh because it did bring back memories of bird watching as a scout.

"Yes, Alex, I had a great time scouting and being outdoors. We would camp overnight in the woods in New Jersey. I used a sleeping bag, two blankets, and straw as a pillow."

"Ewww, that's awful!" says Haleigh. "Straw as a pillow!"

Alex laughed. "Did you look like a scarecrow when you woke up?"

"Yes, I probably did! We began our day by making a campfire with flint, steel, and some twigs."

"Doesn't Smokey the Bear say not to make fires in the woods?" asked Alex.

"It's OK if you're careful. We had to cook our food over the fire. We made bread that was not too tasty but we were hungry, so we ate it anyway."

The real fun was exploring and learning to live outdoors. Our troop leader showed us how to track animals and which directions they were headed. We would find berries and mushrooms and learn to distinguish between the edible ones and the poisonous ones.

"Do you know what a compass is?" I asked. They all chimed at once, a loud No!

"It shows us what direction you are heading and keeps you from getting lost."

Out in the woods, I would leave nothing to chance, making notches in the trees and dropping crumbs (only to find out later that birds ate the crumbs).

Alex said to me, "Grandpa, *I'm* going camping this summer. I'm going to Hershey Park, and we are going to camp at a hotel for three nights!"

As I chuckled, Haleigh confirmed, "Me too, Grandpa!"

Alex is Haleigh's idol. Whatever Alex does as an older brother, Haleigh wants part of the action.

I went on to tell them about how we used flags to send Morse code, which is a way of sending messages usually by electric ticker, but also with flags, and how we used a semaphore flag, which is another way of sending messages. We would go to the top of a hill and use the flags to signal and transmit our message to other Boy Scouts at the top of another hill.

Haleigh said to me, "Grandpa, what happened if it became cloudy—did you use your cell phone then?"

"Grandpa didn't have cell phones; that's why they used Morse code to communicate," smiled Alex.

"Morse code," said Rebecca, "an old way to send messages with flags." Rebecca takes after her mother, Helaine, who always had an answer. I cannot wait until Rebecca grows up like her mother. Her mother was always, always chatting.

In a change of conversation, Alex starts telling me about his savings. I asked him, "Do you have money?"

He said, "Oh, yes—I have $212 saved up!"

"That's a lot of money, Alex! How did you get it?"

"Oh, it's pretty easy—every time my mother wants me to try something new to eat, she gives me $5! So, I've learned whenever she gives me something new, I just say no, even if I might like it, and this way if I say no and I try it, she gives me $5. Someday I'm going to be rich, Grandpa, by saying no!"

Oh, to be a kid again!

My mind wanders off into the past—to Brooklyn, my hometown, my house just two blocks from Ebbets Field, where the Brooklyn Dodgers played. My friends and I did so many things at Ebbets Field, like playing behind the field in the parking lot, dreaming that someday we'd be a Brooklyn Dodger.

"Oh, how I remember like it was yesterday, watching my Brooklyn Dodgers. I always wanted to be a pitcher for the Brooklyn Dodgers, and Ebbets Field was, to me, a palace—my only palace."

"I understand, Grandpa. I'm going to play for the Devils someday!" Alex declares. He is a true New Jersey Devils hockey fan and knows all the statistics of the game, just as I knew the statistics when I followed baseball and the Brooklyn Dodgers.

"Hey, do you know there is a place called Camden Yards in Baltimore, and that's where the Baltimore Orioles play now, and there is a new place called Citi Field in Flushing, Queens, where the New York Mets play now? And both of their brand-new stadiums are based on the original design of Ebbets Field. So things come and things go, but some things always stay the same."

"Just like you come and go, but you stay the same, Papa Larry." Rebecca stroked Mesa on the head. I swear I hear Helaine talking. It is like Helaine is whispering in her ear, telling her what to say.

I went on to tell them about how I used to go to the library and just read and read when I wasn't outside playing or doing chores. I would just dream of all the places I wanted to travel to and experience. All the adventures I wanted to take. All the things I wanted to do and try. Just like the robin in her nest, how I would try, even if I fell. I would rather climb the mountain, skin my knees, bloody my nose and say, "I tried." And how I would just stand right back up and try again.

The baby robin was like me, left on its own to find its way out of the nest. My mother and father were separated when I was a kid, and I was the only child, so I was left on my own, in a sense, to find my way. As I tried to fly away from the nest, I learned a little more every day, tried a little more every day.

The little robin chirps in my hands. I set it down carefully on the grass. It trips and flops, then hops a few steps, then flaps its wings and flies off. And so, I begin to tell my story.

Revisiting My Childhood

You can take the kid out of Brooklyn, but you will never take Brooklyn out of the kid.

—Anonymous

One day after lecturing, I was sitting at a bar at a hotel in Vienna. While at the bar, the bartender came over to me and said, "A man would like to buy you a drink." I was taken by surprise and shocked. The man came over.

He said, "Remember me? Your name's Lawrence, isn't it?"

I said, "Yes."

"My name's Frankie. We grew up as kids in Brooklyn."

Frankie then brought over his wife, Ingrid, whom he introduced to me. We chatted for a long while.

Ingrid said, "You know, Lawrence, every time François (she now calls him François, not Frankie) feels good about what he has accomplished in life, he says with a tear in his eye, 'If the guys from Brooklyn could see me now!'"

I also had a tear in my eye, because through the years, whenever I thought I had done something pretty good, I too would say to myself, "If the guys from Brooklyn could see me now!"

When I got back home to New Jersey, I decided to go back to Brooklyn to revisit my childhood. I drove onto Ocean Parkway, which has changed a great deal.

"How has it changed, Grandpa?" Haleigh looks up at me with her big bluish-green eyes. "Is it really old now like you?"

Alex gently grabs my hand. "It is older than Grandpa, right?"

With a big grin, I tell how different it is now. "Well, it has been around for a while, but when I was a kid, Ocean Parkway and Avenue Z was the fancy section of Brooklyn right next to the water. Fancy at that time meant you lived in an apartment that had an elevator. You lived across the street from the park. The rooms were big and airy and you had maybe one window air conditioner and one TV in the house, but they were rare in those days. In our house, we did not have any air conditioner or TV."

Haleigh's strawberry blonde hair bounces from side to side as she dances around saying, "Grandpa, in those days we would be the fancy people."

Now, Ocean Parkway from Avenue T through Avenue Z is Sephardic (Spanish/Middle Eastern Jews); from Avenue T through Avenue M it is Ashkenazi (German/Eastern European Jews). From Avenue M through Avenue F, it is Muslim, and from Avenue F through Avenue B it is Russian. After Avenue B it is African American. As a kid, we did not have any Asians or African Americans in our area. In fact, the only minority was the Jews—all four of us. Today our section is mostly African American, people who want to start their life and give their children a better life than they had.

In many ways, it's really the same—it has not changed. The color changed; the values are the same. The culture is different. But they all want a better way of life, and they want their children to have more than they, as parents, received from their parents.

I reached Church Avenue and Flatbush Avenue to look at what used to be my old walking grounds. Garfield's Restaurant is now a Chase Bank. I could not find Erasmus Hall. Erasmus Hall used to be the area high school. It was a fantastic high school. As I drove up and down the avenues, I noticed mostly African Americans. I passed Lincoln Road and Flatbush Avenue, going to my old home on Sterling Street. I finally arrived at Sterling Street, between Bedford Avenue and Rogers Avenue. The cleaners and shoe shine parlor I used to walk by as a kid are now a funeral home called the House of Hills, Inc.

As I passed the Colonial Arms Apartments on Sterling Street and Rogers Avenue, I saw where my Scoutmaster, Paul Sofrin, used to live.

"Morse code," yells Rebecca.

"Did he talk to you in Morse code, Grandpa?" Haleigh asks while doing pirouettes around Alex.

"Don't be silly, Haleigh, he talked to him like we do." Alex shrugs his shoulder and keeps walking alongside me with his hands in his pockets, avoiding Haleigh.

"We sometimes talked in Morse code, but mostly, like regular people, we spoke to each other."

Paul Sofrin was a sensational leader and a great role model for me when I was a kid. Whatever he preached, he did. When we had to climb over broken trees, trudge through holes and ruts, and go across brooks, Sofrin, like an Israeli officer, led us. (The Israeli officers led from the front in battle. That is one of the reasons there were so many extra officer casualties.)

Sofrin always had a smile on his face, and if he cut himself, he would just brush himself off and say, "Okay, guys, let's do it!" And when we had the opportunity, he'd let me lead and I tried to emulate him, except I had a competitive spirit, and whatever he did, I wanted to do better. If he climbed a tree six feet up, I would climb the tree twelve feet up. If he broad jumped over a three-foot-wide brook, I would broad jump over it when it was ten feet wide and land in it and get all wet and twist my ankle.

He kept saying to me, "Larry, why can't you just be yourself?"

And I said to him, "Mr. Sofrin, I am being myself—I always want to be better than I was the day before. My greatest challenge is not other people; my greatest challenge is me."

Mr. Sofrin said to me, "I pity your parents—I know why they never had any more children. I wouldn't have, either!"

At Sullivan Place and Rogers Avenue, there used to be a movie theater and a bakery, but they're gone now. They were replaced by a food center and a little hardware store. At 157 Havemeyer Street, where my grandfather and my mother had a store, the building is now called Natan Borlam Co., Inc., Children's & Ladies Wear. They are still selling the same things that my mother and grandfather sold.

"But Grandpa, how can they sell the same things if people already bought them?" Haleigh stops in front of Alex and does a demi-plié, then jumps up again into pirouettes.

"Oh, no, that's not what I meant. I mean the same types of things."

"Pickle juice!"

Amazing! This was the store that my mother sold to Mr. Borlam over fifty-four years ago in 1955. I went into the store, and there it was—the same store, only air conditioning was added. There was the outside where I had my pushcart, where my job was, first, to make sure that people didn't steal, and second, to lure customers in with the cheap prices. When they went into the store, there were more expensively priced items. I remember I used to go up to the second floor, where my mother used to have a long ladder to get into the attic. You had to be really skinny to get into it. The same ladder was there—the same attic was there. I remember my mother and this store in 1955, and here I am at the store in 2008. That's a lot of years later!

In chatting with Mr. Borlam, I happened to mention to him how my mother enticed people into the store. Mr. Borlam said, "Larry, nothing has changed—attitudes have changed, but salesmanship is still the same." He said people came to him from all over Long Island, New Jersey, and Westchester because he had special clothes at sensational prices—the same thing my mother had.

I mentioned to him that the area had changed, that at one time it was more working-class people. Mr. Borlam replied, "That hasn't changed either—with today's economy, even if you make good money, you still have a poor working class, and what you have to do is that you've got to give people value. Not value that you think, but value that they think. Because people will pay you more, Larry, if they feel that they are getting more of a value."

Mr. Borlam and I had a picture taken of us together. He was a man in his early nineties and he still goes to work literally every day. He mentioned to me that he bought 157 Havemeyer Street for $9,000 in 1955, and now you don't want to know how much it's worth. He still has the same kind of clientele; the people come from as far as 50-100 miles away. Our meeting was heart-rending; he was teary-eyed; but it was truly like going home again to where my mother, my grandfather, and I had worked when I was a kid.

Coming home—you can only come once. You can never come home literally after that.

Haleigh reaches out and lays her right hand on Mesa, lifts her left leg and arm into the air, posing. "I go home every day, Grandpa!"

Alex, with his hands still in his pockets, quickly says, "He doesn't mean the home you live in, he means the home you grew up in."

"I go home every day to the home I grow up in."

"Home," Rebecca beams her captivating smile, "a place where I live with Mommy and Daddy."

"When I was your age, my home was in Brooklyn. So, in a way, Brooklyn is still one of my homes. It just isn't the same anymore. But today, my home is in New Jersey."

"Pickle juice."

My kids were brought up in Livingston, New Jersey—the suburbs. Livingston is about an hour and a half from New York City, two hours from Philadelphia, and it is in many ways a wonderful place to live with respect to culture and travel. My kids had all the advantages of schools, culture, and travel. But they will never have the indelible experience of growing up in Brooklyn and seeing the world, emotionally and physically, a thousand times without leaving Brooklyn. The great adventure in Brooklyn and New York City was that you could explore it all by yourself. This feeling of not having to depend on others to help you have fun was very special.

A 2008 picture of my mother's store, which was purchased by Natan Borlam in 1955

Natan Borlam (right) and I enjoy a visit back to memory lane, 2008

Standing next to the original ladder I used to climb into the attic of my mother's store, 2008

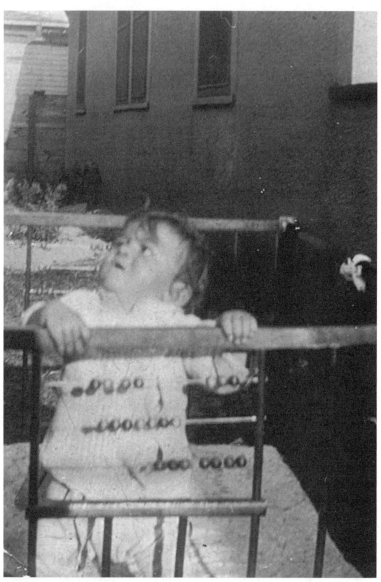

In my playpen at age three, 1934

Childhood Memories

When I was young, I ran around like crazy. At my age, if I run around, I am crazy.

—*Lawrence S. Harte*

My parents separated when I was about four years old. Neither of them ever got divorced, and I spent most of my young childhood as a latchkey kid, going to school and coming home to an empty house. But this way, I was able to enjoy things for myself.

Rebecca tugs quickly on my pants and says, "A latchkey kid goes from school to home to an empty house."

"That's right, Rebecca. A latchkey kid is one that goes from school to home, where he or she is alone while the parents are away at work." I couldn't help but smile. She is so inquisitive, like her mother, Helaine, and a chatterbox too.

As a kid, we lived in a second-floor tenement. In the summertime, since we did not have air conditioning, it was so hot that we used to sleep on the fire escape to get some air. In the wintertime, the window frames had so many holes in them that I used to sleep with my sweater and socks on.

"I sleep with my sweater and socks on too," Alex confesses.

As a kid in Brooklyn, my job was to clean the furnace in the basement, take the coal and ashes out, and put new coal into the furnace. It was hot and it was full of soot.

"Why would you do that? What's a furnace, Grandpa?" Haleigh takes Rebecca's soft little hand and twirls her around like a ballerina.

"The furnace was the way we heated the apartment house. I shoveled coal into the furnace for heating hot water for the day. Then I would run upstairs (we didn't have elevators) and wash up before going to school."

"That seems like a lot of work for hot water. I just turn my knob to the right in my bathtub if I want hot water."

"It was a lot of work, but it was what we had to do in those days. We didn't have water heaters like you have today."

"I'm glad we have water heaters, Grandpa. I don't think I'd like shoveling coal or getting dirty."

"In those days, we did not have any refrigerators either; we had ice boxes."

"You sure didn't have much when you were a kid. It sounds like a lot of work to live in Brooklyn!" Alex keeps his poky pace alongside of me.

"I sure did have a lot of work to do as a kid, but Brooklyn in those days was magical. It was my home."

When I was bored, I would try and memorize the names and telephone numbers in the phone book. Today, I have difficulty remembering my own number. I would then try and tear the telephone book in half. Today, I am lucky if I can lift two telephone books.

I used to have these large pieces of ice that I would put in sacks and stick in the dumbwaiter to bring them up from the basement to our second floor. Of course, that is where all the garbage went, and when the ice got to the second floor, there were bugs all over it. I just washed it off, chopped it up, and I never told my mother. I guess I was just lazy as far as having to carry the ice upstairs. What a genius I was—that is, until my mother came out and found bugs from the garbage on the ice in the box.

Haleigh looks at me with a deep stare. "Papa Larry, if Brooklyn was magical, couldn't you just poof the ice to the second floor?"

"Brooklyn was magical, but not in the fairy godmother kind of way. It was magical because we were street kids taking care of ourselves and sharing our dreams. We saw a lot, did a lot, and dreamt a lot."

"Pickle juice!"

In those days, we did not have TVs or computers. We had a large radio, where I used to listen to the likes of *The Lone Ranger*, Jack Armstrong, Lum and Abner, *The Shadow*, Uncle Don, Walter Winchell, Gabriel Heater, Jack Benny, Fred Allen, Bob Hope, and Kate Smith. There was no TV—I had a chance to dream and be creative.

Alex's brown eyes glance at me in puzzlement. "No TV or computers! Did you have iPods or MP3 players, Grandpa?"

"No, not even iPods or MP3 players."

As a youngster growing up in Brooklyn, I was an only child. I didn't have a brother, nor did I have a sister, but I had brothers and sisters in the little library around the corner from my house.

"I have a brother. Alex is my brother."

"Yes, Haleigh, and you are my sister. Grandpa, it must've been quiet when you were growing up not having a sister or brother."

"I have two brothers too," Rebecca eagerly blurts out, "Tyler and Casey!"

Literally, on every rainy day when I had nothing to do at home, I was in the library reading all kinds of books. I could not afford to buy the books, and it was a nice place to study because where I lived was very noisy. Since no one was around to tell me what to do, it was really my home away from home. Sometimes it really *was* my home. The librarian would advise me on school matters. Sometimes she would give me money for a snack and let me stay until she closed the library.

I especially loved to read science and adventure books. One of my favorite novels as a kid was by Commander Ellsberg; it was all about submarines and adventure. I especially liked adventure books of the unknown, of people trying things where they didn't know what was going to happen. And I loved science books. Even in those days, I loved the classics, even though I was just a kid. I loved Greek history, too.

"Do you think I'd love to read the classics like you?"

"One day you can tell me, Alex."

I read the *Iliad*, way before they asked me to do it in college. I loved reading about "The Thousand and One Nights" in *Arabian Nights*. It was so adventurous and so exciting. I did go to the movies, but to me, reading was something absolutely sensational. Another book that I liked was *Aesop's Fables*. It was just simple stuff of adventures and quotations, and of what people do in certain life situations. I liked the practical parts—it just plain excited me. I loved to read; I loved to dream.

The library was a place where I dreamt, I wrote, and I read. I read about what I would like to do some day, and how I would do it. I didn't know how to do it then, but I always read. My favorite person to read was Benjamin Franklin. To this day, I remember lines from his *Poor Richard's Almanack*. To me, Benjamin Franklin was the American equivalent of Baldassare Castiglione, the Renaissance courtier. Franklin was so good at so many things.

"Grandpa," Alex says, "I want to know all about Benjamin Franklin. I'm going to do a book report on him."

"Alex," I reply, "go for it!"

"You must be really smart, Grandpa," Haleigh says as she squints her eyes while looking up to me trying to squish the blinding sun away from her view.

When I was eleven years old, my friends and I would take a five-cent subway ride to the St. George Hotel pool in downtown Brooklyn. Imagine a whole day of swimming and a workout room for a dime! This included a locker and the rental of an itchy wool bathing suit. We would go there in the wintertime to swim and to meet girls. The huge pool varied from three to ten feet deep. The pool had a high diving board in the middle of the deep end, and two low boards on either side. It was here that I learned to dive and that I hit my head on the bottom of the pool. Maybe that's why I act different at times. The pool had amazing waterfalls. To a young kid from Brooklyn, this pool was the Taj Mahal right there in my town.

When I wasn't in the library or playing sports, sometimes I would take a subway train to Greenwood Heights in Brooklyn to check out the Green-Wood Cemetery because I heard that there were so many celebrities buried in that place. I'd say, "My gosh, this was the place to be!" I didn't know it, but the Central Park area was designed after the Green-Wood Cemetery. Central Park was built in 1857 and declared a National Historical Landmark in 1963; Green-Wood Cemetery was built in 1838 and declared a National Historical Landmark in 2006.

The Green-Wood Cemetery lies several blocks southwest of Prospect Park. When you walk through the cemetery, you can see a Civil War memorial monument, and a great view of Manhattan, but you are really also on the site of the first and largest major battle of the Revolutionary War. We really are in history.

There are some neat people buried there. There is Henry Ward Beecher, who was an abolitionist, and Henry Chadwick, who was known as the Father of Baseball. Walking around, my friends and I saw the burial ground of DeWitt Clinton, who eventually became governor of New York. There was Charles Hercules Ebbets, who was the first Brooklyn Dodger owner. Ebbets Field was named after him. There was the editor of the *New York Tribune* and founder of the Liberal Republican Party, Horace Greeley (who popularized the saying "Go West, young man"). It is a neat place. Samuel Morse, who was the inventor of the Morse code and the single-wire telegraph system, is buried there too. So is William Marcy Tweed, Jr. (known as "Boss Tweed"). That guy was really a big power player in New York City for many years. He ended up being convicted of stealing millions of dollars from the New York City taxpayers through political corruption and died in the Ludlow Street Jail. The cemetery also gives a great view of the Statue of Liberty.

Brooklyn had it all in those days, from happy things to cemeteries that showed me a little bit about history. In those days, movies were ten cents plus a penny tax, which was eleven cents. Hot dogs were a nickel. A corned beef sandwich was fifteen cents. An egg cream was three cents. A subway and a ferry were five cents. We could buy small rolls for a penny. There was a trolley car that we used to get on for five cents. Ebbets Field, where the Brooklyn Dodgers played, was fifty-five cents in the bleachers.

"I'd be rich in those days!" Alex blurts out, recollecting his savings. We take a rest at the edge of the path in a shady spot with two benches.

"We'd all be rich in those days."

Oh, those were the days. I lived in a part of Brooklyn that, to me, was absolutely universal. I had everything any child would want, and more. As an example, I was able to walk to my public school. I was within walking distance of one of the most beautiful libraries in the world, and a beautiful museum. Two blocks from the great Prospect Park, the Botanical Gardens, and the zoo. Four blocks from a huge baseball field. Two blocks from Ebbets Field. One block from a bowling alley, and one block from a roller skating rink. A block from ice skating in the wintertime. One block from tennis. Two blocks from horseback riding and boating and listening to beautiful music in the park. For just five cents, a subway ride away from fishing, swimming, and sailing; lying on the beach; and watching the girls, for just five cents. All was within fifteen to twenty minutes. Life was such that any child, by himself, could go anywhere in Brooklyn, and cross over into Manhattan to see the theater, the concerts, and all of the extra effects.

As we sit on the bench, Mesa nudges my arm with his wet nose for attention. I stroke his fur, and Haleigh starts to give him hugs and kisses. "Grandpa, it sounds like you lived in the middle of everything fun. Where did you live in Brooklyn?"

"I lived on a street called Sterling, Haleigh." Rebecca runs around in front of our bench and tags Haleigh in hopes of a play date.

"Tell us more, Papa Larry," Rebecca squeals as she keeps running in random tandems.

At the site where Ebbets Field Stadium once housed the Brooklyn Dodgers. Today the site is occupied by the Ebbets Field apartment houses. 2008

The intersection of Havemeyer and Third streets, Brooklyn

STERLING STREET

Know your environment: A policeman stopped a guy and asked him, "Didn't you notice the stop sign as you went through?" The guy said, "I noticed the stop sign; I just didn't notice YOU!"

—*Anonymous*

I grew up at 131 Sterling Street in Brooklyn. My life was idyllic. I lived between Rogers Avenue and Bedford Avenue. On Sterling Street, at the end of the corner at Rogers Avenue, we had a barber shop where I used to go for thirty-five cents and a nickel tip. Many times I didn't have money, but I told the barber I would bring it next time. Next door to Peter Digiti's barber shop was our candy store, where we got the newspapers and our ice cream sodas and candy, and made it a little bit of a hangout. We got ice cream sodas for five cents and plain sodas for two cents. *The New York Times* and the *Herald Tribune* were three cents, and the *Daily News* and the *Daily Mirror* were two cents.

Across the street we had the tailor. My mother used to get my clothing OTT—off the truck—and God bless that tailor, he made everything fit. Next to him was a shoemaker. I would come in with the biggest holes in my shoes, and he fixed them up and patched me up.

"How sad, Grandpa, you had holes in your shoes," Haleigh sighs with a sad look.

"Don't be sad, Haleigh." Rebecca consoles Haleigh and gives her a big hug.

"Grandpa has nice shoes on now. Look, Haleigh, no holes," Alex reassures his sister as he points to my shoes.

On Bedford Avenue we had a grocery store where we got our

groceries. Bread rolls, would you believe, were a penny apiece. Next door was a bowling alley where we could bowl, and nearby was a little restaurant where I got one of my first jobs. They fired me because I was too slow getting the money from the people.

We had a bar at Empire Boulevard and Bedford Avenue that served steaks and chops. I used to go in there once in a while to see if they had any extra food that I could take home. Next to the bar was an automotive place. I would just walk by because we didn't have any cars, and the cars really didn't interest me at that time. But I sure changed later in life.

Around the corner from my house was a beautiful roller skating rink. On Empire Boulevard there was a trolley car that ran all over Brooklyn. It went from Empire Boulevard to my mother's store on Havemeyer Street in Williamsburg, which at that time was literally a Jewish ghetto section. Today, it is a very hip area.

At Empire Boulevard and Bedford Avenue, there was a huge gas station where we would take old cans and pour the oil drippings onto the ground, and I would try to convince people that I had discovered oil. Imagine, oil found in Brooklyn.

Rebecca snickers, "You're funny, Papa Larry. You discovered oil."

Across the street was a huge Firestone station. I remember the Firestone because one day some neighborhood kids and I just happened to be throwing rocks. I can't believe it, but one of the big windows at Firestone broke. Sometimes, I still think that someone might be wondering who did it.

"You shouldn't have been throwing rocks, Papa Larry," Haleigh scolds. She is a true stickler for the rules.

On Sterling Street, just up one block from where I lived, was a tennis and ice skating rink. At the end of the street, where it met

Franklin Avenue, there was the Bond Bread bakery with a beautiful smell. You could buy bread one day old, but to us it was a great smell. There was a lady there who sold candy apples. Whatever she didn't sell, she would hand out to us. For me, as a kid, life was really idyllic.

A block from my house on Bedford Avenue was a Catholic church. I think I was the only Jewish kid on the church's basketball team. I wasn't the best athlete, but man was I tough and was I fast.

"You went to Catholic church?" Alex questioned with a tone of disbelief.

"I didn't go to Catholic church, Alex. I just played on the basketball team."

"Basketball," Rebecca squeals, "a bouncy ball game with a hoop."

The priest and I soon became good friends. I think he tried to indoctrinate me to become a Catholic, but I tried my very best to have him become a Jew. The priest would tell me all about Catholicism, which was an education. I tried to tell him all about being a Jew from my point of view. Our views, naturally, were biased, but we came to have great respect for each other. I remember that one day, the priest said, "Practice and pray, and your dreams will come true." I said, "Practice, practice right, and pray that the ball goes into the hoop." I told the priest I could not become Catholic because my mother made boiled chicken and chicken soup every Friday. We never ate fish on Friday.

On Rogers Avenue, across the street from the barber shop and the little candy store, was my little library. Since I grew up by myself, I would spend almost every rainy day in the library. They got to know me so well that they never even asked me for my card. Two stores up from the library, at Rogers Avenue and Empire Boulevard, was a diner called Toomey's. That was a place where my buddy and I would go and buy their biggest order of French fried potatoes for twenty cents with lots of ketchup and salt. We would just walk for blocks and dream the dreams.

"I love to walk, Grandpa," Haleigh exclaims as she jumps up from the park bench and walks back and forth quickly.

"Me too!" Rebecca giggles and follows Haleigh.

"I like to walk too, Grandpa, especially in the park with you," Alex says softly and smiles as he stays seated next to me on the bench with Mesa lying down at our feet.

The comfort foods that I had when I was a kid still bring pleasant memories as an adult. There were specific foods that each had their own associated activity that I cherished when I was young. To this day, I love hot dogs with mustard and sauerkraut. They remind me of the nickel I spent for a hot dog at all the Brooklyn Dodger baseball games and at Brighton Beach in the summertime, swimming and getting suntanned. I used to buy bags of French fries, ketchup, and salt. I would walk with a friend literally for hours, talking of life and what we were going to do when we grew up. Today, I try to eat healthy foods, but I still leave a little bit of room for a few French fries.

One Wednesday a month, I would race home from school to have a can of corn soup. It was the elixir of my youth. Today, I will go out of my way to find a restaurant that serves corn chowder. If I did not eat anything else, my meal today would be complete. When I was a child, my mother would give me rice pudding when I wasn't feeling well. Today, when I feel glunky or achy, guess what I order—the magic cure-all, rice pudding.

"It's a good thing you walked a lot when you were a kid."

"You're right, Alex! I think that's why I am in such good shape now. I used to walk a lot when I was a kid, especially to the places that had all of the good food."

My favorite full meal as a kid was spaghetti and meat balls. A whole gang of us would go to an Italian restaurant. I think the restaurant we ate at was a front for the Mafia. When we went out, we would eat a huge amount of food for little money. As we ate, large men with big cigars walked by us and into a large back room.

"What's the Mafia?"

"Well, Haleigh, the Mafia is a mean group of people that you don't want to upset because they can hurt you. They like to use people to do bad stuff for them. Basically, they are people you should stay away from."

"What's a 'front'?"

"A front, like the restaurant, is a business the Mafia owns to make them look legal, but they actually do things against the law there."

"Oh! You're right, Grandpa; they are people you should stay away from."

We used to spend our nights close to the candy store, or listening to the Brooklyn Dodgers by radio. When I had three cents, I would buy a chocolate egg cream, which was a mixture of chocolate syrup with a little milk and seltzer.

Rebecca repeats, "Chocolate egg cream—chocolate syrup with a little milk and seltzer."

"That's right. They were so delicious. I still try to find places today that serve chocolate egg cream."

"Yummy! I like chocolate."

Further up on Rogers Avenue, a block up toward Sullivan Place, was our bakery. Every Sunday morning I would walk to the bakery and bring home those cinnamon rolls, which to this day I still love. I would break them up into small pieces so they would last longer.

Two doors away from the bakery was Rogers Theater, our movie theater, where it cost us ten cents plus a penny tax. Can you imagine—eleven cents to get in! Of course, close by to the tennis courts on Washington Avenue was our delicatessen with cold sodas. Oh, did I love it there! Yum, yum, yum.

A block away from the delicatessen was our old temple, located on top of a grocery store on the second story. That was our first temple. Later on, the temple became pretty wealthy and went on to Ocean Avenue, which is a fancy place opposite the park. That's where our final temple was located. On Empire Boulevard, just a block away, there was Prospect Park, the Botanical Gardens, and a zoo. Washington Avenue was also where the rich people lived. They lived opposite the Botanical Gardens.

Prospect Park, just two blocks away, had a beautiful lake where we used to go rowing and have water sports. We could go fishing at the lake and horseback riding.

"That sounds like a fun park."

"It was, Alex. They had a beautiful music stand where, during the summer, they played concerts on the weekend. Of course, it was a great place for picking up girls."

"You're silly, Grandpa!" Haleigh exclaims.

"I am silly, aren't I?"

We used to walk through the Botanical Gardens and admire the different leaves of nature. The school would take us for nature study to the zoo and the gardens there. If we walked up from Washington Avenue and Eastern Parkway, which was possibly nearly three-quarters of a mile to a mile, there was a beautiful museum and the Brooklyn Public Library. We'd go there on weekends and any special days if we wanted to learn or just be in areas of culture.

On Franklin Avenue we used to walk up a little bit more, and there was another movie theater, the Parkside Movie. My school was on President Street, between Franklin Avenue and Washington Avenue, about nine blocks away. Would you believe I walked to school, walked home for lunch, walked back from lunch, and came back from school? So all this walking didn't leave me much time for lunch.

On Washington Avenue, a block from the delicatessen, was a theater called the Patio Theater, which was another movie theater. We had so many movie places around, it was just really great. In 1940, I remember standing on Franklin Avenue. There was a huge crowd. A motorcade was driving by. I asked someone there, "Who is driving?" And he said, "The president of the United States, President Roosevelt." I got on my tippy toes. I think I saw him. Or, maybe I saw the top of the guy's head in front of me. What memories!

For transportation, you could not believe it. One block away on Empire Boulevard, we had a trolley car that took us all over Brooklyn. Two blocks away, we had the BMT, a train line that took us into Manhattan; Brighton Beach; Coney Island, where we could frolic in the sand; and Sheepshead Bay, where we could watch the fishing boats come in. Two blocks the other way we had the IRT, a train line that again went to the other side of Manhattan. I lived two blocks away from my transportation to the whole world. I could go by train to the ferry and go across on the ferry, all for a nickel. At Nostrand Avenue and Montgomery Street was a trolley barn, where all the trolleys would come at night. It was kind of eerie how the trolleys got so close in together.

"I live right by my transportation to the whole world too, Grandpa, and it doesn't even cost me a nickel," Alex quietly states. "All I have to do is go in our car, and Mom and Dad take me to the whole world."

Haleigh quickly adds, "Me too!"

"I'll go in the car, too," Rebecca declares. Haleigh takes a break from walking back and forth and sits on the bench with her legs kicking up and down. Rebecca watches Haleigh and tries to mimic her by sitting down by her side and kicking her legs up and down as well. Those two have so much energy.

Two blocks away on Bedford Avenue, between Sullivan Place and McKeever Place, was the great Ebbets Field. This was the place of my youth, where I used to live, dream, and work selling sodas and newspapers. Eight blocks down, on Empire Boulevard, was the Seventy-first Precinct Police Station, where the police used to round us up if we did anything goofy. In a way, it was a good idea because they kept us in line.

"That's a good thing, Grandpa, since you like to throw rocks at stores," Haleigh says, reminding me of my mischievous ways. "Did your other friends throw rocks too?"

"Haleigh, Grandpa didn't throw rocks all the time. He only said he threw it that one time," Alex retorts in defense. "Right, Grandpa?"

As I think back to my youth and how the boys and I were always doing stuff—good or bad—I can only answer, "That's right, Alex."

"What were your friends like Papa Larry?" Rebecca interjects with a sense of curiosity.

As we get up from the shaded park bench and continue our walk down the beautiful path, I begin to tell my tale of the boys of Brooklyn. "Well, Rebecca, they were a different kind of kids than nowadays."

131 Sterling Street, Brooklyn, where I grew up, 2008

Toomey's Diner, where I used to eat French fried potatoes as a kid

Trolley cars in Brooklyn, 1940s

KIDS I GREW UP WITH IN BROOKLYN

They say the best men are molded out of faults and for
the most, become much more the better for being a
little bit bad.
                    —*William Shakespeare, in* Measure for Measure

As a youngster, I remember once sitting on a stoop on a warm summer evening, just chatting away with the neighborhood kids. One of the parents came over and asked us what we wanted to do when we grew up. When they came to me, I said, "I don't know; I've got lots of dreams, but I really don't know." One of the other kids said, "It doesn't make any difference what Lawrence does. Whatever he does, he is going to be great at it!" I was embarrassed—I was only ten.

On those warm summer nights, a bunch of us kids would sit out on our stoops on Sterling Street listening to the noise of Ebbets Field and the Brooklyn Dodgers crowd roaring two blocks away. We would listen to the voice of "Red" Barber, nicknamed "The Ol' Redhead," who was the radio sportscaster for the Brooklyn Dodgers. The Dodgers were our dream, our hope, our present, and our future. In the pauses between Barber's beautiful voice, the sound of the bat, and the cheer of the crowd, we would talk to each other about our dreams and what we were going to be some day.

We would sit out and sweat in those days. Our dreams were in the air there as each of us would just talk about what we wanted to be some day, about how some day we would leave Brooklyn to go around the world.

"You went around the world, Grandpa!"

"I did. I made my dreams come true, Alex. I loved to dream and talk about traveling the world. I can still picture those hot nights with the roaring crowds and the voice of Red, just being a kid."

We were a special breed. None of us knew we were poor because we were all the same. We were all rich in dreams, love, and sharing the dreams of the Dodgers, waiting until the year when the Dodgers would win the World Championship, and we, too, would conquer the world because we could do it.

Stanley Holden lived next door to me in the apartment house. He eventually became a professor of physics at Wilkes-Barre University. He was proud, big into hi-fi and flying airplanes, very smart, and the only other Jewish kid on the block. I remember his parents used to order Chinese food on Sunday and invite me over. Unfortunately, I could never reciprocate because we never had Chinese food, and nobody in my home ever invited anyone.

Walter Hedenberg lived on the corner of Bedford Avenue and Sterling Street. We went to grade school and Brooklyn Tech together, and we were buddies during that time. I lost track of him after high school.

Richard and Wesley Truesdel lived two apartment houses away from me. Their father, Mr. Truesdel, was a print shop teacher at Brooklyn Tech, and he was one of the reasons I went there. His two sons were both on the rifle team and excellent students. Of course, they went to Brooklyn Tech, too.

There was Herb Van Schack. He was a good guy, and he could throw a ball over a sewer and a half. The distance of the sewers was thirty yards apart. He was really our quarterback. Could that guy throw a pass! I never knew whatever happened to him. I never even knew what high school he went to.

Then there were the other guys. They were kind of tough but nice guys. Tommy Montagary, Jim Ahern, Ray Judge, Joe Curran, and Billy

Cottle. All of these guys made up our group.

On the next block, one block up, the more educated, wealthy kids lived. There was Jerry Manning, who also was a great quarterback. He could throw a sewer and a half. There was Don Jaffe, who went to private school. He was a bright guy. There was David Cooper. I heard he was from Cooper Blades. Cooper Blades, as I understand it, was like Gillette Blades is today. That's what I heard. There were the Sher and Hammer brothers, who were all first-class athletes. There was Roger Malkin, who eventually became an oral surgeon. These are the kids I played with from day to day. We had fun, we fought, and we all left Brooklyn. I have no idea where any of them are today, or if they are still living.

"Grandpa, if Brooklyn was so magical, why did everyone leave? It is sad you don't know where your friends are today."

"We all just kind of parted ways in life, Haleigh. Brooklyn was magical for us as kids; it was a place to grow up and dream. It was a place to call home. But as we got older, life changed and other places became home."

Some of the kids went off and became cops. Some became firemen; some became crooks who went to the Mafia.

"Mafia! Bad people!" Rebecca blurts. Since neither of her parents baby her, she is quite the speaker for her age. She absorbs everything and loves to say words and then describe them. It's incredible what kids remember. "I don't think I like the Mafia, they are bad people, Papa Larry."

"You got it. Bad people."

Some became lawyers, some became judges, and many began to work as civil service agents for the city. Working for the city in the civil service in those days was a special, special plum. Everything was a payoff; nothing in New York in those days got done without paying off the person who had to inspect something that you wanted. As for me, I wanted to be a plastics engineer. I read *Popular Mechanics*, *Popular Science*, and *Scientific American*. I loved those magazines! I wanted to change the world, and, of course, I wanted to be president, but can you imagine a Jewish kid being president in 1940?

"How about now, Grandpa? Can I be president? I'm a Jewish kid and it's not 1940."

"You can be anything you want to be, Alex. All you have to do is want it and go for it."

Well, as I said, we were street kids. A lot of dreams, a lot of living, a lot of surviving. Being on the streets meant you had to know how to survive. And survive we did.

The Lawrence Harte definition of street smart:
1. Be a cunning tower, as in a submarine.
2. As you trawl through life, keep looking all around you.
3. If in doubt, attack. If you are weak, run like heck.
4. Always forgive. Never forget.

The street life had its moments. Once, I was playing in the school yard, and someone with a knife stuck me up for five cents. I gave him that nickel. About a month later, I found him and I took his head and pounded it into the pavement, almost giving him a fracture. I wasn't going to let him get away with what he did to me. Yes, it was five cents, but among us kids it was also a matter of respect. Today, I hear modern-day athletes talking about respect; it comes from their youth.

"Mommy and Daddy tell us we should not hit."

"And they are right, Haleigh. It's different nowadays. You don't live on the streets like I did."

"If I hit someone, I know I would be punished. I don't want to be punished. Were you punished a lot?"

"Like I said, we were on the streets. No one was at home. Your great-grandmother worked at her store long hours, so I brought myself up."

"Grandpa didn't have his mommy and daddy at home like us, Haleigh," Alex cuts in. "Grandpa got to go outside on his own."

Taking things was second nature to a kid on the streets. I remember my first bicycle, which I borrowed from a fruit stand whose owner refused to pay me for working for him. Someone had left it overnight. I forgot to bring it back and borrowed it until they wanted it back. There was another time in Woolworth's when I went in to buy some toothpaste. A kid, who I did not know was watching me, said, "The coast is clear—SINK IT!" "Sink it" meant quickly sink it into your pocket when the employees of the store were not watching or the boss was not watching.

"Sink it! Pocket!" Rebecca repeats.

"You took things that weren't yours? You can't take things that aren't yours, Grandpa." Haleigh interrupts Rebecca.

"That's true, Haleigh, but in those days that's what kids on the street did."

"I'm not sure Mommy and Daddy would like what you did as a kid."

From the mouth of babes—I just had to laugh. "I don't think so either."

"Pickle juice!"

One day, my group and I were caught throwing stink bombs into peoples' houses who thought we were too noisy. A stink bomb was photograph film wrapped in toilet paper and then lit with a match. It made a skunk's smell seem like perfume.

"That must've smelled pretty bad." Alex sniffed as if the skunk were nearby.

"It doesn't smell like perfume, Papa Larry," Rebecca runs around yelling while a young couple quickly walks by us in hopes of evading a skunk attack.

The police picked us up in a paddy wagon and took us to the police station. To show us a lesson, they put us behind bars. That odor convinced me to never, never again cross the law. I remember saying to my friends, "I have an Uncle Louie. He'll come down and get us out." My uncle came to the police station. I told him the story. Uncle Louie, who was a lawyer, said to the sergeant, "Keep the boys another hour. They deserve it." To this day, I believe Uncle Louie would have kept his own mother in jail.

"Uncle Louie was a smart man. You did bad things. He wanted to punish you," Haleigh declares.

Another time when I was fourteen, my friend's brother took him and me to a swinging hotel in the mountains. I remember being told to stay in the room where he gave us all the food we wanted, and all night long I heard gambling, screaming, yelling, and cajoling, and signs of alcohol and smoking. Where was this place when I was twenty?

As a kid, I used to play pool in pool parlors with my group. It was extremely smoky, but you learned a few things that you needed. You learned eye-hand and gut relationship. And to follow your gut when the chips were down, because you could always tell when there was a pool shark. They missed each shot by a half inch. Watch out, because they were going to take you when the money was on the line.

We were tough kids always looking to make money. Our best business was a little shady. When people parked their car on our street for the baseball games, we would ask, "Can we mind your car?" If they said yes, they would give us five cents. If they said no, they came back from the game to find no air in their tires.

"Did you make a lot of money?"

"We sure did, Alex. Most people always gave us the five cents. After all, we came from Brooklyn!"

We were all street kids; we played hard, we fought hard, we hugged hard. There was no discrimination; we just called each other all kinds of vile names, but the bottom line was if you could run fast, if you could fight hard, or if you were rich enough to supply the ball and the bat, you were equal. In those days, we could walk the streets day or night and be safe. We did not need adults to watch us or arrange play dates for us. The only play date we had, we arranged ourselves: "I'll meet you after school and have it out." Because of this typical life, we became very self-reliant and independent. If we fell, we had to pick ourselves up. There was no person to help us. They were working or at home. We could fight hard, and the next day we would play together and dream out loud about the life we might have when we grew up.

"Sounds like you did a lot of bad things, Grandpa. Did you do good things like play?"

"As kids on the street, we did a lot of things we shouldn't have done. We really didn't have anyone watching us. But we didn't always do bad stuff. We use to play a lot too, Haleigh."

"Of course you played a lot, Grandpa. You were a kid like us."

"I did, Alex, and I loved to play games and sports like you."

AT PLAY

At this age, I use flippers to keep pace with the 20-to-30-year-old swimmers. There is a rule that if you get lapped twice, you must move over a lane. If I go any slower, I will end up in the shower.
—*Lawrence S. Harte (swimming at the YMCA in 2007)*

On Sterling Street, there was a place where we played boxball, stoopball, punchball, stickball, Ringolevio, Johnny ride the pony, and red light. We played boxball, where we chalked out in the street a square with different bases. A pitcher would throw the ball to a batter, who had to hit it with an open hand, try to get it through the infielders, and try to run home before the ball arrived. We played stoopball, where we would try to hit the edge of a stoop with the ball and if it went flying across the street onto the brick building, that would be a home run. It required a great deal of eye-hand coordination.

On the street, we played all kinds of games, from boxball to punchball to stickball, where we hit from sewer to sewer. The street was our playground. The cars were our bases. The sewers in between were our home plate and second base. And we showed our male prowess by how many sewers we could hit. I once saw a person hit two sewers. That was our concrete playground. We played punchball in the middle of the street. We would get up at one sewer and punch the ball with our fists closed, and we would try and get through all the guys who were on defense. If they caught it on the fly, we were out. And we would have bases. First base would be a car, second base would be another sewer, third base would be a car, and home plate would be a sewer.

We played Ringolevio, where somebody was "it" and you had to try to find the guy. You could tackle him until you got him, and once you got him, then he would have to run after you. We played Johnny ride the pony, where somebody would be up against the wall and you put your head in their stomach, and someone would put their head behind you and we would keep riding on top of each other. We played red light, where someone would close their eyes and count to ten, and then say, "Red Light!" If they caught you moving, then you had to do all these things yourself.

Our other concrete playground was at the schoolyard of P.S. 241. Some eight blocks away we used to play basketball, again on concrete. In late February and the beginning of March, we would shovel off the snow and begin playing basketball with our short sleeves in freezing weather. But when you are young, you don't know any better. You just do it "because." You just do it.

Weather was no deterrent to kids at this age, and, although I wasn't the biggest guy in the world at 5' 7", I worked on a 16-foot jump shot from the left side. I worked on it and worked on it and worked on it. Back then, the winning team stayed on the court in three-man basketball. Some days, when we were respectable and we were lucky, we could stay on the court all morning or all afternoon. Like I said before, I wasn't the biggest guy in the world, but I never gave a free layup. I would clobber the guy. I didn't want him to make the two points. In those days, in three-man basketball, we didn't shoot fouls. The only thing that saved me was my 16-foot jump from the left side, which I practiced every day.

When we were a little bit older, we would play baseball on a sandlot and we'd play football in the park without helmets or shoulder pads, and we tackled. That was the way it was in those days. There was no protection—just youth and our dreams, and having fun. Maybe that's the reason I act funny sometimes these days.

Behind Ebbets Field on Montgomery Street was a gravel lot. We used to use the back of Ebbets Field's concrete base as a pitching base, because we didn't have a catcher. In this gravel stone lot we played baseball and football. We slid into gravel stones, always skinning our knees and bloodying our noses, but that was part of being a boy. I came home every evening with bruises and cuts from sliding on stones.

Also in Prospect Park and Parkside Avenue were the parade grounds. We used to play what today is called American Legion baseball. We never had enough gloves, and since I was a lefty, I hardly ever had a glove. As a youngster, I was a left-handed pitcher. I would use a righty glove and quickly switch and try to throw with my other hand. After a while, I got adapted to using my right hand to throw with, and that's one of the reasons that today I am ambidextrous.

"Ambi what?"

"Ambidextrous, Rebecca. It means I am able to use both my hands the same. I could pitch with my right or left hand."

"Ambidextrous!" Rebecca repeats with glee.

"You got it!"

I had no choice. We used to use gloves as bases. We had one bat and one ball, and if we lost that ball, the game was over. In those days, the rich kids had the ball and bat. They were lousy athletes, but we sucked up to them because, without them, we couldn't play the game.

"Wow, you had a lot of fun. I want to visit Brooklyn, Grandpa." Alex grasps his hands and puts his arms out and swings them back to make the motion of swinging a bat.

"It sure was different from the play dates and games they play nowadays."

There was a time when we were playing an all African-American team. I was pitching for our team, and there was a pickup of African-Americans. I hit the first three batters. I remember the coach from the African-American team came up to me, put his arms around me, and said, "Son, why don't you try and pitch a little bit outside? You'll be a better pitcher." Well, I did pitch on the outside, and the balls came over the plate, and they beat the shit out of us! I shouldn't have listened to him.

"Ooh, you said a bad word!" Haleigh catches my slip without hesitation.

"Oops, sorry."

Once when I was pitching and the ball came back to me very fast, I put up my left hand to try to catch the ball. The problem was the glove was on the right hand. My pinky literally came off the rest of my hand. I went home to my mother and when she saw that, she said, "Lawrence, get out of the house. Go to the hospital; you're getting blood on the linoleum." And I walked some ten blocks to the hospital where I had a towel around my finger. They sewed it up. To this day, I have a scar of youth on my pinky. Maybe next time I will use the right hand when a ball comes at me. Besides baseball, we also played tackle football in Prospect Park—of course, without helmets.

Sometimes we used to play handball against one backboard. We would play in the school yards and in the summertime we would play at Brighton Beach in Coney Island. Some of the best handball players in the whole country came from Brighton Beach. I remember as a kid watching Vic Hershkowitz play. He became the American champion and later went into the United States Handball Association Hall of Fame. The association considered him "the greatest all-around player in handball history." Besides Vic, there were other players that were just plain sensational. Literally, the best in the country played handball at Brighton Beach. My being ambidextrous was a real plus. I could use both my left and my right hand. Considering my lack of discipline toward the game, I became pretty good because I could use both hands. Most people in those days could only use one hand. And I climbed the ladder, but it wasn't my first love. It was just a way to get suntanned, have fun, and meet some girls.

"I want to try handball," Alex blurts out. He eagerly takes his hands out of the batting position and swings his hand as if to hit a ball with it.

"One of these days I will show you."

"I want to play too," Haleigh yells, running up alongside Alex and imitating his hand movement.

"Okay, I will show you too."

"Handball sounds like a lot of fun, Papa Larry."

"It is fun, Rebecca."

"What else did you do besides all those sports, Papa Larry?"

"I was maybe eleven or twelve years old when I tried the sport of fishing, Rebecca."

I went on a fishing expedition in Sheepshead Bay in Brooklyn. Someone gave me a fishing rod, so we went out fishing in a boat with a little motor. My friend was older than me. He was about fifteen, and I figured, well, there must be big fish out in the ocean. So I got the biggest line in the world. Looking back, I probably could have caught a shark with that line! Actually, I think I caught a one-pound fish, but to me, that fish was as big as a shark! I was so excited. I brought it home to my mother and she yelled at me that I was getting fish oil all over the floor. I think my mother threw it out. She would never eat something fresh from the waters when she could go to a fish market and buy it for five times the price.

"I love to go fishing with you, Grandpa," Alex divulges. I remember going fishing at a lake and showing Alex how to cast his pole. His little face and brown eyes lit up when a slight tug pulled on his pole. As he would reel in his catch, the expression on his face was invaluable. It was as if he had just won the lottery.

"I love to go fishing with you too."

Besides sports, at times I would play chess with my Uncle Louie. I was bored by it because I wanted to win. When I was six, my Uncle Louie taught me chess. I would come home from school and there was a chess table on part of the kitchen table. I would have a snack to eat and we would play chess. It was an ongoing game. Sometimes day after day we would play the same game with the same strategies. He wanted me to think out of the box. With me, it was just a game, but he was smarter than I. He was trying to teach me something about life, about thinking logically, thinking dramatically, and sometimes taking a calculated risk.

When I did not know what a word meant, my Uncle Louie would never tell me, and he would say, "Look it up in a dictionary." He wanted me to go after knowledge rather than being spoon fed. His philosophy was that winning wasn't important; the process of thinking was. It wasn't until years later that I realized that winning is great, but the process of thinking outweighs the winning because it stays with you forever.

"I like chess," Alex exclaims. "I'm really good at it."

"I don't get it," Haleigh announces. "Why play chess?"

"There are many purposes in playing chess. One is thinking

outside the box."

"Outside of what box?"

"As an example, if I make a move, my opponent can make maybe three moves. What is my reaction to any of those three moves?"

"I still don't get it."

"Can you explain it more, Grandpa?" Alex asks.

"Here's a practical example—if I put my foot into a puddle, what happens?"

"You get wet," Rebecca utters with joy.

"I can splash myself. I can splash somebody else. I can get my foot wet. What do I do if these three things happen? This means that you have to think a step ahead. That is the advantage of chess. Many times it has nothing to do with chess; it has to do with thinking ahead."

"I wouldn't step in the puddle," Haleigh impulsively points out.

"Haleigh, Grandpa didn't really step in the puddle. It's just an example," Alex tries to explain as Haleigh begins to spin into pirouettes once more. "Grandpa, is it like the Brooklyn Dodgers, when they were okay, got better, and won and then had to move?"

"It is a little bit, but not exactly. The Brooklyn Dodgers were in a league of their own. You should have seen them play. It was exciting to be a young kid and have Ebbets Field as your neighbor."

School marquee of P.S. 241, part of my old stomping grounds, 2008

Showing off my acrobatic skills with a friend (bottom), 1944

Fishing at Verona Park with Alex Harte (right), fall 2004

THE BROOKLYN DODGERS

If I were playing third base and my mother were rounding third with the run that was going to beat us, I'd trip her. Oh, I'd pick her up and brush her off and say, "Sorry, Mom, but nobody beats me."

—Leo Ernest "The Lip" Durocher
Brooklyn Dodgers manager (1939–1947)

All of us, as kids, wanted to play with the Brooklyn Dodgers, whether they were good players or bad players. I tried my best.

"Baseball, Papa Larry. I like baseball!" Rebecca's wavy golden brown hair bounces as she skips around and repeats, "Baseball!"

"That's right, Rebecca. Baseball! I love baseball and I loved the Brooklyn Dodgers."

"I love baseball too. My team is the Mets, Grandpa," Alex blurts out. He loves team sports and he puts forth a great effort. He enjoys collecting tons of baseball items. He takes after his father, Doug. Neither one of them was interested in my stamp collection. Go figure!

This was my first true, true love—my beloved Dodgers. Being born in Brooklyn and living blocks from Ebbets Field, how could one be anything but a Brooklyn Dodgers fan? It was a sign of the times that we came from a very modest neighborhood and the Dodgers always seemed to come in SECOND. Our philosophy was—wait until next year!

"Grandpa, why did you love the Dodgers so much?"

"Haleigh, for many in Brooklyn, the Dodgers were representative of us, because we weren't at the top, but someday we were going to make it to the top."

"Did you make it, Grandpa?"

"I hope I did. And, in a way, I owe it to the Dodgers. They gave me hope and filled my dreams with faith when I was a kid."

Years later, when Walter O'Malley took the Dodgers to Los Angeles, some writers said the three most evil men of the twentieth century were Hitler, Stalin, and Walter O'Malley. I don't think so. There were reasons why O'Malley moved, but he certainly left a tremendous void in Brooklyn.

The Dodgers, before becoming the Dodgers, were first called the Brooklyn Bridegrooms, the Brooklyn Superbas, the Brooklyn Robins, and finally the Brooklyn Trolley Dodgers, before their name was shortened.

"They sure had a lot of names."

"That they did, Alex. But in the end, they became the Brooklyn Dodgers."

In 1912, Charles Ebbets, who owned the Dodgers from 1902 to 1925, announced that he was going to purchase grounds to build a new concrete and steel stadium, but he needed money, so he sold half the team to Ed and Steve McKeever. That's where the name for McKeever Place, which was on the side of Ebbets Field, comes from. The team was based at Ebbets Field, which opened April 9, 1913.

"That was a long, long time ago."

"It was a bit before your time and mine, Haleigh."

"It's much closer to your time, Grandpa."

"True! I enjoyed living only a couple blocks away from Ebbets Field and my Brooklyn Dodgers."

I was about five years old when Casey Stengel was hired away from my Brooklyn Dodgers. He later turned out to be the greatest of managers. Can you believe that even "The Bambino," the "Babe," was hired in 1938 as the first-base coach and was a part of the Dodgers?

On April 30, 1940, James Otto "Tex" Carleton of the Dodgers pitched a no-hitter, blanking the Cincinnati Reds, 3–0. As an eight-year-old, I asked my friends, "What's a no-hitter?" I didn't know until that day.

"Papa Larry, what's a no-hitter?"

"A no-hitter, Rebecca, is a pitcher who pitches without anyone getting a base hit. That means it's a really good pitcher."

"A no-hitter means a good pitcher," Rebecca confirms.

The Dodgers won the pennant in 1941 and were managed by Leo Durocher. Imagine—in 1941 they had an attendance of 1,214,000 and they left Brooklyn some years later. They lost the World Series to the Yankees 4–1, but those were the days; Brooklyn had a place deep in my heart.

They were a great team. They had Mickey Owen as catcher and Dolph Camilli as first baseman. Camilli lived one block away from where I lived—can you imagine a baseball player doing that? Billy Herman was second base. Cookie Lavagetto was our third baseman. Pee Wee Reese was our short stop and once signed a ball for me; I wrote a note about him to *The New York Times*.

Dixie Walker was our right field outfielder, and he was so popular with the Brooklyn fans that it brought him the nickname "The People's Choice." He was named the 1944 National League batting champion, was considered five times for the MVP award, and was an All-Star player for five consecutive years, from 1943 to 1947. He was an outstanding hitter.

And Pete Reiser was our Rookie of the Year. He was magnificent. Unfortunately, he had hit the wall too many times and he retired prematurely from baseball. What a great future Reiser had; he wasn't just good—he was fantastic!

In left field was Joe Medwick, a consummate pro—he batted .318.

The pitchers in those days were awesome—Kirby Higbee, Whitlow Wyatt, Kurt Davis, and the bullpen reliever, Hugh Casey. Other guys on the team were Luke Hamlin and Freddy Fitzsimmons, who subsequently owned a bowling alley right around the corner from where I lived.

These were the great Dodgers; the Dodgers I loved, took pride in, and lived for. These Dodgers were so great that the following became All-Stars: Dolph Camilli, Billy Herman, Cookie Lavagetto, Joe Medwick, Micky Owen, Pee Wee Reese, Dixie Walker, and Whitlow Wyatt. They were an extraordinary bunch of individuals.

"Grandpa, I wish I could've seen the Dodgers in Brooklyn with you."

"I wish you could've seen them too, Alex."

The Dodgers finished first in the National League in 1955. They were managed by Walter Alston. They had an attendance of over a million people.

"A million, that's a lot of people."

"The Dodgers had a lot of fans, Haleigh."

The Dodgers finally won the World Series for the first time over the New York Yankees, 4–3, in 1955. I cannot tell you the joy that I had. I got phone calls and cards from all over the world from kids I grew up with in Brooklyn, because this was our day of not finishing second, but finishing first, and, of course, beating the damn Yankees. I was in dental school at the time, and even my mother, who could care less about baseball and never called me—I could have had a broken ankle, but she would not have called me—called me up from her store. This was a special day and all of Brooklyn was truly happy for us on this day. We were the capital of the world. This was our team of destiny; we were not to be denied.

"I think it's a special day when the Mets beat the Yankees, Papa Larry."

"It was a grand day, Alex. We had a great parade in Brooklyn that year, and people literally came back from all over the world to celebrate the event and commemorate a special period in our lives when everybody—just sitting on the stoops as kids—used to yearn for the time when our beloved Dodgers, our boys of summer, would bring home the World Series to Brooklyn. We had finally realized those yearnings. And to this day we still dream of that day when, oh man, people from all over the world joined, rejoiced, and cheered and cried—we were the champions of the world!"

Unfortunately, two years later, the Dodgers left Brooklyn for the West Coast, never to return. On September 29, 1957, the Dodgers lost their final game to Pittsburgh, 2–1, before moving west. Roger Craig started, and Sandy Koufax relieved. The Dodgers left Brooklyn forever. The Dodgers played in the National League from 1890 until 1957. They won twelve National League pennants and one World Series before moving in 1958 to Southern California to become the Los Angeles Dodgers.

On April 20, 1995, the Dodgers president, Peter O'Malley, donated the Brooklyn Dodgers 1955 World Championship plaque, the only such plaque that was ever in Brooklyn, to the borough in which it was won, saying, "The plaque belongs in Brooklyn, and it came home."

I knew nearly all the 1941 Brooklyn Dodgers (when we lost the World Series to the Yankees) and the 1955 Brooklyn Dodgers (when we won the World Series) and of course all of those in between.

"You knew the Dodgers?"

"I sure did, Alex. In those days, they not only worked at Ebbets

Field in Brooklyn, but they also took us into the ballpark. In those days, they did not make so much money, and they literally lived on our block. Can you imagine a ball player living on our block today? They were just good people, trying to make a living and enjoying the game of baseball."

"I wish I had ball players living near me."

I remember meeting Pee Wee Reese, a future Hall of Famer, in 1947. I met him at Ebbets Field when the players were coming off the field. I asked for his autograph and he said to me, "Son, what do you want to do when you grow up?" I replied, "Gee, I don't know...." When I told my mother the story that night, she put her arm around me, kissed me, and said, "Lawrence—study, because it's not going to be baseball!"

Then in 1950, I met my favorite center fielder, Duke Snyder. Yes, there was Willie Mays of the Giants and Mickey Mantle of the Yankees, but to me, the Brooklyn bums and Duke Snyder were my very favorites. Remembering when I spoke to him in Brooklyn and at Cooperstown has always been a sensational feeling with me.

Years later, I even met Sandy Koufax and Don Drysdale. They were the great pitchers of the Brooklyn Dodgers and of course the Los Angeles Dodgers. I met them in Florida. Sandy Koufax was a quiet, soft-spoken guy. Don Drysdale was the dynamic and chatty guy. In those days, if their team got one run, they would win. Koufax and Drysdale went on to become more famous and were inducted into the Baseball Hall of Fame.

I went to the Hall of Fame when they inducted Don Sutton of the Brooklyn Dodgers, and I will never forget Sutton's speech, in which he said, "I came to work every day with my lunch pail, and I walked in the steps of greatness, the greatness of Koufax and Drysdale. I could never be as great as them. The best I could do was work as hard as them."

They say you can never go home again. Yes, you can, but only once. For one night, the past and present came beautifully together. On August 14, 2009, I took Alex and Doug to a New York Mets baseball game at Citi Field. Alex was thrilled.

"I loved it, Grandpa. I got a baseball with an autograph, two hot dogs, French fries, and ice cream."

All healthy foods! I had to laugh. "That's right, Alex. And your dad, Doug, and you wore your New York Mets hats and shirts. I wore my Brooklyn Dodgers shirt and hat from 1955 when the Dodgers won their first World Series."

The rotunda of the new Citi Field was built to duplicate the rotunda of Ebbets Field in Brooklyn of the 1930s and 1940s. The new rotunda had old pictures of the favorite players of my youth. I posed with Alex in front of the pictures of Duke Snyder and Jackie Robinson.

So many people in the packed crowd came over to me to shake my hand and touch my old Brooklyn Dodgers shirt. They related stories of their parents, friends, and themselves, when at an earlier age they went to Ebbets Field to root for the Brooklyn Dodgers. So many of these people hugged me with a tear in their eyes and, in turn, I had a tear in my eye, reliving the time in our past when we were the boys of summer.

"I remember when you pointed to center field, Grandpa, and told me about your time as a kid."

"What did you tell him, Grandpa?"

"Haleigh, I told Alex that as a little kid I could see center field from the tar roof of my four-story tenement. I would listen to Red

Barber, the radio voice of the Brooklyn Dodgers, as he described a home run being hit into Bedford Avenue. I saw the home run as it was being hit over the fence. It was my type of television without having television."

"It was real TV!"

"It was more than real TV, Haleigh. It was the Dodgers. It was my life as a kid."

"Watching the Dodgers was like watching real TV to Papa Larry," Rebecca yells again as she continues skipping around. "My daddy, David, likes baseball too."

"Yes, it was like real TV, Rebecca."

"What else did you do, Papa Larry? It sounds like you had fun playing games and watching real TV when you were a kid."

"I did more than play and watch the Dodgers, Haleigh. There was so much to do in Brooklyn. I was always doing something. In fact, I used to be a Boy Scout."

"A Boy Scout? What's that?" Haleigh grabs my hand, awaiting an answer, while Alex keeps making swinging motions as if to hit a baseball with a bat and Rebecca skips around us to her own imaginary music. A light breeze brushes by us as we enter the park boardwalk with Mesa in the lead.

Ebbets Field, Brooklyn

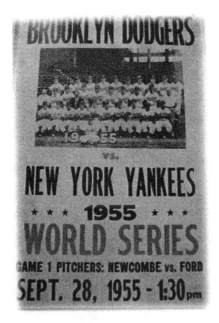

*Dodgers World
Series poster, 1955*

The Dodger Victory Book, 1942

*Three generations of
the Harte family,
(left to right)
Douglas, me, and
Alex, cheering on
the New York Mets
at Citi Field, 2009*

BOY SCOUTING

Boy Scout Oath:

On my honor I will do my best
To do my duty to God and my country
and to obey the Scout Law;
To help other people at all times;
To keep myself physically strong,
mentally awake, and morally straight.

One of the greatest things that I have done was to join the Boy Scouts. It was a lot of fun. Some of what was taught I already knew in advance; some of it I learned. Being kids from Brooklyn, we had certain attributes. We used to go to a jamboree, where scouts would come from other areas besides Brooklyn. They would have contests involving throwing a knife or an axe into a tree from a certain distance. We kids from Brooklyn would always win, and the other scoutmasters would say, "How come?" And our scoutmaster would say, "They practice every day!"

I began Scouting in 1943. Looking back, it was one of the most exciting, stimulating, and thought-provoking parts of my life. A kid from Brooklyn had the opportunity of learning all about the outdoors, about himself, about how to work by himself and with himself, and how to work with a lot of people, in a group setting. We lived outdoors, we breathed outdoors, we cooked outdoors (although my cooking was horrible and still is), and we had adventures. For a boy, that was exciting.

"I might want to join the Boy Scouts," Alex states with interest. "Do I have to be eleven or twelve?"

"You don't have to be eleven or twelve, Alex. You can go earlier."

"Can I go, too, Grandpa?" Haleigh asks.

"The Boy Scouts is only for boys, but you can join the Girl Scouts."

"Yeah! I'm going to the Girl Scouts."

I had a scoutmaster named Paul Sofrin, and he once gave me a book on bird study, which I still have, because I came in first in a paper drive. I collected more newspapers than anybody else in the whole troop. Why? I still don't know why, except I wanted to be the best, even if it was in collecting newspapers. I literally stayed up all day and all night because I wanted to win first prize for gathering papers. My scoutmaster wrote in my little bird book, "To Larry because you are a real American Boy Scout."

I remember when I had gone to Staten Island to earn the Bird Study merit badge. This was after taking a subway, a ferry, and a bus and walking two miles to reach a gentleman on Staten Island. He asked me, "Larry, what do you know about birds?" I said to him, "I know there are two kinds of birds—pigeons and jailbirds." He laughed, and spent the whole day and next day teaching me about birds, about which way animals run and walk in the forest, and about how to survive in the forest. Being a city kid, I will always remember the experience of learning how to survive in nature.

"I love birds. They're beautiful. They have so many pretty colors."

"That's not the type of birds I meant, Rebecca."

"I like all kinds of birds," Rebecca shouts. She lifts her arms up and begins to flap them as if she were a bird, circling Mesa on the boardwalk.

"Grandpa, I know what pigeons are because we see them in the park, but what are jailbirds?"

"Well, Alex, jailbirds are criminals, or bad people, who are living in jail."

"That's not a real bird, Grandpa," Haleigh informs me.

"I knew it wasn't a real bird, but it was the only one I could think of at the time."

"Pickle juice!"

"It's okay, Grandpa, at least you knew about pigeons," Alex adds.

Once I had the opportunity to become a patrol leader because I spoke up when other people would still be thinking. Since then, I have had a philosophy: think, then make a decision. In other words, if I make errors, I would rather they be errors of commission, while I'm doing something, rather than of omission, not doing anything. I would rather walk the mountains, climb the hills, bloody my knees, scrape my nose—anything, as long as I'm making an effort—than not do anything. At the end of the day I'd be able to say, "I gave it my best," rather than, "If only."

In the Boy Scouts we used flint and steel to make a fire. One day I was practicing in my mother's bathroom on the linoleum floor and I set fire to part of the floor. I was sick. I doused the fire and opened the window. What was I going to do? I cut out a piece of tile from underneath the bathtub and carefully replaced the burnt tile in the middle of the bathroom, then glued it in. Would you believe it, it was years later before my mother found out! See, I knew I could work with my hands.

"Papa Larry, you set a fire. They get hot!"

"Yes, Rebecca, a fire is hot. It's important not to play with fire or else you can do something bad like I did, or even worse."

"Did you get in trouble?"

"Not really, Alex, but your great-grandmother did let me have an earful. I bet I would've been in big trouble if she had caught me when

I did it."

"I don't like to get in trouble," Haleigh blurts out. "That's why I always try to be good."

Alex tugs on my pants and gestures for me to bend down to him. As I bend down, he softly whispers, "She's not always good, Grandpa."

"I see," I whisper softly back to Alex. He gives me a grin of contentment and we continue to walk down the scenic boardwalk.

Scouting is great. It teaches you to think for yourself, and it was a lot of fun for me because I had to learn to live and survive in the wilderness, to mark trees so that I could make my way through the forest, and to use a compass. We learned about animals, about all kinds of birds, and about eating in the wilderness. We learned where to find wild animals and docile animals. We learned about first aid and to stay in shape, but more than that, we learned how to survive by ourselves: how to keep warm, how to keep cool, how to use water, how to make different foods.

Living in the woods with nature was exciting, fantastic, and absolutely thrilling. We hiked, sometimes seven miles a day, sometimes fourteen, sometimes more. We used to walk over the George Washington Bridge on our hike to the wilderness. At that time the wilderness was in Fort Lee, New Jersey—can you believe it?—which today is all built up. But that was my wilderness, where we would dream of being like Daniel Boone or of being in the French and Indian War.

"Who's Daniel Boone?"

"He's a legendary folk hero, Haleigh. Daniel Boone was a hunter and frontiersman. There were great tales about his adventures in the woods."

"Can you tell us some of his adventures?"

"Maybe one day, Haleigh."

"I want to hear more about Grandpa, Haleigh," Alex interrupts.

"Me too!" Rebecca stops circling Mesa and runs over to us.

We came across a brook one day and we all had to go to the bathroom. I, as a group leader, said, "Follow me." We all did what we had to do. We nicknamed that brook "Camp Pissing Water." Today it is the site of a high rise apartment. Times do change, but the memories remain.

"Why didn't you use a bathroom, Grandpa?"

"We didn't have any bathrooms around, Haleigh."

"Pickle juice!"

Possibly because I was an only child and I had to rely on myself, I absolutely enjoyed the Boy Scouts. Being a Boy Scout was a blast. I went through the ranks of Scouting. It was exciting because it meant that I was achieving something that I was working hard for. My parents were pretty smart, even though they did not know much about Scouting. They did know that it kept me off the streets, out of trouble, and interested. Between Scouting and sports, I didn't get into as much trouble as I could have. It also helped us kids to take our minds off of the war in Europe and Japan in those days.

During World War II one of our jobs as Scouts was to deliver food to the troops that were stationed with anti-aircraft guns in Prospect Park. They had artillery stored in case planes came over from Germany. Prospect Park was only two blocks away from my house. At night, our job was to help the air raid warden make sure that all windows were blacked out so that no light came through them. In those days, we had a blackout, where everybody kept their lights out so that the Germans couldn't spot us. It's amazing to me now, looking back.

"Were you scared, Papa Larry?"

"It was a horrifying situation, Alex, but that was the time we were growing up in, and we just went through it naturally."

"I think I would've been scared, Grandpa."

"I have to admit, it was a scary time. In fact, I even invented ice balls as weapons against the Germans."

In the winter, I used to make snowballs. One day it occurred to me that if I mixed stone pebbles into a snowball and then drenched it with salt water, I would have an ice ball. I told my scoutmaster of this idea, that if the Germans came, we could throw these ice balls at them. My scoutmaster told me we might hurt the Germans if we used the ice balls. I remember looking at him with my eyes ablaze saying, "I don't want to hurt them; I want to kill them!" Needless to say, no other neighborhood gangs wanted to have snowball fights with us.

"Did you hurt any Germans, Papa Larry?" Rebecca asks.

"No, I didn't have the opportunity to use my ice balls."

"Did the Germans hurt a lot of people, Grandpa?"

"They did, Rebecca. They hurt a lot of people."

I did have one experience that, unfortunately, I will never forget. There was a boy in our building who was killed at Pearl Harbor, on December 7, 1941. I remember when his mother received the news. She cried, and all the women in the building came and hugged and consoled her. I went up to her and couldn't say a word; I just put my arm around her, and she put her arm around me. To this day, I don't deal well with tragedy. I still put my arms around people and hug them, but I find it difficult to say the right thing. I just hug with my heart, my soul, and my arms.

"World War II sounds really bad, Grandpa. Why were people fighting?"

"Well, Haleigh, there were some bad people hurting a lot of good people. They were hurting people from their country and other countries. At one point, the good people decided it was time to fight back, and that is how the war started."

"I wish there weren't any bad people."

"Me too, Haleigh."

"War sounds dumb, Grandpa."

"It sure does. But unfortunately, as long as there are bad people in this world, there will always be war."

"Does everyone kiss and hug at the end? Alex and I kiss and hug after we fight with each other."

"No, no one kisses and hugs at the end."

"Papa Larry, I want to hear more about the war when you were a kid," Alex interjects.

As we near the middle of the boardwalk, we come to a wide area with a watchtower and benches overlooking a lake. Mesa and Rebecca stop to watch a fish jump out of the water, while Alex and Haleigh sit beside me, eager to hear about my time as a kid during the war.

Boy Scout medal award certificate, Waste Paper Campaign, 1945

Boy Scout Certificate of Leadership, 1945

GROWING UP IN A WAR

Wars are won not by brilliant strategy,
but by those who make fewer mistakes.
—*Lawrence S. Harte*

Mom had a cousin who was a bombardier on a B-17 in World War II. I was impressed by his candor and humility—he was a real hero. Later on in my life, I went to the world-famous Oshkosh Air Show in Wisconsin. I met a Congressional Medal of Honor winner. I thanked him for being a hero and saving our country. He replied, "Son, I was put in a position. I had to react without thinking. If I thought, I probably would never have done it."

"Grandpa, we have our very own war hero in the family," Haleigh exclaims while she taps her hand on the bench trying to get Rebecca's attention. "What's a bombardier, Grandpa?"

"A bombardier is someone who is part of a crew that drops bombs during the war using bombsights."

"How do they know where to drop the bomb?"

"They did it by the use of a Norden bombsight, which is a technical way of accurately telling where to drop the bomb."

"Pickle juice!"

We used to take a subway train out to Floyd Bennett Field, in Brooklyn. The Naval Air Force, which was stationed there, sent planes to scour the waters off the Atlantic Ocean in search of German submarines and aircraft. We were able to get close to the field because, in those days, they didn't have the security that they have now. I remember seeing those brave pilots who had come down out of their planes and just looked like everybody else, except that they were my heroes.

Growing up as a kid during World War II, I used to have a map that would show where the Allies and the Japanese were. With me, it was a constant game, but unfortunately, it was a game where lives were lost, where there were defeats and there were victories.

"What are allies, Grandpa?" Alex tugs on my shirt to catch my attention.

"Allies are the people that are fighting on your side in the war."

I followed the war on my map to the end, where at least physically there was peace in August of 1945. I was seven years old when the Munich Agreement was signed, in which Chamberlain and Duvalier of France accepted Germany's annexation of parts of Czechoslovakia. That was in September 1938. By March 15, 1939, Hitler had broken the agreement by annexing part of Bohemia and Moravia. On September 1, 1939, Germany invaded Poland. Two days later the Allies declared war on Germany. Incidentally, at that time of the war, France had more troops than Germany, but it didn't help. In August of 1940 the Battle of Britain began with a tremendous bombardment of England.

During this period, Adolph Hitler was the dictator of Germany. Although Hitler was a bad person, he would not have been able to implement his military and extermination objectives of the Jews and other minorities without the tacit consent of the military, the economic elite, and some of the German people.

On December 7, 1941, while I was listening to a professional football game on the radio, the Japanese invaded Pearl Harbor. During this time, Japan wanted to be a superpower. In order to achieve this status, they needed oil and minerals for their energy and raw material needs. The U.S. blockaded these areas from Japan. This action was one of the reasons that led Japan to attack Pearl Harbor.

We knew in advance that they were going to invade, but we thought it might be in the Philippines, so they really tricked us. It was a devastating attack. We lost five of eight battleships.

On April 18, 1942, we launched the Doolittle Raid, where land-based bombers set off from an American aircraft carrier to bomb Tokyo. This provided not as much of a physical lift as an emotional one for the American people. Finally, on June 4, 1942, we engaged in the Battle of Midway, where the Japanese lost four aircraft carriers to our one. That certainly was the turning of the war. On June 6, 1944, we staged the D-Day invasion, when the Allies landed in Normandy, and, on May 7, 1945, the German forces unconditionally surrendered. After dropping two atomic bombs in Japan, we were victorious and World War II ended in August of 1945.

When the war stopped, we had a victory block party. To this day, I don't remember a party as glorious as that party. But while we were happy for victory, we were sad for our men and women who were lost during the service of our country. Like many things in life, it was a bittersweet experience, but it was a moment to remember. I remember drinking beer—if my mother only knew! So, I threw up—what the heck.

"Grandpa, you drank beer as a kid?" Haleigh questions in a scolding manner.

"I did things I shouldn't have done as a kid."

"You were a bad boy, Grandpa."

"Not all the time, Haleigh."

"Grandpa, you lived through a lot of history," Alex interrupts. "There was so much war. Were you scared?"

"Of course, I was scared. Since I was a young child, I lived much of my youth living in a world filled with war. World War II wasn't the only war I lived through. In fact, we're living through a war now too."

Rebecca, bored at looking at fish jumping in and out of the water, walks toward me and utters, "Papa Larry, there are bad people in war, just like the Mafia."

"That's true, Rebecca."

"What war?" Alex questions.

"The war in Afghanistan, which started on October 7 in the year 2001."

"That was the year I was born!"

"It was, Alex."

"Do we have to turn off our lights like you did, Grandpa?"

"No, Haleigh, it's a different type of war we are fighting than when I was young."

"What other wars were there, Papa Larry?"

As I lift Rebecca up onto my lap and Mesa sits beside the bench on the boardwalk, I look at my grandchildren and answer with a soft, sad tone, "Too many!"

The Arab–Israeli War of 1948

I was sixteen when the Arab–Israeli War began on May 15, 1948. On May 14, Israel proclaimed its sovereignty. On May 15, the United Nations partitioned land into two areas, a Jewish and an Arab state. The Arabs refused to accept this, and the armies of Egypt, Syria, Jordan, Lebanon, and Iraq, supported by others, invaded Israel with the intention of destroying it. The historical context for this was that after World War I, the Ottoman Empire had fallen, and the League of Nations had given England and France the authority to respond as they saw fit. The modern Arab world and the Republic of Turkey were created at that time. The League of Nations granted France mandates over Syria and Lebanon, and granted the United Kingdom mandates over Mesopotamia (Iraq) and Palestine (which was later sudivided into two regions: Palestine and Transjordan). It was in the Palestine section that Israel was established.

In March of 1948, many of the Jews in the Middle East had served with the British on the side of the Allies. The Grand Mufti in Palestine had cooperated with the Germans and made broadcasts during the War advocating the killing and annihilation of the Jews. Many of the Jewish soldiers who had fought with the British in World War II, later on fought in the Arab–Israeli War of 1948.

"Why would they want to kill the Jews?" Alex gave a horrified look. "Grandpa, I'm Jewish!"

"Me too," Haleigh looks at me with shock.

"Well, it had to do with land and religion issues, which have festered for centuries."

Through the years there were many wars between Israel and its neighboring states. Israel almost always won, and this was a tremendous humiliation to the Arab people. Many of the Arabs in Israel moved to Arab states, which kept them under the yoke and purposely kept them poor to perpetuate this anger and make it more difficult for them to just be part of their new Arab country. The relocated Arabs felt this treatment as humiliation, and they believed that one way to avenge this humiliation was to turn religious. Some practitioners of Islam also turned to terrorism, believing that this was a way of making the world see them and not forget about them. To this day, we have this terrorism in a large part of the Middle East. We have a lot of Jihad around the world and there are many reasons for this, many political, many religious.

"Is that why there is the war in Afghanistan?"

"Yes, Alex, terrorism is one of the reasons we have the war in

Afghanistan."

"Is it ever going to stop, Grandpa, or am I going to grow up in war like you?"

"I hope it stops soon. Unfortunately, war never has a good ending because so many people die to fight for their countries."

I think that one strong way to counteract terrorism is to have complete alternative uses of energy. We should not have to use oil as a bargaining tool with enemies of our country. We need politicians who have the gumption, the leadership, and the intellect to drive this idea forward. I believe our country would be able to do it; we just need the leadership to work with us on it. We have nothing to lose; we have everything to gain—peace and a better way of life for our children and their children.

"I hope it stops soon so no more people have to die."

"Me too, Haleigh. Me too."

As the glistening rays of the sun begin to dim in the daily ritual of sunset, we finish our walk on the boardwalk and our day in the park.

"I want to hear more about your life as a kid, Grandpa."

"I will tell more another day, Alex. Right now, we have to hurry home for dinnertime. Everyone is waiting for us."

"You promise?"

"I promise, Haleigh."

The Show Must Go On

Act! Act! You have the wrong place.
We are not allowed to act here.
                    —from the movie *Children of Paradise*

Nicholas stands in front of the mirror and says to himself, "Now, that's what I mean." I get to see Nick on rare occasions, only when I am visiting Kathy Phillips (who is Nick's grandmother), in Florida. As he prepares for his performance in a local musical production, Nick begins to sing a tune to get his vocal chords warmed up. He has a great voice. If I had his voice, combined with my drive—God! I could've been on *American Idol*. Watching Nick get ready for his debut, I couldn't help but remember the times when I was on a stage.

"Did you know, Nick, that I began my show business career in third grade?"

"Really, Dr. Larry, what did you perform in?"

"I was in a play. My line was 'What do I see? I see stars.'"

"Were you any good, Dr. Larry?"

"I apparently did not say it loud enough. The teacher whacked me across the head. For a split second, I saw stars, the moon, and all the planets at twelve noon. In those days teachers could do that to you. I thought it was perfectly normal, and the next time I thought I better open my mouth wider."

"I'm glad you stuck with being an orthodontist; it seems to work better for you," Nick chuckles.

At age eleven, I found out that I was a listener in music class. A listener was someone who sang so off-key that it messed up everybody else, and they told you to listen and not sing. What a blow to my ego.

"Did you stop singing when this happened?"

"No, Nick, I didn't stop singing. Instead, I immediately decided to do something about it. I just was not going to take it. I decided to practice the school songs until I got them right. If I did not practice a song, it sounded terrible to me even in the shower."

"Did you practice by yourself, or did you have help?"

"I played the accordion, and the right hand is like a piano, so I practiced on my accordion on my right hand until I was able to sing a song. And I just sang and sang that song. Nowadays, I can sing a few songs only because I practiced. People think I can really sing, but I really cannot."

"Your secret is safe with me," Nick whispers with a big smile and places his finger over his mouth to say *hush-hush*.

As we leave the house and ride to the theater, Nick can't help but wonder if that was the end for me in show business. "Dr. Larry, you tried so hard to practice those songs so you could sing them well; did you give up with performing after that?"

"Actually, since high school, I liked theater and song and dance. The problem was that song and dance didn't like me."

"So, you still tried?"

"Of course, I wasn't going to give up. I was in some high school and college productions that I can't recall, except for the varsity show in college."

"What did you do in the varsity show?"

"At eighteen, I tried out for a varsity show at Columbia, where I worked on the French can-can dance. Was that ugly!"

"I take it you didn't do too well. So was this the end for you?"

"You would think, but apparently I didn't learn my lesson. So, I just moved from dance to song."

"You tried singing, again!" Nick puts his hand over his face and nods his head from left to right in clean musical movements. Even when he isn't trying, he shows so much rhythm and talent.

"While I was at Columbia, I had the opportunity of being a stand-in at the Metropolitan Opera. As an extra, they paid you $5 and all the sweat you could accumulate. I tried to sing but they said, 'Mouth it, baby, mouth it!'"

"Hmmm. Sounds like that was the end for you."

"Not really. But as much as I liked to perform, whether I was good or bad, I truly enjoyed being a spectator of the performing arts. After college, I worked at the Astor Theater in Brooklyn. They had summer stock (a theater that presents productions only in the summertime), and they performed *Mister Roberts* with its lead Ensign Pulver. I went there every day for some thirty days and my God, I can almost see the lines in front of me to this day."

"What did you work as in the theater?"

"I worked in production at the theater and with props. I felt that

I could be an understudy, even though it was a professional theater, if someone were to get sick. It just never happened though, but I tried. I thought that was a fast way to Broadway, being an understudy in a small theater in Brooklyn."

While I was in Pennsylvania for dental school, I used to go to performances of the Philadelphia Orchestra, where Eugene Ormandy was conducting. I bought seats in the bleacher section; not the best seats in the house, but they were worth it. They were the only tickets I could afford, and it was wonderful. In those days, the Philadelphia Orchestra probably had the best violin section in the world. In fact, I think they still may have one of the best violin sections in the whole world.

"Since song and dance didn't work out for you during college and, it seems, neither did theater, did you stop trying to break into show business?"

"Believe it or not, joining the Air Force after dental school didn't stop me from my theatrical pursuits."

"Really?" Nick gave a look of surprise. "You must really love show business, Dr. Larry."

"At twenty-five, I directed and produced the Air Force show in Rome, New York, with no experience. I was the only one that opened my mouth and volunteered for this position."

"How was the show?"

"It was okay. One thing you learn in the military is never to volunteer. I went against a cardinal rule—shame on me! In the military you really don't have much free time because you have your other military duties, so we worked on the production literally all night long."

"What was the show about?"

"The show was about a vagabond guy who goes every three years from base to base, and how he tries to enjoy life, make love with his wife, and show her the wonderful parts of life by going from show to show, or from base to base."

"It sounds interesting," Nick replies nicely with a face of disinterest. "Did your audience like the show?"

"Fortunately for me, the show never went on the road. We were lucky that the show stayed in one place. If we had gone on the road, it would have been an auto crash."

"I guess after this, you finally called it quits?"

"Not really, I've never really left the world of show business. Since I wasn't as talented as you and had to work harder than most others, I just realized how much I truly loved it."

"You'd have to love show business, Dr. Larry, to go through what you've gone through."

"I always thought that maybe I'll get my big break one day."

"Did you?"

"In a way, I did. When I got out of the military and went into practice, I directed TV shows for children in Morristown, New Jersey."

"That sounds like fun. How'd you get into that?"

"Since I had just started my practice, I had lots of time and I heard that in Morristown they needed someone to work with children. Since I was a kid at heart, I decided to just work with the kids. It was a local television station, so I really volunteered because the other people, I guess, were not as enthusiastic as me, although probably more talented."

"I think it's great that you never gave up, Dr. Larry."

"I don't believe in giving up, Nick. It doesn't really matter what other people think of you; it only matters what you think of yourself.

And, I always knew that, even though I wasn't as talented, I could still do it with a little perseverance and hard work."

"If you could do it, Dr. Larry, then so can I."

"You definitely can Nick." It filled my heart with warmth and joy to hear those words from his mouth. "I kept on doing different things within the show business world throughout my life and enjoyed every minute of it."

"What else have you done?"

"When I was about forty, I went into the Little Theater in Livingston, New Jersey, to try my hand at theater once again. I performed in *Brigadoon* and *Kiss Me Kate*."

"What part did you play?"

"I played Ralph, the stage manager, in *Kiss Me Kate*."

"I don't know the show, but it sounds like a great part."

"It was for me. We used to practice every day for about three months for our show. I really couldn't sing or dance that well, and I had to be right next to the piano to sing on key. The piano was stage left. I was supposed to come on stage right, but I kept coming on stage left so I could be close to the piano."

"That sounds like you, Dr. Larry."

"I had to be resourceful. When we had our auditions and I was singing, people looked at me and said, 'Oh my God—is that Larry Harte? Thank God he has a day job!'"

"It's true; it's a good thing you have a day job, Dr. Larry," Nick looks at me seriously. "It sounds like you would've starved if you had tried to make it in show business."

"You may be right, Nick. But I do remember the great songs from *Kiss Me Kate*. It was the most exciting part of my theatrical experience, although minimal."

I remember the songs "Another Op'nin', Another Show," "Why Can't You Behave?", "Wunderbar," "So In Love," "We Open in Venice," "Tom, Dick or Harry," "I Hate Men," "Were Thine That Special Face," "Kiss Me Kate," "Too Darn Hot," "Where is the Life That Late I Led?", "Always True to You in My Fashion," "Bianca," and "I Am Ashamed That Women are So Simple." And my favorite, "Brush Up Your Shakespeare." If you practice these songs for four months, four nights a week, with people that you enjoy, it becomes part of your life, part of your psyche, part of your past, and part of your present.

As we walk through the doors of the theater and Nick parts ways with us to get ready for his big debut singing "Yesterday" by the Beatles, I still couldn't help but reminisce about my times in the theater and the wonderful music, performances, and shows that I experienced throughout my life.

I recently saw *Kiss Me Kate* at the Paper Mill Playhouse and got a kick out of the guy who played Ralph the stage manager. This guy's credits included Broadway's *Beauty and the Beast* in London, *Showboat*, *Peter Pan*, *Guys and Dolls*, *Cats*, *A Chorus Line*, and *Kiss of the Spider Woman*. Can you imagine—he needed all those credits to play my little Ralph the stage manager role. Humph! The only credits that I had were from high school and college.

Today I very rarely go to a movie because I seem to like the old movies more. I think most people like old movies because, in the days portrayed in those movies, time stood still, and the movies meant something because you had so much time to enjoy them and listen to them. Today life has such a fast pace that by the time you put your hand out to shake hands with someone you've met, he or she has already moved past you. Life then was just slow. Today, people are time starved; life is so fast that we don't remember what we had for breakfast. In those days, I could quite often see two movies plus a newsreel or a sports reel for ten cents and a penny tax. The movies in those days were neat; looking back, they were sensational!

In 1939, I saw *Beau Geste* with Gary Cooper, Ray Milland, and Robert Preston. It was a wonderful movie about the British upper class and was a fairly authentic description of life of the pre-1914 Foreign Legion. I guess I was at a very impressionable age. I actually thought that I was in the movie.

There was also *Dark Victory*, with Bette Davis, about a Long Island hedonistic socialite. It was an intense drama. I was a kid from Brooklyn. I had no fancy social life; I couldn't say thee and thou. I said, "My God, maybe someday I'll be able to say these fancy words in a fancy social life."

There was *Drums Along the Mohawk* with Claudette Colbert and Henry Fonda. *Gone with the Wind* with Vivien Leigh, and Clark Gable as Rhett Butler, and a black slave mammy played by Hattie McDonald. *Goodbye, Mr. Chips*, a portrait of a well-meaning shy and proper Latin schoolmaster, Mr. Chips, who devoted his life to his students. *Gunga Din*, one of my very favorites, partly based on the poem by Rudyard Kipling, which featured Cary Grant and Douglas Fairbanks, Jr.

Hunchback of Notre Dame, the film adaptation of Victor Hugo's classic tale starring Maureen O'Hara. *Mr. Smith Goes to Washington*, a really funny, sentimental story with James Stewart and Claude Raines. *Of Mice and Men*, a film adaptation of John Steinbeck's Depression classic, with Burgess Meredith and Lon Chaney, Jr. *Stagecoach*, a great Western film with John Carradine and Claire Trevor. *The Wizard of Oz*, such a great little children's fancy with a fantastic cast—Judy Garland, Bert Lahr, and Ray Bolger, to name a few.

Wuthering Heights truly is a great romantic love story movie based on Emily Bronte's tragic Victorian novel, featuring Laurence Olivier, Merle Oberon, and Geraldine Fitzgerald. And there was *Young Mr. Lincoln*, adapted from Lawrence Hardy's original story of the early years of Lincoln, with Henry Fonda. It was a GREAT year at the movies! Looking back, 1939 was a noteworthy year for an impressionable young Jewish boy growing up in Brooklyn.

The 1940s kept in step with 1939 for great movies. There was *Abe Lincoln in Illinois*, with Raymond Massey. *All This and Heaven, Too*, with Bette Davis, a nineteenth-century production set in France. *Fantasia* was a creative, innovative animated classic from Walt Disney with some Tchaikovsky and Stravinsky in the music.

The Grapes of Wrath, which was adapted from John Steinbeck's Pulitzer Prize-winning novel, is an epic story of the migration of a drought-stricken Oklahoma family that tries to get to the promised land of California, seeking farm work during the Depression. *The Great Dictator* with Charlie Chaplin was absolutely hysterical. Chaplin plays a dual role as a poor Jewish ghetto barber and a Hitler look-alike. And there was *The Great McGinty*, featuring Brian Dunleavy.

Knute Rockne, a favorite all-American movie featuring Pat O'Brien and Gail Page, was about the legend of Rockne and Notre Dame. *The Mark of Zorro* with actor Tyrone Power—man, was it swashbuckling and adventurous! *Our Town*, which is based on the Thornton Wilder novel, won the Pulitzer Prize, and was truly a unique movie. *The Philadelphia Story* was a comedy with Katherine Hepburn and Cary Grant. *Pinocchio* was humorous and, again, an animation, a true kid's classic. *Pride and Prejudice* was adapted from Jane Austin's novel, with Greer Garson, Maureen O'Sullivan, and

Marsha Hunt. There was *Rebecca*, by Alfred Hitchcock, with Joan Fontaine and Laurence Olivier. *The Santa Fe Trail*—that was so exciting, with Errol Flynn, Ronald Reagan, William Marshall, and Raymond Massey. And *The Thief of Baghdad*—oh, was that hilarious! This British fantasy film was just a kid's dream, and it still is to this day.

In 1941, *Citizen Kane* with Orson Welles was one of the best films ever made. It was an American drama about the private life of a newspaper publisher, William Randolph Hearst. Also, there was *All That Money Can Buy*, with Walter Huston and James Craig, and *The Maltese Falcon*, which starred Humphrey Bogart and Mary Astor in a great detective mystery. *Sergeant York* was every boy's favorite, with Gary Cooper, as was *Suspicion*, another great suspenseful film by Alfred Hitchcock starring Cary Grant. Man, is this a thriller!

In 1942, there was my all-time favorite *Casablanca*, with Humphrey Bogart and Ingrid Bergman. Wow! I'm still looking for Rick's Café in Casablanca. I've yet to find it. This year produced other classics like *Bambi*, another Disney production, and *Gentleman Jim*, about the heavy weight boxer Gentleman James Corbett, with Errol Flynn. *In Which We Serve*, directed, I think, by Noel Coward, was a drama about World War II. *King's Row* was the story about a small rural Midwestern town, with Robert Cummings, Claude Rains, and Ann Sheridan. *The Magnificent Ambersons* was the story of a wealthy Midwestern Victorian family and how a family fortune disappeared.

The Man Who Came To Dinner—oh, was that witty—featured Monty Wooley, Grant Marshall, and Billie Burke. *Mrs. Miniver*, with Walter Pigeon and Greer Garson, was about living during World War II in a British village outside London. Who could forget that! *Pride of the Yankees*, starring Gary Cooper, was about Lou Gehrig. I love this movie, even though I am a Dodgers fan; seeing it still makes me cry. It was heart wrenching.

The Talk of the Town is an amusing comedy with Cary Grant. *This Gun for Hire* is a mystery from Graham Green's novel, I think. *A Gun for Sale* with Allen Ladd is another brilliant film. *To Be or Not to Be* is a satire about exposing the Nazis that lampoons the Third Reich, starring Jack Benny and Carol Lombard. And, *Yankee Doodle Dandy*—did I love this! It's the story of George M. Cohan, a great song and dance man played by Jimmy Cagney and Walter Huston.

In 1943 there were films such as *Cabin in the Sky*, which is an all-black side-splitting musical with Eddie Rochester Anderson from Jack Benny fame. *Forever and a Day* deals with people in a great manor house in London from Napoleonic times to the World War II blitz of London. *For Whom the Bell Tolls* is a story from Ernest Hemingway's classic novel of the Spanish Civil War, with Gary Cooper and Ingrid Bergman. *Heaven Can Wait* is a fantasy comedy about a wealthy playboy, featuring Don Ameche and Gene Tierney. *The Human Comedy* is based on the original story by William Soroyan that deals with events of World War II and the need to cope with responsibilities; it starred Mickey Rooney, Van Johnson, Donna Reed, and James Craig.

Madame Curie was a historical biography of the famous scientist who discovered radium and changed the health picture of the world, with actors Greer Garson and Walter Pigeon. *The Oxbow Incident* is about two cowboy drifters, Henry Fonda and Harry Morgan. *Shadow of a Doubt by Alfred Hitchcock* was a suspenseful work! It stars Joseph Cotton and Theresa Wright and focuses on a small town in California. *The Song of Bernadette* is about a place in France that deals with miraculous visions. And *Watch on the Rhine*, based on

Lillian Hellman's Broadway play, was one of the really good anti-Nazi drama films of the war.

During 1944 there was *Arsenic and Old Lace*, a film that was good, macabre fun. It was about a lonely gentleman who lived in a Brooklyn home that employed mercy killings, and Cary Grant and John Alexander were in it. *Double Indemnity*—what a suspense film—starred Barbara Stanwyck, Fred McMurray, and Edward G. Robinson. *Gaslight*, a real Victorian thriller, was set in London, with Ingrid Bergman and Charles Boyer. *Going My Way*—ah, a classic film—starred Bing Crosby as a down-to-earth priest. *Hail the Conquering Hero* is about a World War II Marine Corps 4F reject and how he works and believes that he is a hero; he is even nominated for mayor. *Jane Eyre* is Charlotte Bronte's classic story about Victorian times, with Joan Fontaine, Margaret O'Brien, and Orson Welles.

Lifeboat, by Alfred Hitchcock, was all about Allied boats that are sunk by a U-boat and the story behind that occurrence; it starred Tallulah Bankhead, John Hodiak, and Walter Sleyzak. *Meet Me in St. Louis*—what a great romantic, musical movie that was. I love that story! It was the story of four sisters living in St. Louis, with Mary Astor, Judy Garland, Margaret O'Brien and Lucille Bremer. Don't forget *National Velvet*. It dealt with horses and starred Elizabeth Taylor and Mickey Rooney. It probably was the film that launched Elizabeth Taylor's career. *To Have and Have Not* was a first-class film based on Hemingway's novel, with Lauren Bacall and Humphrey Bogart. What a combination!

Now, in 1945 there were *Anchors Aweigh*, a musical comedy with Frank Sinatra and Gene Kelly; *And Then There Were None*; *The Bells of Saint Mary's*, with Bing Crosby; *The Lost Weekend*, with Ray Milland; *The Picture of Dorian Grey*; *Spellbound*, another Alfred

Hitchcock classic; and *A Tree Grows in Brooklyn* by Betty Smith, which was special to me because I grew up in Brooklyn.

Among the notable movies of 1946 was *Blue Skies*, with Bing Crosby, Fred Astaire, and Joan Crawford. The dance numbers "Putting on the Ritz" and "You Keep Coming Back Like a Song" were phenomenal. There was *Breakfast in Hollywood*, with Rita Granville, and *The Hardy Girls*, with Judy Allan, John Hodiak, Ray Bolger, Angela Lansbury, and Cyd Charisse. It was set in the Wild West days. *The Jolson Story* featured Larry Parks and Evelyn Keyes.

The Kid from Brooklyn featured Danny Kaye and Virginia Mayo and the great song "You're the Cause of It All." That Danny Kaye was a sensational actor. *Night and Day* was an excellent film with Cary Grant and Judy Simms, with all the well-known Porter songs. *The Road to Utopia* starred Bing Crosby, Bob Hope, and Dorothy Lamour. *The Stork Club* featured Betty Hutton and Don Defore. And there's the movie *The Sweetheart of Sigma Chi*, with a great record for Frank Sinatra. *The Ziegfeld Follies* by Flo Ziegfield featured a legendary cast—Fred Astaire, Red Skelton, Jimmy Durante, Fanny Bryce, Lena Horne, Esther Williams, Judy Garland, Lucille Ball, Gene Kelly—and the great song that came out, "This Heart of Mine."

Then 1947 brought us *Crossfire* and *Gentleman's Agreement*, with Gregory Peck. And I remember *Miracle on 34th Street*, a tender Christmas story.

You can't forget the movies of 1948 like *Easter Parade*—I still sing "In Your Easter Bonnet." Judy Garland was a wonderful singer. And there were others, such as *Hamlet*, with Laurence Olivier; *Johnny Belynda*; *I Remember Mama*; and *The Snake Pit*—man, was that scary.

I have to mention a few movies from 1949, including *Adam's Rib*, *Kind Hearts and Coronets*, and *The Third Man*. There were also classics like *Alice in Wonderland.*

All of these past movies are such great memories. They were always available a few blocks away from home—at The Rogers Theater, which was four blocks away; The Patio Theater, which was about ten blocks away; The Kenmore Theater, which was about a mile away; and The Kings, which was probably about a mile and a quarter away. We always walked and talked going to those movies, and what a bargain! We didn't realize how great these movies were until we saw them as old-timers today! Oh, the smell of show business. To have been on stage, dancing and singing like Danny Kaye or Fred Astaire, or to be Humphrey Bogart in *Casablanca.* I may not have had the most successful career in show business, but I felt like I was always on center stage right in the middle of all of these classics, right in the front row of the theater. What memories!

In those days, the movies were an escape from the war in Germany and Japan, from the state of being a little guy in a small area of Brooklyn, where we took our culture for granted. To a kid, not much really happened except for the Brooklyn Dodgers. Going to the movies was my world away from a little town. I could be one of the characters, and I could go all over the world. I experienced the adventure and felt that someday I too would travel the world. And I was excited at how the actor could play so many roles and "chameleon-ize" into so many different people. Watching the interactions of the characters, I began to try to understand what makes relationships work and how people succeed in different areas.

What an education. I learned that sometimes people succeed by acting because part of life is acting; part of life is chameleon-izing. And I learned from these movies that when you were nice to people and gave them respect and made them feel important, they would go out of their way to be extra nice to you. It was a win-win situation.

The movies stimulated me to try to get involved in understanding different kinds of people, and by doing that to understand myself. Also, by understanding different kinds of people, I could relate to them more easily and, hopefully, make it easier for them to understand me. Seeing movies also stimulated my desire to travel around the world. Even though I couldn't sing or dance, I wanted to travel the world and see its beautiful scenery and different cultures. And I knew that someday, when I had reached the end of my travels, I would still come back to my country, where my heart is.

Nicholas Andrews,
Kathy Phillips' grandson,
2009

Making a Living

If you could try and learn one thing a day,
you would be astounded at what you have learned after
many years.

—Lawrence S. Harte

"Good morning, Grandpa!" Alex moves toward me and gives me
a hug. "I am going to work with Daddy today."

"Are you?"

"Yes, today is 'Take Your Child to Work Day' at my school."

"Do you know what you want to do for work when you're older?"

"I want to be a player for the Devils," Alex exclaims, swooshing
his arms as if he were holding a hockey stick in play. He has always
been a fan of the New Jersey Devils hockey team. In fact, he also loves
the New York Mets baseball team and the New York Giants football
team.

"I think that's great Alex. Is there anything else you want to do?"

"I don't know. There are so many things I like. Grandpa, did you
always work as an orthodontist?"

"Not always."

"What did you do before?" Alex follows me into my office, watching me with his big brown eyes. He quickly sits in a chair positioned in front of my desk and cuddles his body into the curvature of the frame, awaiting a response.

"I worked at a few jobs before I became an orthodontist."

"What kind of jobs?" He squirms around a bit, trying to adjust his body to the chair to find the perfect position.

As I look back at the number of jobs I've had and the number of jobs I was fired from, it is apparent, to make an understatement, that I was destined to work for myself because, apparently, no one else wanted me to work for them. However, although some of my jobs were short-lived, I did learn a great deal from them.

"Well, Alex, when I was about seven years old, like you are now, until I was seventeen, I used to work at my mother's store in Williamsburg, Brooklyn. The store was Grand Central Station in action and noise."

"That sounds like a busy store. What kind of work did you do at your mommy's store?"

"My job was to watch the pushcart filled with merchandise that was in front of the store."

"All you had to do was look at a pushcart. That seems like a pretty easy job. Too bad Mommy and Daddy don't have a pushcart for me to watch."

"Not exactly. The items on the pushcart were cheaper than the prices of the items in the store. My job was to lure the customers into the store and make sure they did not steal from the pushcart."

"Oh! Were you good at your job, Grandpa?"

"In the beginning I was very shy but when I caught someone

trying to steal a pair of pants, I screamed and ran after the guy, even though I was only seven. It just wasn't right for someone to steal something. Once I got over my original shyness, I kind of liked the job of talking to people and trying to bring them into the store. It was like a challenge to me, and I kept busy."

I found that people, if you are nice enough and listen to them, would be on your side. I also learned to be on the same wavelength as people. I would be like a chameleon and change my accent and tone depending on the customer. If they were quiet, I was quiet. If they were loud, I was loud. I found that they liked people who they felt were like them.

"I don't think that works with Haleigh, Grandpa. I try to always be nice and listen, but she still does what she wants. I'd have to always be noisy if I tried to be a chameleon with her."

"I think the people that went to the store are a little different than your sister." I couldn't help but let out a laugh underneath my breath.

"I guess, Grandpa. Did you like working with your mommy? I like working with Daddy."

"My mother was a tough cookie to work for. *Good* was not a word she used; everything had to be great. Now I know where I get that trait from. I didn't get paid; it was just part of being the kid of a mother who worked six days a week."

"You didn't get paid! What did you do for money? Daddy told me I would get paid today if I worked really hard. He said that he works hard to earn good money and if I work hard, I will make good money too."

"He's right, Alex. It takes hard work and determination to make good money. As a kid, if I wasn't working at my mother's store I was looking to make money somewhere else. I would sell ices and lemonade to people going to the Brooklyn Dodgers game."

"How did you sell them?"

"I would put up a big sign that said 'Are you thirsty? Go Brooklyn Dodgers!' And, since I was on a corner, I would place barrels on the sidewalk that forced the people to walk by my stand. So, I gave myself instant traffic for business."

Once I ran out of flavors, so I used red Lavoris mouthwash with sugar. I learned that day that some people will drink anything if you market it well.

"Mouthwash! That doesn't sound good; you must've been a good businessman, Grandpa. What else did you do for money?"

"One job I truly loved was selling peanuts at Ebbets Field. It was a great job. You could see the game for free, get paid, and get the players' autographs."

"That sounds like a great job! I would love to watch a game for free, get paid, and get autographs! I want to sell peanuts!"

"Let's just start with going to the games and see where it goes from there."

"Okay, Grandpa, but I can't wait to tell Daddy I'm going to sell peanuts."

"I'm sure he'll be amused to hear that Alex. It was a great job, but it didn't stop there for me. At twelve years old, I had my first real job at Western Union in Manhattan. It paid fifty cents per hour, or $20 a week. I gave $10 to my mother."

"Why'd you give money to your mommy?"

"I had to; she asked for it. And, if my mother asked for money, I just gave it to her."

"I would give money to my mommy too. What did you do for Western Union?"

"I delivered telegrams in midtown Manhattan. I even delivered telegrams to Doris Day and Rock Hudson."

"Who are they, Grandpa?"

"They were famous actors during my time."

"So they must be pretty old actors."

"They aren't around anymore, but they would've been pretty old."

That job taught me the concept of service and how to get tipped well. I found out that if you smile, look people in the eyes, make them feel important, and say their name well, they tipped well. I learned that giving good service meant being on time, being attentive, listening well, and learning to speak only when something was important.

Then at thirteen, I began my career as a cook grilling and selling hot dogs at Nedick's.

"Grandpa, you were a cook?"

"Yes, a cook. I know; it's hard to believe I grilled hot dogs."

At lunch time, people left their work for possibly thirty or forty minutes. They didn't want to wait for a hot dog, and so, between putting the hot dogs on, grilling them, preparing them, giving them the mustard and sauerkraut, and taking the money, I worked at a fast pace. I also learned a lesson of life. One day I sold all the hot dogs on my grill. My boss said to me, "Always get other dogs on the grill so that you never have to stop selling." It never occurred to me that when you are running short, you better go downstairs and bring up the rest of the hot dogs. That day they asked me to go find a hot dog job somewhere else.

Selling hot dogs showed me how to work under a great deal of pressure while trying to understand peoples' needs and wants. The place that we worked in was very small. You couldn't work there if you were overweight. It was hot, there was no air conditioning, people wanted and demanded service, and my boss wanted and demanded service. He said, "People don't want to wait for something when they have limited time. They want a hot dog that's hot, with sauerkraut and mustard and a smile, they want correct change, and they want it fast!

"It's hard to believe you cook at all, Grandpa."

"I learned to leave the cooking to those who are good at it."

"That's smart Grandpa. I think it's better to eat the food than to cook it."

"Me too."

"Did you cook anything else, Grandpa?"

"That was the end of my cooking career. Now, since I loved the Good Humor ice cream truck that used to come around my neighborhood when I was a kid, it was only logical to work for them. So I got a job as an ice cream driver."

"You drove an ice cream truck?"

"Yep, and it was a catastrophe!"

"What happened? Did you eat all of the ice cream?"

"No, but that's a good idea; too bad I didn't think of it. The ice cream truck got stuck on a bridge, and I turned off the engine, which turned off the cooler. The ice cream melted, and I was fired on the spot! Good Humor was not in a good humor that day. So I went on to other jobs."

"That is funny, Grandpa." Alex snickers at my ill-fated attempt to be an ice cream truck driver. I can't help but join him.

"If you think that was funny, you've got to hear this one. I got a special chauffer's license to drive a Pepsi Cola truck, and I realized the only way you could make money was by being fast, getting rid of the bottles and getting on with your route so you could get another route. So I thought I would be tricky and put all the bottles on one side for each delivery. This way I wouldn't have to waste time going to the other side of the truck. The idea was sensational, except that the truck practically keeled over because of the weight problem, and the bottles splattered over the walk. A new job was beckoning for me, because they fired me from this one."

"You didn't have much luck as a driver did you, Grandpa?" Alex, unable to keep a straight face, filled the room with his joyous laughter. I was happy to see that my adventures ended in a more amusing light now than in those days.

"No, I didn't. I gave up driving trucks after that. Then, there was a time I was a pinsetter and waiter at a bowling alley near Ebbets Field, the Fitzsimmons Bowling Alley. As a pinsetter, they gave me five cents a game for backbreaking work."

Once in a while, a wise-guy would bowl the ball while I was setting up the pins. No problem. The next time I would set the pins apart. The S.O.B. was NEVER going to get a strike!

"What's an ' S.O.B.', Grandpa?"

"I think that's a good question to ask your dad, Alex."

"Why?"

"I'm not too sure how to explain it to you. I think your dad will do a better job."

"Okay, Grandpa."

Well, I went on to be a waiter there. But there were problems with that job too. First, I wore glasses, and I did not want to wear them so I could look good. The problem, however, was that I could not see. Second, the restaurant required that I pay for the food before I brought it to the customers. I kept watching the customers so they would not leave without paying. But I was too slow, so they gave me the boot.

"You should've just worn your glasses."

"You're probably right."

A big learning experience occurred when I worked with Busch Credit Jeweler. As a high school sophomore, I was a stock clerk there. One day, the manager of the store was having trouble selling a diamond ring to a customer. As the customer was about to walk out, the owner said, "Mr. Lawrence, could you possibly help this fine lady who needs advice as to what ring she should buy?" I walked over, not knowing a diamond from a piece of glass. The lady bought a ring. I got really cocky that I had sold a $2,000 diamond ring for cash. The manager came over and had the customer give $200 down on the ring, with the rest to follow in payments. This arrangement turned it into a $3,000 ring. I learned from this that the store will make more money with extended credit than with a complete cash sale. But more importantly, I learned a valuable lesson: never be afraid or ashamed to ask people for help.

"I ask Mommy and Daddy for help when I need it, especially if Haleigh won't leave me alone."

"I think it's great that you're not afraid to ask for help."

"Like I said, Grandpa, when it comes to Haleigh, sometimes the only thing I can do is ask for help." Alex gives an exasperated look as he reminds himself of his sister's many antics.

Now, I had a job once in the wintertime that taught me that he who puts hot hand on cold car has stick-hand-to-car sickness. The antidote? Pour boiling water on hand. The outcome? Third-degree burns in ten-degree temperatures.

"Ouch! That sounds like it really hurt. What were you doing?"

"My job was to put gas in the car and check the oil. It was a busy thoroughfare, and I didn't have time to put gloves on because I was going back and forth. I wasn't thinking when I put my hand on the car, but I would never do it again because part of my hand's imprint is still on that car, wherever it is."

"I'm going to make sure I wear gloves whenever it's cold."

"That's a great idea, Alex."

"One summer I worked in a tar pit laying tar on a road in ninety-degree weather, with cars splattering tar drops over me."

"What happened that summer?"

"I learned there has to be a better way to make a living!"

"Like an orthodontist, Grandpa?"

"Yes, like an orthodontist."

In the summers of 1945 and 1946, I went to the beach literally every day when I was not working at my mother's store. Since I liked to swim, I worked as a lifeguard.

"I like to swim. Can I be a lifeguard?"

"I'm sure you can when you're a little bit older."

I wasn't the best swimmer, but I could swim forever; I had a tremendous amount of stamina. I was pretty fast too.

"How'd you become a lifeguard?"

"In order to be a lifeguard, we had to take a test by going out in little boats to people and showing how we could give artificial respiration. We also had to run fast and be able to pick up somebody who was carrying extra weights. It was like a physical education test."

I loved it because I loved a challenge and it kept me in good shape. It was kind of neat because you had a chance to get a suntan. In those days we just bronzed ourselves, not knowing anything about the radiation of the sun or the problems of cancer. We always had all the good-looking girls hanging around us.

"Did you ever save anyone's life?"

"Fortunately, I never had to truly save anybody. Good Lord, I wonder what would have happened if I had tried to save somebody!"

There were many times when I went out to get people who were semi-drowning and brought them in. I didn't think it was a big deal because I didn't think they were in much trouble. If we had waited longer, they probably would've been. So I was lucky. I got there in time to rescue the people I went in after and just had to bring them in. Sometimes they would be kicking and screaming, so I would put their head underwater to shut them up for a moment."

Every time I had to swim out, I would remember our chief saying, "You can try to save someone, as long as you save yourself first. If there is a choice, take care of yourself because if you can't take care of yourself, you can't take care of anyone else." This philosophy has stayed with me all my life. If you don't take care of yourself, how can you take care of others? It is not narcissistic and it is not selfish; it is realistic, and if you do it in a fair and honorable way, you gain and the world gains.

"My family takes care of me!"

"They sure do, Alex."

I spent a good many of my summers being out in the open. I love the outdoors. I was a water safety instructor and a lifeguard when I was in high school at the local beach, Brighton Beach. I applied for the jobs because I saw them advertised in the school newspaper. The weather was great and the girls were fantastic. Everybody respected the lifeguard. I guess in those days a lifeguard was something special. First of all, you sat up on a big chair so people had to look up to you. And girls at the beach in those days were, who knows, befuddled by that. The salary was pretty good. I don't remember the exact amount, but it was between fifty cents and a dollar an hour.

I'll never forget when I was waterfront director at Camp Geneva in Pennsylvania, a very exclusive girls' camp. I responded to an ad in the newspaper that needed a waterfront director.

"Is this job the same as a lifeguard?" Alex asked.

"No, it was a little different than a lifeguard. It was hard to be a waterfront director because, not only did you have to have a water safety instructor license, but you had to have experience in teaching, swimming, sailing, rowing, canoeing, and water safety."

"I changed my mind. A water safety Instructor sounds better than a lifeguard. You get to do fun stuff like sailing."

One day the director said to me, "Larry, we would like to have our annual water ballet. So, Larry, put on an annual water ballet." I won't say that my first attempt was great, but the parents who were visiting their children thought it was awesome, so awesome that they lined my pockets with lots and lots of shekels—coins. I learned how important it was to be good to kids, especially in front of their parents. Also, since the camp was all girls, I learned a great deal of protocol. Being a boy with no other girls in the family besides my mother, I learned how to use proper protocol and etiquette with people.

"You're lucky you were a boy with no other girls in the family besides your mother."

"You'd think."

"I know, Grandpa!"

The director said to me one day, "You cannot keep a t-shirt over your Speedo bathing suit because it doesn't look good." They made me tuck my t-shirt in. I've always had trouble with Speedo bathing suits. I used to wear them when I swam in the pool.

Later in life, I was at Doug's country club and I was in the pool with a Speedo. They told him, "Have your father wear something a little bit nicer the next time he comes in, and a little bit less revealing."

"I think you need to change your Speedo bathing suits, Grandpa."

"I did change them."

I once went to a friend's country club in North Carolina and they said, "Buy him another Christmas present—a REAL bathing suit!" So, as you can see, my Speedos left a lasting impression. I finally found a large bathing suit with pockets, and while I was swimming I felt a vibration in my suit. It was my cell phone. The next day I bought a new cell phone. And people think Speedos are a crime.

"I guess the Speedos kept your phone safe."

"Yes, that is true. I learned it the hard way. But everyone else is much happier without the Speedos, except my cell phone."

The next year I was at Camp Robinson Crusoe in Sturbridge, Massachusetts. This was the most exciting camp and probably the most exciting summer of my life. Josh Lieberman was the owner and founder of the camp. He had a philosophy that valued being with nature, singing, music, and sports for sports' sake instead of just for competition. I learned about nature, philosophy, and life.

"He sounds like a good man, Grandpa."

"He sure was. His words are still in me: look at the whole, look at all of nature, and nature will be with you always. And do something each day that makes you feel good about yourself and lets you give to others."

"I always feel good about myself, and Mommy and Daddy tell us all the time it is good to give to others who need."

"Your mommy and daddy are pretty smart people."

One summer I was a medic at Boy Scout camp in upstate New York. I was suturing wounds as a first-year dental student. What guts! I was a dental student, not a medical student, so really I shouldn't have been suturing wounds—because the first wound I sutured was the first wound I sutured. I never really had training in it. My work ranged from taking care of sutures and all kinds of wounds that kids would get from cuts and bruises to giving them tetanus shots for stepping on wires. I guess I was gutsy because I really was out of my element. Fortunately, everything came out fine.

"I think you were gutsy."

"I thought so too, Alex. It was a really good experience."

An unforgettable experience was one time that I worked as an intern, I should say extern, at Montrose Veterans Psychiatric Hospital as a psychiatric aide. Yes, in a psychiatric hospital. The pay was sensational because who wanted to work there? The patients were unreal. I realized that the line between genius and insanity is a very thin one. There were people who were brilliant physicians, attorneys, and judges in life, and they had just gone over the top. When they were "on," they were great. When they were off, they threw butter at you, and that was only the beginning.

"I don't think I'd like butter or anything else being thrown at me. It doesn't sound like too much fun working there."

"I can only say that it was an interesting experience."

There was also my holiday job working in Harlem at Christmastime carrying letters into the tenements. The pay was time and a half because of the neighborhood at that time. I remember there were two kinds of letters, bills and checks from the government. My boss used to say, "Kid, drop all the letters in the hall of each hallway and get your butt out of there as fast as possible."

"Did you drop all the letters in the hall?"

"Oh yeah, and I ran really fast too. It wasn't the safest place to be at the time."

"So, they gave you the job because you ran fast, Grandpa."

"Come to think of it, maybe that's why they gave me the job."

So, from the looks of all the jobs I've held you could call me a jack-of-all-trades and a master of integration, for these experiences were the catapults to my success. These experiences were invaluable.

"I'm glad you're an orthodontist, Grandpa," Alex smiles. "That way I can come to work with Daddy and spend time with you too."

"I think that's the best part about being an orthodontist, Alex."

As he wiggles his small frame off the adult-sized chair, Alex maneuvers himself around the desk and gives me a big hug. His small, olive-toned hand reaches for mine. Without haste, he leads me out of my office into the area where his father is working. He looks at me, looks at his father, and softly inhales a breath of contentment and pride.

Memories of Temple

Some people like the Jews, and some do not. But no thoughtful man can deny the fact that they are, beyond any question, the most formidable and the most remarkable race which has appeared in the world.
—*Winston Churchill*

The cool, brisk air rushes past our bodies as we walk to the steps of temple. The golden, amber rays from the sun light our path into prayer and penitence. Beside me, I see two generations of Jews honoring their beliefs and religion—my children holding hands with their children, as my father once did with me.

"Grandpa, did you go to temple with your family when you were a kid?"

"Yes, Haleigh, I went to temple with my family. I used to go most of the time with my father."

"You've been a Jew for a long time, Grandpa."

"Of course he has, Haleigh," Alex cuts in. "He's been a Jew since he was born, like me and you."

"Grandpa, what was it like to be Jewish when you were a kid."

"Well, Haleigh, when I was growing up, people weren't very nice to Jews where I lived."

"That's horrible!"

"Don't you remember what Grandpa told us about the war and the mean people?" Alex interjects.

"War has bad people and mean people," Rebecca states as she trips over a step and takes a quick fall. She cries an instant tear, jumps up, and begins to run up the steps once more.

"Pickle juice!" Haleigh nods her head in disbelief.

Growing up Jewish was not easy in a world that was not always pro-Jewish. I encountered some problems during my earliest days in Hebrew school, on the streets, in the schools, on the job, and in the military. As a boy, I used to wear my best clothes on Shabbos, which was Saturday. The neighborhood kids would sometimes taunt me and use anti-Semitic words against me, like "Dirty Jew!"

"Why did they call you a 'dirty Jew,' Grandpa? Didn't you take a bath? I know that Mommy and Daddy make me take a bath so I'm not dirty."

"Yes, Haleigh, I did take baths." I couldn't help but laugh a bit. "They called me a 'dirty Jew' because they were trying to hurt my feelings."

"That makes no sense, Grandpa. If you weren't dirty, why would they call you dirty to hurt your feelings?"

"I just don't know."

"Grandpa, what did you do when they were mean to you?" Alex inquires with a serious tone and look. Pulling his left hand out of his pants pocket, he grabs my right arm and keeps his pace in line with mine.

"I would complain to my mother about these taunts."

"Did she help, Grandpa?"

"Well, Haleigh, she would say, 'Sticks and stones will hurt your bones, but names will never harm you.' Some kids were imitating the feeling of their parents. In times of depression, some of the majority would take out their frustrations on the minorities. The Jews were one of the minorities."

"Grandpa, did they keep bothering you and calling you names?" Alex squeezes my arm a little bit tighter, still wondering why people would be unkind to me because I was a Jew.

"I took it for a while until one day I realized I ran faster than anyone else and could fight like heck. I was ten years old, on top of the world, and they would never bully me again. I would not give in."

"Fighting is not the answer," Haleigh scolds. "Mommy and Daddy always say that fighting is bad and someone can get hurt."

"Mommy and Daddy are right. Fighting is bad. The only difference is that I grew up on the streets, and a kid that grew up on the streets of Brooklyn during my time didn't have the same opportunities that you have, Haleigh. My only choice back then was to fight so that they wouldn't bother me anymore."

"Wasn't there anything else you could do?"

"I did other things too, because I knew fighting wasn't a good answer."

Every Jewish child has two names followed by the name of a parent. It was a Jewish way of revering the generations and paying homage to our past. My Jewish name is Lazer Ben Josef, Lawrence son of Joseph (my dad). Since being Jewish didn't win over many people in my early years, I decided to change my last name from Hartstein to Harte. I asked my dad for permission! He said, "I want you to be happy. I want people to judge you by what you are and what you stand for. Go with my blessings. The family name will be carried on not by a name, but rather by the character behind the name. Lawrence, I love you."

"Grandpa, does that mean we are really Hartstein and not Harte?" Alex catches the connection.

"You are from the 'House of Harte,' Alex." A large grin covers his face from cheek to cheek.

"Jews go to temple on Holy Day!" Rebecca continues to run around as we approach the entrance of our temple. Others from the congregation walk by, chuckling in agreement at Rebecca's affirmation.

As a kid, my dad would drag me to temple on the High Holidays, Saturday mornings, and all other Jewish holidays. I must say, it was a great job to work for a Jewish organization like the YMHA (Young Man's Hebrew Association); you got all the national holidays off, plus all of the Jewish holidays off. I bet holidays took up to six weeks a year. That's a lot of time off plus vacations. My dad was very religious; he was an Orthodox Jew. He did not ride, work, write, or even turn the lights on from Friday evening to Saturday night. He used to pray every morning with his talis. I said to myself, "When does he have time to go to work?"

"Your daddy was very strict. I'm not sure I could go without TV or music for such a long time. That's a whole day!"

"You exaggerate, Haleigh," Alex retorts. "We've gone a whole day without TV or music."

"Pickle juice!"

Among my fond memories of my family are the Passovers we celebrated together. When I was a little boy, my Gran Pappy would sit at the head of the table during Passover services; he was the elder of the house. I kind of liked Passover because it was the only time I got a present during the year. It is a tradition that when the elder of the house hides a middle portion of three *matzos* (brittle pieces of unleavened bread), called the *afikomen*, whoever found the *afikomen* got a present. Since I was the only kid, I got the *afikomen* and the present. Whatever the present was, it was sweet to me because I never got a present on my birthday.

"Presents are fun to get. I love parties."

"It was always fun to receive a present, Rebecca."

"You never got a present on your birthday?" Haleigh's wavy hair crosses over her face as the wind brushes against her fair complexion.

"It was okay, Haleigh. We didn't have a lot of money and I was happy with whatever my family gave me."

"I love to get presents, Grandpa!" Haleigh exclaims.

"Me too," Rebecca adds in agreement.

"Grandpa, did you always like being a Jew?"

"Of course, Alex, I have always been proud of being a Jew!"

"I am proud to be a Jew."

"As you should be, Alex."

Well, like I said, my dad *schlepped* (took) me to temple every Saturday and every Jewish holiday. I thought it was kind of fun, but at times I was bored out of my mind. On the bottom of each page of the book of the Siddur (the prayer book) was something called the Ethics of the Fathers, the Perkei Avot. It was all about fundamentals and ethics and attitude, and I used to read that all the time. It kept my boredom to a minimum, and it did teach me a great deal about ethics and philosophy.

"Grandpa," Haleigh whispers softly, gesturing for me to lower my head down to hers, "don't tell Mommy and Daddy, but sometimes I get bored at temple too."

I softly whisper back into her delicate ear, "It'll be our little secret." Haleigh props her body up in perfect stature and continues our walk through the temple doors. As we begin to find our seats toward the back of the temple, I feel a slight tugging of my pants from behind.

"Yes, Haleigh?"

"Grandpa, why do we sit in the back?"

"Because it's home." Haleigh follows me to our seats and cuddles up against my side. Rebecca runs from her seat next to her mother and me, while Alex takes his place by my other side.

"What do you mean, 'it's home,' Grandpa?"

"Well, it's where my family always sat—now yours—and where I always have felt comfortable sitting.

"As I got older, I began to get disenchanted with a few so-called devoted religious people of the temple. I felt that during the week some connived and were not nice people, but they made a lot of money."

"Money is made on paper and is the color green," Rebecca quickly responds while eavesdropping, then jets back to her mother.

"What does connived mean, Grandpa?"

"It means when people think of bad ways to take money from you. It can be done by such things as not telling the truth, or trying to take advantage of vulnerable people, Haleigh. On Saturday, these few would come to pray and ask the Lord his forgiveness. I thought this was hypocrisy."

"What is hypocrisy?"

"Alex, hypocrisy is when someone says they are going to act one way, but they end up acting completely different."

"They don't sound like good people."

"No, they don't, do they?"

However, the biggest disenchantment was not these conniving people but rather a rabbi. One day when I was eleven, I asked the rabbi a question, "Why was it important to be kosher and eat kosher foods?" He said, "Lawrence, it is not for you to question; it is for you to do." He could have said that in ancient times it was not healthy to eat certain foods. He could have told me it was the tradition of the religion, but I resented him saying, "If the rabbi tells you to do it, never question the rabbi." From that day on, I began to question religion. It took me until I had children to come back into the fold.

When I was about twelve years old, I happened to listen to a Sunday morning radio program on Ethical Culture by Jerome Nathanson. This guy made sense. Ethical Culture is a movement based on the ideal that the ultimate aim of human life is to create a more humane society. Some of the ideas were the following:

1. We relate to others in a way that brings out their best.

2. We will, at the same time, elicit the best in ourselves by trying to elicit the best in others. We encourage a growing untapped edge of spiritual development, an inexhaustible worth.

3. Human worth is where all people are taken to have inherent worth, not dependent on the value of what they do. They are deserving of respect and dignity and their unique gifts are to be encouraged.

If it wasn't for family guilt, I might have become an Ethical Culturalist. To this day, those words seem right to me. As you get older, since you can't work as hard with your hands, you have more time to be spiritual. It is a shame we have to wait so long to be spiritual when spirituality can add fullness to your life at an early age.

"It's okay, Grandpa." Haleigh gives me a quick belly rub to comfort me. "It's okay. You are in temple now."

"Yes, we are in temple now, and that's what's important."

My first synagogue was at Lincoln Road and Flatbush Avenue on the second floor of a walkup. The synagogue was only for the hearty. Even I had trouble walking up the two flights of stairs. We sat in the last row of the synagogue on a window sill for the High Holidays. There were two reasons for this. One, the price was right (in those days the closer you were to the Holy Ark, the more expensive was the seat). Two, I could open the window to let some fresh air in. In those days, there was no air conditioning and taking a shower was not a prerequisite for being close to God.

"I don't think I would've liked going to temple with you when you were a kid."

"Why not, Haleigh?"

"Because it would be hot and smelly."

"I can understand. It was awfully hot and smelly from where I sat. Even though it wasn't the best environment, the point was that I was there."

As the temple became more prosperous, it moved to a new location on Ocean Avenue. The temple was opposite the park. In those days it was very fancy. We could almost not afford to get in the doors. Fortunately, God's vision was so broad that God could still see us and hear us from the last row. Since this was an orthodox temple, the men and women did not sit together. I remember two sisters in temple whose dad was a big giver. They always sat in the front and were kind of cute. Their family was involved with the social and spiritual activities of the temple.

My parents weren't involved in anything at temple; they just came and sat and prayed in the back of the temple. On many holidays, we had a Yizkor service (a prayer for the departed). My mom and dad prayed for their parents who had passed away; it was a Jewish way of never forgetting your roots and your past, even though we live in the present. It is a continued tradition from thousands of years ago. I hope that my children will do it for me when I pass on.

"I'll do it for you, Grandpa," Alex swiftly exclaims. "I will never forget you."

"Me too!" Haleigh adds.

"Me too!" Rebecca repeats.

"I know you will," I reply as my heart fills with warmth and joy, knowing that my grandchildren will keep their word and remember their roots by never forgetting their Grandpa.

As times changed, the Prospect Park Jewish Center had to move because of the population change. It is still an Orthodox temple with a high school for girls in East Flatbush. The membership of the present congregation has dwindled. But my thoughts and memories of my congregation when I was young are of a congregation that filled each seat and had standing room only in a second floor walkup, close to God. Now, I belong to a Conservative temple where the whole family sits and prays together, but still in the back of the temple.

"We feel at home when we sit in the back of temple." Rebecca makes her last attempt at eavesdropping and freedom before Helaine sits her down to prepare for the ceremony.

To this day, I always sit in the back of my present synagogue, even though I donate a great deal and could get a seat in the front row. For my family and me, it is tradition to sit in the back where we are at peace and feel at home—just as it was when I was growing up.

I must admit, though, one of the most influential events in my life related to my being a Jew. In later years, when I learned of the Holocaust, where millions of Jews were led to slaughter, sometimes without much of a fight, I vowed that that would never happen to me or my loved ones. I vowed to try to find a way to help the less fortunate. To this day because of my heritage, I give to charity and help not only Jewish people but others, whatever religion or race they are, find an opportunity for a better life.

"I like going to temple and sitting in our home," Haleigh beams.

"Grandpa."

"Yes, Alex."

"It doesn't matter where we sit in temple. It always feels like home when you are around."

As the rabbi commences, I feel two soft hands on both sides reach mine, their fingers intertwining with my fingers. We sit and listen, as a family, at home, close to God.

Visiting the Wailing Wall, Jerusalem. The wall, built in 19 B.C.E. by Herod the Great, received its name as a description of the Jewish practice of mourning and bemoaning the destruction of the Temple at this site. (I'm near the center, second row from the Wall)

Lighting a candle on the menorah (nine-branched candelabrum) representing the second of eight days of Chanukah, 1989. The menorah has been a traditional symbol of Judaism for over 3,000 years and is the emblem of Israel. According to Jewish history, there was only enough sealed (not desecrated) olive oil left to fuel the eternal flame in the temple for one day after the desecration of the Jewish temple in Jerusalem. The flame burned, miraculously, for eight days. This gave enough time to make new pure oil. Therefore, the menorah has eight branches, representing those eight miraculous days the flame burned, with the ninth candle, known as the shamos *(servant) light, which is used to light the other candles.*

Education in a Nutshell

Leaders are like teachers. They can only show us the
doors—it is up to each of us to decide which door to open.
—*Anonymous*

It is a beautiful Sunday morning with colored leaves adorning
each tree; an invigorating dry, zesty wind encompasses our bodies
and a radiant sun penetrates the opaque clouds of autumn. Haleigh,
Rebecca, and Alex fill the playground with their flamboyant laughs
and rambunctious energy. Oh, to be a kid again in Brooklyn, playing
stoopball on the streets or baseball on a concrete lot.

"Grandpa, will you push me on the swing?"

"Of course, Haleigh."

"Papa Larry, will you push me on the swing?" Rebecca repeats
after Haleigh as she jumps off of the jungle gym and follows her
cousin to the swing set.

"Of course, I will."

"Grandpa, will you push me too?" Alex asks as he slithers down

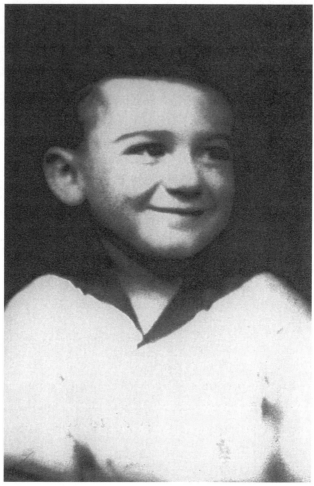

In my infamous sailor suit, 1936

the twisted slide with an easygoing swiftness.

"I sure will, Alex."

"I wish we could do this all the time, Grandpa, but tomorrow we go to school."

"That's okay, Haleigh, because school is fun too. We can always come to the playground another time."

"I don't go to school tomorrow, Papa Larry, but I do have to go back home to Pennsylvania."

"Yes, Rebecca, you do have to go home tomorrow and I will miss you a great deal."

"Don't worry, Papa Larry, I'll be back soon."

"Of course," I reply with a slight chuckle.

"Did you go to school, Grandpa?" Haleigh quickly changes the subject back to school.

"That's a silly question, Haleigh. Of course Grandpa went to school. How do you think he became an orthodontist?" Alex jumps on the petite, rubbery rectangular seat aged with Mother Nature's elements.

"Yes, I went to school."

"Did you like it?" Rebecca questions, as she looks forward to her days starting kindergarten.

"I did. It was different than school today."

When I was a child, I lived eight blocks from the school. There were no buses, and we had to go home for lunch. It wasn't so bad; the only problem was that they used to give us vanilla milk or plain milk, and I hated plain milk. I once took some chocolate syrup in a little bottle to school, and the teacher said to me, "You can't do that." She took the chocolate syrup away from me and used it herself.

"I love chocolate milk!" Haleigh soars forward toward the sun's ray peeking through the sky, almost touching it with the tip of her toes.

"I love chocolate!" Rebecca licks her lips as she indulges the thought of eating a rich, sweet piece of chocolate.

"They let you go home for lunch. That must've been really nice. I think Mommy's food is so much better than cafeteria food." Alex pushes his legs out as he dips down into the center swing and attempts to gain rocket momentum.

"It was a nice break from being in class."

I was bored in elementary school because it did not seem to challenge me. It seemed as if most of the things the teachers tried to teach bored me. I usually got A's in the subjects, except for penmanship, where I got a C.

"Mommy and Daddy say I have pretty handwriting," Haleigh declares with a note of pride.

"I'm not too bad either, but I could still use some more practice," Alex confesses. "But if I become a doctor like you and Daddy, I don't need to have good handwriting."

"There are plenty of doctors out there who have good handwriting, Alex. I don't think practice ever helped me though. To this day, even I have a hard time reading my own writing."

"Mommy and Daddy always tell us 'Practice makes perfect,' Grandpa," Haleigh exclaims. "Good practice makes perfect!"

"You're probably right, Haleigh. I'm sure I didn't practice as much as I should have on my handwriting."

"I can help you if you want, Grandpa," Haleigh offers.

"Sounds great!"

"You have to take it seriously though, Grandpa, and practice a lot."

"Of course," I answer. I couldn't help but show a slight grin of amusement on my face. Here was a kindergartner showing me up on penmanship.

"I practice writing every day, Grandpa. I also practice Chinese and the violin," Rebecca boasts, trying to reach the clouds with her feet as she swings upward toward the sky. While the swing descends, she leans her head back, giggling lightly.

In kindergarten they threw me out of school because I kept asking lots of questions. I was beginning my educational career as a "kindergarten dropout." My mother's fear was not that I wasn't going to kindergarten, but who the babysitter was going to be. She was furious.

"I ask a lot of questions."

"And they haven't thrown you out of kindergarten, Haleigh?"

"You're silly, Grandpa. The teacher tells me that I have a healthy mind. I think she is a doctor too."

"I guess your teacher should've talked to mine."

"I don't think my teacher is that old, Grandpa."

"You used to make your mommy mad a lot, Grandpa."

"I did, Alex, and it was never on purpose."

Once, in fifth grade, the teacher asked me, "Lawrence, what are you doing?" And I said, "Nothing." And she said, "Exactly; you have been doing this all term long! Bring your mother in." Again, my mother was furious because, after all, she was missing work. Mom worked six days a week, eleven hours a day.

I was kind of a ringleader in school. I became so good at getting out of trouble that the teachers usually caught the other guys. Aside from kindergarten and fifth grade, most of my problems came on Sundays. I think my mom could not wait to get back to work on

Monday to escape the "Sunday Traumas." My earliest recollection (not just what my parents told me) of such a day was when I was five years old. I had a sailor suit on one Sunday afternoon at Brighton Beach. I led all my friends, all dressed in their Sunday best, under a very cold shower. They and all their clothing got wet. After that day they were no longer my friends—their parents told them to stay away from me because I was a troublemaker.

"Grandpa, you shouldn't have gotten everyone wet," Haleigh reprimands me. "I wouldn't be happy if I got wet in one of my pretty dresses."

"It sounds like fun to me," Rebecca says, imagining herself in a pretty sailor dress with matching tights and shoes.

"I think it's kind of funny, Grandpa," Alex chuckles. I remain behind them as I give my arms a rest while they continue to demonstrate the principle of kinetic energy.

"It seemed like fun at the time and looking back now, it was kind of funny. But Haleigh makes a good point. It wasn't a good thing to do to my friends. My mother didn't find it too amusing either."

In fifth grade I thought I was a klutz, but all of a sudden, I was able to run faster and hit a ball further than anybody else. Then in seventh grade my whole life changed, when my teachers, Mrs. Kennedy and Miss Clausen, had me teach math and science to my fellow students. I guess that was their way of keeping me out of trouble. I finally loved school. I was not bored anymore.

"I'm so happy now," Haleigh rejoices upon hearing about my new-found love for school in seventh grade. "I was worried for you, Grandpa, because I love school. I don't know how you couldn't love school."

"I love school too, Grandpa. I have a lot of friends at school I get to play with," Alex agrees.

"I liked playing with my friends too. Most of the neighborhood kids went to school with me since we'd walk to school. I guess it just took a while for me to like going to school."

I became president in eighth grade, and my life changed when I went to Brooklyn Tech. All of a sudden, I went from just being nobody to being somebody special. Especially to boys who were athletes, I was so important. Golly—I had arrived!! Even the girls began inviting me to parties and dances. I was so immature with girls that the main thing I remember from these events was the food and being forced to dance with the girls.

"Grandpa, I think you're special!"

"Thank you, Haleigh. I think you're pretty special too."

"I think we're all special," Rebecca adds as the light, cool winds cross over her face with each swing, leaving her with rosy cheeks and a slightly pink nose.

"How did life change when you went to Brooklyn Tech, Grandpa?" Alex bends his legs to slow down on the swings. Haleigh and Rebecca follow his example. Slowly, they begin to swing lower and lower.

"Well, it was a different school with different kids. I changed too."

"How was it different?"

Alex takes a slight leap off the seat and runs around the swing in my direction. Haleigh continues to wait for the swing to come to a complete stop. Rebecca impatiently jumps off the swing, landing a perfect ten and looks around to find her next adventure. Alex and I walk over toward the sandbox as Haleigh runs past us and plops down on the sand digger. Alex takes a seat in front of his sister and begins to dig as well. He gestures for me to join in. Rebecca comes twirling by and finds an empty sand digger near her cousins, across from mine. As I try to adjust myself in the adolescent-sized seat, I can't help but feel like I am a child again.

BROOKLYN TECH

Learn under the sun; practice under the clouds.
—*Lawrence S. Harte*

I had the opportunity of going to Brooklyn Tech, a special high school that required an entrance test. This was like getting $30,000 a year in private tuition. It was the best education of my life. Kids came to Brooklyn Tech from all over New York City and the suburbs. There were rich and poor kids. The core thing we all had in common is that we had to take a special exam to get in. In taking and passing an entrance exam, you felt important.

When I first entered Brooklyn Tech, I thought, "This is great!" Here was a high school that, on the first day in the auditorium, the gym teacher, Mr. Milde, got up and said, "Good morning, MEN!" I couldn't believe he called us men. We were a bunch of thirteen-year-olds who still hadn't shaved and had acne all over our faces.

"Didn't they have any girls at the school, Grandpa?"

"Not during that time, Haleigh. Most of the schools separated the girls and the boys."

"That doesn't seem fair. I have a lot of friends. Some are boys. I like to play with all of my friends. How could I play with them if we were not together?"

"I understand, Haleigh, but when I was growing up, it was not the same as today."

"Pickle juice!"

The principal said, "This is a tough school. Look to the left and the right of you. The odds are one of you will not be here in four years." I said to myself, "I feel sorry for those guys because I will be here."

"Were you still there in four years?"

"I sure was, Alex. Like I said, I felt sorry for those guys that didn't last."

"That's because Grandpa didn't take kids into the showers with their good clothes on when he was there."

"No, I was a good boy, Haleigh. In fact, the classes were really tough, so I worked hard and I was on my best behavior, most of the time."

"I'm on my best behavior most of the time too, Papa Larry," Rebecca says as she motions the jaws of her digger down into the sand.

The courses were rigid and the school was tough. The instructors didn't stand for any shenanigans. Once, I was given detention because they said I had cut a class three months before. I told the principal I did not cut the class and asked, why notify me three months later? I said it was not fair. The principal said to me, "Life is not fair." I served the detention.

"What do you mean 'cut a class', Grandpa?"

"To cut a class, Haleigh, means to not show up to the class."

"Where do you go?"

"Anywhere you want to go."

"Were you allowed to cut a class?"

"No, we weren't allowed to cut a class."

"Did you cut the class, Grandpa?" Haleigh stops her mechanical rhythm with the sand digger and takes a long deep look at me.

"No, I did not cut the class. I think they thought I was someone else. But that's the past and I had to just take it. There was no point in arguing, especially since I wanted to stay at the school."

Brooklyn Tech offered courses in mechanical engineering, chemical engineering, aeronautical engineering, and college preparation. We had subjects all day, with no study period. I took four years of math, English, mechanical drawing, shop, physics, and gym and three years of chemistry, French, History, and God knows what else. I also took four strenuous years of a gym class in which we had to practice high bar, parallel bars, horses, and rope climbing, to name just a few of our activities. I remember climbing the ropes without using my feet. It was not a big deal to me, but apparently it was to others.

"Mommy and Daddy tell me I have to wear my shoes all the time," Alex professes. "They say we have to keep our feet clean and be careful not to step on anything sharp."

"Well, as a kid, I didn't have much, and like I said, my shoes were filled with holes. So, a lot of times, I inserted paper in my shoes to fill the holes. You are lucky, Alex, because you have good shoes to wear and they don't have holes."

"Some of my shoes have holes," Haleigh admits. "But they are special holes that make the shoes look pretty. They are for decoration."

"Some of my shoes have pretty holes too. Papa Larry, are you sure you didn't have pretty girl shoes like Haleigh and me?" Rebecca inquires.

"I think the holes in your shoes are not the same as mine. I didn't wear pretty shoes with decorations. In my day, we had holes in our shoes and our clothes from exercise. Today, you buy clothes with holes to look good and they're expensive."

"Pickle juice!" Haleigh murmurs.

"Grandpa, you said you worked hard. Were the classes hard for you?"

"No, not really hard, just challenging, Alex."

One of my biggest issues in school was my bad penmanship. So I developed a strategy. I used to date girls who could write or type well. And so my worries were over.

"I think I'd rather practice my handwriting more, Grandpa, than date a girl."

"That sounds like a better plan than mine, Alex."

Haleigh interrupts, "Did you like your teachers at school, Grandpa? I love my teachers and they love me."

Now, I did have some interesting teachers at Brooklyn Tech. There was our math teacher, a brilliant man who enlightened me, but he was always scratching himself. We used to call him "Itchy Balls." Mr. Herbert was my French teacher. He tried to have me speak French without a Brooklyn accent. Then there were Mrs. Bloom and Mr. Daly, my English teachers, who insisted that I speak and write English rather than Brooklyn-ese.

And, of course, there was Mr. Starr. Mr. Starr was my history teacher. He used to ask me, "Lawrence, how do you know so much about history?"

I told him my Uncle Louis was a history teacher at another high school. He would lecture me every day.

Mr. Starr used to say, "Lawrence, you should become a lawyer; you cannot stop talking or arguing!"

"Maybe Haleigh should be a lawyer, Grandpa."

"Why's that, Alex?"

"She doesn't stop talking either."

"I do stop talking. I don't talk in my sleep," Haleigh asserts, defending herself from her older brother.

"That's about it, Grandpa. But it should be quiet during bedtime, so that doesn't count, because we're sleeping."

"I'm sure Haleigh doesn't talk all of the time, now does she, Alex?"

"If you say so, Grandpa, but you don't have to listen to her every day."

"Pickle juice!"

"I don't stop talking either, Papa Larry. I think I'll be a great lawyer," Rebecca declares.

"I think God gave both of you mouths for a special reason. Whatever you do in life, I am sure you will both be very successful."

"Grandpa, did you do anything fun at this school?" Alex questions. He quickly changes subjects in order not to infuriate his sister any more than he already has done.

At Brooklyn Tech, I became involved in sports. I was captain of the table tennis team. What did I learn from ping pong, or table tennis? To focus. When you play back and forth at a very fast pace, you're in a trance. You're in a zone and you must focus. You cannot think of anything else. It guides you into a tremendous amount of eye-hand coordination and flexibility. It is a sport that anybody of any size can take up, one that you can play for the rest of your life. It develops excellent mental and physical attributes. I recommend this to all kids and families.

The interesting thing was that I had never had a ping pong table at home, and that was the sport I was least interested in. I just developed my skill because I worked hard at it; I didn't have any innate talent. The only opportunity for practice that I had was in between other sports at school.

"Table tennis sounds like fun!"

"It was a lot of fun, Haleigh."

"Will you teach me to play some day, Grandpa?"

"I'd love to teach you one day, Alex."

"And me?"

"And you too, Haleigh."

"Don't forget about me, Papa Larry!"

"I'd never forget about you, Rebecca."

I also took up swimming the backstroke for the first time. My coach said that if anyone went any slower, they would go backwards. Once, he wanted me to swim the medley that consisted of the backstroke, freestyle, and the butterfly or the breast stroke. I was so bad with the butterfly that I thought I would drown. I would run to the bathroom to hide from the coach. Aside from swimming I also tried out track. I thought I was fast in track. I was, but the African-American kids always ran the anchor (the final leg of a relay); they were just faster. So I ran wherever they wanted me.

"It's silly trying to swim the butterfly, Papa Larry."

"Why is it silly, Rebecca?"

"Because everyone knows that butterflies fly and don't swim." Rebecca chuckles with amusement picturing her grandfather trying to swim in the pool like a butterfly.

"I didn't really try to swim like an actual butterfly, Rebecca. There are different ways to swim in a pool and one of them is called the butterfly because of how pretty it looks."

"Butterflies are really pretty. I love their colors," Haleigh comments.

"Grandpa, what else did you do?" Alex swiftly places Haleigh back on track with the conversation after her slight veer off into a fantasyland filled with butterflies.

"I did a lot of things. There was so much to do at Brooklyn Tech!"

Besides sports, I wanted to be involved in making changes. So in my senior year I ran for president of the school. Funny thing, when I ran for president, the administration looked up my attendance record. They actually could not believe it; I was never absent from school! It wasn't because of my health; it was because of fear and guilt. I had felt that my mother would KILL me if I didn't show up at school.

"I think she would've killed you, Grandpa."

"I think so too, Alex."

In any case, I ran my campaign by getting a campaign manager in each of the activities I was involved in. Classmates were involved whom I knew well. I pledged the following: more help with college admission, more dances with girls' schools, and more of a chance to see the great parts of New York City on weekends. A president is never really liked completely. The best you can do is be respected.

"Did they respect you?"

"I hope they did, Haleigh."

"Did Mommy and Daddy go to your school?"

"No, Haleigh, your mommy and daddy went to other schools."

"Pickle juice!"

Students from Brooklyn Tech were definitely not your regular kind of kids. Years later, I took my kids to a high school reunion, and one big guy who had been on the football team came over, put his arms around me, and said, "Larry, do you remember when we were the best there was?"

And my kids said, "You WERE?"

And I said, "I was???"

Another guy who was last in our class was at the reunion. He was so bad he couldn't even copy my paper, and yet now at our reunion he was dressed fancily and had a terrific young girlfriend. He was head of waste management of a large city.

I said, "How did you do it?"

He said, "Larry, it was easy—I hired people who could count and who could write. I did the easy work and I did it smiling, and I did the managing."

Go figure! Not too long afterward, I went to a Brooklyn Tech cocktail reception that was sponsored by a poor kid from Brooklyn who had made good. He had an apartment on Park Avenue. He said, "Larry, let me show you around the apartment." He took me into the bathroom and showed me a Picasso.

I said, "Why do you have a great Picasso in the bathroom?"

He said, "Because, Larry, EVERYBODY has got to take a leak!" We definitely were a special kind of breed.

"I don't get it, Grandpa. Who is Picasso and why did he have it in the bathroom?"

"Alex, Picasso was a famous artist and his paintings are worth a lot of money."

"So why was it in the bathroom?"

"Like he said, everybody has to take a leak! He meant that since everyone eventually has to go to the bathroom, then they will all see the painting that cost so much money."

"Grandpa, it still sounds silly to me."

"Well, Haleigh, he figured everyone would see how rich he really was because he put such an expensive painting in a place like a bathroom that wasn't very important."

"Wouldn't it be easier to just tell the people how rich you are?"

"Probably, Haleigh, but I guess he preferred to show it."

"Pickle juice!"

"I don't think I'd put a Picasso in the bathroom, Papa Larry," Rebecca announces.

"I don't think I'd put one in the bathroom either."

"What did you do after you finished school, Grandpa?"

"That's a good question, Alex. I went to another school. I went to the university."

"Is that how you became an orthodontist?"

"Yes, it was one of the schools that helped me become an orthodontist."

As we jauntily rise from our seats, Haleigh and Rebecca begin to shake their feet relentlessly. The fresh, creamy sand covered our shoes and attempted to gain entrance to our feet. Alex and I look at them and then at our feet, and we both begin to do the hokey-pokey by putting our right foot out and shaking it all about; then we put the left foot out and shake it all about. In unison, we escape from the sandbox and head toward the playground set. Its wooden beams stand tall and confident, awaiting the next child.

Alex grabs the rope net and begins to climb as Haleigh follows closely. Rebecca investigates her surroundings and chooses to climb the metal stairs rather than the rope ladder that is currently occupied by her cousins.

Wearing my athletic award sweater from Brooklyn Tech, 1948

Brooklyn Tech

COLUMBIA COLLEGE

One of my classmates said, "Larry, if you had talent, you would be dangerous!"

(2008 Columbia class reunion)

After graduating from Brooklyn Tech, I went to Columbia College, which was an Ivy League school. I had some trepidation, not about the intellect part, but about the social part. At seventeen and being from Brooklyn, I was not quite ready for the social aspect of the education experience. The kids were dressed in white bucks, gray flannel pants, and blue sport jackets. Fortunately, I do not recall how I dressed. It was a learning experience.

"I think you dress nice, Grandpa."

"Thank you, Haleigh. I'm not so sure how nice I dressed when I was at Columbia, but I know I dress much nicer now."

When I was eighteen and a freshman at Columbia, I had a blind date with a young lady from a finishing school called Dalton. When I picked her up at her brownstone, she had a flood in the living room. I later found out that it was actually a babbling brook!

"What's a babbling brook?"

"A babbling brook is like a small river inside of your very own home, Rebecca."

"Why would anyone want a river in their home?"

"It was for decoration. It was like having a little bit of nature on the inside."

"If they wanted nature, Papa Larry, they could've just walked outside."

"That's true, Rebecca."

Her dad asked what I wanted to drink. With my background of milk and beer, I said, "Whatever you are drinking would be fine for me, sir." He gave me a double scotch with soda. It reminded me of the castor oil that my mother used to coax down my throat.

"What's castor oil, Grandpa?"

"Something you don't ever want to taste, Haleigh."

"Pickle juice!"

On another occasion, I went out with a young lady from Sarah Lawrence, and she said to me, "Larry, do you like opera?" And I said, "I LOVE opera!" I lied. It was a Saturday night, and I had been involved in sports that afternoon. When the lights went out, so did I. It was our first and LAST date.

"You shouldn't lie," Haleigh scolds. "Mommy and Daddy say that lying is bad."

"Lying is bad. I wasn't thinking, and I thought I would impress the girl."

"Mommy and Daddy say, 'There is no excuse for lying.' I think that is an excuse, Grandpa."

"You're right, Haleigh. But I've learned now not to lie."

"Good, Grandpa, because Mommy and Daddy would be upset if they knew you lied." I caught my laugh below my breath in an attempt to keep the serious tone and not undermine Haleigh's lesson.

"I think it's best if we just keep that a secret then."

"I think so too, Grandpa."

Another time, I went out with a girl from Barnard and we went with a whole group to a party at the Waldorf Astoria Starlight Room. I had to borrow money from her because I didn't have enough to pay for the evening. When I saw the price of the drinks, I wanted to drink Alka Seltzer.

"What's Alka Seltzer, Grandpa?"

"That's a medicine that calms a sour stomach, Alex."

"So why did you want to drink it when you saw the prices?"

"Because the drinks were so expensive that they turned my stomach sour."

"You're crazy, Grandpa," Alex laughs as he slides down the metal pole and acts like a heroic fireman who's being called into duty.

Another time, I was invited to an estate in Connecticut, where I had to borrow a white tennis outfit. Who knew that dungarees were not acceptable tennis attire?

"What are dungarees?" Haleigh takes her turn at the pole with a graceful slide and twist at the end.

"Dungarees are blue jeans. They weren't popular to wear when I was younger like they are now."

I was good at darts and pool. I couldn't lose. While playing pool with the girl's father, he said, "Son, you play pool like you came from Brooklyn." I did not answer. I knew I was in trouble when the mother of the girl said to me, "So, Lawrence, what club do your parents belong to?" I had no idea what she was talking about, so I stuttered and sheepishly said, "Well, they are in the process of changing clubs." Later on I learned they were talking about country clubs. I enjoyed the swimming pool, I enjoyed the tennis courts, and I enjoyed the lawn, but at that stage of my life I wasn't ready socially for these people who were very nice and very caring to me, but I wasn't mature enough socially to accept them.

"Daddy belongs to a country club."

"Yes he does, Alex."

"Isn't that the country club that didn't want you to wear Speedo bathing suits?"

"Yes, it is." Oh, how the inquisitive minds of children absorb and retain information a little too well sometimes.

Besides the elite dating, I remember once when I was a freshman eating at the athletic training table. We had soup. The soup came, I put the spoon in, and sipped with the spoon toward me. My nose was literally in the soup. The boy next to me, who had come from a private school, probably Hotchkiss in Massachusetts, said, "Larry, you push the spoon AWAY when you have soup." Years later at a reunion, he came over, gave me a hug, and said, "So, Larry how was the soup?"

"That's just silly, Grandpa. Why would you push the spoon away to have soup? Everyone knows you have to bring the spoon to your mouth to eat soup."

"It was a special way that rich people ate their soup. It was considered proper etiquette, Haleigh."

"I like the way I eat my soup."

"I do, too."

Columbia was a tremendous education, not only intellectually, but socially and culturally. I discovered certain areas that I was not able to find when I was living in Brooklyn. I noticed that there were very few Jews at Columbia at that time, that the power of Columbia was in the fraternities, and that most of the strong fraternities were not Jewish. But I learned a lot. I learned how to get along with people, how to say what I wanted to when I wanted to, and how to keep my mouth shut.

One of those instances of learning to keep my mouth shut occurred when I was a freshman. I got up before the whole class and I said, "I would like to be president because I was president before." One of the guys in the back row said, "Sit down! So were we all!" By the way, I never became president.

"That wasn't very nice to tell you to sit down," Haleigh protests as she climbs the rope net once more, this time trying to compete against her brother.

"No, it wasn't nice, but I still learned a lesson. I also realized I wasn't in Brooklyn anymore."

When I was a freshman at Columbia, we had what they called a "sophs-freshman rush." For this event there was a tall greased pole on South Field, which was in the middle of campus. A little Columbia beanie hat was placed on the top. The Sophs got around the pole and held hands, and we freshman had to try to break through their ranks, get to the top, and get the beanie.

I was one of the leaders of the freshman class trying to break through the "Sophs," who had their arms around each other in a circle. I did what we do in Brooklyn. We got all the heavy guys in a wedge. We drove that wedge, like a ply wedge, right into one section of the Sophs that had the smallest guys. We went right to the poles with our big guys pushing. And then with the big guys there, we made a pyramid where the little guys got onto the big guys and a little guy got to the top and got the beanie. Man, it was military warfare, and it was fun. It was a fight; it was a blast.

"Grandpa, that sounds like fun! Can we grease this pole and put a beanie on top?"

"Not today, Alex, maybe another day."

"I want to put grease on the pole, Papa Larry. It sounds like fun," Rebecca adds as she runs over to the rope net ladder to climb up to the pole.

"I don't want to put grease on the pole. I would get dirty," Haleigh declares in protest.

"Don't worry! No one is putting grease on the pole."

"Pickle juice!"

Another time at Columbia, I had the opportunity of having my picture on the front page of the Sunday *New York Times Magazine*. The story was about the Korean War. I don't remember what I said. I just remember the photographer saying, "Hey kid, don't smile too much when you take the picture."

"Were you famous?" Haleigh questions as she cautiously observes the pole, making sure no grease had been added.

"I wouldn't say famous, but for me it was exciting to be in *The New York Times*."

There were so many advantages in going to Columbia. I had the opportunity of being on a council with Dwight Eisenhower, who was then president of Columbia.

"Is President Eisenhower important?"

"He was to our country, Alex. He was the thirty-fourth president of the United States."

"Wow, he was important!"

Another great advantage in being at Columbia was having GREAT teachers: Van Doren, Gilbert Hyatt, and the future 1955 Nobel Prize winner in physics, Polycarp Kusch. I remember getting a note from Professor Kusch saying, "I am glad that SOMEONE has a concept of harmonic motion. My congratulations!" I also remember that one of my classmates in physics, Melvin Schwartz, won the Nobel Prize in physics. I know how he did it too—while I was sleeping at two in the morning, he was still in the physics lab.

"What's the Nobel Prize?"

"The Nobel Prize, Haleigh, is an international prize that is considered one of the most prestigious awards that can be given in a specific field."

"Pickle juice!"

Columbia opened many doors for me and led to great future prospects. Once, I went out for a job at Dow Jones, and the person whom I met there had gone to Columbia. So for him, it was almost a given that I was part of the fraternity, part of the family. I was offered the position, which I graciously declined. Going to school at Columbia certainly provided great opportunities and a vista of chances that I probably would never have had somewhere else.

One day I was wrestling my coach, Dick Waite. I was half his age and twice as strong. All of a sudden, the coach had me in an uncomfortable hold. I said, "Coach, I thought you taught me everything." He said, "I taught you everything, but not everything." I learned a lesson. A master can teach his disciples everything, but certain things can only come with the experience of time.

"Columbia sounds like a great school, Grandpa."

"It is a great school, Haleigh!"

"Can I go to Columbia, Grandpa?"

"Of course you can, Alex."

"Did Daddy go to Columbia?"

"No, Daddy went to Boston University, but your Aunt Helaine went to Columbia."

"I love my Aunt Helaine," interrupts Haleigh. "I want to go to Columbia too."

"I'm going to Columbia like my mommy," Rebecca interjects.

"I think wherever you guys go will be great. It doesn't have to be Columbia."

"Is that when you became an orthodontist?" Alex rubs his hands back and forth before grabbing the pole one last time.

"At first, I wasn't too sure what I wanted to study when I was at Columbia. I eventually figured it out."

I remember once my dad asked what I was majoring in when I was a freshman at college. I told him philosophy. He said, "Come home; I will put you on a truck for fourteen hours day and you will learn philosophy." The next day I changed my major.

"Is that when you became an orthodontist?"

"Not really, Haleigh. But I was well on my way to becoming an orthodontist. I still had to study a few more years to become one."

"You really did like school, Papa Larry. You were in school a long time."

"I did a fair share of time in school, Rebecca. It was well worth it too."

"Did you stay more years at Columbia?"

"From Columbia, I went on to the University of Pennsylvania Dental School, Alex."

"Daddy went to Penn!" Haleigh shouts as she awaits her turn on the pole.

"He sure did!"

As Alex reaches the ground and Haleigh begins her last descent, the clouds begin to get denser and fight with the sun for dominance. Bored with the pole, Alex turns to the monkey bars with Haleigh in pursuit. Rebecca looks at the pole and also decides to skip across the jungle gym to the monkey bars. As I watch under them making sure they can hold their weight, I become tempted to try the monkey bars too.

Columbia College students and I (front left) get a few minutes of fame in print in The New York Times Magazine, *1951.*

My many hats

Proud graduate of Columbia College, with my father, Joseph Hartstein (left), 1953

With my uncle Louis Grossmark (left), and my mother, Jean Hartstein (right), who now had a doctor in the family, 1953

UNIVERSITY OF PENNSYLVANIA DENTAL SCHOOL

A complicated mind is full of intellectual manure.
An uncomplicated mind is full of random diarrhea.
—*Lawrence S. Harte*

When I was in grammar school, I wanted to be a plastics engineer, which, in those days evoked the response, "What is he talking about?" When I went to Brooklyn Tech, I said, "I want to be a plastics engineer." At Columbia, I thought of working with the State Department, learning languages, serving my country, and possibly becoming a lawyer in the Department. However, I discovered two facts that concerned me. The State Department was rife with anti-Semitism, and, because that time was the middle of the McCarthy era, people in the State Department were subject to harassment after many, many years of service. Many of the times the charges were completely unfounded, but careers were ruined.

"Grandpa, what is anti-Semitism?" Alex inquires.

"Anti-Semitism is when people do not like you because you are Jewish. They don't respect your customs or traditions."

"Grandpa, there were a lot of mean people when you were growing up. I still don't understand why people don't like Jews. I know you told us it is because of religion and land, but it still doesn't make sense to me."

"I don't understand either. I just hope that one day, people can respect other people's beliefs and not judge them for what they believe in, but rather for who they are and how they act."

"I agree, Grandpa. I like everybody. I don't like that someone would not like me because I'm a Jew."

"I like everybody, too!" Haleigh exclaims as she reaches for her last monkey bar.

"I like everybody and everybody likes me. It's silly not to like people for being a Jew, Papa Larry," Rebecca proclaims.

"Grandpa, you said something about the McCarthy era; what is that about?" Alex begins to climb up the ladder to attempt the monkey bars once more.

"It was a time when our country was in war and communism was a threat. Communism is when the government takes over and controls everything. A senator named Joseph McCarthy began accusing people of being communist—someone who believes in communism. And so, many people started acting a little crazy, thinking communists were trying to take over our government."

"That's crazy and scary!"

"Yes, it was a crazy and scary time."

"What made you choose orthodontist?"

I went to a book called *How to Pick a Vocation*. I found out from this book that most people chose their professions by eliminating what they knew they didn't like and choosing something from what was left over. One question in the book was, "Do you like kids?" I answered yes. "Do you like to work with your hands?" Yes. "Are you a little bit of a goofy guy once in a while?" I answered yes. And the result indicated that I should be an orthodontist. So, I became an orthodontist.

"Maybe I can read the book too. I want to be a lot of things, Grandpa."

"I think you'll have plenty of time to figure out what you want to do, but a book can always help, Alex."

"I want to be a ballerina. I don't need a book. I just need ballet shoes and music to dance to," Haleigh announces as she jumps off the ladder and lands in a graceful pose.

"I think you'd be a beautiful ballerina, Haleigh."

"I think you'd be a beautiful ballerina too," Rebecca states as she jumps off the monkey bars as if she were a professional gymnast landing her perfect ten.

The way you began your year at dental school was the way you finished. The instructors graded you by their first impressions. One day, someone took my work and presented it to be graded. He got a B and I got an A. He was furious.

"You were smart, Grandpa." Haleigh hops from one end of the monkey bars to the other waiting for her brother to finish his climb.

"I figured I had just made a good first impression."

"First impression?"

"When someone meets you for the first time, they either like you or they don't. They judge you by how you look and act. That is a first impression."

"I'll always make a good first impression then, Grandpa, because I love people and they love me."

"You sure will!"

"Do you have any stories of dental school, Grandpa?"

"Well, Alex, I think I have a few funny moments I could share." Alex quickly crosses over and descends from the monkey bars. Haleigh runs up the wooden ladder to the deck of the playground and puts her head through a fiberglass tunnel opening. Alex looks around and debates where he's going to venture next.

One day at the clinic, I was doing a filling restoration, which restores a tooth to its original state. The instructor came over with a mirror, looked at the filling, and said, "Scratches!" So I polished it up a little bit more. He came back ten minutes later and said, "Scratches!" and threw the mirror down. I polished it up a little bit MORE. Twenty minutes later, he came back and said, "Scratches!" So I said, "What are you talking about—scratches WHERE?" And he said, "Scratches in the mirror!"

"Scratches!" Alex laughs, "Grandpa, you thought he was talking about your filling. That's funny!"

"Yes, that's just one of the goofy things I did in dental school."

"You're goofy, Grandpa." Haleigh laughs with us, although she is completely oblivious to the joke.

Rebecca joins in on the laughter and says, "Papa Larry, I love how you are so silly. You always make me laugh."

There was another time when a patient came in and we gave her removable upper and lower false dentures. She said, "Doctor, I hear ringing!" And one of my instructors said, "Ma'am, that's perfectly normal, but tell me, does it sound like ding ding or ding dong?"

"Papa Larry, what did she say it sounded like?"

"Alex, it was another joke. The instructor used her concern of hearing ringing with the sound of a doorbell, since a doorbell rings."

"A doorbell goes ding dong, Grandpa," Haleigh blurts out as she crawls through the fiberglass tube.

"Oh, I see. Dental school is for people who are goofy!" Alex reasons as he walks toward the spinner.

"It sure is! You see now why the book told me to be an orthodontist."

"It's a smart book, Grandpa. Were there any times it wasn't goofy?"

"Of course, Alex."

The Alpha Omega Dental Fraternity sponsored a nonprofit dental clinic for people who could not afford dental care. As juniors, we worked on those patients at night. Aside from helping the patients, it gave us extra experience, which helped us get way ahead in school. It was a win-win situation for the patients and for us.

In the summer of my junior year, I drove with three of my classmates to Waukesha, Wisconsin, to a mud bath hotel.

"A mud bath hotel?" Rebecca's voice echoes through the crawl tunnel as she searches for Haleigh.

"A hotel that offers mud baths."

"Why would you want to take a mud bath, Papa Larry? You would still stay dirty. I like to use water and soap to get clean."

"It's a special type of mud," I respond with a slight chuckle. "Afterwards, you rinse off with water."

"Why not just use water first and not use mud, Grandpa? It sounds silly if you still have to rinse with water," Haleigh adds.

"I guess it's because they say this special mud makes your skin nice and soft."

"My skin is already nice and soft. I think I will stick with water."

"Haleigh, let Grandpa finish his story," Alex interrupts as he places his hand on one of the metal bars that help a rider hold on for dear life as the spinner goes around and around.

"Grandpa, you didn't finish your story," Haleigh responds as she eyes her brother, darts down the playground platform, and heads to the spinner, refusing to be left out.

They had an Alpha Omega Dental fraternity meeting at the hotel. I used one of my friends' cars. I was always a goofy driver.

"You're just goofy, Grandpa," Haleigh announces as she reaches for a metal bar on the spinner. Noticing their hesitation, I gesture for them to climb onto the spinner and hold on. Rebecca runs up to the spinner and leaps onto it. I lightly turn the mechanism and begin the dizzying the ride.

Driving through Indiana with friends, I drove on the middle marker. A policeman said to me, "Son, do you know you're driving on the middle marker? Are you drunk, or are you just a lousy driver?" And the other three guys said, "There's no better lousy driver than him." The guy laughed and I didn't get a ticket. And, to this day, unfortunately, I still drive on the middle marker. So I wasn't just goofy in dental school; my goofiness extended to my driving as well.

"Grandpa, we know you're a goofy driver. Daddy says it sometimes too," Haleigh shouts in glee. Her rosy cheeks flatten from the force of the wind from spinner's momentum. "Whee... Whee...," she shouts as around and around they go. Alex just holds on without an ounce of horror, enjoying the ride as Rebecca smiles and giggles louder as the spinner goes faster.

Since I had finished all my required clinic courses at the end of my junior year, in my last year I only had to spend half of my time in school finishing up some academic courses. I spent the extra time going to cultural events and sitting in on advanced university classes.

"What did you do then, Grandpa, since you only spent half of your time in school?"

"Well, Alex, I finally got a chance to learn about Philadelphia, to learn a little bit about the arts and sciences, and get some intellectual feeling back in my life."

"Rebecca lives in Philadelphia!" Haleigh states with an air of assurance.

"Yes, she does."

"I do. I live in Philadelphia, and New York sometimes too," Rebecca announces.

At dental school I had an experience that I will never forget. The wife of a friend of mine was spending a huge amount of money on clothing and jewelry. It was so bad that they had to go to a loan shark to pay their bills. The loan shark eventually came after them and threatened to harm my friend if he did not pay.

Having grown up in Brooklyn, I happened to know someone who might take care of this dire situation. I called up a guy that I used to play with on the streets of Brooklyn. I said, "Billy [that was not his real name], this is Lawrence." After a silence that seemed to last forever, Billy said, "Hello, Lawrence."

I explained to him what had happened. He listened carefully and said, "I will call you within the hour." Some forty minutes later, the phone rang. Billy said, "Tell your friend to pay the principle without the interest. Have a good life, Lawrence." Billy was saying to me that this was a favor to me for old times' sake; don't call again. I never did.

During this time at dental school I needed to make some money, so I used to make gold trinkets like hearts, cars, and inscriptions and sell them to a Philadelphia department store. The store used to advertise the trinkets in the newspaper and made lots of money from my work. One day, I went to the store and told them that that situation wasn't fair. The manager said, "Son, who are you going to sell to while you're at school?" Just to appease me, he gave me a little money. I learned an important lesson—sometimes what you do is not as important as who you know.

"You made gold hearts, Grandpa. I want a gold heart," Haleigh screeches as she goes around and around.

"I want a gold heart too. I love hearts," Rebecca shouts.

"I don't make them anymore. I only made them when I needed money during dental school."

"Pickle juice!" Haleigh smiles as the spinner goes around and around.

"Papa Larry, did you have to do anything else for dental school?"

"I had to take a state exam to legally practice dentistry, Alex."

As a senior, I had to take the state exam. In those days, you had to take a state exam to practice dentistry in most states. Connecticut was very difficult to get into in those days because they wanted to limit the number of new incoming dentists. One of my friends' dads was on the state board there, and he said to me, "Larry, do the restoration, no matter what it looks like." When I came in for the interview, he and I talked about my going up to Cape Cod to visit his family. All the other guys who applied were asked impossible questions that were impossible to answer.

"Was it impossible for you?" Haleigh motions for more as the spinner begins to decelerate in speed.

"Not for me; fortunately, my question was not impossible to answer. I was just lucky. I learned at this time that who you know is as important as what you know."

"Is that when you became an orthodontist?" Alex balances his body as he sits unaffected by the spinning.

"Not yet! I became a dentist at this time. After dental school, you have to study more and specialize to be an orthodontist."

"That's a lot of school."

"It sure was, but it was well worth it. I didn't go straight to school though to be an orthodontist."

"Why not?"

"Dental school was four years, Alex, and when it was time to graduate, I did not have any money. So I volunteered for the United States Air Force, where I eventually became a captain."

"Did you still want to be an orthodontist?"

"Even during this time, I thought of going into the specialty of orthodontics when I got out of the Air Force, which I did."

My parents came to my graduation from dental school, as they also did for high school and college. I spent graduation days saying goodbye to my girlfriends. In dental school, I dated very fancy, nice girls from the main line. If I had been socially ready, I could have been in real estate, business, or show business. Instead, I had to work for a living! I told them I was joining the Air Force. They literally had a "Harte" attack.

When my mother found out at graduation that I was joining the Air Force, she cried that I could die on a remote island and she would not be able to get a *minyan* together (a communal prayer that requires a quorum of ten adult Jews) to come to pray at the funeral. In any case, both of my parents were proud that their son had become a doctor.

"I'm proud of you, Grandpa!"

"Thank you, Haleigh. I'm proud of you too."

"I'm proud of you, Papa Larry," Rebecca repeats.

"And I'm proud of you!"

Alex quietly studies my face as the spinner begins to slow down. Turn by turn, his curious eyes catch mine while his mind continues to ponder about orthodontic school.

"Papa, Larry, where did you go to orthodontic school?"

Haleigh and Rebecca jump off the spinner giggling before it comes to a complete stop. Alex watches Haleigh and Rebecca skip toward the playground area as he waits for the spinner to complete a final motion. As we walk to the playground, Alex grabs my right hand and lifts his head, intently waiting for a response.

University of Pennsylvania Dental School, 1957

In the lab at UPenn Dental School, 1956

Counting patient charts at UPenn Dental School

EASTMAN DENTAL CENTER, UNIVERSITY OF ROCHESTER

The word "try" is not a word. The word "good" is not a
word. "I will" and "great" are words.
—*Lawrence S. Harte*

I applied to orthodontic school while I was in the Air Force. The orthodontic residency was extremely difficult to get into because the program only took the top people in their classes. In addition, I made it even more difficult for myself.

"How did you make it more difficult, Papa Larry?"

"Well, Rebecca, I wanted to go to a program that was free. The Eastman Dental Center, at the University of Rochester, had one of two programs in the entire U.S. that you did not have to pay for."

"How did you get into Eastman, Grandpa?"

"I got into Eastman, Alex, with a little bit of luck and a lot of hard work."

In applying to Eastman, I mentioned that I had worked at the Philadelphia Center for Research in Child Growth (now the W. M. Krogman Center for Research in Child Growth and Development) under its founder, Wilton M. Krogman, a world-famous physical anthropologist, and Dr. Viken Sassoni, a world-famous orthodontic researcher. I wrote that I took X-rays of the skulls of monkeys and people.

To my surprise, I received a call from Dr. Basil Bibby, who was the director of the Eastman Dental Center (now the Eastman Institute for Oral Health). He invited me to see the school, and even picked me up at the airport. I could not understand why he was so interested in me. I later found out that the school was looking for somebody with monkey experience.

"Did you like working with the monkeys, Grandpa?" Alex asks with a tone of disbelief.

"I love monkeys," Rebecca shouts as she runs up the steps and waits behind Haleigh, ready to take on the twisted slide with no fear. It's incredible how much she takes after her mother, Helaine.

"Grandpa, you worked with monkeys?" Haleigh questions as she glides down the twisted slide.

"The truth be told, the only monkey experience I had was watching monkeys in a zoo or in a vaudeville act."

While at Eastman, I took over the night dental practice of one of my classmates, Dr. Len Fishman, to earn more money. Dr. Fishman's son is the famous leader of Phish, the internationally acclaimed rock band. Fishman used to tell me that his son used to make a lot of noise when he was growing up. Now, Phish is getting paid big money for making that noise.

"Haleigh makes a lot of noise, Grandpa. Do you think she'll get paid big money too?"

"I hope so, Alex!"

My whole life changed at Eastman. I was in a profession that required science, esthetics, and marketing. I loved all three. I could not believe that people were going to pay me for having fun for the rest of my professional life. I was honored to be part of the orthodontic family.

"Papa Larry, you said that Eastman was free, right?"

"Yes, it was, Alex."

"Then why did you go to the Air Force before you went to Eastman? You said that you went to the Air Force because you didn't have money to go to orthodontic school, but it was free and you made money working in Dr. Fishman's night practice."

"That's a great observation, Alex. When I finished Penn Dental School, I guess I joined the Air Force because I was single and adventurous and wanted to see the world."

"Grandpa, did you always want to join the Air Force?" Alex keeps a poky pace by my side as Haleigh and Rebecca run back and forth, their energy seeming more boundless than ever.

"I did, Alex. I was a little bit older than you when I started thinking about joining the Air Force."

"Why, Grandpa?"

As the sun ascends and the clouds dominate the sky, we say farewell to the playground and walk toward home as I relate my adventures flying high in the Air Force.

Flying High

Integrity First
Service Before Self
Excellence in All We Do

—*U.S. Air Force Core Values*

I guess I began thinking of joining the Air Force at the age of twelve. That was the year they came out with World War II airplane spotter playing cards. Each card had three silhouettes on the face, a front view, a side view, and a view of the bottom of an aircraft that would be seen by a ground observer. So if I were a pilot, I could tell what kind of a plane it was. I was excited about flying from an early age.

"Grandpa, you collected airplane cards like Daddy collects sports cards," Alex exclaims with excitement.

"That's right, just like your dad."

"Do you still have the cards?"

"I don't have the cards anymore, but I remember some of the planes."

The B17 bomber was called the Flying Fortress. It had four

engines. There was the U.S. fighter Wildcat, which was a fighter plane. And I remember one of my favorite U.S. fighter planes, the P38. It was called Lightning. It had two engines and a twin tail. To this day, I have a replica of the plane in my den.

"I saw the plane in your den."

"You sure did, Haleigh. It's one of my favorites. What a neat airplane!"

"I've seen the plane too, Papa Larry. I love to ride in planes. My favorite time is when I get to see you," Rebecca informs me as she skips alongside us.

"I love to see you too!"

There was the dive-bomber called the Nautilus. It was the A24. It was the one that used to go after Japanese aircraft carriers. Another favorite of mine was the bomber B25 Mitchell.

"Why is that one a favorite, Grandpa?"

"That was one of the planes I took across the Pacific, Alex, when I was in the Air Force. I remember sitting in the compartment with just my Air Force khakis on. I nearly froze to death."

"That was silly, Grandpa. You should have worn warmer clothes."

"Yes, Haleigh, I should've worn warmer clothes. I didn't know it was going to be so cold."

"Mommy and Daddy always make me wear warm clothes when it's cold outside, Grandpa. Didn't your mommy and daddy teach you to wear warm clothes?"

"They did, Rebecca. I guess I just wasn't ready for the weather."

I remember the U.S. bomber B24. They called it the Liberator. Those were the bombers that went over Romania and bombed the Ploesti oil fields.

"Why did they bomb the oil fields, Papa Larry?" Alex watches his sister twirl and twirl and twirl ahead of us. She stops at a post, puts her hand out for balance and does a graceful ballerina kick in the air, then returns to her twirling. Rebecca skips behind her contemplating whether she should continue skipping or to start twirling like her cousin Haleigh.

"Well, Alex, during World War II we were fighting the Nazis of Germany. The city of Ploesti, Romania, was a significant source of oil production for Nazi Germany, so we bombed the oil refineries to try to eliminate their source of fuel."

"That makes sense, Grandpa."

"The Nazis sound like bad people, Grandpa," Haleigh mumbles in mid-turn.

"They were, Haleigh."

"Why were they so bad?" Rebecca wonders.

"There's a theory that the Nazi Party, which came to power in 1933 in Germany, was formed by a group that was angry about the Treaty of Versailles."

"What's the Treaty of Versailles, Papa Larry?"

"The Treaty of Versailles was one of the peace treaties that helped end World War I, in which the Germans fought against the Allied Powers."

"The Germans seem like angry people."

"No, not all of the Germans were angry people, Haleigh, but there was an angry group at that time. These people thought the treaty was a Jewish/communist conspiracy to humiliate Germany at the end of World War I."

"That sounds silly, Papa Larry. The treaty was for peace. Why would it be to make fun of them?"

"I agree, Alex; it is silly. But that was the way some of them felt, and that was one of the reasons the Nazi Party came to exist."

"It doesn't sound like a party to me," Haleigh asserts. Lifting her arms in the air, she forms an arch over her head, then slides one foot up the other leg midway to her knee, creating a triangular shape.

"It's not a party like you think, Haleigh."

"I know it's not, Grandpa, because parties are for fun and not for mean people."

I also remember the Focke-Wulf Fw200 German bomber. It was a four-engine bomber that went long distances. And, of course, the favorite German fighter was the Messerschmitt Bf109. That was probably better than some of our planes in those days. And of course, the Stuka, the German blitzkrieg dive-bomber, was the one that went after the Junkers, our cargo ships. Probably my favorite fighter of all time was the British fighter Spitfire. Those were the ones that saved England during the German blitzkrieg against London after the fall of France. That was a very heroic plane.

"You have a lot of favorite planes, Papa Larry."

"I guess I do, Rebecca. I love airplanes, so I guess my fascination with these planes is what lured me to join the Air Force. They were such beautiful and powerful machines. I was mesmerized by them."

"What did you do in the Air Force? Did you fly planes?"

"I wasn't a pilot, Alex, but I did get to ride in a lot of planes and travel to different places in the world."

My days in the Air Force were very interesting and truly fantastic. I was in the Air Force for two years. I went in as a kid and left as a person with a huge amount of experience. I graduated dental school in June, and in July I became a lieutenant in the Air Force and went to basic training.

"What's a lieutenant?"

"A lieutenant, Alex, is a commanding officer rank, and it's one rank under the captain. After one year in the Air Force, providing you didn't mess around with the general's wife or got court-marshaled, you became a captain. I always feared that someday I would be court-marshaled because I asked so many questions. In the service it is understood that you are not supposed to ask questions; you are just supposed to take orders."

"Haleigh wouldn't make it in the service, Grandpa."

"Why do you say that Alex?"

"Because she likes to talk and ask a lot of questions."

"You may be right then, Alex, but she does follow the rules, and the service is all about following rules."

"If you think so, Grandpa."

"Asking questions is not a bad thing, Alex. Because I asked so many questions, at one time they wanted to transfer me to the intelligence group. My commanding officer felt it was a win-win situation. He would get rid of me and the intelligence group would get somebody who was just goofy and asked lots of questions."

"Did they transfer you, Grandpa?"

"No, I didn't get transferred, but they at least thought about it."

In the Air Force you really lived for today. Most base tours lasted two to three years, and it was difficult to have buddies since you moved around so much. It was like a special esprit de corps because every three years you would change stations and eventually you would meet someone from twenty years ago.

Haleigh stops as she hears the discouraging words, peers into my eyes and discloses, "I see my friends every day. I wouldn't want to move from my friends. I love my friends."

"I saw my friends in school every day too, but once I

graduated, we all went our separate ways. Some of us stayed in touch though."

"Pickle juice!"

Alex, taking one hand out of his pocket and shuffling a couple of fingers across the bottom of his nose to scratch the tingling sensation from the wind, asks, "When you graduated from dental school and went to the Air Force, how did you go? Did your mommy take you?"

"When I graduated from school, before I got into the Air Force, I bought myself a very fancy red convertible. I didn't have much money, but I had some extra during the time of my senior year in dental school. I worked at the Philadelphia Growth Center and at a fertility clinic, to save up money. I had always wanted a convertible since I was a kid. I bought the convertible because I had never had anything new in my life."

"You never bought something new before?"

"No. For the first time in my life, I bought something new, not used, not OTT, not Off The Truck, it was mine. I felt on top of the world."

"What did you drive before it?"

"Before the convertible, I had a clunky 1940 Plymouth Coupe. The way the car stopped was by my putting my foot through the bottom and stopping it."

Rebecca yells, "You had a car like the Flintstones. They stop their cars with their feet too."

Being compared to a cartoon set in prehistoric times was not what I expected; however, the Plymouth Coupe was not too far from being ancient.

"Close, but not exactly like their car, Rebecca. It was just falling apart. I remember buying it for $250. It was a bargain, but it fit the expression, "You get what you pay for!" But it was what I could afford at the time."

I drove up to Griffiss Air Force Base in Rome, New York. It was the first Air Force base I was stationed at. Rome was a great town, and Griffiss was a great base, but they say that, if you sneeze on July fourth, you miss the summer because the weather is so cloudy and so full of snow.

"That's funny, Grandpa. It must really be cold there in Rome."

"It did get pretty cold there, Haleigh."

Rome was a town that life passed by. It was a town with one newspaper, the *Rome Sentinel*, and one movie theater. If it wasn't for Griffiss Air Force Base, I think the town would have gone away. I kind of liked that sleepy town. It gave me time to meditate and think. I was there about a year. Mark Twain could have had a sign on top of the Savoy Restaurant that said, "If you have one year to spend, spend it in Rome, New York, and it will feel like the rest of your life."

"Did you have any fun there, Papa Larry? It sounds like there wasn't a lot to do there."

"I must say that life did go by, Rebecca, but I made sure to enjoy it every second of the day."

Once, I went to Whiteface Mountain, a mountain close to Rome, New York. I was trying to act like an Olympic skier. I was a pretty fast skier and was trying to show off on ice. I lost my edge, I lost my footing, and down I went. I lost my vanity. What I wouldn't do for attention! It was like show business. Unfortunately, I tore ligaments in my left knee. Of course, that show business act lasted about eight weeks in a cast. They carried me down on a sled stretcher, with the applause of the crowd saying, "What a klutz!"

"I am good at skiing, Grandpa. Too bad you didn't have me there to teach you," Alex grinned.

"Maybe I wouldn't have torn a ligament with your tutoring," I snickered.

The officer's commissary offered items that didn't get damaged as easily as I got hurt. I bought, in 1957, an Omega watch. To this day, it is still working. It cost me $35. I also bought a huge Grundig AM radio there, and I schlepped it from Germany all the way to the United States to my mother. My Uncle Lou, when he passed away at 106 years young, had the Grundig in his apartment.

"Did you do anything else besides skiing, Grandpa?" Alex inquired as he looked at his sister skipping and hopping ahead of us with their cousin Rebecca.

"I also used to go waterskiing to pass the time in Rome. We used to go to a local lake called Lake Delta. One day I was waterskiing and fell, and I let go of the rope. I was a pretty fair water skier. I ended up doing a handstand in the water. Silly me!"

"Grandpa, I don't think skiing on water or snow is safe for you."

"No it isn't. It isn't safe for me."

I will say that not all was fun and games though. Honestly, taking orders was difficult for me, especially if I felt that the person giving orders didn't know too much or had no idea what he was talking about. There was so much waste because people were not accountable and did not have to pay for their actions personally. So I protested. Our commanding officer made a decision on logistics. I protested. Finally, an old-time master sergeant who had been in the service for many years said, "Son, cool it. You are not going to change anything, so go with the flow." I learned to go with the flow and that sometimes in life you just have to tread water. The experience did help me understand what the service is about—the philosophy of discipline and obedience. Now I understand completely because, without that, you cannot have a military.

Haleigh proudly states, as she skips passed us once more, "I always obey Mommy and Daddy." Alex gently tugs at my arm and softly replies with a solemn face, "Not all the time, Grandpa."

There were some great memories though. I must have dated three quarters of the whole nursing barrack in my last three months at Griffiss Air Force Base. Oh, to be young! I was bored, so what better was there to do than to date? I was single; I really had no attachments. There was nothing else to do.

"What about Grandma or Kathy? Weren't they with you?"

"I didn't know your grandmother or Kathy at that time, Rebecca. I didn't meet your grandmother until a few years later. And I didn't meet Kathy for many, many years after."

Another time, during my Air Force days in 1957 through 1959, we made a liquor run to Greenland. We went to Greenland because the plane was going to Thule, Greenland, ostensibly on a training mission, but also to bring back liquor. My job, because I was a junior officer, was to make sure that we got all the liquor needed to bring back to the base in Rome, New York. One time, coming back from Greenland, we ran into severe storms and had a choice of lightening the load of the plane by getting rid of either the alcohol or the fuel. You guessed it— we got rid of the fuel! We just had enough fuel to land the plane.

"Everyone must've really been thirsty!"

"They sure were thirsty, Alex."

"They were lucky you had enough fuel to land."

"So were we! It was one of my many fun adventures."

I must admit though that the Air Force had its rough side too. One of my positions as a dental officer in the Air Force was, unfortunately, death identification. It involved identifying people who had died in air crashes. Many of the people I had to identify had been my friends at the officer's club.

Haleigh's face drew sad as she refrains from skipping and hopping. She cries, "That's horrible, Grandpa!"

Rebecca joins Haleigh and cries, "That's really horrible, Papa Larry!"

"It really was horrible. I remember one day that is so vivid in my memory; it will stay with me forever."

"Please tell us, Grandpa," Haleigh's tone turns serious and her eyes begin to shine as small pools of water form in her lower eyelid.

"Okay, I will," I respond in a mournful pitch. "It's a sad story though."

I had to identify a fighter jet pilot who was a good friend of mine. His girlfriend at that time said, "Larry please, say it's not Bob! Say it's not Bob!" But it was Bob and, in the Air Force and in the military, when someone dies, the shock waves travel around the world. Within three or four days, his friends came from all over the world to pay respects at the church.

When there is a tragedy or someone dies in the Air Force, four jets fly over, and one of the jets in the back tails away. This is called the missing plane or the missing person, and it is in honor of your brother who has passed away in the service of his country. This was done for Bob. Our eyes were red and tears flowed down our faces, but the memory of an officer, a friend, someone who died in the service of his country, in the service of our love and the family of man, would last forever.

"That's so sad, Grandpa." Alex stops walking and grabs my arm to give me a hug. Haleigh clings to my other side and cries once more. "It'll be okay, Grandpa," she says. Rebecca looks at us and nods to me with a sad grin, letting me know that everything is okay.

"I'm okay, Haleigh. It's just a sad memory. There were plenty of good memories too."

Alex unhinges himself from my body along with Haleigh, and we continue on our walk home. Wanting to forget the feeling of sorrow, Alex adds, "Grandpa, you told us you visited many places. Where else did you go in the Air Force?"

"I traveled and was stationed throughout the world."

Another place I was stationed was the Gunter Air Force Base in Montgomery, Alabama, for the Air Force Officer Training School. When we were graduating, the commander began telling us about war. In the middle of his speech, he asked if anybody was from Brooklyn. I raised my hand. He said, "Son, you know it all. You do not have to listen." Brooklyn's reputation was infamous.

"You're lucky you're from Brooklyn," Haleigh points out.

"Why is that?"

"You know it all, Grandpa. That's what they told you."

"Growing up in Brooklyn, it was rough, and I did learn a lot, but I don't know it all, Haleigh. You're always learning in life. No one really knows it all."

On another note, while I was in Alabama, I had an opportunity of having a blind date with the person who made our Air Force uniforms. She was a Jewish girl from Montgomery. On our first date, I came with my officer's uniform, and she came in an evening gown as if we were going to a ball, but we were just going out for a soda. The South really is classy and conservative. Can you imagine—if we had had the chemistry, I could be living in Montgomery, Alabama, y'all.

"The South sounds like a great place. I like to dress up, Papa Larry."

"And you always look beautiful too, Rebecca."

Alex, trying to get away from Rebecca's dress-up conversation, interjects, "Grandpa, where else did they station you?"

"I spent some time at the Wright-Patterson Air Force Base in Ohio."

"Why did you go to Ohio?"

"It's where I took the flight chamber test."

"What is a flight chamber test?"

"Before you can fly in a jet plane, you must be trained in a flight chamber. You are placed in the zero gravity chamber and then you take off the oxygen mask and find out which part of your body feels oxygen deprivation first."

"Is that important?"

"This is important to know because it tells you where and when you are going to feel the loss of oxygen."

With me, it was the back of my neck. A guy from Mississippi was my partner, and he had to watch while I took off my oxygen mask. He was so slow he scared the heck out of me. I switched to be with a guy from Maine. That's probably why I am living today.

"I'm so happy they put you with the guy from Maine."

"Me too, Haleigh."

Talking about living, once we had a crash landing in Madison, Wisconsin. We were flying from California to Rome, New York, when we experienced engine trouble. As we went around the field, they put foam on the field, and crowds began to gather. When we came in and didn't crash, I got the feeling that the crowds, like at a boxing match, were not happy. There was no blood.

"Why would they want to see blood?" Haleigh stares at me horrified.

"Sometimes people are weird."

"They sound weird, Grandpa."

"I don't want to see blood," Rebecca exclaims.

"I don't want to see blood either."

"Did you have any other crash landings?"

"I did, Alex, in Tainan."

Once I was on a plane that landed in Tainan, which is a small city in Taiwan, in a monsoon rain. In those days, Red China was shelling the islands of Quemoy and Matsu off the coast of Taiwan. We came in for a landing on a mud field that was complete mush. That was my big war experience. I got dirt on my camera. And I followed my brave pilot out of the cockpit as he said, "Follow me." He stepped into mud past his waist. I decided to go out the back entrance. At least the mud was only to my ankles. I still have itchy feet. I swear it is from the dirt that is still underneath my nails from the crash landing in Taiwan.

"You are so silly, Grandpa. You have itchy feet."

"I do, Haleigh."

"Pickle juice!"

I went to Manila in the Philippines to explore some of the historic areas of World War II. I visited Corregidor Island. Now it is a memorial for American and Filipino soldiers who fought against great odds during the war. I visited the area of the Bataan Death March, which happened on April 9, 1942, where some 75,000 Filipino and Americans were forced to endure a sixty-mile hike. Thousands died from starvation, dehydration, untreated wounds, and wanton execution. I visited a cemetery where many of the Americans were buried. War is a bad atrocity. There was nothing good about this. It left a feeling of emptiness in my heart, in my soul.

"War isn't good, Papa Larry."

"War is never good, Rebecca."

Oh, there were so many memories, so much adventure. I was once stationed at the Von Steuben Hotel in Frankfurt, Germany. The Air Force stationed me in the hotel rather than in a dormitory. I left my boots there, and I sent them a letter. They wouldn't send me my boots until I paid for the rental charge for their keeping my boots for two weeks. Can you believe it? Rent for boots!

"Did the boots stay in their own room, Grandpa?" Alex questioned in disbelief. He looks down at his shoes and wonders how much they would charge for his.

"For what they charged, they should've had the penthouse suite!"

At one time I went to a ski resort with some Air Force buddies. This resort had a large bar, and the waitresses tied a glass onto the tops of each of our skis. Each glass was filled with whiskey. Three pilots and I lifted our skis and drank the contents of our glasses all at once. The drink was called a shot-ski. I was drunk before I smelled it. And I admit it—I couldn't match my companions in flying skills or drinking skills.

"Grandpa, you were drunk? Mommy and Daddy would be very disappointed in you," Haleigh lectures.

"Yes, they would. I should've known better."

"Pickle juice!"

Then there was the time my commander asked me to teach his wife the card game of bridge. I was a bridge instructor. She got very interested both in the game and in me. I was so naïve. As a single guy, I dreamt of being court-marshaled or at best, shot.

I also used to go hunting with my commander. He would never let me get behind him. He was afraid I would miss the deer and hit him. Maybe he knew something that I didn't.

"He was afraid you'd shoot him," Alex repeated.

"I think he was. He might've been right. Either way, he made sure I didn't have a chance to prove him right."

One time I was stationed in Tokyo and Tachikawa, and I had the opportunity of meeting a Geisha girl. Geisha girls gave massages, stomped on your back with their feet, prepared your food, were very warm and cordial, and only wanted a present in return, never money. I bought two sets of real pearls, one for this lady and one to bring home to my mom.

"I love to get presents!"

"I'm sure you do, Rebecca."

"Pearls are pretty, too."

"Pearls are very pretty, Haleigh, that's why I bought them for the Geisha girl and my mom. They loved them."

Another time in Tokyo, I wanted to go to the U.S. embassy because I had lost my passport, so I took a taxi cab. The taxi driver wore white clothes and a tie; he was very kind and attentive. The only problem was that he didn't speak English. He told me to get in. After several minutes of driving very fast, he let me out. I had been only two blocks away from the embassy before I got into the taxi cab.

"Did you get to the embassy?"

"I did finally get there at great expense, Haleigh."

"You could've walked the two blocks, Grandpa," Alex reasons.

"I realized that after I spent a lot of money on the taxi driver."

"You're silly, Papa Larry!"

"I felt silly, Rebecca."

I was sent to the Sidi Slimane Air Force Base in Morocco. I was sent there on a Strategic Air Command plane. They only took single guys because they used to pick you up at four o'clock in the morning, and married men were exempted unless it was an emergency. I had to sleep in a dormitory that was brutally hot. It was in a desert and extraordinarily hot. Sometimes the temperature was up to 115 or 120 degrees. I vowed that I would never subject myself to that again. Later on, I would go to the Y, into the sauna, and into the hot steam room. There I was again, doing the same thing I promised I would never do! And I was paying for it.

"How did you stay cool in Morocco?"

"I spent three weeks in the movie theater in Morocco, Haleigh, watching *All Quiet on the Western Front* by Eric Von Remarque. I was there every night."

"Why?"

"Because it was the only place that was air conditioned!"

"Pickle juice!"

I also got an idea of how Moroccans did business through their fish sales. This is how fish sales work: At six o'clock in the morning, there was one price for fish. At two o'clock in the afternoon, because of the flies and because of the high heat, the price of the fish went down, but so did the taste. Your stomach would never be right again. That's the way they did business. Early in the morning was the only time to buy fresh food.

"The next time I eat fish, Grandpa, I'm going to make sure it was bought in the morning."

"I think that's a great idea, Alex."

Morocco wasn't the only hot place I visited while in the Air Force. I was sent to Wake Island, which is a military base and scientific research center. It is about half way between Hawaii and Guam. The Japanese seized it during WWII. There is nothing there except hot sun!

"Papa Larry, did you go anywhere it wasn't hot?"

"Yes, I did visit many places that were not as hot, Rebecca."

Another adventure was on a train from Manchester to London, England. I met a young lady who was the daughter of a British officer and a member of the House of Commons. I asked for directions for the train to London. She gave me directions. When I got on the train, I saw her sitting at a window seat. I asked if I could sit next to her, and she said, "Yes."

Her father, who was sitting nearby, was probably commenting on American cockiness and chauvinism. Whenever he spoke to me, I smiled. They invited me for dinner.

Her father said, "Lawrence, when the United States broke away from King George of England, you gained your freedom, but you lost your civility."

I think my answer to him was, "When the Boston patriots threw over the British tea in Boston Harbor, the patriots were not very civil, and I guess I was part of the genetic culture that came with it."

Can you imagine, if I had stayed in England, maybe I could be a member of the House of Commons! By the way, the British LOVE uniforms, they LOVE tradition, and, in some ways, I, too, love tradition.

"I'm glad you're a member of the 'House of Harte', Grandpa!"

"It's the only House I want to be a member of, Alex." I couldn't help but look down at his big brown eyes and smile.

I had the opportunity to take an Air Force plane for a vacation in Shagaramus in Trinidad and Tobago, where there was an officer's country club. I believed I had died and gone to heaven. It was a beautiful, beautiful place. The beaches were pristine, the climate was great, and I was treated like royalty. While there, I went with some buddies on a walk and there was a HUGE snake across the road.

Everybody walked over the snake, but not me; I took a three-quarter-mile detour because I did not want to go over that snake! I thought that snake was a miniature tyrannosaurus rex. My buddies all laughed at me, but I got to the officer's club first because they ran into road construction after they had walked over the snake and stayed on the same path. That's life sometimes. Subsequently, I brought my whole family back to Shagaramus. It had changed; it made me feel that the saying that you can never go home again was really true.

"But you can, Grandpa. We are going home now."

"We are going home, Haleigh, but I meant something different by that expression."

"What did you mean, Grandpa?"

"When someone visits a place and returns years later, the place normally has changed; it's not the same. This is what the expression 'You can never go home again' means."

"Pickle juice!"

In my final days of being in the Air Force, I was stationed in Mitchell Air Force Base near Roosevelt Raceway. During this short period, I met the grooms who took care of the horses and the riders of a nearby track. I knew who was going to win, who was healthy, and who was sick. In those days, I would bet $100 on a race, knowing everything; I still lost $800 during that summer. It just shows you that you better get a job because betting is not all it's cracked up to be.

"I love horses!" Haleigh and Rebecca blurt out in unison.

"I do too."

"Grandpa, how did you know which horse was going to win?"

"Well, Alex, since I had met the grooms for the horses, they would give me all the inside information on the horses, which helped me place my bet. The only problem was that I still didn't come out a winner."

"What did you do after the Air Force?"

"After I left the Air Force in Long Island, I drove home to Mom and Uncle Louie as they were packing to move to Florida."

"Did you move to Florida with them?"

"No, I stayed in New York to go to orthodontic school. I had to get a job quick. I had to make some money before I went to orthodontic school, so I worked as a dentist in Queens."

"Did you like your job?"

"It was a job. I needed money."

I learned a lesson. When I started working there, the office manager told me that he would give me $5 for every denture I made and $1 for every filling. The problem was that the office manager never gave me any dentures to make, so I was only making $1 per filling. Once again it was demonstrated to me that it isn't WHAT you know that's important, but WHO you know.

"I know you!" Haleigh shouts with glee as we come up to the front walk of the house.

"I know all of you!" Rebecca shouts after Haleigh.

"Grandpa, you were taught that lesson a lot!"

"Yes, yes, I did learn that lesson many times in life, Alex. It is a wise lesson."

As the air begins to shift to a cooler temperature and the sky darkens, we arrive at our destination. Rebecca runs up to the door and rings the doorbell.

"Grandpa, did you hear?"

"Hear what, Haleigh."

"Ding dong!"

The echo of our laughter fills the home as we enter; the door closes behind us as does another chapter in my life.

In my U.S. Air Force uniform, 1957

Enjoying a day off from the Air Force, waterskiing in Rome, New York, 1957

My 1957 fancy red convertible Chevrolet Bel Air. Nicknamed "the '57 Chevy," the convertible was introduced in September of 1956 by General Motors.

In downtown Tokyo, 1957

Being awarded a Charter Member Certificate from the U.S. Air Force, 1958 (I'm on the right)

Memories of My Mom

Every day is sunny; once in a while, the clouds get
in the way.

> —*Jean Hartstein*

Spring returns as the crisp, fresh air transports the aromatic
scent of newly risen flowers and brings out the deep green color in
the trees. Ah, Passover! What a glorious time of year to celebrate with
family. As my children travel with their families to their mother's
home, we gather together, eager to celebrate the Seder.

Celebrated the first two nights of the eight-day holiday, the Seder
is an intergenerational ritual prescribed by Jewish law. This ritual is
laid out in the Haggadah and based on the Book of Exodus. The finest
place settings and silverware are brought out with holiday dressings.
The *matzo*, *maror*, *charoset*, and *karpas*, along with salt water for
dipping and the traditional four cups of wine, are elements of the
ritual in this transmission of Jewish faith from grandparent to child.

As we prepare to read text this evening from the Haggadah with family and friends, I can only think back to when my grandfather would sit at the head of the table, leading the service. Being the grandfather now, I look forward to sitting at the head of the table and carrying on our heritage and traditions.

"I found it! I found it!" Haleigh shouts with merriment as she holds up the *afikomen*, which is a piece of matzoh, hidden so that the kids can look for it. Dessert is now served, and Haleigh is rewarded with a newly ironed five-dollar bill.

"I'm rich! I'm rich!" (Actually, all the kids got the same amount of money.)

We conclude the Seder with a prayer and remain talking about the events of the Exodus until sleep overtakes us. The next morning, I find myself surrounded by my grandchildren as I awaken to the enchanting perfume of freshly brewed coffee.

"Grandpa, we want to know more about our family." Haleigh beams her effervescent smile at me.

"I love my family!" Rebecca screeches while running around the main room trying to expend the energy she was recharged with overnight.

"Please, Grandpa. Tell us about our family on your side. I want to know what your mommy and daddy were like." Alex remains seated on the sofa analyzing the chess game in play with his father.

"Okay, okay. You win. Just let me have my cup of decaf coffee and I will tell you all about the Harte family. At least, what I can remember." Slowly, I sip the invigorating cup of decaffeinated java as the set of three curious eyes stare closely at me, waiting for that last single drop to be consumed.

I remember my mother taking me as a child on our annual two-week pilgrimage to the Catskill Mountains in upstate New York. My mother would hire a big, big car into which six people would stuff themselves. Halfway up, we would stop at the Red Apple Rest—the same restaurant year after year—and my mother would get me the same sandwich, liverwurst and onions. To this day, I have never had it again. I HATED it!

"That doesn't sound very good," Haleigh cringes in disgust.

"No, it doesn't sound good, Grandpa," Alex frowns with disgust.

"It wasn't! I hated it and still do to this day."

"You ate a sandwich with liverwurst and onions, yuck!" Rebecca's nose crinkles as she tries to copy Haleigh's look.

On the first day of vacation, my mother, a very clever person, would give an extra tip to the bellboy, the busboy, and the waiter, and say, "If you give us great service, this is only the beginning!" We DID get great service. Mom could have cared less what I did all day long, as long as I showed up at the three gigantic meals that she paid for. She wanted her money's worth!

"Your mommy was really clever," Haleigh interrupts. "Is that why you're so smart, Grandpa?"

"I don't know, Haleigh. Maybe it is."

Those vacations were memorable. On one of them, when I was about twelve years of age, another guy and I liked the same girl. I beat him in the finals of a tennis tournament. I thought I would get the girl because "to the victor belongs the spoils." I was wrong. The girl felt sorry for him and went with him.

"Tennis is played with a ball and racket," Rebecca explains as she bounces up and down in her chair looking to play with someone.

Even though my mother just had a high school education and an extra year or so of secretarial training, she was a super-smart person. I would come home with homework and she would look at what I had done. Even though she had no idea what it was, she would tear it up and say, "Do it better!"

"Did you do it better?" Alex questions.

"I didn't do it better. After a while, I got smart. I gave her a carbon copy, which she tore up."

"Did she find out?"

"She never found out, or if she did, she never told me."

One day, I came home with a grade of 95 on a paper from school. She said, "Good beginning, Lawrence, now let's get them ALL right." To my mother, good was a beginning; great was an end.

"That's you too, Grandpa," Haleigh points out as she moves from one cushion to another.

"I suppose it is." I couldn't help but laugh.

"Did your mommy have a mommy and daddy, Grandpa?"

"Of course she did, Haleigh. Everybody has a mommy and daddy," Alex quickly responds.

My mother was one of three children. Her family came to America in the late 1800s. My grandfather Aaron, my mother's father, was a Cossack.

"What's a Cossack?"

"Cossacks, Alex, were members of military communities in Ukraine and southern Russia."

"He was in the military?"

"You can say that; it was like a military."

At seventeen, my grandfather left Russia because of the discrimination against the Jews and went to America. He married a woman named Bessie. My grandfather was also a member of the Ushiker Lansker Society.

"What society?"

"The Ushiker Lansker Society, Haleigh. When Jews immigrated to the United States in the second half of the nineteenth century, many of them settled in New York, where they organized a number of societies. The Ushiker Lansker Society was a society that helped with welfare, legal, doctor, and health problems."

"They helped a lot of people."

"That's right, Haleigh. The Jews took care of their own. This is the way they helped each other in the new world."

After my grandfather married Bessie, my grandparents soon had three children. Besides my mom, there was my Uncle Harry, who moved to Florida, a sensational person—very social, very gracious, and a chance-taker who I learned a lot from. Uncle Harry was married to Aunt Bobbie. Aunt Bobbie was not only a beautiful woman, but only had nice things to say about people. They had two children, Steve and Linda.

Steve is a good-looking guy who followed me into the profession of orthodontics. In fact, his three nephews, who were Linda's sons Brad, Rodger, and Ronald, became orthodontists as well. Can you imagine, including my son Doug and myself, we had six family members as orthodontists. Steve and his wife, Lori, have three children, Harrison, Cameron, and Devon.

Steve's sister, Linda, is a sweetheart of a girl who worked at his practice for many years, and was married to Sonny Finklestein, who was one-of-a-kind.

Since I did not have any brothers or sisters, I considered Steve and Linda my brother and sister.

"Who was the third child besides your mom and Uncle Harry?"

"The third child was my Uncle Louie, Alex."

My Uncle Louie, who was like a second father to me, spent lots of time just helping my mother in business and, in some ways, guiding me.

"Did your mom work a lot?" Alex probes.

"Yes. Mom always worked, except for taking two weeks off each summer to go to the Catskills. She also took off to come to my graduations from public school, high school, college, and dental school."

"Did she watch you play games or sports like my mom and dad?"

"No. To my regret, she had little opportunity to see me participate in activities."

"Were you upset, Grandpa?"

"No, I wasn't upset, Haleigh. Mom was the breadwinner of the family. Besides, I know she was proud of me. In later years, when she was in a nursing home, she would introduce me to people as 'My son, Lawrence—the doctor!' That was enough for me."

"Papa Larry is a doctor of teeth!"

"Exactly, Rebecca."

"Did your mom buy you a lot of things?"

"No, Haleigh. We didn't have a lot of money when I was growing up."

Mom had her ways and always tried to save money, even for medical attention. When I was about six years of age I had a real stomachache and was in a lot of pain. In those days, the doctors visited your house. I remember the doctor. He was around 6'4" and 250 pounds. He put his arm around my head and pressed his hand into my stomach and said, "Your son has appendicitis; he needs an operation now. Look at the pain he has." My mother said, "If I pressed my hand into your stomach, you'd have pain too." To this day, I have not had an appendicitis operation.

"Wow, Grandpa, your mommy was a doctor too."

"Not a doctor, Haleigh, just shrewd."

I used to sneeze a lot. Mom took me to a doctor. He said, "Lawrence has an allergy. You have to come each week for a shot for $5." My mother looked at me and then looked at him and said, "My son is going to live with the sneezing." I never got the shots; I never had the allergy. To this day I still sneeze. Interestingly enough, I only sneeze when I go to a restaurant and I get the bill. I must have an allergy to having to pay that comes out in sneezing.

"You're silly, Grandpa," Alex and Haleigh mutter and laugh in sync.

"My kids always laugh at that too."

"Grandpa has an allergy to paying the bill," Rebecca repeats as she continues to bounce up and down.

"I am the only person in the world that has an allergic reaction of sneezing when he has to pay a bill."

"Tell us more, Grandpa. I want to hear more about your mommy." Haleigh jumps up, tags Rebecca, and runs back to her seat. Rebecca begins to giggle and runs into another room.

"When my mother lived in a nursing home in Florida, she used to ring the bell and the nurses wouldn't come. Nobody would come. Finally, one day, she called 911 and you know what happened? From that day on, when Mom rang the bell, they came."

"Yeah!" Haleigh cheers.

To Mom's credit, she would get up every morning and dress like she was going to work when she was younger. This attitude kept her going in a positive way. The old line that says "when you look important, you feel important" fit her. Mom became the ringleader of the home.

My mother's philosophy of life was that people should understand you and you should try to understand them, and you should always be fair and honorable in your dealings with everybody. She believed that people should know where you are coming from and that you would not be pushed around if they think that you are honorable. She believed that you should speak up against injustices, not only for yourself but for your family and your society.

Now, on the other hand, she felt that if you should find that in speaking up you made an error, you should be first to recognize it, to say, "I am sorry," and to make amends to those you have offended. Every problem is an opportunity. There are always problems in life. Quite often, a significant part of our problems is caused by how we deal with the problems themselves. If a problem does present itself to us, we should put out both hands in front of us and say, "Will this problem still be with me in five years?" If it will, then we should try to understand, accept, and work with this opportunity. If we feel it will not be with us in five years, we should put our hands back in our pockets and get on with our lives.

"Do you think the same, Papa Larry?"

"Yes, I definitely do."

Mom had her quirks too. She would try to act very prudish from time to time, saying *thee* and *thou*. I never did tell her that underneath her folded cloth napkins, I used to find the *National Enquirer*, which was a gossipy and sexy newspaper.

"Why did your mommy hide the newspaper?"

"I'm not sure, Rebecca. I guess that was Mom's vicarious experience since she was single for most of her adult life."

"Did you ever tell her?"

"No, I never did tell her."

Even though my mother had her oddities, she was an extraordinary person. She was highly talented and a very hard worker. She was proficient in Spanish and an excellent salesperson with a great eye for design. She worked very hard. Her whole life involved just working, and once in a while caring for me. I don't think she had much of a social life. Her whole life involved just existing and doing the best she could.

"You told me you worked with your mommy," Alex recalls. "What did you do?"

"You worked with your mommy?"

"Yes, I started to work with her when I was just a little older than you, Haleigh. I began working at my mother's store when I was seven years old. It never occurred to me that it was such a bad deal, or that work was so bad. Life was fun; I always had fun and time to play, to work, and go to school."

In the 1930s and early 1940s my mother used to have a little pushcart with very reasonable goods. The object of the pushcart was to attract people and make them want to see more in the store. My mother used to tell me, "Your job, Lawrence, is to get them into the store." Her job was to show the customers in the store what they wanted so they would buy.

"Did she get them to buy things?"

"She sure did, Alex."

Mom had an axiom that she would never tell anyone what size dress they wore or what size she was giving them because some people needed a size that they might not care to admit. For my mother, everybody was her friend. There were no strangers. As a great salesperson, she had the facility within seconds of turning a stranger into a friend by reading them, then being on the same wavelength as them and taking care of their needs and wants.

She once said, "Needs in this world are minimal: to eat, to be clothed, to have shelter, to be reasonably well. But a great salesperson sells wants. As an example, I *need* a car to get me to work, but I *want* a Cadillac. The great salesperson can translate needs into wants so that consumers can feel comfortable that they did the right thing in buying something."

She was the consummate salesperson. If a customer wanted blue and she did not have it, she said blue shrinks, and if the customer wanted pink and she did not have it, she said pink fades.

"Your mommy was very good at her work."

"She was more than good, Haleigh. She was great."

Mom was ahead of her time. She would read the newspapers and learn what the expensive New York stores were selling and then find copies at a fraction of the price. People would come to her from all over to get these copies, which were close to the originals. She said selling was important, but that you could lose everything by having too much inventory.

"How would you lose it?" Alex hangs on every word, interested in the business lesson.

The importance of that is that after a while, inventory, whether it is clothing or butter, loses its value and you lose a great deal of your profit."

"How did she know if she had too much?"

"Her way of checking out the date and cost of inventory was by placing the year with price on the label. For example, if she bought something in 1948, a dozen pieces for $24, she would write down '1948 24.' Nineteen forty-eight was the date she bought the inventory and twenty-four was what she was charged. This would be on every one of the garments. She would divide by twelve and would know that the garment cost her $2. By doing this, she knew how much to charge people every time for everything in the store."

"She really was a great businessperson, Grandpa."

"Yes she was."

She always said that great business people not only saw opportunity, but took advantage of opportunity and were successful. She mentioned that a great deal of value could be had by taking product A and product B and turning them into product C. More often than not, people would pay geometric proportions more for C even though the sum of the values of A and B was an arithmetic sum.

Mom was the first person to mention to me that unless one is prepared to lose, one will never win. I remember how she would tell me the story of selling fish on a sidewalk stand. The fish always cost more early in the morning compared to late in the afternoon because it began to smell in the afternoon. So it was with many things in life. Timing is extremely important.

"Grandpa, did your mommy go to Morocco?" Haleigh recollects what I said about the Air Force and my trip to Morocco.

"No, she didn't visit Morocco. My mother just knew how things worked."

"What about your daddy?" Haleigh inquires.

"Grandpa, what was your daddy like?" Alex cuts in.

"Daddy! Mommy! Me!" Rebecca reappears from the corner, soaring toward us as if she were running out of a burning building.

"My dad was very different from my mother."

"Please tell us more," Haleigh begs. "I want to hear about your daddy too."

"Me too," Rebecca announces while plotting her next tag session with Haleigh.

Rebecca runs into Haleigh and tags her from behind. Haleigh turns her body, taking aim at Rebecca, and hops up. Alex watches the two, pondering whether he should join in or not. As the energy of their ages begins to wind up, we rise from the room and proceed to the backyard so they might unleash their liveliness outside.

Here are a few words and sayings of my mother:

A *fagysynah punim* (a mean-looking face)

Ganefishen eigen (The literal translation is "devil's eyes" or "big eyes," meaning your eyes are bigger than your mouth, referring to when you try to eat too much or order too much.)

A *bruch* on Hitler's *kup* (When things are bad, Hitler should get a headache.)

Mom took me three times a year to the Molly Picon Jewish theater on Second Avenue in New York City. She wanted me to learn the Yiddish language. The learning of Yiddish combined with Brooklynese, English, and Hebrew got me all *fashimiled* (all messed up). To this day, I can speak six languages (including English), but none of them well.

My mother, Jean Hartstein, on her wedding day, 1930

Wedding photo of my parents, Joseph and Jean Hartstein. Back row, left to right, Harry Hartstein, Aaron Grussmark, Louis Grossmark, and Joseph Hartstein. Front row, left to right, Bessie Grussmark and Jean Hartstein, 1930

My grandmother, Bessie Grussmark (close-up from wedding party photo) 1930

With my grandmother, 1934

Memories of My Dad

Control your energy. If you start every day with a sprint,
you may finish every day with a crawl. Every person has a
little bottle of energy. If you use it all in the morning, there's
nothing left at night.

—*Joseph Hartstein*

My dad was a special kind of guy. On Saturday mornings, he used
to drag me to temple, even though I didn't want to go, and on
Saturday afternoon, when I wasn't in sports, we would take walks in
the park and he would talk to me about life. He was a very sweet,
lovable person who just never made it in life and tried to do the best
he could under the circumstances.

"Were you with your dad a lot, Grandpa?"

"I did not see much of Dad as a kid, Alex. My parents were
separated when I was seven, and my dad spent a great deal of time
taking care of his ailing mother. But when I got to spend time with
him, I made sure to make the best of it."

One New Year's Eve my dad took me to New York City to bring in the New Year at midnight. Even though the weather was frigid and it was snowing, I had a great time because I was staying up really late and I was with my dad.

I have to admit, Dad was there for me when I needed him, even if it was for a brief amount of time. I remember having chicken pox and having to stay home from school for a few days by myself. On one of the days, my dad visited for a few minutes and gave me a little cloth puppy. He said, "When you feel like scratching yourself, scratch the puppy instead." To this day, I love to scratch puppies.

"Puppies! I love puppies," Haleigh yells while running from Rebecca.

"Puppies! I love puppies!" Rebecca mimics.

Since my mother was always working, my dad would, on occasion, come to watch me in athletic events. He never said, "Congratulations for winning!" He would only say, "Did you have fun?"

"That's what you ask me," Alex proclaims as he tosses a ball in the air and catches it on its way down.

"Yes, it is!"

"Papa Larry, I always have fun with you," Rebecca declares. "I love to have fun!"

"I love to have fun too, Rebecca."

I remember one day walking with my dad to Prospect Park while he told me about life, about trying to enjoy life and getting as much out of it as possible. He was a Sabbath observer. My dad, may he rest in peace, used to say to me, "Lawrence, your body is a group of gears. Once they break down, you will be in trouble. Try not to be so driven without resting."

"Did you rest, Grandpa?"

"I never listened, Haleigh."

"I always listen to my daddy. You should've listened to your daddy."

"You're right. I should have listened."

"I listen to my daddy," Rebecca adds. "You should always listen to your parents, Papa Larry."

Dad was nice, sweeter than me and far mellower. I was more hyper; I wanted to prove to the world that I could really, really do it. He was very caring toward me, very sympathetic; he never wanted me to work so hard, and he was just the sweetest of men. When I was very young, I indulged in being opinionated and trying to do radical things. My father said, "Lawrence, be careful, because what you do or what you say when you are young will stay with you for the rest of your life." He was right.

"What did you talk about on your walks?" Alex inquires as he continues to throw the ball up and catch it on its way down. Rebecca stops chasing Haleigh and becomes amused by the ball. As it descends, she attempts an interception, only making the ball fumble out of Alex's and her hands. Haleigh rushes to grab the ball and takes off yelling, "Catch me if you can!"

Rebecca springs into action yelling, "I can catch you!"

Alex watches his sister and cousin, then turns his head and waits for my response.

"During our walks, we would talk about different things."

Dad once told me that he was a Mason. I asked him a few times afterwards, "What is a Mason?" He never answered. But from time to time, he mentioned that many of the writers and signers of the Declaration of Independence were great thinkers. Later on, after my dad passed away, I found out that many of these signers were

Masons. Maybe my dad was trying to tell me something.

"Did you ever find out what a Mason was, Grandpa?"

"No, Alex, I never did. I just knew that they were important people."

"What else do you remember about your daddy?"

"I remember my dad used to rock me to sleep when I was a little guy. I guess I had insomnia."

"What's insomnia, Papa Larry?" Rebecca shouts.

"Insomnia is when someone has a hard time falling asleep."

"Grandpa, you had a hard time falling asleep? Were you sick?"

"No, Haleigh, I wasn't sick. I just had so much on my mind. I guess it kept me up at times."

"How did he rock you to sleep?"

"He sang a lullaby to me in Yiddish whose English translation was 'When you become rich some day, whatever you do, your mother and father will always love you. Sleep, Lawrence, sleep.' Dad was a great singer (those genes were NOT transferred to me). He had had some singing lessons when he was young."

"Your daddy was a singer?"

"Yes, Haleigh, he was a wonderful singer. He didn't sing professionally though."

"I love to sing!"

"I love to sing, sing, sing," Rebecca chants.

"Grandpa, how is your daddy different from your mommy?" Alex asks, remembering what I had said about my parents being very different from one another.

"I think my mom and dad had role reversals."

One day Dad and I were riding on a bus with the window open. My dad took the hat off my head and told me that he threw it out the window. A moment later, my hat reappeared. My dad was a magician. So a moment later, I threw my hat out of the window and looked at my dad. To this day, I am still looking for my hat.

Dad at times mystified me. Although he was a very peaceful man, he liked boxing matches. He shared with me that many Jewish immigrants in the first three decades of the 1900s became boxers. At one point, many of the top boxers in the world were Jewish. Dad spoke of Benny Leonard, who was the light heavyweight champion. There was Barney Ross, who simultaneously held the lightweight, junior lightweight, and welterweight titles. And there was Max Baer, who became heavyweight champion and defeated Adolph Hitler's German favorite, Max Schmeling.

Although I loved my dad dearly, I vowed that no one would take advantage of me the way they did of my dad. He was a very kind, soft-spoken man, very giving and very peaceful. He was not a hard-driven family man and, literally, would give you the shirt off his back, even if it was his last one.

Dad once told me that when he was running for class president in seventh grade in public school, some friends who were supporting the other candidate asked him, "Please, why don't you vote for him?" Dad then voted for the other guy and he lost. When it was my turn to run for president in the eighth grade, I voted for myself and won. I had learned a lesson—when I ran for class president, I did not leave a stone unturned in order to win. I learned from my dad. He was so sweet and so wonderful, but people stepped on him. If people stepped on me, it wasn't because I let them; it was because they were that good. I was always going to give everything my best.

"I always give everything my best, Grandpa," Alex asserts as he confiscates his ball from Haleigh. The three begin to toss the ball back and forth.

"Yes you do!"

"Did your daddy have a brother or sister, Papa Larry?"

"My dad, Joseph, was one of three brothers, and he had two sisters, Rebecca."

One of his brothers, Harry, was an attorney. The other brother, Sam, was a dentist. His sister Helen was a hygienist, and his other sister, Miriam, was a homemaker. Aunt Helen, a social person, was married to Arthur and had a son, Allan. Allan was a sweet guy who worked in the post office. Aunt Miriam, who was married to Boris, had a daughter, Diane. Diane is a lovable girl who became a teacher and was the glue of that side of the family. She married Bob.

Dad grew up in New York, and he went to Dewitt Clinton High School. He was a good athlete. He played first base in high school. After high school, he went to dental school at Columbia. His brother Harry, the attorney, ended up being a clerk in the justice system in Brooklyn. Dad and Harry were involved in Democratic politics, and were co-captains for their district.

"What does a co-captain do?"

"At election time, Haleigh, co-captains would go to the people in the area and take them by bus or car to the voting place. After they voted they would give them a free breakfast."

Politics was always the same: I have something to sell; you have something to buy. That's what politics was, and still is today. At an early age, I became embittered toward politics because it was not really geared toward helping people, but toward power, glory, and money. Later on, I realized that, through politics, you can also be good and give help to people.

"I want to be president, Grandpa," Alex declares.

"Why is that?"

"Because, Grandpa, as the president, I can help all the people and everyone has to listen to me."

"You'd be a great president, Alex." Alex smiles and holds his head high with confidence.

"I would vote for Alex for president!" Rebecca exclaims. She throws the ball lightly, and it falls in the middle of their circle. She giggles and begins to run erratically.

"Grandpa, tell us more about your daddy and his family," Haleigh persists.

Uncle Harry, the attorney, never married and lived with his mother.

Dad's brother Sam was a dentist and a great dancer who had one son, David, and subsequently got divorced. I have never seen or talked to this cousin in my life.

"How sad." Haleigh frowns with a look of dismay. "I love my cousin Rebecca."

"It's okay, Haleigh. At least you're lucky to be able to spend time and talk with your cousin."

"I'm lucky, Grandpa."

"Yes you are."

"I'm lucky too," Rebecca adds.

"Yes, the three of you are very lucky."

"Where did your dad's parents come from? Did they come from Russia like your mom's?"

"Not exactly, Alex."

Dad's parents came from Hungary at an early age during the late 1800s. My grandfather's name was David, and he was a pawn broker. His wife was Dina. On my dad's side, his parents, or my grandparents, came from Budapest to the United States. My grandfather David was in the usury business in Budapest. It was one of the few occupations that the government let Jews have. When he came to America, he opened up a pawnbroker store.

"What's a pawnbroker, Grandpa?"

"A pawnbroker, Alex, is a person who gives you a secured loan on a personal item of yours when you need money. He lets you buy back your item within a certain amount of time for the loan amount plus interest, or, if you don't buy it back, he keeps the item and can sell it to someone else."

"Huh? I don't understand," Rebecca says as she squeezes her eyebrows into her eyelids in confusion.

"Well, Rebecca. Let's say you needed money and you could sell something of yours for the money."

"Okay, Papa Larry."

"What would you sell?" Alex inquires.

"Let's say that you were going to sell some baseball cards."

"I wouldn't sell my baseball cards, Grandpa. If I needed money, I would just ask Mommy or Daddy."

"I understand, Alex, but for an example, let's just say that you needed money and you were going to sell your baseball cards."

"Okay, Grandpa."

"My grandfather would buy the cards from you for a certain amount of money, and he would give you this money as a loan."

"I understand so far, Grandpa."

"Good, Alex. Now, he would tell you that you have thirty days to buy back the cards for the same amount of money plus interest, and if you don't buy them back, the cards would be his to sell to anyone."

"Oh! I understand Grandpa. He lets you borrow money, but you have to give him something in case you don't pay him back."

"Yes, something like that."

"Your grandfather was smart, Grandpa."

"I think so too."

As a kid, I remember going to my grandfather's house in Williamsburg, Brooklyn. My grandparents had family parties and a zest for living, but never invited any outsiders. They were very well educated, although they kept to themselves in this small area. This is one of the reasons why I left the family—because they just didn't have many friends, nor were they involved in the outside world. They kept saying the same thing at every party. I would get a headache from hearing the constant repetition. Aside from the immediate family, I never saw people from my dad's side at a party.

Looking back, I made a big mistake. I now know that family is there for you. Part of family life is hearing the same old stories, jokes, and recipes. Part of family life is eating Grandma's greasy chicken soup and getting your cheeks pinched by Grandpa David.

"I love my family," Haleigh interjects as she skips over to Alex and gives him a big hug.

Rebecca scampers over to Haleigh repeating, "Me too!"

"Grandpa, I like to meet new people. Mommy and Daddy know a lot of people."

"Yes, they do. It's good to know a lot of people outside of your family."

"Grandpa, you said your daddy was a dentist."

"I did, Alex."

"Did he have his own business like you?"

"Yes and no. Dad never had real breaks in life. Once he opened up an office that patients could not get to because of road construction and the practice failed."

"He did have a business like you."

"Yes, he opened his own business, but not like me. My father didn't have too much drive, and didn't do well at all in business."

"You did good in business, Grandpa."

"I learned as a kid from working with my mother and watching my father's mistakes."

He just didn't do well in business and, because of this, he and my mom didn't get along. Dad spent too much time caring for his mother and not enough time in the office. He would give his services for free, and he could not ask for money. My mother was tired of supporting him, and in exasperation, she left him.

"Why didn't Grandma ask your daddy's customers for money?"

"That's a good question, Haleigh. Your grandmother worked very hard in her store and didn't have the time to work at my father's business. She had to work in the store to bring in money and support the family. She felt it was your grandfather's responsibility to collect money from his customers like she did with hers."

Alex interrupts, "Where did your daddy work when he didn't have his business?"

"He worked a few different jobs."

Dad, in one of his jobs, was the dentist at the Dannemora Prison in upstate New York. This is a maximum security prison. It's hard to picture my dad, a simple, quiet man, working in a hard-core facility, but it was a job. He also worked as a manager at a movie theater, and he worked as a secretary for the Democratic Party. I remember when my dad had his first business, he had a pack of cigarettes in his little waiting room, and I wrote "Poison" on them. He beat me up, but I was ahead of my time. Nowadays, the use of cigarettes has been proven scientifically to cause many health issues.

"Your daddy smoked cigarettes?" Haleigh asked.

"No, he left the cigarettes in the waiting room for his patients."

"Cigarettes are poison. Yuck!" Rebecca yells and darts from one side of the yard to the other, bored of tossing the ball.

"That's right, Rebecca. Cigarettes are poison."

Now, if I talk about my father, I must mention the Dodgers. Growing up in Brooklyn, my dad was a *fierce* Brooklyn Dodgers fan and, because of genetics and environment, I became a Brooklyn Dodger fan. I used to say to my dad, "Gee, the Yankees must be better—they beat our Brooklyn Dodgers so many times!" My father would get angry and say, "Lawrence, it's pure *luck;* it is plain luck. If we had a little more luck, we could have won all of those games."

"Your daddy was a Dodgers fan!" Alex exclaims in excitement.

"He was! This is where my love of the Dodgers started as well."

To my dad and, really, to all of Brooklyn, the Brooklyn Dodgers were the basic fabric of our society. On Saturday, the rabbis would pray for a Dodger victory, and on Sundays, the priests and ministers would pray for a Dodger victory. The Dodgers were in every part of our family—our brothers, sisters, mothers, fathers, uncles, and aunts. When they won, we were in joy, and when they lost, we were in sorrow. Times change; it's hard to have the same kind of feeling as when a team is part of your family. In my early years, aside from baseball, there were little or no other real sports or extracurricular activities that were available to the average kid. The team was, to many of us, a religion. We were emotionally involved with the Brooklyn Dodgers. It was our team, and in many ways, our second religion.

"Did your dad pass on his love for the Dodgers like you pass on the Haggadah to us now during Passover?"

"Yes, exactly, Alex. Our love for our Jewish heritage is passed on from generation to generation just like our love for the Brooklyn Dodgers."

When my dad passed away, he had $400 in the bank to give to me as an inheritance. Even though I did not have any money, I gave the $400 to his two sisters who had cared for him in his later years. I knew I would do OK by myself. This was the least I could do for my dad.

"Grandpa, I want to hear more about your family!"

"What would you like me to tell you, Haleigh?"

"I want to hear more, Grandpa. I want to hear more about your family."

"Grandpa, what about your Uncle Louie? You said your Uncle Louie taught you a lot."

"He did, Alex."

As I think back to my Uncle Louie, Alex hands me a baseball glove to practice pitching and catching with him, while Haleigh and Rebecca improvise being ballerinas. Inside the house, the family prepares for another evening of Seder.

*My father, Joseph
Hartstein, 1953*

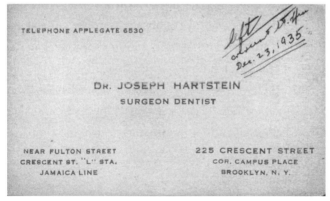

My father's business card, 1935

Memories of My Uncle Louie

> We, the fortunate, have to give to the unfortunate, even if
> we think they are not trying as hard as we would like.
> Otherwise, there will be a violent revolution.
> —*Louis Grossmark*

My Uncle Louis (Uncle Louie) lived to the age of 106. He was blind for many years of his later life, but as a kid growing up, he was tough. I guess part of the advantage of his being around for so long was that I had the opportunity of listening to him repeat many things—in case I didn't get something the first time, I got it the thousandth time. He always said things his way and, even though I disagreed with him, we always had discussions. I guess when you are family you can just let it all out, and we agreed many times to disagree; as in chess, we had many draws.

"Your Uncle Louie lived to 106?"

"He sure did, Rebecca!"

Sometimes I think to myself, "My God! Psychologically maybe I have some of his genetics, and I can hopefully live to a ripe old age, have my wits, and also contribute to society."

"Your uncle was blind?"

"Yes, Alex, he was blind for many years."

Uncle Louie could have been an advocate for blind people. He could have lectured to anybody. He was brilliant. My uncle could have contributed more to society, but because of his poor vision, I guess he just didn't want to go out of his way.

"Grandpa, how did your uncle's eyes go blind?" Haleigh couldn't help but feel how sad it was to be blind. She loved to watch nature and see birds fly and the colors of the leaves change with the seasons. She just couldn't imagine not being able to look at things like she does now.

"My uncle's eyes were always weak as a kid. His eyes became progressively weaker, so that by the time he was in his sixties and seventies, he really could not see at all—just gradations of light and darkness."

As a kid, he was very small and wore very thick glasses, but was a very aggressive kid in school with a big temper, which got him into trouble. He was tough and he got into scraps. They beat the heck out of him most of the time because he was a little guy. But he kept fighting and he gave no quarter; quite often, according to him, he came home bleeding, with his clothes torn.

I must give Uncle Louie credit, because he knew his eyes were getting worse and he learned many tricks, like putting bills in his billfold with dollar bills one way, five-dollar bills another way, ten-dollar bills another way. This way he knew what kind of money he had. He would keep repeating his accounting of his bills to Mildred, who was his nurse in later years who came in for four hours each day, and she would repeat back what he said, and that's the way he memorized everything. He wrote letters and would keep repeating and repeating. That's how he made up for his blindness. He wouldn't use a tape recorder; he felt that was an insult to his intelligence.

"Grandpa, did Uncle Louie have children?"

"No, Alex, Uncle Louie never got married and he really didn't have that many outside friends."

"My uncles have lots of outside friends, Papa Larry."

"Yes, they do have a lot of friends, Rebecca."

When my mother separated from my father, I think Uncle Louie felt a family obligation to see if he could help her out. So he never had children and lived with me and his sister, my mother. He helped her out and she, in turn, helped him because he had physical problems. So she was his eyes. Quite often she was his mouthpiece because she spoke up for him when he needed help.

"Your Uncle Louie loved his sister a lot."

"Yes, Haleigh, he sure did. He tried to take care of me and my mom, and my mom took care of him too."

"Alex takes care of me too."

"That's because he loves you very much."

"Pickle juice!" Haleigh and Rebecca stop dancing and begin to play tag once more. Haleigh pokes Rebecca on the arm, and Rebecca runs laughing into the house. Haleigh begins to hop like a bunny while waiting on Rebecca.

When my mother passed away, at age ninety-two, my Uncle Louie, who was blind, lived alone for the next fourteen years preceding his death. I remember when my mother passed away, Uncle Louie said, "Lawrence, I just got your mother's social security check. I think I'm going to cash it." And I said to him, "Uncle Louie, you can't do that—it's against the law! You could go to jail." I remember my uncle saying, "Not a bad thing. I'm so lonely, and it costs me money to live here. I can go to jail; they'll pay for it, and I'd have people to talk to!"

"Did he cash the check?"

"Fortunately, Alex, Uncle Louie never went ahead with it."

As I related earlier, when I was a kid, my friends and I got into trouble for throwing stink bombs into the neighbors' houses. Uncle Louie came to the jail where the police took us. I told him my story and he said to the jailer, "Keep him in jail another hour—maybe he'll learn a lesson." When Uncle Louie told me of his plans to cash my mother's check, I said to myself, "Ha, here's my chance to get back at my Uncle Louie." But I never did because he didn't go ahead with it.

"That sounds awful. It smelled really bad!"

"It made a big stink, Haleigh."

"I'm glad Uncle Louie left you in jail," Haleigh asserts.

"You are?"

"Yes, Grandpa, because how else would you learn your lesson? You were a bad boy. I'm glad you didn't tell him that story. Uncle Louie just wanted to teach you what was right."

"He did teach me, Haleigh."

I felt sorry for Uncle Louie, but he also taught me a lesson that moves me to this day: that no one wants to be alone. He made the best of it. He was tough and very independent, and because he was independent he was able to live so long. He did not want to give in; he didn't want to die. And if the doctor had told him to stand on his head, he would have tried to stand on his head.

"He wasn't alone, Grandpa."

"He wasn't, Haleigh?"

"No, Grandpa. Uncle Louie lived with your mommy. When your

mommy was gone, he had a lady called Mildred and you still saw him too. You see, Grandpa, your uncle always was with someone."

"I suppose you're right."

"What did your Uncle Louie do for work, Grandpa? Did he work with your mommy?"

"He did help my mom, Alex, but my Uncle Louie was an attorney and a teacher."

Rebecca runs back into the yard from the house. She hears a part of the conversation and says, "Uncle Louie was a teacher?"

"He was a teacher, Rebecca. He taught history for many years at Eastern District High School in Brooklyn."

Whatever I did, he would say, "Is that the best you can do?" If I got a hundred on an exam, he would say the exam must have been too easy. I guess that's the first time I heard it said that good is the enemy of great. When you are good, you become complacent, and the one thing my Uncle Louie didn't want to do was to make me complacent.

"Grandpa, I thought your mommy was hard on you, but I was wrong. Your Uncle Louie seems like he was much harder."

"In a way he was, Alex, but it was a good thing."

"It was?"

"Yes, because it pushed me to be better than good."

Many alumni, judges, authors, and professional people always talked about him as the toughest, most stimulating, and most invigorating teacher. When I met former students who knew him, they said he would challenge them to learn about history, not for dates, but for the social, cultural, and political events of the times. He would pull everything together. His former students said that when they wrote a composition, if they copied something, he would give them a failing grade. He wanted them to INTERPRET history, not just copy history. He wanted them to think for themselves. They said that he used to drive them crazy, but later on this type of education helped them with their lifestyles and in their professions.

They did not like him because he was so grating and annoying and sometimes he would put them down, but they did respect him and, later on, they appreciated what he did.

"Grandpa, your uncle was mean because he wanted people to think?"

"That's one way to say it, Haleigh."

Uncle Louie couldn't stand authority, and never would butter up to it. That's why he never became head of the department. He was his own person. He was so grumpy at times that he drove us crazy.

"You're grumpy sometimes too, Grandpa."

"I am, Alex. I realize that sometimes I get grumpy because I get impatient when I expect people to do what I think is the right thing for themselves, not for me. I guess Uncle Louie might have been grumpy for the same reason."

"I love you even if you're grumpy," Rebecca comments as she gives me a hug.

I think I became my own person not because of my Uncle Louie, but because Mom and Uncle Louie were never around because they worked so hard. In so many ways, I had to raise myself and be my own person. I had to think for myself and, many times I did the wrong thing. But you know, I sure did learn, and I'll tell you one thing—if I did something wrong the first time, I wouldn't do it wrong the second time.

"Grandpa, it's a good thing you learned."

"It is a good thing, Haleigh. I learned the difference between an amateur and a pro."

"What's the difference, Grandpa?"

"An amateur makes the same mistakes every time; a professional makes new mistakes every time."

I tried to correct the many mistakes I made as a kid since I was my own person and really had no one to turn to for advice. So, just like Uncle Louie, I am my own person now. But I think his absence in my life provided a greater impetus for my becoming my own man than his lectures.

"What were his lectures like, Grandpa?"

"Uncle Louie taught Socratic method, Alex."

"What is Socratic method?"

"Uncle Louie would ask a question and, depending on what you said, he would ask a question about your answer."

"Did you learn a lot?"

"Most of the time he drove me crazy because I was impatient and just wanted the answer."

If I asked him what a word meant, he'd say, "Look it up in the dictionary." He would never tell me what it meant whether he knew it or not.

"Did you think he helped you teaching his way?"

"It did help me a lot, Alex. The training he gave me was excellent. It was just so much training that it drove me batty at times."

Later on when I went to school at Rochester, our director taught with the Socratic method and to me, it was a piece of cake. For everybody else, it was a burden; it gave them a headache and a feeling of insecurity. To me, it was like taking coals to Newcastle. So Uncle Louie did come in handy sometimes, although many times he drove me batty because, as a kid, I wanted a quick response and a quick fix. He wouldn't have any of it.

"What is 'taking coals to Newcastle,' Papa Larry?"

"It's an idiom, Rebecca. An idiom is a word or phrase that has a figurative meaning; basically, the word or phrase means something different from what it literally says."

"Okay, Grandpa. So, what does it mean?"

"Well, Alex, 'taking coals to Newcastle' is a phrase that means a pointless action. This saying comes from the town of Newcastle that was a strong supplier of coal. If you wanted to sell coal to them, you'd be wasting your time because they had so much."

"Oh! So, it's like taking water to the ocean. It doesn't need water."

"Exactly, Alex."

"What else did he teach you, Grandpa?"

"My uncle was an authority on modern and American history, with a deep sense of feeling for the common man, Haleigh."

"What kind of feeling?"

"Uncle Louie felt that even if the common man doesn't try very hard, you have to take care of the common man so that his potential will be realized. His thoughts were that even though there are a lot of people who don't work and sometimes don't care, we still have to teach these people so that, hopefully, they will teach their children to take care of themselves, which will create a more fruitful society. He said that if you don't take care of the common people, even though you don't like a lot of things they do, they will rise up and have a revolution and they can take things away that you want and cherish for yourself, your family, and your lifestyle. In a way, he was saying it was insurance; it was moral and economic insurance that you were providing for them and also for yourself."

"What's insurance, Papa Larry?"

"Insurance, Rebecca, is something you pay for that, even though it involves a small loss of money or time, guarantees the prevention of a large, possibly devastating loss."

"Can you explain it in my language, Grandpa?"

"Okay, Alex, I'll explain it the way Uncle Louie wanted me to understand. If you took some of your time to work with the common man, which is a small loss of your time—this is the payment—it would be a guarantee for our society that helps prevent a large decline in the moral or economic structure of our society. This is your insurance. In other words, taking time to teach people to be good and do the right thing helps our society do good instead of doing bad in the future."

"Oh! I get it, Grandpa. Uncle Louie was a wise man."

"He was a brilliant and wise man. At the same time, he never really took the time to realize that some people make good points too."

"I think you're a wise man, Grandpa," Haleigh smiles.

"Me too," Rebecca says in agreement.

Many times, Uncle Louie would tell me what he did when he was teaching at Eastern District High School. He would tell me how he would argue with the head of the department on how to teach students and what should be in the curriculum. He was so antagonistic that it was difficult for him to compromise. That's one of the reasons he never became head of the department or a leader or president. He just didn't have it in himself to understand that there is another point.

Looking back, I see that he could have done so much for society by getting involved with people and leading them. A great leader has to be able to understand other people to lead them. If you just stick to your own opinion, people will resent you, and they will refuse the very thing that you could offer. Thus, in some ways, you really are a failure, considering the talent you have. I kept saying, "Uncle Louie, you are giving me an opinion, but you are saying it in such a strong manner that it's very difficult for me to give you my opinion. Even if I give my opinion, I get the feeling you are not going to change yours. So why even give my opinion?"

"Did he ever care about your opinion, Grandpa?"

"I'm not sure, Haleigh. He didn't seem to be open to my opinions."

It seemed that he was rarely open to understanding other opinions. Although I must tell you that despite the fact that he was so obstinate, quite often he was right on target. Uncle Louie gave opinions and the implication was that the issue wasn't open for discussion, so it was very difficult to get close to him.

"Did you agree with his opinions, Grandpa?"

"Not all of the time, Alex. If I didn't think that he was right, I would just say it."

As we both matured, we began to discuss the situation. But in the end, he still stuck to his guns, even though I did change when I thought he had a point.

When I would disagree with him, he would say, "Lawrence, why are you the devil's advocate? Why don't you agree with me?"

And I would say, "Uncle Louie, because I don't! I just think by pushing people down and giving them YOUR opinion, you're not giving them a chance to get close to you. Once people get close to you, they will understand you. But you have to give people the opportunities of letting them get close to you, and THEN you can give them your opinion."

"What is a devil's advocate?"

"Rebecca, a devil's advocate is someone who takes a position he or she doesn't agree with just for the sake of argument."

"Papa Larry, is that another idiom?"

"Yes, Alex, I suppose it is."

Uncle Louie never listened, but I never stopped trying. He was a brilliant man, a teacher and a lawyer. To the day he died, he had all his marbles.

"Grandpa, why did Uncle Louie never get married?"

"I never really found out why, Haleigh."

I always wondered why Uncle Louie never married. Maybe one of the reasons was that he had such thick glasses. He believed that his doctor had insinuated that if he ever got married, he might go blind and wouldn't be able to support his family. I think that bothered him a great deal. And, I think that taking care of his father and then his sister (my mother) gave him more personal baggage. He probably never found the right woman and the right woman never found him. I don't even know if he dated or not.

"But since he never married, I had the opportunity of spending time with him as a kid. He took me to different places over the years. I remember him taking me to the 1939 World's Fair in Flushing, New York, with the Trylon and the Perisphere."

"What are the Trylon and the Perisphere, Papa Larry?"

"They were the symbols of the World's Fair, Rebecca."

"I remember going from exhibit to exhibit. Uncle Louie took me to Horn and Hardart, which was a restaurant chain where you put money into a machine and you got a sandwich out. That was kind of neat. We went to the Fair by subway since my uncle never drove a car, and it took forever, but it was the only way of getting there.

He also took me to get clothing at Rogers and Pete. It was a fancy,

fancy store and he would take me when they had a sale on. I remember getting a jacket and two pairs of slacks. My uncle bargained with the salesman. The salesman said, "Mister, this is the deal—take it or leave it!" We did take it.

Other times, we would go to the Metropolitan Museum in New York and look at ancient relics. Uncle Louie loved some things from the Egyptian era, perhaps because he traveled so many times to the Middle East when he was young in the 1930s.

"Did you like Egyptian stuff, Grandpa?"

"I found it okay, Haleigh. I thought I would have preferred to see more modern things like an airplane, which they never had at the museum."

"Because you love airplanes?"

"Yes, you got it. I love airplanes."

But I trudged along with him and kept looking at the paintings, and he said to me, "Lawrence. What do you see in the painting?" I didn't know what to say because I thought the whole thing was boring. Later on, I got an education in art. But in those days, it was a stomachache that I was getting watching art.

"Did Uncle Louie like sports?"

"He did, Alex."

Uncle Louie was, for his size, a good athlete. He was a good basketball player, very fast. He played on the City College freshman team that had Nat Holman, who eventually became a famous coach. City College was a college in New York City. I think he dropped off the team after the first year because he had to work going through school. According to him, he was a second stringer, but he played tough. He didn't play any other sports, to my knowledge.

"What else did Uncle Louie like?"

"My uncle loved politics and the Democratic Party, Rebecca."

He remained steadfast in his belief that he never voted for an individual, but for a party. In his case, it was the Democratic Party. Uncle Louie believed that the Democratic Party was the party of the people, the party of the common man. He felt he was a common man. He wasn't an oil tycoon; he wasn't a banking magnate. And he felt that the party would help the common man receive better education, health benefits, and financial opportunities. Sometimes the people who ran on the Democratic Party ticket were not that good. But to him, it wasn't the person; the party was more important than the person.

Uncle Louie used to say, "We, the fortunate, have to give to the unfortunate, even if we think they are not trying as hard as we would like. Otherwise, there will be a violent revolution." He once said that people would die for an emotional principle rather than reason for peace. I think he felt that most people would be content if each day they had some food, shelter, and family love (that took care of their present-day needs), and if their worldly needs were met to some degree.

The irony of what my uncle said as far as people dying for an emotional need is that Uncle Louie loved the Democratic Party because it was a party of the people. He believed in the Hamiltonian democracy, or a benevolent dictatorship, where the people of the land would be taken care of. But sometimes he got confused. He wanted it both ways, and it's tough to have it both ways. He wanted the people to be taken care of by a benevolent dictator (the state). The problem was, what would happen when the present benevolent dictator was not in office? Who would be the successor? Uncle Louie also believed that the common man should have complete autonomy to take care of himself. That's why the confusion.

"It sounds like Uncle Louie really believed in helping people."

"He did, Alex. He just had his own opinion on how to help and he didn't listen to anyone else's opinion."

"I think it's good he wanted to help people," Haleigh points out.

"I think it was good too; he just had a hard time expressing himself emotionally."

Notwithstanding his making fun of me when I came in second and third in athletic meets, I really feel he was proud of me. He just didn't know how to express that kind of love for me, but I think deep in my heart that he was truly proud of things I did. For whatever reason, he just couldn't give me that pat on the back, that hug saying, "Lawrence—wow—you were terrific today!" But in my heart, I felt that he was proud of me and what I had accomplished.

"He was proud of you, Grandpa." Haleigh grabs my arm and looks up at me. "I'm proud of you!"

All I can do is smile.

My uncle always had a strong interest in me because in some ways, I was his son. We were at loggerheads many times when I was young, but as the years went on and I went down to Florida to visit him and help him financially, I learned to respect him more and more for his brilliant mind and for the love he felt toward the rest of the family.

But he just couldn't express himself emotionally. For example, Uncle Louie didn't believe in kissing. If I gave him a big kiss, he would always say, "Stop that nonsense, Lawrence!" But he did things his way, and if we listened to him, there was a lot we could learn. He was a special kind of person. He was in some ways my adoptive father.

"Did you visit Uncle Louie a lot in Florida?"

"I visited him as often as I could, Rebecca."

My uncle would always ask me, "Lawrence, how are you feeling?" And I'd say, "Oh, I'm fine." And then, "Tell us about Douglas and Jon and Helaine." He wanted to know what they were doing and, when they were kids, he would give them savings bonds. He was big on savings bonds, and on books. Uncle Louie was so proud of his grandchildren and what they were doing. He wouldn't outwardly say, "Wow, they're terrific. My God, they're fantastic!" But he always had an interest in them, and he was always concerned about their welfare. He gave them each enough books to fill a public library.

When Uncle Louie died, he didn't leave me a penny, even though my mother gave her money to Uncle Louie. Maybe he felt the education of hard knocks was enough payment and that what he had given me over his lifetime was worth more than an inheritance.

Just before Uncle Louie passed away, he wrote a special letter to Alex. I think it was a premonition of his death, but it was a beautifully written letter that my uncle dictated and that Mildred, his nurse, wrote. It was very special.

"Did he write me a letter, Grandpa?"

"You weren't born yet, Haleigh. Uncle Louie only knew about Alex."

"Pickle juice!"

"Did he know about me?" Rebecca questions.

"No, you weren't born yet, either."

"How sad," Haleigh notes, "Uncle Louie didn't know about me or Rebecca."

"What did he write me, Grandpa?" Alex asks to get back to the conversation of the letter.

"He wrote you a beautiful letter, Alex."

> *To my very dear great-grandnephew, Alexander,*
>
> I am the brother of your great-grandmother, Jean Hartstein. She was a wonderful woman! She was loyal and devoted to everyone in the family. Her son is your grandpa Larry; his son is your daddy, Doug, and you are my great-grandnephew.
>
> This is your Uncle Lou talking. The sunbeams and moonbeams have disappeared. The rainbows are gone. I wish you well and now I plead with the almighty to direct the sun, the moon and the stars to shine on the four corners of your world and your life and all those near and dear to you. I hope the good lord will grant you good health, good fortune and "nachas and parnussa" and a long life on earth.
>
> As you traverse the skyways, the highways and the seaways, I hope you will improve what you see as you make yourself a better man, and make your family a better family, and make the country a better country, and make the world a better place to live, with peace and good will on earth!
>
> I enclose a check for $1000. I hope that you use it in any way you like to make your world and everyone who knows you happier. This is in honor of my sister, your great-grandma Jean and my brother your uncle Harry.
>
> I say bon voyage wherever you go along the way and pay my respect to your family. My best to you and all those near and dear to you.
>
> > *Love,*
> > *Uncle Lou*

As I move to the shaded area of the yard, Rebecca scurries into the house and back out of it yelling, "I want to play more!"

"Grandpa, did you spend a lot of time with any of your other family members?"

"I had some memorable times with family, Alex."

"Tell us more, tell us more," Haleigh repeats.

Rebecca and Haleigh fall into a tickle fight. Their laughter echoes through the yard. Alex moves over to my side of the yard and gestures to continue tossing the baseball.

Uncle Louie Grossmark took this photograph of troopers giving the "Heil Hitler" salute in Berlin, Germany, 1934

My Uncle Louis Grossmark,
1940

Louis Grossmark
(back) taking a break
from riding a camel in
Egypt during an
excursion with friends,
1929

Louis Grossmark (right) and a friend in Italy, 1932

Memories of My Uncle Abel

The art of show business is a business of personal relevance.

—Abel Green

Although I didn't see him many times in my life, I have to mention my mother's cousin Abel Green. My Uncle Abel, who was really my mother's first cousin, was called the black sheep of the family because he was in show business. I called him Uncle Abel because, I guess, "second cousin" was not respectful enough. As an editor for *Variety* since 1932, a songwriter, composer, author, and producer, my Uncle Abel was a popular and respected man in the theater, music, and publishing industries throughout the country. *Time* magazine even wrote once that if the show business bible was *Variety*, then Abel Green was its "King James."

"Your cousin sounds like he was famous," Haleigh stops tickle fighting with Rebecca.

"Uncle Abel was a big theater and music man," Rebecca blurts as she catches her breath.

"He was a very well known and respected man during his time. Everyone wanted to know him, except my mother."

Uncle Abel used to wear a bowtie, smile, and present a strong handshake. He was quite a popular man, except with my mother. My mother used to say to me, "Lawrence, stay away from that part of the family. They are just into things that I don't want you to do." And so I saw him only three times in my life.

"What was the first time you saw him, Grandpa?"

"The first time, Alex, was when I was a young kid."

My Uncle Abel possibly saw my mother once every three years. He never visited us, and we never visited him. The first time I met him, I looked at him with a jaundiced eye because it seemed to me that he spoke big, fancy words, and I was not sure what he was saying.

"And the second time," Haleigh utters in anticipation to beat her brother in asking.

"The second time I saw Uncle Abel was when I was seventeen years old."

My mother moved to Florida with my Uncle Louie and she wanted to make sure there was someone to take care of me in New York City since I was going to Columbia College. When my mother moved to Florida, my dad was working at a high-security state prison in upstate New York, so there really wasn't anybody to keep an eye on me. There were some of my dad's cousins, but since I didn't have any relationship with them, it was hard to form a new relationship. I really didn't have that much in common with them. So, my mom sent my Uncle Abel a note. I guess she forgot for a moment who he was and what she had told me.

"What did the note say?"

"Well, Haleigh, the note was a success, even though I don't know what my mother wrote, because my Uncle Abel invited me to a party."

"Grandpa, did you go to the party?"

"I did, Alex, and what a party it was! There were famous people; it was exciting."

I remember it was very smoky, with lots of alcohol and lots of beautiful women with few clothes on. I didn't like the smoke because it seemed to get into my eyes. I was impressed by the number of bottles of different types of alcohol at the party. I only knew beer and milk and what they called whiskey. The beautiful women were really very pretty. They seemed to have lots of makeup on, they talked about trivial things, and, when someone walked away from them, they would say, "That bitch!" All the women would say to each other was, "My God, how beautiful you look!" But as a woman would walk away, one would say to another, "My God, she looks like a dog!" I guess that was part of the Hollywood scene.

"Grandpa, you said a bad word!"

"Oops! I did, Haleigh, and it was mistake."

"We won't tell, Grandpa," Alex proclaims as he continues to throw the ball back and forth.

"Mesa is a dog," Rebecca recites as she listens in on the conversation toward the end, fortunately for me.

"Did the women really talk bad about each other, Grandpa?"

"They sure did, Haleigh. There was a tremendous amount of competition. There were a lot of beautiful women and a lot of talented, handsome men, but only connections for a few, and connections and luck really did help in getting a person to stardom."

To me, this world was like "La-la Land"; it wasn't the real world.

I just took it for what it was that day. The people really didn't faze me at all. These people were people. They were in a profession. They had to think one way and act another way, and they were human beings like anyone else.

In those days, Uncle Abel knew all the Hollywood greats and they were at his party. Hollywood stars like Gregory Peck, Maureen O'Hara, James Cagney, Clark Gable, Elizabeth Taylor, Frank Sinatra, and who knows who else could have been at the party. My uncle introduced me to so many of them, but I have no idea what their names were anymore. The guests came from all over the world. There I was, just a kid who didn't know better. He had friends who were directors and producers in Hollywood and, of course, the great actors of our times. He was good friends with Irving Berlin and Maurice Chevalier.

"Wow, Grandpa, you met famous Hollywood people!"

"It was a great experience, Alex, but I did not realize it until later in life, even though at the time I was nonplussed about this experience. My mistake was that I told my mother."

"Did she get mad at you, Grandpa?"

"My mom didn't get mad, Haleigh, but she was worried. She did ask, 'Wow, Lawrence, did you get their autographs?' Even in those days, I would not lower myself to get an autograph because people thought I was famous too. I just walked around the party introducing myself."

"Why did your mommy worry?"

"Well, Alex, my mother wanted me to stay away, because she thought they would impress me in the wrong way: I would quit school, I would go to Hollywood, and I would become a bum."

Looking back, I think maybe I could have become a RICH bum,

but I'll never know. It was kind of fun for those two days. I would have liked more of it, but I enjoyed the two parties I went to. If I hadn't told my mother, who knows, today I might be a producer or director instead of an orthodontist. Look at all the people I could have known, or look at all the people that I could have gotten in trouble with!

"I like you as an orthodontist, Grandpa," Haleigh shrieks.

"I do too, Haleigh."

"Grandpa, you said you saw him three times. What was the third time?" Alex keeps a count of my visits to Uncle Abel as he tries to pitch a beginner's curveball. He grips the baseball, leaving the index finger off. He places his middle finger along the bottom seam of the baseball and his thumb on the back seam. As he throws the pitch, his thumb rotates upward and his middle finger snaps downward, while his index finger points in my direction. What a great pitch!

"You saw him once, twice, three times." Rebecca begins to run in circles as if she were dizzying herself.

"The third time was at another party, like the one I mentioned."

If nothing else, I could have learned English with my Uncle Abel. His writings were just brilliant. He had an extraordinary command of the English language. He's known for the famous headlines "Wall Street Lays an Egg" of 1929 and "Sticks Nix Hick Pix" of 1935. He is also known for his outstanding reviews. He wrote reviews on legendary films such as *The Great Ziegfeld*, *How Green Was My Valley*, *Yankee Doodle Dandy*, *Gigi*, *All About Eve*, and *Modern Times*. I remember them all.

"I've never heard of any of those movies, Grandpa, but I'll take your word for it," Alex announces.

"Those must be really old movies, Grandpa," Haleigh adds as she begins to chase Haleigh in her circle.

"Yes, they are old movies, the classics."

Besides his writings, he also organized theatrical news coverage of European and South American capitols. My Uncle Abel also co-authored and produced the *Philco Radio Hall of Fame*. He was not only a great theatrical trade reporter and editor for *Variety*, but he was also a composer and a musical collaborator with many people in Hollywood. In 1952, my uncle joined ASCAP (American Society of Composers, Authors and Publishers). His chief musical collaborators were Jesse Greer, Pat Ballard, Fletcher Henderson, and Al Stillman. Some of his popular song compositions are "Variety Stomp," "Encore," and "Variety is the Spice of Life."

"He wrote songs, Grandpa?"

"He sure did, Alex."

"Your uncle was really talented."

"He was such a talent. He was our black sheep, our special, special sheep of the family."

The family hardly brought Uncle Abel up in conversation because he was the other side of the family, and we really never had any social relationship with him. My Uncle Louie always thought that Uncle Abel was a brilliant man, but that he didn't know what the real world was about. I once said to my Uncle Louie, "He may not know what the world is about, Uncle Lou, but he is involved in it and he is trying to do something about it." Uncle Abel brought the world beauty from his art and talents, which is still enjoyed.

"Did you ever see Uncle Abel again?"

"No, like I said, Alex, I only saw him three times in my life. Today, I have no idea where Uncle Abel or any of the relatives from that side of the family are, or where they live or what they did. They were just a part of my past that came and went."

"Tell us more," Haleigh screeches.

"Tell us more, tell us more," Rebecca echoes.

When I throw a fastball to Alex, he watches the motion of the baseball while it is in flight and tries to guess its path. Keeping a visual on the ball, he adjusts his direction to receive the ball and puts his glove out in front of it, open and ready to seize it. Good practice makes perfect!

Abel Green, 1940s

*Elizabeth Taylor and
my uncle, Abel Green*

Memories of My Grandpa Aaron (Gran Pappy)

Don't make little things into big things, unless they are fun things.

—Aaron Grussmark

My grandfather Aaron (on my mother's side) was a tremendous person. It wasn't until years after my grandfather's death that I found out he had leukemia. He always looked gaunt and yet he never acted sick or complained. He always wore a smile no matter how he felt. He passed away a few years before my bar mitzvah, during the middle of World War II, which left a void in my life.

"What's leukemia?"

"Leukemia, Haleigh, is a cancer of the blood."

"Is that bad, Grandpa?"

"Yes, it is bad."

"Pickle juice!"

As a young man in Russia at the age of fourteen, Gran Pappy became a Cossack.

"He was in the military. Right, Grandpa?" Alex jogs his memory, recalling when I had spoken earlier of my mother and her family.

"It was a type of military, but not like the Air Force. He was a member of people who were noted cavalrymen that originated from the Ukrainian steppes. They were known to be from southern European Russia and adjacent parts of Asia whose people formed militaristic communities."

"What do you mean by 'cavalrymen,' Papa Larry?"

"That means he rode on horseback. He was a great horseback rider. This gene was never transferred to ME!"

"A horse is big and fast." Rebecca begins to gallop across the lawn trying to copy the movement of a horse.

"I love horses!" Haleigh gallops behind Rebecca.

The word *Cossack* means adventurer or guerilla. The Cossacks were utilized as a special military force in Russia. One day, I asked my grandfather, "Gran Pappy, why did you join the Cossacks?" He said, "Hell, I didn't join, they drafted me. That was one of the reasons that I left Russia. The army was very anti-Semitic."

"Grandpa, the Jews weren't liked too much in the old days, were they?"

"Let's just say, Alex, the Jews went through a great deal of suffering to get where they are today."

My great-grandparents and my grandfather were born in a small town in Ukraine near Russia. It was spelled Kamianets-Podilskyi, and had a population under 100,000. It was located on the Smotrych River in southwestern Ukraine. The town that my grandfather came from was the place where the first and largest Holocaust mass-murder event in the world took place.

"What's the Holocaust, Grandpa?"

"The Holocaust, Alex, is the term used to describe the genocide of millions of Jews and other minorities in Europe during World War II by Nazi Germany, under the command of Adolf Hitler."

"What's genocide?"

"Genocide means the deliberate destruction of an ethnic, racial, religious, or national group. In other words, they killed off a group of people on purpose because of their ethnicity, race, or religion."

"Genocide means killing people!" Rebecca hollers as she continues to gallop.

Haleigh stops galloping and turns to me with a look of gloom and asks, "Grandpa, did they really kill millions of people?"

"Yes, Haleigh, they did."

"They are bad, bad people," Haleigh comments in disbelief.

"They were more than bad, Haleigh."

"When did they attack your grandpa's town?" Alex inquires with a disheartened quality in his voice.

"It occurred in August 1941, where some 27,000 Jews were killed." Alex's and Haleigh's eyes drop down in sorrow as they hear the depressing news.

My great-grandfather and his parents were farmers. At the age of seventeen, my grandfather left most of his family to come to a new world. He left with some of his brothers because of Russian persecution. He came to New York City on a steamer, where he traveled in the bottom of the ship with the low-class passengers, and settled in lower Manhattan. Since he had no trade, he would purchase things at a low price and try to resell them for more money in order to survive.

"Did your grandpa see his family again?"

"No, Haleigh, he never got to see them again, except for his brothers who came with him to New York City."

Gran Pappy Aaron didn't talk about his parents and family too much. One day I asked him about his parents and he said, "Lawrence, I cried for them because I would never see them again, but I had to go on. They insisted I go without them; they were too old. Since they died, I have said a *kaddish* (Yiddish for *prayer*) for them every day of my life."

"What did your grandpa do for work?"

"During the early days of World War II, Haleigh, Gran Pappy was a fire warden. He was so patriotic that he tried to enlist in the war, but he was too old. So he took his job as fire warden very seriously."

"What did a fire warden do, Grandpa?"

"His job was to make sure that all the windows were blacked out at night, so that the Germans would not see anything if they attacked."

Every day, he would take extra newspaper with him during his patrol and if he saw lights, he would cover the windows up with the newspaper. Sometimes I would yell at him, "You're taking the newspapers and I can't read them!"

And my Gran Pappy would respond, "Lawrence, don't worry if you can't read the newspaper. If you look at the newspaper a month from now, the only thing different will be the names and dates. There will still be stories of rape, war, and vengeance. And, once in a while on the back page, you will see something happy. Better you should read good books about history and life. You will learn more and the stories will stay with you longer."

I was a voracious reader of books, but being a kid, I still wanted to read my newspapers. So I just listened and remembered what he would tell me, but it didn't really register at that time. He always said to me, "It's better to read old books because they stay with you longer. Newspapers you put in shoes and I put on windows. You don't see people put books in shoes and on windows because those books bring the light of life to you." To this day I still read books and newspapers. I guess I never came around to agreeing with my grandfather about newspapers. I love to read and be informed. I wonder what my Gran Pappy would say today if he were alive and saw me reading on the Internet!

"I think your Gran Pappy would be upset, since you still read the newspaper, Grandpa Larry," Alex retorts.

"Didn't you have Internet when you were young, Grandpa?"

"We didn't even have computers, Haleigh."

"No computers! What did you do?"

"I did a lot of things without computers."

From the ages of three to eight, I had the wonderful opportunity of spending a lot of time with my Gran Pappy. He was retired and would talk with me and philosophize. Although he was not an educated man, he was very smart. Gran Pappy stayed until maybe up to eighth grade in school, but since his family were farmers, he was needed more to work in the fields. But he did make sure his children had a formal education. He always insisted that one should have a good education and good health.

"You always tell us we have to have good health and a good education too, Grandpa."

"That's right, Alex."

Listening to my Gran Pappy, I heard seven generations' worth of education, love, and hand-me-down philosophy. When I was about six years old, my Gran Pappy told me about urine and its benefits. He said, "If you ever have a cut or a *penkher* (*blister* in Yiddish) you can use your urine as an antiseptic." I just looked at him like it was unbelievable. Wow!

"What's antiseptic?"

"Antiseptics, Rebecca, are what some people put on their cuts to make sure they don't get infections."

"Pee, Papa Larry! Pee on me if I have a cut?" Rebecca looks up at me with her big round blue eyes in wonderment. Although we were only a few years apart in age when we both heard about urine as an antiseptic, our minds thought alike.

Haleigh, with a serious crinkle in her nose, looked up at me in disgust and said, "That is not right, Grandpa. People don't pee on themselves!"

"Did you ever pee on a cut, Grandpa?" Alex's curiosity gets the better of him as he considers using urine as an antiseptic.

"I guess once in a while I thought of doing this, but I said to myself, 'I'd rather bleed to death.' So I never did it."

Looking back, my Gran Pappy was right. I recently looked up his belief in urine as an antiseptic on the Internet. It is true! I guess I just didn't have the guts to do it.

"It is true?" Haleigh looks at me with skepticism.

"Yes, it is!"

"Pickle juice!"

"I don't think I'd have the guts to do it either, Grandpa."

"I'm glad you understand, Alex. I still haven't done it to this day."

Another time, I saw Gran Pappy peeing on the grass. I said, "Gran Pappy, what are you doing?" He said, "It's good for fertilizing the grass, but not for fertilizing good manners." After this, I saw my grandfather pee on the grass a few other times. I respected him, but I couldn't understand why he peed on the grass. I asked him, "Why don't you go to the bathroom?" He would look at me and say, "Here we have bathrooms in America, but were I was from, we barely had outhouses. Grass and bushes were our outhouse." Funny thing though, a few years later when I was a patrol leader with the Boy Scouts, I led my whole troop during an outing in the woods to a brook and had everyone urinate in it. We called the brook, "Camp Pissing Water." It was then that I understood my Gran Pappy a little more. When you've got to go, you've got to go!

"I've got to go! I've got to go!" Rebecca announces as she scurries into the house.

"What else did your grandpa teach you, Grandpa?"

"Besides urine, Alex, Gran Pappy Aaron also taught me *shpei es oys*, which means *spit it out* in Yiddish."

"What did it teach you?"

"It taught me to spit things out if I wasn't feeling good."

Gran pappy Aaron said, "If you are sick, full to the stomach, get the poison out of your system. Spit it out, cough it up, throw up— just get it out!" It sounds raunchy, but it does work. Boy was my Gran Pappy right. Through my life, I sometimes did as he said and spit it out in a handkerchief or whatever I had available. It did make me feel better. When I couldn't spit it out, I would swallow it again. But I would try to spit it out once more if I could.

"Did your grandpa talk to you like you talk with us, Grandpa?"

"He did, Haleigh. I always enjoyed spending time with my Gran Pappy."

Gran Pappy Aaron would talk and I would listen. He would tell me what life was about. Sometimes when we'd go for a walk, if I fell down, he'd say, "Get up Lawrence! We've got a lot of nice things to do today. We haven't enough time to stay in one place." And, I would just get up and keep going.

I remember our nature walks in the park. Gran Pappy loved nature. He would show me paw prints of squirrels, possums, and raccoons, and show me which way they were going. I learned a great deal about nature and life from him. He would try to teach me how plants grow, how animals lived in the wild, and how to try to exist if one did not have the normal accoutrements of survival. He would take a branch, cut it in half, and show me the green, the sap, and the brittles, and how to make a fire.

"Didn't you learn all of those things in Boy Scouts, Grandpa?"

"I did, Alex. In fact, my Gran Pappy's enthusiasm for nature is what led me to join the Boy Scouts of America."

One day in the park, I was throwing stones into a pond. Gran Pappy took a stone and skipped it across the water and said, "Happiness, Lawrence, is skipping stones across the pond, not throwing them in." I must've been a real klutz because I never could get as good as him in skipping stones. I did love those walks in the park. For me, happiness was walking and talking with my Gran Pappy.

"Happiness is talking with you, Grandpa."

"Thank you, Haleigh. I'm happy when I'm with you too."

"I'm always happy," Rebecca exclaims with glee as she runs back to us from the house catching a small part of the conversation.

"What kind of stuff did you talk about with your grandpa?"

"We talked about everything, Alex. We talked about life, nature, books, and even what I wanted to be when I grew up."

"We talk to you, Papa Larry, about all of those things too," Rebecca points out.

"Yes, we do, just like I did with my Gran Pappy."

One day my Gran Pappy asked me what I wanted to be when I was a big boy. At that time, I had many aspirations. I would go on about how I wanted to be a fireman because they drove a big red truck and made lots of noise.

"I love fire trucks!"

"Me too, Alex."

The next day, I would change my mind and tell my Gran Pappy how I wanted to be a garbage man because they look at all the great things you can pick up that others throw away. And it was free!

"Free is good, Grandpa, but I don't want to be a garbage man."

"Why not, Haleigh?"

"Because they get dirty, Grandpa."

"Their job is smelly too, Papa Larry," Rebecca adds.

Other days, I thought about being the president of the United States because I hated to take orders and loved to give orders. The president also traveled a lot and I wanted to see the world. And if I couldn't be president, then I wanted to be an explorer. I was always interested in adventures like going to little islands and climbing mountains. I would go on and on about the different things I wanted to be day after day. I would give my grandfather a *kop veytik* (*headache* in Yiddish) because each day I wanted to be something different.

"Grandpa, I always want to be something different too. Do I give you a *kop veytik*?"

"No, Alex, you don't." I couldn't help but chuckle. It amazes me how much children soak in when you talk with them. I must've been a sponge just like them when I was young, soaking up everything I was told.

Gran Pappy Aaron would remind me each time, "Lawrence, follow your dreams, but always remember the difference between needs and wants. You may want a bigger bike, but do you really need it? Be practical with your dreams. It's not important what you want to be Lawrence; it's the dream you visualize. You can change your mind every day, but by dreaming and visualizing you have a hope that carries you to a brighter future." At that time, I would just listen because he was such a great narrator, even though I really didn't follow what he'd say.

"What else did he tell you, Grandpa?"

"Besides following my dreams, Haleigh, Gran Pappy would always tell me to be strong mentally and physically. Right and left."

Gran Pappy would say, "If you keep yourself in good health and discipline your mind, you can do anything you want with your dreams. But you must practice every day to be good every day. Do not put off for tomorrow what you can do today. This way you do not have to remember what you have to do because you already have done it. Do things right the first time and they will not be left to do the second time."

"I practice every day to be good, Grandpa," Haleigh declares.

Alex gives a slight chuckle and says, "She doesn't practice that well some times, Grandpa."

"I practice to be good every day too, Papa Larry," Rebecca boasts.

Gran Pappy Aaron also taught me to strive for everything, to be all you can be. He would tell me, "Lawrence, the worst that will happen is that you do not make it. The best is that you tried." In those days, it didn't make any sense what he said to me. Since I was very competitive, I figured he was just telling me to do my best, not worry if I failed, and try again. And, this is what I did. I always knew there would be another day. I just tried my best and remembered Gran Pappy and his words of wisdom: "People will beat you, but don't beat yourself. You will see you will win more than you will lose."

"Daddy tells me all the time that I'm a winner because I always try," Alex boasts with confidence. "Grandpa, I always feel like a winner, even if I lose."

"That's because you are a winner!"

"I'm a winner too!"

"Yes, Haleigh, you're a winner too!"

"And me too, Papa Larry," Rebecca interjects. "I'm a winner too!"

"All of you are winners!"

On occasion, Gran Pappy would tell me that education of the mind and the soul never leaves a person and transcends generations. He would explain, "The Jews have always been a minority. What keeps them together is a discipline of strong education and strong moral values. People can take your money, your clothes, your house, but they can never take your mind and your soul. These riches will stay with you and your family forever."

"Does that mean we're rich, Grandpa?"

"We are, Haleigh, but not in the material sense."

"What do you mean, Grandpa?"

"We're rich in family. We have a great family that follows the Jewish traditions and heritage and values very close to our hearts. We know the difference between right and wrong and we try to help others. This is what makes us rich, not money."

"Money is good too, isn't it?"

"Yes, money is good too."

"I'm rich, Papa Larry," Rebecca declares. "I'm rich in family."

"Yes, we all are rich in family, Rebecca."

I guess because I grew up poor, I never really worried too much about material things. I really didn't even feel like I was poor. I cared more about dreaming, living, learning, and sticking to my beliefs. As a kid, I had holes in my shoes and I would stick newspaper in them to fill the holes. But I always read the newspaper first before I stuck it in the holes. So I guess I somewhat understand what my Gran Pappy was saying about people never taking your mind and soul. I never stopped wanting to learn, so I would just read. I would read anything.

One time, I showed a kid my stamp collection. He took some of the stamps and I wanted to kill him. But I just stepped back and said, "It's only stamps. It's only stamps." I was upset the kid stole my stamps, but in the end, they were just stamps.

"I'd be upset if he took my stamps, Grandpa."

"I was upset, Alex. But they were just stamps."

"Do you remember everything your grandpa taught you?"

"Much of his teaching and philosophy stuck with me in life."

The philosophy of *tsedakah* (*righteous giving* or *charity* in Yiddish) is an important philosophy that I have lived by and also shared with others. Gran Pappy Aaron would say, "Out of every dollar earned, give first to savings, second to charity, and third to live by." He would go on to explain, "By saving, you hoard your nuts like a squirrel for a rainy day. By giving charity, you are helping people not as fortunate to live and hopefully take care of themselves some day. Living off the fruits of your labor and enjoying your family is what life is all about." I shared this philosophy with my kids, as well as with some patients and students. I really feel that my kids thought I was goofy, and my students too. But I know that this philosophy stuck with my children and they do give to charity, and I am proud of them.

"Daddy tells us we have to give to charity," Haleigh confirms.

"I'm glad to hear that, Haleigh. Now I know that Gran Pappy Aaron's words live on not just with me or my children, but with the three of you as well."

My time with Gran Pappy Aaron was very special. I would listen to him talk and ask him questions. I wanted to learn everything I could from him. I asked so many questions that he said to me with love, "*Dir hoben a groys moil!*" *(You have a big mouth!)*

"I'm told I have a big mouth."

"By who, Haleigh?"

"By Alex."

"I guess we both have big mouths then, Haleigh."

As a grandfather today, I have found out that my grandfather was right and ahead of his time. When I was young, I didn't listen. Although I didn't act, I remembered many things, things that were good and things that were bad. This came with having a good memory. And with this good memory, I kept the things my Gran Pappy said to me always in the back of my head. And now as a grandfather, I share this hand-me-down philosophy from Gran Pappy Aaron with my grandchildren.

"I like the hand-me-down philosophy, Grandpa," Alex says as he takes a break from pitching. He decides to sit down on a chair and motions for me to join him.

"I like it too!" Haleigh begins to gallop once more as her sidekick, Rebecca, tries to catch up with her.

"Giddy up! Giddy up!" Haleigh and Rebecca command in unison.

"Grandpa, you told us how your grandpa and grandma met."

"Yes, Alex, I did."

"You also told us how your mommy and daddy met."

"I think so."

"So, how did you and Gran Mommy meet?"

"How'd you meet Kathy, Grandpa?" Haleigh interjects.

"That's a good question, and it's a long story."

"We have a lot of time, Papa Larry!" Rebecca assumes since no one has called for us.

As the shade wraps itself around the outdoor furniture, Alex and I enjoy a peaceful rest on the chairs as Haleigh and Rebecca continue to gallop like wild stallions across the yard. Since time hasn't traveled quickly in this backyard, I am left with no choice but to give in and tell the story.

My grandfather Aaron Grussmark, 1898

Relationships

One night with Venus and a lifetime with Mercury.
—an old saying used by Louis Grossmark

Dating, marriage, and divorce—it was a very interesting adventure right from the beginning with my ex-wife, Judi. In hindsight, there were many signs that forecasted our relationship. My first date with Judi was a blind date. She was referred by my friend Brian, who became my best man at our wedding. Brian had had a blind date with Judi once, and they just became friends. He thought she was a great gal, but there was no chemistry between them, so Brian thought she might be good for me.

"What's a blind date, Grandpa?"

"A blind date, Haleigh, is when two people who have never met before are set up by someone who is a mutual friend."

"You didn't know Grandma before going on a date?"

"No, I just knew about her from my friend Brian."

"Pickle juice!"

"What was your blind date like, Grandpa?"

"It was actually a very nice first date, Alex."

Judi lived in Forest Hills Gardens in New York City. She lived in a very nice area near the Forest Hills Tennis Stadium, where they held international matches. When I met Judi, I thought I had won the trifecta!

"What's a trifecta?" Haleigh clings to every word.

"A trifecta is when a person is bidding on a race and they choose the first three winners in the correct order they finish."

"What did you win the three things in, Grandpa?" Alex wasn't too sure how trifecta fit into my meeting his grandmother.

"Well, she was pretty, she came from a cultured family, and she lived near a famous tennis stadium. Her father was a businessman and her mother was a teacher."

"How old were you when you met Grandma?"

"Judi was twenty-one and I was twenty-eight when we met."

I showed up in my Air Force captain's uniform for our first date. I wanted to impress her; however, I don't think she was impressed by my uniform. And, unfortunately her parents had little use for the military either.

"Why didn't they like the military?"

"They didn't think military people were very smart people, Haleigh."

"Pickle juice."

Judi's family was cordial but aloof when I met them on our first date. I took her out for a movie and a bite to eat. My first impression of Judi was that she was cute and very nice. She was wearing a dress that looked beautiful on her. We were out about three hours on the date and I thought the date went okay, not bad. She invited me in for dessert. I met her father, who told me in no uncertain terms, "Son, I am staying up all night in the living room to read, so you can leave when you are ready." I stayed only for a half hour and I ate the dessert, even though I am not a dessert eater, because I thought I would irritate the dad if I had stayed and not eaten the dessert. There was an expression about dating that said, "If you are not getting anywhere, shake hands and call it a night." So I did just that. I wanted to be respectful and not overstay my welcome.

"Did you see her again, Grandpa?"

"Of course he did, Haleigh. How else would she be your grandma?" Alex quickly responds.

"Yes, I saw her many times before we got married."

"Did you get along with her parents, Grandpa?"

"I would like to think I did. I know her father grew to like me, but I never really felt her mother did."

During our younger years, Judi's mother used to yell at her because she was never satisfied with what Judi did. Her mother was always nitpicking. In contrast, her father was a delight and a gentleman; eventually he liked me a lot. I used to stick up for Judi with her mother, whether Judi was right or wrong. Her mother did not seem to like that. However, we had many things in common. We both liked math, had high energy, and were very social. One thing I really liked about her mother was that she was an awesome cook. In some ways I was jealous of her because she spoke with Judi two or three times a day. In retrospect, I was dead wrong for being jealous because all daughters have done that from time immemorial. I guess in early times they signaled by bonfires, and today by cell phones.

When her mother was going downhill and in the beginning stages of Alzheimer's, Judi's brother took her to North Carolina to live in a house near his office. We hardly ever visited her mother after she moved, even though she lived for many years thereafter. We went down to visit once during wintertime. She looked at everybody, but didn't say a word to anyone. Then she looked at me and went to the closet, got my coat, gave it to me, and said, "Goodbye." It was the first and last word she said to anybody.

"Did she really tell you 'Goodbye'?" Haleigh glances at me in disbelief.

"She really did!"

"Tell us about another date with Grandma, Grandpa."

"On our second date, we went to Bear Mountain State Park to a pool."

In the pool, I found myself teaching a handicapped little boy to swim. I saw the boy in the pool and had no idea where his parents were. He would not let go of the edge of the pool. I befriended him because I felt sorry that he was handicapped and no one was paying attention to him. I guess Judi was watching me, although all my attention was on teaching the boy how to swim. Later on, Judi said she fell in love with me at that time because it was so great how I acted with the boy and I would be a wonderful father.

"Did you marry her after the second date, Grandpa?"

"Not after the second date, Haleigh. Judi and I went on many dates after that."

"What kind of stuff did you do on your dates, Grandpa?"

"Well, Alex, we went out dancing at Tavern on the Green, we went to the movies, and we spent many days at the beach."

"When did you marry Grandma?"

"I courted, proposed, and married her all in the same year, Haleigh. I met her at the end of May and I proposed to her in August and we were married in December."

"Did Grandma meet your parents?"

"When my family met Judi, my mother said to me, 'Lawrence, she's too skinny. How is she going to pull horses on the farm?' My mother felt that anyone that was skinny wasn't in good health. But my family loved her anyway."

"Pickle juice!"

"Papa Larry married Grandma!" Rebecca squeals in glee. Haleigh and Rebecca take a break to sit with Alex and me in the shaded part of the yard and listen to more of how their grandparents met.

"Why didn't you stay married, Grandpa?"

"That's an excellent question, Alex."

I knew there were premonitions of what was to come in our marriage. At the wedding, my best man, Judi's father, and her brother all fainted from the heat. Judi wanted to turn around.

"Did Grandma leave?"

"She wanted to, Haleigh, but I said, 'No, it's show time!' What a way to begin a wedding and a marriage."

In our early days of the marriage, I was a tennis fanatic. I would come home late after playing tennis after work. I would play tennis with the other guys in the town for about an hour about three nights a week and I would get home about 8:00 or 8:30 in the evening. Judi did complain to me about my playing so much tennis.

"Did you stop playing tennis, Grandpa?"

"I didn't stop playing, Alex. Ideally, I should've told her she could learn and I'd play with her. Instead, I told her I worked forty-eight hours a week and I didn't think it was too much to ask to be able to get rid of some of my excess energy."

"Did Grandma understand?"

"No, I don't think she understood. In fact, she got so fed up that, one day, she set fire to my tennis racket."

"She set fire to your racket, Grandpa?"

"She sure did, Haleigh."

"Did it make you stop playing?"

"Nope, I bought a new racket the next week and began playing tennis again."

"Did Grandma get mad again?"

"Looking back, I don't think there was any jealousy on either of our parts, but there should've been. I think the only reason she was fed up with my playing was because I wasn't giving her much attention, since most of my time was spent at work. Shame on me!"

"Shame on you!" Rebecca mimics.

But I think Judi loved that I took charge, was great with kids, and provided for her. She thought I had an enormous amount of energy, a tremendous will to succeed, and a lot of discipline. Maybe she also admired that I wouldn't take "No" for an answer, although that last trait is not always good in a marriage. I think she would have preferred that I spend more time with her rather than just listen to her.

"Did you fight a lot, Grandpa?"

"We didn't fight a lot, Alex, because she kind of yelled and I just kind of listened."

I figured if I talked, I was going to lose anyway, so I might as well lose fast. She could be sensitive. And—in jest—because of this, sometimes I didn't sleep too well at night because she was a crack shot with a rifle. I used to keep one eye open. I wasn't too concerned though, because if she shot me, who would support her?!

"Grandma would shoot you?"

"No, Haleigh, it was just a joke. Grandma wouldn't shoot me."

"Why was Grandma sensitive, Grandpa?"

"I'm not sure, Alex. I think it was the artist in her. It is said that artistic people can be sensitive."

"How is she artistic, Grandpa?"

"Her hobbies are painting oils of landscapes and people, and she played the classical piano."

"Did you like being with Grandma?"

"For the most part, we did enjoy each other's company. We had religion, the arts, bridge, education, and travel in common. Our philosophy of life was similar because of our backgrounds, and we both agreed that a person should be open to other people's opinions even though you may disagree with them."

"Was there anything you didn't have in common?'

"She didn't like warm weather, per se, and I used to go down to Florida to visit my mother, who lived in a nursing home, and my Uncle Louie, who was blind."

I sometimes would say to her, "Hey, how about us spending some time in the winter in Florida?" And she would say to me, "Send me a card! Send me a card!" Once, we were adventure touring in the jungle of Malaysia, going through water with leeches, and we had to cross a rope bridge. We were going from one side of the jungle to the other and there was only one way to go. You couldn't go back. She was deathly afraid of heights. I walked across the bridge and she was behind me.

She said, "What's going to happen? What are you going to do with me?"

I said, "Come on over!"

She said, "What happens if I don't want to come over?"

So I said, "Send me a card!" She eventually crossed the bridge without turning around.

"Did Grandma go anywhere else with you, Grandpa?"

"Believe it or not, Haleigh, she did. Even though she didn't like deep water or high altitudes, I schlepped her all around the world."

Once, we were in Capri off the coast of Italy on the water in a small pontoon boat when a high amount of rain came. Judi was a poor swimmer and was scared the boat would capsize, but she hung in there. She put her head in her hands and eventually we came out okay. I have to say she was a gamer. And, although she smoked quite a few packs of cigarettes a day, she never lost energy when we went on our trips.

"Grandpa, what was Grandma like when she was young?"

"In the beginning of our marriage, Alex, she could have cared less about animals, but after a while, she had her own zoo."

"What made her like animals?"

"Her dad was a naturalist and a gardener and it just came naturally to her. Raccoons, opossums, groundhogs, you name it. She even went on a tour showing people how to respect boa constrictors and other wild animals."

When we were married, she was a volunteer at the Turtle Back Zoo in West Orange, New Jersey. That is how she got involved with the animals and boa constrictors. Considering she didn't like high altitudes and didn't like the water, she was very comfortable with wild animals. Looking back, these wild animals were probably a substitute for me because I was a wild animal!

"Papa Larry was a wild animal!" Rebecca shouts, jumps up, and begins to run around. "Did you help her with the animals?"

"I did sometimes."

One time Judi showed me how to put a boa constrictor around my stomach. All of a sudden it got very tight and I could have sworn the boa constrictor was in cahoots with my ex! It scared the heck out of me. My survival instincts kicked in and I pulled the boa down. I cursed and I prayed. I had to pull down the boa so it could go around my feet, rather than up toward my neck where it could crush my throat and squeeze me to death.

"That sounds scary, Grandpa!"

"It was, Haleigh!"

"It's funny that Grandma wasn't scared!"

"She wasn't. It's wonderful that this quiet little girl became a naturalist."

"Did Grandma study about animals?"

"To my knowledge she took a volunteer course on how to care for animals."

Grandma did go to college, and she graduated as a teacher of Early Childhood Education. At the beginning of our marriage, while I was in residency, she taught at a school in Fairport, New York. I think the first year and a half of our marriage was the best time of our life together. We had very little income, we were loving to each other, and we spent a lot of time with each other.

After my residency, Judie was a stay-at-home mom. She later volunteered as a wildlife rehabilitator, healing birds and other animals and sending them back into the wild. Our house was really a zoo in many ways, since it was the main sanctuary for the animals. It was probably more of a sanctuary for the animals than for me.

"How long were you and Grandma married, Grandpa?"

"We were married about forty years before we decided to get divorced."

We tried to work things out, but it didn't work. She wanted the divorce, and I agreed with her. We had grown apart and the heart strings were tattered. It was too difficult to tie them together again. The divorce proceedings went okay. I am sure neither of us was completely satisfied, but that just means it was a good divorce settlement. During the divorce, our communication was sometimes testy. But once the divorce was over, it was really cordial. From my point of view, I gave more and settled for less. But for me personally, the peace in the family was well, well, worth it!

"Was Daddy okay with your divorce, Grandpa?"

"All the kids were unhappy about the divorce, Alex. They thought many times we were good actors because we didn't share our concerns with them and didn't show we were unhappy until it was too late."

In retrospect, we both spent so much time giving so much love to the kids that we seemed to forget about loving each other. Even though our marriage didn't work out, in a way we did win. The kids, although they live in different areas, have a deep bond for each other. They would go around the world to help each other at any time.

"They are together now, Grandpa," Haleigh points out.

"Yes, they are together now."

We are very fortunate with our three kids. They are motivated, even though I had to push them sometimes when they were younger. We got them educated—one's a physician, one's an orthodontist, and one's a super businesswoman with a double degree from Columbia. As parents, we hit the lottery. I hit the trifecta again!

"Trifecta!" Rebecca shouts and raises her hands up in the air as if she just won a race. "I love my mommy and my uncles."

Judi is an intelligent person. Although she was the only one in the family who did not go to an Ivy League school, I always said that she was the most intelligent. She would do *The New York Times* crossword puzzle in ink on Sunday mornings. She completed the puzzles correctly and fast When we had to look up words in contests, she always came in first and I came in last. She was a fantastic speaker and was very practical in bringing up three kids.

When we got married, she let me do all the banking because she probably wasn't interested in writing checks. She was frugal, but she sometimes drove me batty because she would go somewhere an hour away to buy a dress at a bargain and then not bring it back. She bought a lot of inexpensive things and it seemed she went shopping almost every other day. I thought this was goofy. But in the overall realm of things, it was so silly for me to think that way. She was just trying to get a good deal to save money.

As we were getting close to the divorce, she seemed more interested in finances. (I'd like to think I taught her so well that she became great at it.) After the divorce, she became a financial expert. She picked up finances so fantastically, in fact, that I always felt like asking HER for advice. Just kidding!

"You're a great teacher, Grandpa!"

"Thank you, Haleigh."

When I first met Judi, she was pretty, petite, quiet, and non-adventurous. She did not seem to like confrontation and taking chances. When we divorced, I think she changed; she was talkative, had a take-charge attitude, drove a car like a racecar, took care of all the finances that she didn't before, and traveled all over the world.

Now that we have gone our separate ways (fortunately or unfortunately), we have a better relationship, a better understanding of each other, and I know that I have matured. The relationship now is nice. During the marriage we didn't take enough time to sit around the house and grow with each other; we just became respectful and cordial to each other rather than loving. Now, we laugh, we joke, we are respectful, we talk about the kids, she invites me to her house (which used to be our house) for High Holidays, and our communication is much better and more objective.

"I like that you and Grandma have fun together, Grandpa."

"It's nice to be able to laugh and joke around with your grandma, Alex. I am happy we are still on good terms."

"How do you and Kathy get along, Grandpa?"

"I guess Kathy was attracted to me because I was upbeat and loved kids. She is modest and quiet, and also an artist; she paints oils and landscapes. We enjoy doing so many things together and are able to do so because the children have grown up. Kathy likes to go to the theater and concerts. She even wants to play sports with me and joins me in doing silly things at times."

"You are silly!" Rebecca giggles.

"I am silly! I like to be a kid and have fun. Kathy has a lot of kid in her too—not as much as I do."

We travel around the world and share an interest in photography. (She is a much better photographer than I am, but so is everybody else.) We also love reading, riding bikes, walking, and being with our grandchildren.

As I've gotten older, I have matured and have learned to express more feeling and caring for people. This was a long process though. I began to change when I realized that there were more years behind me then ahead of me. I realized that I couldn't take my health for granted and that every day I am with a child or a loved one should be a special day and a special blessing. I also recognize that it's all right to be with extended family members even if they tell the same story over and over and over again. I understand that I don't have to be president of every organization, or the president of the United States, God forbid! And, I've learned to appreciate every day; each day should be taken as a special day of love with the people that are important to you.

"Every day is a special day!"

"Yes, Haleigh, every day is a special day."

In our early childrearing years, I was so involved with my work and my professionalism that I didn't take the time to chill out and do other important things. My goals in life have also changed. Now, I want to enjoy life, stay in good health, write, travel, sculpt, listen more, talk less, and love more. With Kathy, I am not working as hard, although sometimes I am home and spend just as much time there on office matters. It is now a relationship and that's what relationships SHOULD be—a relationship.

"I like Kathy," Rebecca blurts out.

"When did you meet Kathy, Grandpa?"

"I first met Kathy when she brought her daughter to the office, Alex."

"What did you think of her?"

"She was so happy and personable—her good humor impressed me."

Kathy even got braces. At one point, I hired her to work in the practice and she had quite a knack for it. Eventually she became the Head Honcho!

Kathy is an artist, and I went to her art show (she had won the award for best impressionistic piece in the show). We both had some interest in each other in New Jersey. It wasn't until Kathy moved to Florida that a relationship really developed. Since she moved to Florida, I've had the best of both worlds. I like warm weather, and we can visit her family and my family on the East Coast. I can also take time off from my work because I am a workaholic. It's another trifecta!

"Grandpa, you've won a lot of trifectas!"

"I guess I have, Haleigh. I must be really lucky."

Kathy is the one who wanted me to write my memoirs. As she says, "You are a walking history book!"

"You're writing a book, Grandpa?"

"Yes, I am, Alex, and it's about my life."

"I think that's a great idea, Grandpa."

"Grandpa, do you fight with Kathy?"

"No, Haleigh, not really. Even though my relationship with Kathy is fine, I still had better watch out. All of a sudden, this quiet, shy, petite person might become a gangbuster, a financial expert, and a racecar driver! I must say that she is a crack rifle shot and pistol shot too!"

"Grandpa, why did you not get along with Grandma all the time?"

"I think we got along for a while, but I'm really not sure what happened."

I came from a family that did not really have interactions with friends or relatives. My parents were separated. My mother worked all day, and my father was not really around very much. So I was alone most of the time. We did not honor birthdays or give presents, and we were basically loners. We were not involved in any civic, cultural, religious, or other activities when I was a kid. We did not have a car and didn't travel much. And because of that, we just learned to be by ourselves.

"How sad!"

"What's sad, Haleigh?"

"You were by yourself."

"It wasn't too bad, Haleigh. I got to read a lot, and I love to read."

My vacation each year was either two weeks in the Catskill Mountains or two weeks during which we took a train to Florida to see my cousins. My family was a group of loners. When I got married, I did not have any money, so money was a concern with me, even though I was going into a lucrative profession. Because of my upbringing as an only child in a family that didn't have much interaction, it was difficult for me to express my emotions because I did not want to show my vulnerability. I was used to surviving and being by myself. And it is very important when having a relationship with somebody that you show vulnerability, because that's what relationships are for.

"You didn't let Grandma know how you felt, Grandpa?"

"No, I guess I didn't, Alex. I had this shell and I was afraid of breaking it."

As a kid, I was afraid of opening up to someone and being hurt, so my shell grew strong. This affected me as I got older and had other relationships. I found it difficult to have a deep feeling or concern for another when I was unwilling to express my vulnerability. I now know that it's very important to do this because that's what relationships are about.

Looking back, I should have laughed more, cried more, and understood that family is family, even if it means listening to a hundred jokes by the same uncle. You love and accept your family members and enjoy every day you have with them.

"I enjoy every day I have with you, Grandpa."

"I enjoy every day with you too, Alex."

In any relationship, you have to bring a feeling that comes from the heart, not from the mind. When I was a kid, they said I was very smart. As I grew older, they said I was very smart. I began to believe in it. I began to preach to people and advise people. I began to criticize people when I thought they were not doing something as well as me. I began to give people their marching lessons for the day. This is no way to have relationships.

You have to accept people for who they are, and quite often, when you give people the opportunity, they will do something almost as well as and sometimes better than you. Being able to do this takes time. It takes maturity. We must be who we want to be and be comfortable with ourselves and respect other people for who they are and what they are. That's what life and love are about.

"I'm comfortable with myself!" Haleigh confirms.

"Me too, Grandpa!" Alex agrees.

Haleigh hops up and hurries over to Rebecca, who continues to run around like a wild animal. As Rebecca finishes dancing like a monkey, she begins to act like a lion and roars, "Roar!" Haleigh takes the lead in the pack and bellows, "Roar!"

"Papa Larry, when you were married with Grandma, you said you spent a lot of time loving your children."

"I did, Alex."

"What is it like being their daddy?"

"It's a lot like the way Doug feels about being your daddy. There's nothing that compares to being a father, except being a grandfather."

While the display of animal kingdom antics shifts to another species, Alex and I decide to practice ball a little more. He takes his glove and slides it onto his tiny hand, makes a fist, and punches it into the palm of the glove.

With Judi, in Rochester, New York, 1962

Kathy and me on a Mediterranean cruise, 2009

Fatherhood

This is my quest,
To follow that star—
No matter how hopeless,
No matter how far.
                    —excerpt from the lyrics of "The Impossible Dream"

Fatherhood is filled with joys and challenges. I hit the trifecta with my children. Doug, the oldest is a well-respected orthodontist in New Jersey.

"That's Daddy!"

"Yes it is, Haleigh."

Jonathan, my second born, is a doctor who specializes in infectious diseases.

"That's Uncle Jon!"

"That's right, Haleigh."

And Helaine is a super businesswoman with her own private consulting firm.

"That's my mommy! Mommy is a super woman!"

"Yes, Rebecca, that's your mommy."

My parenting style was based on my experiences in life. As the family would say, I was the Jewish mother in the family.

"Wasn't Grandma the Jewish mother, Grandpa?"

"She was, Haleigh, but it's just a figure of speech."

"Pickle juice!"

I seemed to be the Don Quixote of the family, pushing my children to reach the impossible.

"Who's Don Quixote, Grandpa?"

"Don Quixote is a man who lived a life full of dreams, Alex."

I wanted the kids to search the world for windmills to enjoy and make this world a better place to live in.

"Why would you want them to search for windmills, Grandpa?"

"The word 'windmills' is used differently, Alex, and means to search for your dreams no matter what anyone tells you."

I wanted each of them to have their very own dream; whether it was larger than life or less than spectacular didn't matter as long as it was their own dream. And I didn't deny them the possibility that their dreams wouldn't come true. I wanted them to keep dreaming their own "Impossible Dream." By pursuing it, they would stay inspired in life and live life to the fullest, making this world, in turn, a better world for everyone to live in.

"I'm going to search for my 'Impossible Dream', Grandpa."

"I wouldn't expect less, Alex."

"Me too, Grandpa, but I don't think anything is impossible for me."

"I think whatever you try for, Haleigh, you'll be a great success."

"Pickle juice!"

"Who took care of everyone, Grandpa?"

"I worked a lot and took care of the family by being the provider."

It goes without saying that their mother was the stable one in the family. While I was at work, Judi took care of the home and domestic aspect of bringing up the children. She made sure that they had clothes to wear, food to eat, a place to stay. Whether it was helping with their homework or ferrying to different activities, she took care of the home front. My job was easy—I only had to pay for everything. She did the hard work.

We traveled as a family because I wanted my children to see the world.

"To find windmills, Grandpa?"

"Yes, Haleigh, to find windmills. To see the opportunities."

When the kids were young, we hired a person who spoke only Spanish to be a nanny. Her duties were to help with the chores and teach the children fluent Spanish. After four years, the nanny went back to Columbia. When she left, she was speaking broken Spanish and the kids were speaking broken English.

I encouraged them to be their best and to be themselves. Still to this day, I feel like I've won the lottery three times. My children are successful, happy, and living life to the fullest. What more could a father ask for!

"Grandpa, tell me about Daddy!"

"What do you want me to tell you about your father, Haleigh?"

"How was Daddy when he was growing up?" Haleigh responds with curiosity.

"What was Mommy like?"

"You want to hear about your mommy, Rebecca?"

"Yes, Papa Larry. I want to hear about Mommy."

"Grandpa, can you tell us about Daddy, Uncle Jon, and Aunt Helaine when they were growing up?"

"Of course, Alex."

Suddenly, silence descends on the scenic landscape as youthful ears wait to hear the gossip of family. Alex swooshes the ball into my glove while Haleigh and Rebecca sit on the sideline, intensely wanting to know more. For seconds, all that was heard was the flight of a ball and the breath of children eager to be told a story.

Enjoying a day with my children at the Seaquarium of New Jersey, (left to right) me, Helaine, Jon, and Doug, wearing matching nautical hats in the spirit of the trip, 1968

My Son Douglas

Selective hearing and selective amnesia can be a great stress-saver during the day.
—Douglas Harte

Douglas was born in Rochester, New York. Doug, as I call him, was born with a full head of hair. At that time, I wanted a transplant because I was losing mine. He was our first child, poor kid—all my dreams, all my feelings went into him. Fortunately for Doug, we had two other kids after him to give him some breathing room. Since he was the first born, I tried everything, drawing upon all my educational and life experiences for him.

I wanted Doug by the age of six to swim the English Channel even if I hadn't done it. I taught him how to swim at the age of four. He was a pretty good swimmer.

"What's the English Channel, Grandpa?"

"The English Channel, Haleigh, is a part of the Atlantic Ocean that separates England from northern France, and it's about twenty-two miles wide where people swim in it."

"How long is a lap in a pool, Grandpa?"

"It depends on the pool, Alex. An Olympic-size pool is about fifty meters long."

"How many meters are in a mile?"

"It takes about 1600 meters to make one mile."

Alex looks at me in amazement. "The English Channel is really long."

"It is quite a stretch of water, Alex."

"That's a lot of swimming for Daddy."

"Yes it was, Haleigh. I soon realized that swimming laps in the pool for Doug was fine for me. I was just happy he swam laps in the pool."

I then tried to get him interested in stamps. My dad gave me stamps from his father when I was eight years old. My Uncle Harry Hartstein gave me a stamp album. I began to collect stamps from the United States and all over the world. I found out that the best-looking stamps came from the poorest countries. Each day, I would look at the stamps. And each month when I had ten cents, I would buy a package of stamps and carefully, gingerly paste them into the album. I would sit down and dream of going to each country on each continent. I would sail the seas. Trek the land. Fly through the air with my special carpet, my magical carpet to see and enjoy the world.

"Like Aladdin, Grandpa?"

"Like Aladdin, Haleigh."

"I want to fly on a magic carpet," Rebecca giggles and looks up into the sky.

The world of dreams was for me like the brother and sister I didn't have. In a way, it was better than having a brother and sister because I could talk to them, but they could never talk back to me.

"I can understand, Grandpa." Alex replies with a bit of irony as he looks at Haleigh and then looks at me.

"Do you still collect stamps, Grandpa?"

"Sometimes I do. I did that more when I was a kid though."

The other day I looked at my stamp album, and much to my dismay, I saw notes. The notes showed the country's capital, population, adjacent rivers, lakes, and seas, and main products, which were mostly manufactured or agricultural goods. Now I know why I was so good in geography. It was plain fun as a hobby for me. I can see where I got my taste for being a National Geographic traveler.

"I like collecting sports cards, Grandpa. I think it's fun."

"I know, Alex, just like your father."

Having been an avid stamp collector since I was a child, I suggested to Doug he might want to take up stamp collecting. I showed him my stamp collection. All he said was, "Nice." A year later I showed him my stamp collection again, in hopes the interest would spark. And, again, he said, "Nice."

"Daddy didn't collect stamps?"

"No, Haleigh, your daddy didn't want to collect stamps."

Doug said, "It looks nice, Dad. But I really would like to take up collecting baseball cards and other sports." He was better at collecting cards then I was in that he wouldn't let his parents touch them and throw them out like my mom did.

"You let your mommy throw your cards out!"

"I didn't have much of a choice, Alex. I should've been smarter and hid them well."

I could have retired early if my mother had not thrown out all my cards, which are priced at a fortune today. I guess my mother wanted me to work for a living. Parents have a devious way of getting their way.

"Daddy collected cards?"

"Yes, Haleigh, Douglas bought boxes of baseball cards each year and still buys them to this day."

Doug never throws anything away. Someday he is going to need a room to take care of his card collection. If it wasn't going to be stamps, it was going to be something else. It took a while, but I finally got through to him.

"I'm glad Daddy collects cards, because I collect cards with him now too."

"I think that's wonderful, Alex. It's something fun to do with your father."

"What else did you do with Daddy, Grandpa?"

"We did so much. In fact, all the kids were always busy and into many activities."

When Doug was six, I took him to Adventure Guides because I wanted to show him nature and the mountains. Adventure Guides was an organization affiliated with the YMCA. It was a way for fathers and sons to camp and bond together. We camped overnight in little tents, cooked food over the fire, and got stung by all kinds of insects. We were in nature. The bathroom was the woods. I love the outdoors.

"I like the outdoors too, Grandpa, but only to look at nature. Nature is pretty. I don't think I would like to be stung by insects or go to the bathroom in the woods."

"I love nature. There are so many pretty flowers and trees," Rebecca chants.

"Did Daddy like camping, Grandpa?"

"Yes,, I also think Doug liked being with me and his friends, Alex."

I thought he might join the Boy Scouts when he was a bit older; however, the times that Doug grew up in were different than when I was a kid. None of his friends went into scouting. In my day, scouting was the "in" thing to join. We had uniforms, we were in a great war, and it made us feel special and wanted. I thought this nature experience would make Doug want to go into scouting like I did. But he had other ideas. Adventure Guides was great for the dads though, because we would put the kids to sleep early and then play cards and drink.

"Grandpa, you just like scouting."

"I guess I do Alex. I really loved the Boy Scouts and the times I went camping with my kids."

"Did Daddy ever do anything silly?"

"Actually, Alex, he did do some silly things."

"What did he do?"

"I remember once when Doug was a small kid, he used to insert the car key into the electric socket. The result sent him across the room flying. We thought he was going to be an electrician or an astronaut, if he lived."

"Did he ever stop?"

"Eventually he figured it out. You'd think on the first try he would've learned."

"Do you have any nicknames for Daddy, Grandpa?"

"Doug was my Tai-Pan, Haleigh."

Doug was about five years old when I started calling him Tai-Pan. When he asked for a raise in his allowance, I said to Doug, "You can only get a raise when you do something constructive." I then went on to tell him the story of *Tai-Pan* by James Clavell. The story was about the East Indian Company. A father said to his son,

"Someday you are going to be head of a noble house, but it will not be by inheritance; it will be by working and striving and being your best." Doug just looked at me and said, "Yeah, Dad." He went to his mother and she gave him the money.

"When I need money, I go to Mommy too," Alex declares with a grin.

"Well, I had hoped he would learn from the story of *Tai-Pan*, but he was smarter and just went to his mother."

Years later, when he was having sibling fights with his younger brother and sister, I pulled the same Tai-Pan tactic on him, and the kid fell for it. When the kids used to argue and fight, I said to Doug, "You are Tai-Pan, you are the leader. You have to be above it all." And he fell for it. My God, ha, ha!

"Daddy really fell for it?"

"He sure did, Alex."

It's amazing that what you say to children when they are younger comes back to them when they are older. When Doug became a dad and one night was trying to put Alex to sleep, I heard Doug say, "Alex, some day you will be head of the Noble House of Harte, but it will not be by inheritance; it will be by strong work and strong deeds." I said to myself, "Son of a gun—I got through to him!" I laughed and I cried.

"Grandpa, did Daddy really say that to Alex?"

"Believe it or not, Haleigh, he did."

"Did Daddy play sports or do fun things, Grandpa?"

When Doug was small, his mother and I wanted to give him everything that we thought a boy should have. We gave him piano lessons and all kinds of sports lessons. We schlepped him from museum to museum. For a while in little league, Doug played third base between that base and home, halfway between the two. His coach said to me, "Larry, your kid is fearless! I have never seen someone play so close!" And I said, "That's impossible. I know my son." Subsequently, we took Doug to the eye doctor, who gave him glasses, and after that, he played behind third base.

"That's funny, Grandpa. Daddy played away from third base because he needed glasses."

"It wasn't too funny then, but it is kind of amusing years later, Alex."

"Did Daddy have a bar mitzvah, Grandpa? We went to a bar mitzvah and Mommy and Daddy said that Alex will have a bar mitzvah one day."

"Yes, Haleigh, your daddy did have a bar mitzvah."

Doug wanted a special bar mitzvah, so we had his bar mitzvah party at a pool. It never occurred to us to ask if the kids could swim— we almost lost a few. He really did great at his bar mitzvah. He had a great touch with religion, and remained kosher like his mother and sister. Jon, on the other hand, would eat anything that was dead or alive. To this day, Doug is the kid who goes with me to the temple on the High Holidays. It is a very special feeling for me to be next to my son, who has the same feelings that were given to me by MY dad.

When Doug was about thirteen, I said to him, "You know, now that you have become a man and you are bar mitzvahed, we want you to be Keeper of the Photos of the family tree, so from now on, you will be in charge of the family tree. The kid listened. Doug became a photographer and the person who kept the records of the family events.

"Do you think Daddy will ask me to be the Keeper of the Photos?"

"I'm sure he will, Alex."

Doug also became a world-class sailor, doing ocean sailing and night sailing in calm and rough weather. He was very involved in sailing and belonged to a team that won a national championship. When the family was young, we were in the middle of a large storm on the water in the Caribbean. Doug, at the age of fourteen, guided us to safety while his mother was down in the hatch saying Hail Mary's. She was willing to change religion if it would have helped us survive.

"Daddy was sailing at fourteen?"

"Yes, at fourteen, and he is a great sailor, Alex."

"Did Grandma change her religion, Grandpa?"

"No, Haleigh, she's still Jewish; but Grandma thought about it if it would help her survive that sailing trip."

"Pickle juice!"

"Was Daddy good in school, Grandpa?"

"Doug was a good kid at school and very sociable."

During grade school and high school, Doug went out of his way to make friends that he still keeps in touch with today. He walks the extra step to keep the relationships going. In high school, he was in the photography club, which gave him the basis for being the excellent photographer that he is today. He played soccer and tennis. He was easy to bring up, compared to his siblings, Jonathan and Helaine. Doug listened—sometimes I don't know why he listened, but he did listen.

"I listen, Grandpa."

"That's great, Haleigh."

I must laugh when looking back. I remember when Doug joined the pre-med club at the high school. This club spent an extraordinary amount of time at the Saint Barnabas Medical Center in Livingston doing volunteer work and at times watching surgical procedures in the amphitheater. Doug got light-headed and his knees began to wobble at the sight of blood. That experience did it as far as Doug ever becoming a physician was concerned.

"Uncle Jon didn't get woozy did he?"

"No, Haleigh, he didn't get woozy. I guess that's why he's an infectious disease doctor and your daddy is an orthodontist."

"Pickle juice!"

During high school, Doug went to live in Spain with a couple who spoke no English. Doug studied Spanish in high school. He thought it would be a good idea to spend some time in Spain. We found a group that worked with fifteen year olds. They would place them in a Spanish home for the summer. Doug went by himself and stayed in Salamanca, Spain, with a poor Spanish family.

"Did Daddy learn Spanish?"

"Yes, Haleigh, he did. He had to speak Spanish to survive, since no one spoke English."

"Did Daddy like his trip?"

"I think he did. While he was in Spain, the family took him to the local hospital because he had digestive problems from the food and water."

Even though he was sick most of the time in Spain, we did not know it until he came home. He had a great time because he was by himself, and according to Doug there were no drinking laws. At the end of his stay in Salamanca, Doug went on a one-star cruise to Italy, France, and Spain. He fell in love with the archaeology at Pompeii, and the Italian women, and continues to save all kinds of artifacts from different parts of the world that he or the family brought back.

"Did Daddy go to your university after high school, Grandpa?"

"Yes and no, Alex. He went to Boston University first and then he went on to Penn."

After high school, Doug went to Boston University because he loved Boston. Doug loved Boston because of its revolutionary past and its beauty. Because of this, he looked forward to going to school in Boston. At Boston University, Doug was on the sailing squad. They wore wetsuits and sailed in the Charles River in November. Because of his background in sailing, he wanted to become an oceanographer.

"Daddy wanted to be an oceanographer?"

"He was very interested in this field, Alex. But after he found out what oceanographers made, he decided to go to dental school."

I was so pleased when he chose dental school instead of oceanography. In the back of my mind, I thought, "Gee! Maybe he will become an orthodontist someday." I kind of liked it when he went to study at the University of Pennsylvania dental school, which was my alma mater. I was pleased that he wanted to learn about other areas of dentistry, such as implants and surgery. He took an interest in an internship at Orange Memorial Hospital in implants and surgery. This background would help in treating patients. Then he went on to Penn to continue his orthodontic training. I could not have been happier. I now had someone to sell the practice to, and he had to buy it!

"Did he buy it when he finished school?"

"The day he graduated from orthodontic school, he took off for four weeks."

Doug is a saver, not only of knickknacks, but of money. He took off a month before beginning to work with me because he felt intuitively that that was the last month he would take off before he retired from orthodontics. Looking back, it was a smart move by

Doug.

"Why, Grandpa?"

"Well, Haleigh, he then came back to the office, and I gave him the keys, and said, 'Doug, it is YOURS! We are going away for three weeks. Work hard, and let me tell you, one way of learning is on the job. This is called truly learning on the job.' And learn he did!"

"Pickle juice!"

Doug has become a great orthodontist. I am so proud of him. Anybody who could work with ME every day and listen to all my preaching every day and still be around is a special person.

Recently, Doug and I went out for a beer. He said, "Dad, I gotta tell you something. It's about time that you buy me out." I said, "What? It's supposed to be the other way." Doug's reply was, "Well dad, I'm ready to retire, but I want to keep it in the family, so who else would be better than you to buy it back?" Doug's comment about me buying him out was very funny. I said to Doug, "Read the fine print of our contract. It says *you* buy me out when I'm ready."

"Maybe I'll be an orthodontist one day, Grandpa."

"Maybe, Alex."

"Daddy does a lot too, Grandpa, not just at work."

"Yes, he does."

Doug has been very active in the community, in Jewish activities, in charity, and the dental society. He was president of the Essex County Dental Society and president of the Alpha Omega dental fraternity, and he is also involved in teaching and giving lectures.

"What's Alpha Omega, Grandpa?"

"The Alpha Omega dental fraternity, Haleigh, is a professional dental fraternity where the students help each other in dental school; it is also a social base for getting together. They also have guest lecturers from the dental field."

Doug became president of the different societies because of his interest in dentistry and the knowledge that you have to get your name around to get referrals from other dentists and colleagues. Doug now teaches at the University of Pennsylvania orthodontics school in clinical orthodontics. I'm proud of him, of my son following my footsteps. It is the ultimate compliment to me.

In fact, when he was a junior at Penn Dental school, he gave, with me, a full-day lecture to the American Dental Association at their national meeting in Miami. Doug helped me with this full-day presentation on custom mouth guards. It was well received. He had to speak before a large audience, which gave him a great deal of self-assurance. This experience of speaking and feeling that he was well received made him feel good about himself. Later on, Doug was named one of the best orthodontists among the best doctors in the *Who's Who of Dentistry* in New Jersey. This is a great honor because your peers vote for you.

"Daddy's the best!"

"Yes, Haleigh, he was named one of the best."

"Uncle Doug is the best," Rebecca reiterates.

"How did Daddy meet Mommy, Grandpa?"

"Doug met his wife, Ronni, on a singles trip to Israel."

Doug and Ronni have a great deal in common. They love sports and entertaining and are terrific parents. Culturally, they enjoy the same things in music and art. Ronni is a special person, very giving and always concerned about my health and my feelings. I adore her. They have two great kids, Alex and Haleigh, and Ronni is a terrific mom.

"I love my mommy," Haleigh shouts while crossing her arms

across her chest as if she were hugging her mother.

Ronni is a very special person. Doug schlepped Ronni into the jungles of Central America. What woman would go to the jungles of Central America? Doug has also schlepped her on seven-demerit trips that are the direct opposite of five-star trips and on sailing vacations, and she has gone along. These trips were as bad as they can get and she went along, at least the first time. Ronni, like Doug, likes skiing, sailing, golf, and tennis and is quite good at most of them. She and Doug share these interests.

"Did you go on trips with Daddy, Grandpa?"

"Yes, Haleigh, I did."

Even though I traveled with my children as they were growing up to show them the world, I still have the wonderful opportunity of sharing the world with them as adults. In May of 2007, Doug and I went out to Seattle for an AAO (American Association of Orthodontists) meeting, with a pit stop in Portland, Oregon, first. We had a great time.

In Oregon, we saw Mount Hood, Mount Saint Helens, magnificent waterfalls, and the Cascades. We went to the Columbia River and we hiked on the Oregon Trail. I felt like Doug and I were Lewis and Clarke, exploring the wild, beautiful Northwest of our country. The skies were a perfect ten. We spent quite a few days in the Oregon area, walking the trails and enjoying the sites. The background of the mountains against the azure blue sky with small, cumulus clouds was majestic. The temperature was in the high fifties. The cascades of water flowing down the mountains reminded me of my early days of camping as a Boy Scout.

"You camped outside with Daddy, Papa Larry?"

"Not outside, Alex, but it was still camping to me. It was nice.

Even though we stayed in hotels this time, Doug and I were camping together."

"Oregon sounds pretty, Grandpa."

"It was beautiful, Haleigh."

"It sounds beautiful," Rebecca yells and sprints up and begins to run around me and Alex as we continue to throw the baseball.

In Oregon, we also saw the Hughes H-4 Hercules, nicknamed the "Spruce Goose," which Henry Kaiser envisioned and Howard Hughes designed and completed in 1947. It only flew about a hundred feet during World War II, and it stands in good condition at the Evergreen Aviation Museum in McMinnville, Oregon. I always wanted to see the Spruce Goose. It brought back memories of my interest in flying and my days in the Air Force. Doug loves history, and I think he enjoyed this trip back in time.

"What else did you see, Grandpa?"

"We went to a few places, Alex."

We also visited the Portland Japanese Garden, which, I understand, next to gardens in Japan, is the most beautiful Japanese garden in the world. The garden is located within Washington Park. It was quiet, there was solitude, and we had the smell of roses. The perfume of the warm Pacific air was going through my hair—well, what there was left of my hair.

"I want to see the garden, Grandpa!"

"One day, Haleigh, maybe we'll visit it."

"Pickle juice!"

We went to the Portland Classical Chinese Garden, which is right in the middle of Portland. It reminds me of a place in China: no cell phones, quiet, and in some ways similar to Japan, because they both are Asian. Both have places for solitude, thinking, and contemplating, a great repast for me, but really for all of us. It is a sensational place for anyone to visit, stay, think, dream, and truly smell the roses.

"Can we visit that garden too, Grandpa?"

"Yes, of course, Haleigh."

We visited some five or six wineries, and I swear Doug must have bought up all the Pinot Noir. Some of the wineries we went to were Lange and Rex Hill. We went on so many wine-tasting tours that we were smashed by twelve noon. We still have some wine left over from the trip and Doug's wine-buying spree. He bought so many cases of wine, I thought he was going to take out a second mortgage on his house. He now has a beautiful wine cellar with hundreds of bottles of wines. I find it amazing that having been a kid from Brooklyn who grew up on beer and milk, I now have three sophisticated kids with a strong knowledge and love of wine.

"Daddy loves his wine cellar, Grandpa."

"I love his wine cellar too, Alex."

"Grandpa, you said you went to Seattle too. Did you vacation in Seattle?"

"Yes, we went on to Seattle for the meeting."

Oregon was truly one of the neatest vacations we ever had. We walked, we hiked, we drank, we talked, we had a blast, Doug and I. After adventuring through Oregon, we set off for the meeting in Seattle, and I did my best to introduce him to my colleagues. I think I've run out of people to introduce him to.

"What was the meeting about?"

"The orthodontic meeting was about new technical trends on straightening teeth."

"Did you like Seattle? Was it like Oregon?"

"Seattle wasn't like Oregon, but it was a nice place, Alex."

Seattle was a great town for museums, ferry rides, and a fantastic fish market. At the fish market, men would throw forty-pound salmon to each other like they were potato chips. Fish and chips in Seattle are different from anywhere else in the world. The taste of a freshly grilled salmon on a bun cannot be described. The salmon came from the Columbia River. I'm not big on fish and chips, but I had it TWICE, once with halibut and once with salmon. Both were super fresh. The halibut was from Alaska and the salmon came right off the river. I never knew that fish and chips could taste that good!

"Tell us about another trip you took with Daddy, Grandpa."

"Another fun time, Haleigh, was when Doug and I were marshals at a Pro-Am golf tournament for two days."

During those days we were able to chat with many of the pro basketball and pro football players. We were also marshals at the U.S. Open at the Baltusrol Golf Club in Springfield, New Jersey. Here we had the opportunity to meet and chat with the great golfers of our time, Tiger Woods and Phil Nicholson among others.

"Is there a trip you remember the most of all your trips with Daddy, Grandpa?"

"Yes, Alex, one of the most memorable trips thus far with my son Doug was our trip to Vero Beach, Florida."

Vero Beach is the spring training base for the Los Angeles Dodgers, as it was for the Brooklyn Dodgers. And now, just like when the Brooklyn Dodgers had their last year playing in Brooklyn, we visited there the last year that the Los Angeles Dodgers would train in Vero Beach. Doug and I went to pay homage to the Dodgers and, in some way, to replay a dream that I've had for sixty years.

"What team were they playing, Grandpa?"

"On this day, the Dodgers played the Red Sox, and the Dodgers won. That was great!"

They had Larry King, a talk show host, introducing himself as a guy from Brooklyn. They had Vin Scully, who broadcasted games when I was a kid in Brooklyn. But what made this event so special is that, some sixty years ago, the Brooklyn Dodgers had first come to Vero Beach, Florida. In those days, the Dodgers had players like Furillo and Robinson, Reese, Snyder, Padres, Camilli, and Hodges. They were the boys of summer and, I too, in my youth, also was a boy of summer. They played recklessly, they played with enthusiasm, they played with love, and it ended with their first World Series victory in 1955.

So, on March 8, 2008, with my son, I went back sixty years to memories of my childhood, of my dreams, where once again I was one of the boys of summer. I have tears in my eyes and a pang in my heart for all these years, for all these dreams, not only for the Dodgers, who came from Brooklyn, but for my friends and myself. We began together as little kids on the block, and as the years went on, our bodies have changed. Our mental acuity may change, but our dreams stay the same, for we once were, also, the boys of summer.

Alex at eight years old was in a little league baseball game. The bat he used seemed to be bigger than he was. He gave a mighty swing and hit a line-drive double into left field. The next kid got a hit, and Alex turned third base and slid into home plate. His knee hit the catcher's shin guard. Alex was writhing in pain. His dad, Doug, and I ran onto the field. We were concerned that he had broken his leg. Eventually, most of the pain subsided with the use of ice packs. As Alex was carried off the field, he received a standing ovation from the people in the stands and from both teams. Both teams stopped the game and came over to shake his hand. This was American sportsmanship at its best. I had a tear in my eye. I got the feeling that Alex might have been thinking, "Gee, I should get hurt AGAIN someday! Nobody ever applauded for me like this!"

"I was thinking something like that Grandpa," Alex admits with a small grin on his face.

"What about Mommy? Tell me about Mommy, please!" Rebecca shrieks as she continues to run around Alex and me.

"Tell us about Aunt Helaine, Grandpa."

"I'd love to tell you about your aunt, Haleigh."

Rebecca comes around the corner behind Alex and runs into Haleigh. She tags Haleigh on the shoulder and takes off once more. Alex and I decide to take a break and make ourselves comfortable in a seat in the shade. Haleigh springs from the ground and runs after Rebecca. Rebecca stops running, and Haleigh rams right into her from behind. The two fall to the ground and begin to tickle each other, giggling the entire time. As a fresh breeze sweeps through the backyard, the echoing laughter paints the background of a story of a daughter, a mother, an aunt, and a friend.

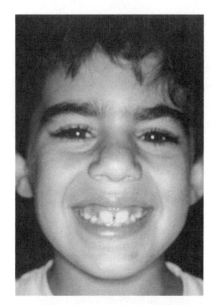

Douglas Harte,
age six, 1968

Our family home, the "House of Harte," Livingston, New Jersey, 2001

With Douglas (right), getting comfortable at a conference in Bermuda, 1994

Alex (left) and Haleigh Harte show off their fashionable styles, 2006

Alex (left) and Haleigh give a big hug for the camera, 2007

Alex and Haleigh, 2009

One of the "boys of summer," reliving the memories of my beloved Brooklyn Dodgers, Vero Beach, Florida, 2008

My Daughter, Helaine

I am going to make this day a great day.
—*Helaine Harte*

My daughter, Helaine, was born in Livingston, New Jersey, at St. Barnabas Hospital. In first grade she was taught the I.P.A. (International Phonetic Alphabet), a technique for sounding out words. It worked wonders with my daughter. On her first test she spelled the word "ancestors" as "aunt sisters." Notwithstanding two Ivy League degrees, she still can't spell.

"I can spell, Papa Larry," Rebecca shares with pride as she rolls around with Haleigh in their tickling battle. "I can spell my name—R-E-B-E-C-C-A!"

"That's wonderful, Rebecca."

"I can spell too!" Haleigh stops for a moment, thinks hard, and spells out, "H-A-L-E-I-G-H."

Alex turns to me with a smirk on his face and declares, "I can spell my name too, Grandpa, along with other words."

"I think it's great that all of you are fantastic spellers. Helaine could've used your help when she was younger."

"Grandpa?"

"Yes, Alex."

"How did my daddy and Uncle Jon get along with Aunt Helaine?"

"They got along like brothers and sisters should get along, I suppose. Most importantly, they loved and cared for each other very much."

Helaine is a true sister. Every time she did something wrong, she would always blame her older brother, Doug. We wound up killing Doug because we felt that Doug should know better because he was the older person. Poor Doug; Helaine always got him in trouble. Helaine's bedroom, which was the size of a closet, was always messy. She blamed Doug for messing it up. Hence, Doug would get in trouble. Doug and Jon would be sitting watching a show on television and Helaine would saunter over and change the channel to what she wanted. Doug would change it back and Helaine would cry—Doug's fault again.

"I understand what Daddy went through with Aunt Helaine," Alex states as he nods in recognition of the similarities with his sister's behavior.

Helaine, even though she was younger than her older brothers, was their protector. The bully of the neighborhood once was taunting her older brothers. Helaine promptly took a shovel and clobbered the guy on the head. She was about nine and the bully was about thirteen. That ended any bullying of the Harte family!

"That's my mommy," cheers Rebecca, "the protector!"

"That she was, Rebecca, the protector of the Harte family."

"Did Aunt Helaine really hit a guy in the head with a shovel,

Grandpa?"

"She sure did, Haleigh."

"Pickle juice!"

Helaine, although very loved by her brothers, was by all definition the little sister. Once, we were taking a trip through the Virginia countryside and stopped at a rest stop. There was so much arguing going on in the back, we thought we would give them a rest. We finally got back in the car, and it was so quiet and we were so happy until I turned around and realized that we had left Helaine! Her brothers never said a word.

"Is that why it was so quiet?" Alex laughs hysterically while thinking about how he would do the same to his sister just for some peace and quiet in the car ride.

"Yes, Alex, your aunt was quite the chatterbox and instigator with her brothers."

"Grandpa, do you think the way they act is because they're girls?"

"Well, Alex, that's a good question," I respond carefully, contemplating the answer.

"Grandpa, do you?"

After a considerable amount of deliberation, I feel safe in saying, "I think they are just very beautiful and creative females that have a lot of energy."

"So it's not because they are girls?"

"Let's just say that everyone is unique and has their own way of acting."

"What happened to Mommy," Rebecca interjects impatiently as she waits to hear about her mother's abandonment in Virginia.

"Yeah, Grandpa, what happened to Aunt Helaine?" Haleigh adds with a hint of impatience. Rebecca and Haleigh try to catch their breath as they move toward our seats.

We went back, and there she was—sitting on the sidewalk at the front of the restaurant, caring less. Helaine had to endure her two older brothers as much as they had to endure their younger sister. Once, on a family cruise around the Greek islands, we had an extra room for the children. The room only had two beds, which the boys would use, so we put a cot in the middle. Voilà! Helaine had a bed too, but the boys gleefully stepped on her all night long getting out of bed.

"Poor Mommy!" Rebecca shouts.

"Did Aunt Helaine get a shovel and hit them over the head, Grandpa?"

"No, Haleigh, your aunt fought back probably with a pillow or something softer. But in the end, she was outnumbered two to one."

"That isn't fair, Grandpa."

"No, it isn't, Haleigh, but it does help build character."

Helaine was used to getting the short end of the stick. The boys had bedrooms in our first house, and she had a closet. Once on a family trip to Hollywood, we decided to eat dinner at a very expensive restaurant. When Helaine saw the prices, she knew the deal—she would be getting the bread plate and sharing everyone's meal. Her only hope was that they ordered something she liked.

"Did anyone ever order what she liked?"

"Someone always ordered something Helaine liked, Haleigh."

"Why couldn't Mommy order her own food?"

"Sometimes, Rebecca, the food would be really expensive. In order to save money, your mommy would just eat from our plates."

"Did Mommy want to eat from your plates?"

"I don't know, Rebecca. I don't think your mommy really cared too much that she did. It was just the price of being the youngest.

Helaine is a strong and independent woman. Things never really seemed to faze her. She is a thinker, a doer, and a survivor.

"Me too!" Rebecca exclaims.

"Yes, you are a lot like your mother, Rebecca."

One day Helaine's mother and I received a call from the principal of her school. She said we must come to the school. It brought back memories of when my mother had to go to school because the teacher had said I was a troublemaker. I said, "Oh my God, a chip off the old block!"

"Was Mommy in trouble?"

"No, Rebecca, she wasn't in trouble."

The school called us in advance to tell us that Helaine would be receiving recognition at a ceremony and asked if we could come. This was fifth grade. It was a special ceremony that was not the usual protocol for the school. As Helaine would later say, "I reached the pinnacle of my life in fifth grade; it was downhill from then on." I used to laugh when she made this comment because I used to tell my kids, "I reached the pinnacle of my life in eighth grade. It was downhill from then on for me." We went to the special ceremony at her school and to our surprise Helaine won all the honors in academics and extracurricular activities. We were so proud.

"Wow! Aunt Helaine is really smart, Grandpa."

"Yes, Haleigh, she is very smart."

"I bet she got a lot of attention that day."

"She did, but she wasn't interested in the attention, Haleigh."

Helaine didn't want to sit around being praised for her achievements; she just wanted to go and chat with her friends. It was no big deal to her, but it was a big deal to her family and even to the boys. To Helaine, it was no big deal at all—she just was herself.

"Tell us more, Papa Larry," Rebecca hollers with excitement. "I want to know more about my mommy!"

"There's so much to share. I'd love to tell you more."

Helaine has always been competitive, both in academics and extracurricular activities. In high school, Helaine played field hockey. They called her "The Enforcer," which meant if anybody hit any of her classmates, she took care of them. My god—imagine a girl called The Enforcer! That is our Helaine.

"My mommy is 'The Enforcer,'" Rebecca proudly screeches.

"Aunt Helaine was tough," Alex acknowledges.

"Yes, she was tough and talented. She loved sports."

Helaine enjoyed field hockey and did not practice a lot. Like everything else in life, she'd rather play the real game and not practice that much.

"Mommy always tells me, 'Practice makes perfect,'" Haleigh advises us.

"It does, Haleigh. But your aunt didn't really go by that motto too much."

"Pickle juice!"

"What other sports did Aunt Helaine play?"

"Besides field hockey, Alex, she played volleyball."

Helaine would literally dive for the volleyball regardless of possible injuries. She gave it her all in sports. One day I came home early from work for lunch, which I never did. Lo and behold, Helaine was also home. She was resting for her big field hockey playoff game. I am a tremendous sports fan, but I am even a bigger fan of education, which is what she should've been getting during that lunchtime at her school.

"Did she get in trouble?"

"Yes, Haleigh, she did get in trouble. I would not let her play in the game."

"Was Mommy sad she didn't get to play?"

"She was sad, Rebecca."

Boy was I unpopular in the family and probably the neighborhood too! Another time I remember that my popularity poll went down was when Judi and I went out one evening. We came home to a town party, at my house! We weren't even invited. Helaine had a little gathering of a lot of people. There were beer bottles thrown all over the lawn, which I picked up. Then I had to drive the kids home who had been drinking. The police were called to the house by neighbors and fortunately they gave me the benefit of a very big doubt. That was the first and last party Helaine had at our house without us being there.

"Sounds like Aunt Helaine is a little bit like you, Grandpa," Haleigh informs me.

"What do you mean?"

Alex quickly steps in and blurts out, "She did bad things as a kid, just like you."

"I guess she did." I couldn't help but grin and feel proud of the comparison.

"Don't stop, Papa Larry," Rebecca demands, "you still have more to tell us about Mommy."

"Besides being busy with sports and academics and other activities, Helaine decided to get a job."

Helaine could not sit still; she was continually in motion. She had to always be doing something. Aside from academics and extracurricular school activities, she found time for jobs after school and on the weekends. Apparently it never affected her grades. She never told us she had a job until she had the job.

"Why did she get a job?"

"She worked for many reasons, Rebecca."

I used to use guilt to induce my children to make money, no matter how little or how much they earned. I guess this guilt, along with her excess energy, was the catalyst to her getting jobs. She enjoyed the challenge of working in the local stationery store and the dress shop. She also enjoyed the money. She went through many after-school jobs and even worked in a fancy restaurant in West Orange, New Jersey.

"Mommy worked at a restaurant?"

"Yes, Rebecca, she did."

When she was old enough, Helaine worked as a waitress at a fancy restaurant, which she loved because it was fast-paced, she made lots of money, and it meant she could stay out until two a.m. She mentioned that when the restaurant ran out of coffee, they would dilute whatever they had and call it decaf. Now when I order decaf I always ask, "Is it regular?" when the waiter or waitress pours it. It keeps them on their toes.

"Papa Larry, did Aunt Helaine go through jobs like you did when you were young?"

"Well, Alex, unlike me, I never found out if she was fired from a job like I was or if she left for something else."

"Grandpa, I want to hear more about Aunt Helaine and the other stuff she did when she was young."

"What do you want me to tell you, Haleigh?"

"You told us about school, sports, and her jobs. What about other stuff she did?"

"Besides jobs, Helaine spent part of her high school experience in Washington, D.C."

"Why did she go to Washington, D.C.?"

"To hobnob with politicians, Haleigh."

Helaine was a congressional page to Congressman Peter Rodino of Watergate fame (he was the chair of the impeachment hearings that led to President Richard Nixon's resignation), and a senate intern to Senator Frank Lautenberg during the school year and part of the summer.

"Grandpa, how did Aunt Helaine become an intern and page?"

"I don't know how she found out about this opportunity to work in Washington, D.C., Alex."

"She was young, Papa Larry."

"She was young, Rebecca. But she was old enough to go since she was in high school."

"Did you go with Mommy?"

"No, I didn't go with her, nor did her mother. Helaine went all alone."

One day she hopped a train to Washington and got the job. She went by herself and stayed in the student dorms while working. Helaine, to her credit, got both of these positions by persevering, taking a train to Washington, and taking a chance. She liked the excitement and the pay.

Helaine has a montage of photos that were taken of her and many of the leading politicians at that time. I remember a picture of her with Senator Dole, Senator Lautenberg, and Congressman Rodino. There were many others. In my opinion, what she learned from Washington was that it is very difficult for a congressperson to concentrate on creative laws and leadership when he or she is running every two years for office. She felt that senators had more time to spend on issues since they only had to run for office every six years.

Helaine, in so many ways, was what I had wanted to be, and I seemed to nudge her a lot. When I was a kid, I wanted to go to Washington and serve my country and perhaps even become president. I didn't do it because I didn't have the financial and parental guidance. I guess I encouraged Helaine in that direction.

"Papa Larry."

"Yes, Rebecca."

"Why do you tell Mommy she has a dirty left ear?"

"Your mommy and I have a standing joke between each other."

"What do you mean?"

"Well, Rebecca, one day I made a joke about Helaine's left ear. Helaine said it was silly. To this day it is still a standing joke between us. I say, 'How is your dirty left ear?'"

"What does it mean?"

"It was a way of endearment because she could do no wrong in my eyes, even when she was dead wrong."

"Did Aunt Helaine go to your college, Grandpa?"

"Yes, Alex, she went to Columbia College."

"What did she do in college?"

"She was very active at Columbia, besides traveling and studying abroad."

During college, Helaine also attended Cambridge in England and the Sorbonne in Paris. She spent from May to August at the schools studying French and European history at the Sorbonne and political science and philosophy at Cambridge.

At Columbia College, aside from academics, she was involved in sports and many activities and councils. She was also the manger of the Columbia wrestling team.

"Was Mommy a good manager?"

"She was quite the manager, Rebecca."

"How did Aunt Helaine keep up with so much?"

"She was good at organizing her time and getting others to help her out once in a while."

At times she would have family members help her with her essays. It seems to me that she never studied, but she got great grades. She would bring home topics, and her brothers would read the books and write the essays. Years later, Doug and Jon would say, "We got an 'A' at Columbia!"

"Daddy and Uncle Jon are funny, Grandpa."

"Yes they are, Haleigh."

"Mommy sounds a lot like you, Papa Larry."

"You think so, Rebecca?"

"Yes, Papa Larry. Mommy travels a lot like you."

"Yes, that is true."

"Mommy also got in trouble as a kid like you, and Mommy went to your school."

"Yes, that is true too."

"You see, Papa Larry, Mommy is a lot like you."

I think that in some ways Helaine did look up to me and wanted to follow in my footsteps. She decided to go to Columbia, my alma mater, as an undergrad. She also stayed in my hall, Hartley Hall. I was involved in wrestling at Columbia, and she became the manager of the team. Looking back, I am so proud and honored that she wanted to emulate me in some small ways.

"What did Aunt Helaine study?"

"She studied business and political science, Alex."

At Columbia, while studying for her undergrad degree, she took Chinese at my request. Another mistake of mine. I meant well, but you never know what the wrath of the gods can do!

"Why was it bad?"

"It was bad because she went to China during a bad time, Haleigh."

After Columbia, she went BY HERSELF to the Beijing School of Economics. Helaine wanted to increase her knowledge and use of the Chinese language. She was tired of eating at Chinese restaurants to practice, and so was the family. She wanted to learn the Mandarin language and how the Chinese do business.

"How did Aunt Helaine go to the school?"

"She researched and applied to the school, Alex."

The Beijing School of Economics was a very difficult school to get into. People from all over the world tried for the chance to be accepted by this school. She found this school, apparently, like most things in her life, by researching and bird-dogging. Many countries of the world sent their very best students to this school. In fact, she met her future husband, Bogdan, who came from Bulgaria, at the school. Bogdan was the pride and joy of Bulgaria. He sure wasn't the pride and joy of me.

"Mommy's husband is Daddy," Rebecca argues.

"Yes, your daddy is her husband now. Your mommy and your daddy were married to other people before. That is how you have two half brothers."

"That man was Mommy's husband first?"

"Yes, he was Mommy's husband first."

"Tell us more about Aunt Helaine in China. What did she do

there, Grandpa?"

"While in school in Beijing, Haleigh, Helaine worked for CNN as an information gatherer."

Since there were very few Americans in China with a background in Chinese, Helaine was a perfect prospect for CNN. As an aside, while Helaine was in China, the CIA came to our house to investigate Helaine and our family. They knew more about us than we did about ourselves. In fact, if I could find that CIA investigator, he could probably write a better history of our family than any of us!

"Do they know about me?"

"They know about everyone, Rebecca."

"That's scary!"

"It is scary, Haleigh, but at the same time, they protect us."

"Pickle juice!"

Also, while Helaine was in China, I had the opportunity of having a photo taken with President George Bush, Sr. with his arm around me. I sent this picture to Helaine in China. When the Chinese people saw that President Bush had his arm around me, it meant that I was the "honored one," and from that time on, Helaine's status grew.

"That's cool, Grandpa!"

"I thought it was pretty neat, Alex, to meet the president and have a picture taken with him too."

During the time Helaine was in the school and worked for CNN, she was also in the middle of the Tiananmen Square massacre, where the Chinese war was taking place. She was in the middle of the firing of guns and tanks.

"Was Mommy okay?"

"We could not get in touch with her for quite a few days, Rebecca."

Helaine finally was able to get through the tank blockade and to an airport. Her mother had her on six flights to different countries to get her out of China. She was lucky to get on a plane. Incidentally, all the other major countries got their nationals out, except for the United States. Does this tell you something about the diplomacy of the United States?

When Helaine flew into JFK airport in New York, she arrived to a heroine's welcome. The press and television media were alerted that the first American to leave China would be on this plane. This was big news in our country because there was a news blackout in China, and the Americans wanted to hear what was really happening at Tiananmen. All the news and TV media were there. When Helaine got off the plane, she looked exhausted. But when she saw the family and all the television coverage focusing on her, her eyes lit up, her smiled broadened (notwithstanding the lack of sleep for over forty-eight hours), and it was show time! She had her face on the front page of the New York newspapers. She was interviewed by so many TV stations and programs that the family had to get away on our own vacation. The media was camping out outside our house. We have a family story that wherever Helaine goes out in the world, some kind of problem always breaks out. We think that she was a CIA front girl for trouble.

"That's because she takes after you, Grandpa," Haleigh deduces. "She's used to getting in trouble just like you."

"That may be true, Haleigh."

"What about Mommy's first husband?"

"What about him, Rebecca?"

"How did Mommy meet him? When did Mommy marry him?"

"She married him soon after coming back from China."

After China, she got married to a Bulgarian. I went to Bulgaria a few times with Helaine and my son-in-law, whose dad had tremendous connections to the secret service and the executive and legislative body of Bulgaria. His father was a colonel in the army and assigned to the Bulgarian ministry of defense in Sofia.

"His father sounds like a very important person."

"Yes, he was an important person, Alex."

We went to parties in Sofia, in the Bulgarian mountains, and in Washington and New York. The country, although it was trying to become democratic, was as corrupt as could be. The black market was everywhere, but it was exciting. I got to meet the president of Bulgaria, Zhelyu Zhelev, all the rest of the executive staff members, and many in the legislative departments. I had the opportunity of going to the Bulgarian embassy, and they treated us like we were just cousins coming for a visit. My only regret—my only one—is that since Helaine divorced my son-in-law, I may have lost the opportunity to be the ambassador to Luxembourg under a Bulgarian passport. There went my big chance! But it was worth my daughter's divorce.

"You could've been the ambassador to Luxembourg?"

"It's a joke, Haleigh. I really wasn't going to be the ambassador to Luxembourg."

"Pickle juice!"

"What was the wedding like for Mommy?"

"In preparation for her wedding to Bogdan, Helaine had her friends and Bogdan's family stay at our house two weeks before the wedding."

Helaine never was known as a stranger. After fifteen minutes with people, she was their friend and was able to work with them, and they liked her. Guests came from all over the world. They slept in sleeping bags, except for Bogdan's parents, for whom my ex had a special bedroom built in the basement. At the wedding, Helaine introduced us to friends from Bulgaria, England, France, Spain, Germany, Japan, China, Canada, Colombia, Chile, and other countries that I don't recall. The wedding was amazing in that all of these people spoke English. They spoke it very well compared to Americans who try to learn foreign languages and sound as if they are speaking pig Latin when they talk.

"Was her husband an important man in Bulgaria?

"Yes, because he was the son of an important man. He was also an analyst for A.S.I. International Trading Company. Bogdan was a summa cum laude graduate of Rutgers University."

"Why didn't you like him, Papa Larry?

"I never liked him, but Helaine was my daughter and she said she loved him."

Fortunately, they had no children when they were divorced. Helaine deserved better. She helped him out with his citizenship— by marrying her, he attained his U.S. citizenship. Also, with our family's prodding and helping with essays and applications, he got into Harvard Business School and graduated. Helaine, like all our kids, was a real giver. For a while, they communicated with each other after the divorce. I have no idea where he is or what he is doing now.

"I'm glad Mommy met Daddy!"

"I am too, Rebecca."

I didn't want to see my daughter's marriage suffer, even though I didn't like Bogdan. I always wanted the best for her. I remember how after Helaine's breakup with a boyfriend when she was younger we were talking in her room. Her heart was breaking, and because I loved her, so was mine. All I could tell her was how beautiful she was and that she would find someone better someday. She just sobbed in my arms. Sometimes as parents we feel so helpless. I felt this way too when she decided to marry Bogdan.

"What did Aunt Helaine do while he went to school?" Haleigh asks.

"Your aunt worked while her husband was in school."

Helaine's first job was in Cincinnati, Ohio, at Procter and Gamble—the Harvard of marketing—in brand management. She was accepted at this job after graduating from Columbia College and the Columbia Business School. Helaine's major at Columbia was political science, and she minored in Chinese. She received a B.A. at Columbia College and a Masters in Business at Columbia Business School. She and her husband commuted from Cincinnati to Boston when Bogdan was studying at Harvard. This was quite a place, Cincinnati. A quotation of Mark Twain says it all: "If you have one year to live, live it in Cincinnati, and it will feel like the rest of your life."

After Procter and Gamble, Helaine went to Boston to work, while Bogdan finished his studies at Harvard Business School. After he graduated, he was accepted into a prestigious consulting firm in New York, and they moved to the New York area. The job did not last long, however, and neither did the marriage. He stayed home and apparently "forgot" to show up for work.

"It doesn't sound good."

"No, it doesn't, Rebecca."

"What did Aunt Helaine do in New York?"

"Helaine went into the liquor industry, in marketing, Alex."

Her first job was at Diageo, which marketed Romana Sambuca. This took her to Europe—Italy and France—more times than some people brush their teeth. She then worked for a vodka company out of San Francisco, although she continued to live in New York. At this point in their life, she and Bogdan got divorced. She was out west for her job more times than most people floss their teeth. Helaine then went into her own private consulting business in New York City, where she markets products of wine and beer from the Orient, the U.S., and Europe.

"Mommy goes to a lot of places."

"Yes she does, Rebecca, and she has a lot of friends too."

Helaine has more friends than most people meet in a lifetime. She has friends from grade school with whom she keeps in touch through letters, phone calls, and emails. Through the years, she's gone to many social gatherings where her work also led her to meet different people. She literally knows and keeps in touch with people all over the world, whether it's England or Monte Carlo or Kentucky.

"Tell us more about Aunt Helaine."

"She still enjoys her sports, Haleigh."

Helaine is involved in jogging and triathlons, and continues to be very competitive in whatever she wants. To this day, I still love to tell the story of Helaine when she once was running in a triathlon, coming in way ahead of her boyfriend at that time. He felt miserable that she had beaten him so badly. I said to him, "It's okay—there is always chess!" He said forlornly, "No way—she beats me there, too!" That's our Helaine!

"I want to hear about Daddy."

"Of course, Rebecca."

Helaine subsequently married David, who seems to be an

extraordinarily wonderful person. They have been married for a few years. David is very interested in charitable work. He is a graduate of Georgetown University and is now attending the Wharton School of Business. He has two fine sons, Tyler and Casey, by a previous marriage, and he shares joint custody of them with his former wife. Helaine and David also have a daughter together, Rebecca, and they live in Philadelphia. They also have their house in New York. They live in Philadelphia to be near David's sons and frequently come to New York City to stay in their city home for social and cultural events. Helaine and David love the triathlon, culture, and raising their children.

"That's me! I'm one of their children!"

"Yes, that's you, Rebecca."

As you can see, Helaine is a real go-getter! She takes life in stride and is always full of energy. When Helaine was pregnant with Rebecca, she was still a bundle of energy. Not even pregnancy could calm her down. Like all the kids, she does not complain and goes after life every day, every hour, and every minute.

"Is Aunt Helaine 'Daddy's little girl,' Grandpa?"

"Yes, she is my little girl, Haleigh."

I wouldn't say I was protective of Helaine throughout the years, but I am protective of her from time to time. Once, a while back, Helaine's friend's father scolded her for something she did. To me, it made no difference whether she was right or wrong. How dare he! I was furious and ready to give him a piece of my mind! They had to restrain me. We still laugh about it today. I'm still protective of my Helaine, even though I know she is a strong, independent woman who can take care of herself. To me, she'll always be Daddy's little girl.

"Grandpa, what about Uncle Jon?"

"Jon was quite different from your daddy and aunt, Alex."

"I want to hear about Uncle Jon," Haleigh proclaims.

"Me too, Papa Larry," Rebecca seconds.

As I get my second wind, Alex and I begin to practice ball again. Rebecca scampers into the house, while Haleigh practices her dance moves. A few minutes later, Rebecca skips back into the yard and mimics Haleigh's dancing. Three sets of anxious ears tune in like satellites as I embark them on a journey of learning about their Uncle Jonathan.

*Helaine Harte, four years old,
1970*

Helaine, 1970

RACING ★ ★ ★ FINAL

TRIGGERMAN IN BYRNE DEATH GUILTY
Stories on page 3

DAILY◎NEWS

35¢   NEW YORK'S PICTURE NEWSPAPER®   Wednesday, June 7, 1989

ESCAPE FROM BEIJING

ANTHONY CASALE DAILY NEWS

Back from the gunfire and terror of Beijing, Barbara Catherwood (▲) wipes a tear on arrival at JFK Airport last night. She brought two young sons but husband stayed behind. There was a hug waiting for returning student Helaine Harte (◆) from dad, Dr. Larry Harte of Livingston, N.J.   CLARENCE SHEPPARD DAILY NEWS

New York Daily News *article, 1989*

With my daughter, Helaine Harte (left), who competed in a New York City triathlon as a participant in the Leukemia and Lymphoma Society's team in training, 1996

David Rhode, me, and Helaine, holding Rebecca Rhode

Rebecca Rhode modeling Burberry with a picture-perfect smile, 2008

Rebecca, 2010

My Son Jonathan

Dad, now this is a great wine!

—Jonathan Harte

Jonathan was born in Orange, New Jersey. Jon was named after my dad, Joseph. Since Jon was born, we knew he marched to the beat of a different drummer. When he was about two, the neighbors found him walking down the middle of our street with nothing on. It didn't bother him. He was our hippie. He did things his way, which eventually turned out to be a great way. Jon was definitely a handful. There was never a dull moment in the Harte household. Between Jon and Helaine, Judi and I definitely had our work cut out for us.

"Grandpa, how was Uncle Jon a handful?"

"Uncle Jon used to do things that made us want to kill him some times, Alex."

When Jon was seven, he wasn't paying attention in his class and we took him to the eye doctor, thinking he had problems seeing. The doctor said that he needed glasses. We gave him his glasses, and he lost all THREE sets. I wanted to kill him! After six months Jon went back for a checkup. The doctor said that his eyes had improved so much that he did not need glasses anymore. Basically, Jon was not paying attention in his class. Incidentally, Jon never wore his glasses, and to this day he does not wear glasses. Grade school was a place for dreaming for Jon. He enjoyed daydreaming a great deal and apparently it helped him be what he is today.

"I love school, Grandpa."

"You do, Haleigh?"

"Yes, Grandpa. I like school because I get to be with my friends. I pay attention, too, because our teacher gives us rewards for being good."

Another time, we were at the dinner table, and Jon spilled milk all over the table and onto my pants. I wanted to kill him again, but Jon said, "Dad, I had a good day at school and in sports. I ate all my food and I listened to Mom. Even Ted Williams only goes two for five, and he made the Hall of Fame!" I wanted to cry and say, "I'm sorry."

"Uncle Jon was smart, Grandpa. He got out of trouble."

"Yes, Alex, he did get out of trouble. He always knew what to say."

"Grandpa, what other funny stuff did Uncle Jon do when he was young?" Haleigh inquires.

"Was Uncle Jon silly?" Rebecca adds.

"Your Uncle Jon was always in his own world."

Once, Jon was playing little league baseball. I guess he was dreaming, and the ball hit him in the head while he was playing center field. I don't know what he was daydreaming about, but I hope it was worth it. Then Jon came up to bat with the bases loaded in the last inning. His manager said, "Jon, get closer to the plate!" The pitch came and hit Jon in the head. The team won the game and I wanted to kill his manager.

"Did Uncle Jon's team win, Grandpa?"

"Yes, Alex, they did win the game."

"Why did you want to kill the manager, Grandpa?"

"His manager had him move up on purpose. I wanted to kill the manager before he got Jon killed."

Another time, when Jon was about ten years of age, we were sailing in a race at Captiva Island, located on the west coast of Florida, in a Soling. Doug was in one boat with two sailors from the Great Lakes, and they were leading the race. There were twenty-five-mile-per-hour winds, and five-to-ten-foot waves. My son Jon kept saying to me, "We could win, Dad!" I was trying to just survive, and Jon just didn't know any better. Looking back, neither of us should have been out in that kind of weather.

"Why did you go to that island, Papa Larry?"

"Captiva Island was a great island for weather, sailing, and vacation, Rebecca."

"Did you have a nickname for Uncle Jon?"

"Yes, Haleigh, I did."

Jon was my "Boo Boo." In a fierce snowstorm, he walked with me a mile to a diner. The other kids would never do that; they would say we were crazy. Jon always went. I have a special place in my heart for Jon. "Boo Boo" were my special words of endearment for him.

"I love the name 'Boo Boo,' Papa Larry!"

"I like the nickname too, Rebecca."

"Was Uncle Jon good in school, Grandpa?"

"Jon never got bad grades in school, Alex, but he did have other issues."

There were many times when Jon or his homework just never

made it to school. The dog or the wind took the homework, or he missed the bus, but Jon was himself and he was happy. His teachers wanted to know what he looked like. I am not sure if to this day they could tell you what he looked like. Jon was very laid back. Surprisingly, we were never called in to school to account for Jon's missing homework or his missing the bus.

"What do you mean by 'laid back', Grandpa?"

"Your uncle, Haleigh, basically just went along with things."

As an example, he would keep his hair long, and when his mother took him to the barber to have his hair cut short, he objected, but not strenuously, and the hair was cut short.

"Did Uncle Jon play sports?"

"Yes, Alex, he was a very focused and fierce player in sports."

In high school, Jon was involved in track and extracurricular activities. Jon was always focused on what he wanted. On one of our vacations at Cape Cod, Jon was in a tennis tournament. His tennis ability was okay, but he won the tournament. What I saw in his playing was a fierce sense of concentration and a powerful will to win. This concentration and will is what I saw in him in life whenever he was determined to focus on something. When he knew what he wanted, he got it. All of my children had this passion; they just exercised it in such different ways. Incidentally, none of our kids ever had TVs in their rooms, and none were given a car until they graduated from college.

"Why didn't they have TVs in their rooms, Papa Larry?"

I told Rebecca, "Papa Larry was plain cheap."

"Did they ever complain?" Haleigh asks with a strong interest.

"All the kids would say, 'Everybody else has TVs.' I would give them the same answer, 'House rules.' It is amazing how they took it in stride."

"Pickle juice!"

"Papa Larry, what else did Uncle Jon do?"

"Jon also played the guitar, Rebecca."

"Uncle Jon played the guitar?"

"Yes, he did. Jon never liked large crowds. He loved his guitar; he loved to compose and play on his guitar."

"How long did he play?"

"He played on the acoustic guitar for about three to four years, Haleigh."

"Grandpa, did Uncle Jon always hate large crowds?"

"For the most part, Alex, your uncle did not like large crowds. One of the few times Jon didn't mind large crowds was during the Christmas season, when he attended his favorite show, P.D.Q. Bach, with Professor Peter Schickele. Schickele drew packed audiences. The music was unreal. His humor was sensational. And our family was together. It was Jon's favorite show!"

"Did Uncle Jon work like Aunt Helaine after school?"

"Yes, Haleigh, he did. Jon had many jobs after school, always because HE wanted to. Jon and Helaine were similar in this way."

"Did Uncle Jon always want to be a doctor, Papa Larry?"

"When Jon graduated from high school, Alex, we were not sure what Jon wanted to do with his life. We took him for career testing and, to our dismay and astonishment, the only career that was matched with him was being an undertaker. Can you imagine—a Jewish undertaker? I had concerns about Jon's future, but my hopes far outweighed my concerns. I was willing to accept Jon for whatever he did and however he did it."

"What did Uncle Jon do after high school?"

"Jon went backpacking throughout all of Europe by himself, Alex. Can you imagine going to different countries with different languages and cultures all by yourself at a young age?"

"Did he go to college, Grandpa?"

"Of course, Haleigh, how else would he be a doctor?" Alex replies.

"Pickle juice!"

Jon went to Clark University in Massachusetts, where he blossomed. Jon wanted to go to a small school near Boston. He majored in economics. He had high honors in economics and did very well in school. On one family vacation in Jon's freshman year, on Parent's Day, the whole family visited him. We were supposed to be there at eleven a.m., but I like to be punctual and we got there at nine o'clock. We knocked on Jon's door and he opened it bleary-eyed. There was a girl sleeping in his bed. His excuse was, "Dad, she was too tired to go back to her room." Our son, Doug, yelled, "That's our Jonny—Go Jonny!" I must say, we were all very proud of him, even though we wouldn't say it out loud.

This only reminded me of how Jon could never lie, because we always caught him. When he was younger, he said he was going over to a friend's house to study, and we found him sitting in front of us at a movie with a gal. In his own quiet way, he was a lady's man—the girls flocked to him. I guess this didn't change in college either. Jon was an unusual guy. He had very few male friends, but he always had a girlfriend. To this day, I want to find out what his technique was.

"Where did Uncle Jon meet Aunt Belynda?"

"He met your Aunt Belynda, Rebecca, in Providence."

"How did Uncle Jon become a doctor?"

"He went on to study medicine after Clark University."

Jon went on to Rutgers University, the state university of New

Jersey, to study medicine. After Rutgers, he went to the University of Rochester and the Miriam Hospital at Brown University for his internship. He then went to the Cleveland Clinic in Cleveland to study infectious diseases. Again, he did it his way. I suggested that he become a dermatologist, but Jon always did it his way. Meanwhile, Belynda was studying nursing at Brown University, and she still does nursing part-time in Denver, where they now live. Jon and Belynda met in the apartment house that they both lived in when they were in Providence.

"Where did Uncle Jon and Aunt Belynda get married?"

"They were married in Colorado, Haleigh."

Jon was an adventurous guy; in fact, all the kids were and are today. Jon has become a very accomplished skier and mountain climber. He loves the outdoors and the outdoors loves him. When Jon and Belynda were ready to get married, they decided to have their wedding at the top of Mt. Breckenridge in Colorado, some 11,000 feet up. I said to Jon, "It's February, it's snowy, and you're not going to get too many of the family to come!" He put his arm around me, gave me a kiss, and said, "You got THAT right, Dad!" It was one of the greatest weddings that I ever went to. He was right—not too many people came.

He then settled in Denver with Belynda because of the climate and all that the area had to offer—the snow, the skiing, the mountain climbing, the hiking, and the people. Jon and Belynda have thrived in Colorado. He is involved with travel medicine and with his medical community in lobbying for what is good in medicine. Jon is an expert in travel medicine.

"What do you mean by 'travel medicine,' Grandpa?"

"Well, Haleigh, your uncle helps patients prepare for trips

abroad. People come to him with questions from all over the country."

Jon is also involved in lobbying; he lobbies for offering the best medicine to the public, even though the public doesn't want the best medicine for themselves. Jon is an infectious disease specialist in Colorado. He is a senior partner in a private practice with multiple hospital affiliations. He is held in such high esteem that he is listed in Colorado as one of the best infectious disease specialists in the *Who's Who of Medicine* in Colorado.

"Uncle Jon is like Daddy!"

"Yes, Haleigh, he was recognized in his field too. Your Uncle Jon is very involved in his community and other communities too. Did you know he volunteered to go to Haiti after the disaster that hit on January 12, 2010?"

"Was that the disaster on the island that hurt all of those people?"

"Yes, it was. It was a massive earthquake with a 7.0 on the Richter scale that struck Haiti."

"Wow, Uncle Jon volunteered to go to Haiti?"

"Yes, Alex, he is one of the many doctors who volunteered to leave their lives here in the States to help the less fortunate in Haiti."

"Grandpa, did Uncle Jon have to leave?"

"Well, Haleigh, since Uncle Jon is a specialist in tropical infectious diseases, he volunteered to leave his practice to volunteer in Haiti, which is a tropical island in the Caribbean. Your Uncle Jon packed all kinds of medicine and non-perishable foods, along with a tent and a sleeping bag."

But when Jon got to the John F. Kennedy airport in New York, he encountered a fiasco. The mission was sponsored by the Church of

Scientology. Because of an administrative snafu, the plane departed with some fifty missionaries, ten rescue people without their equipment, and no physicians.

"Is that bad, Grandpa?"

"I think so, Haleigh. The plane left with half of the seats empty and there were no doctors on the plane."

Notwithstanding the end result, I was very proud of my son, who volunteered to leave his wife, dog, and practice to try to help the people, and especially the orphans of Haiti, for a short period of time. Haiti has one of the highest maternal death rates in the world. Poverty, political upheaval, natural calamities, a high incidence of AIDS, and a population that is some 80 percent Catholic—so that birth control or abortion is not usually suggested—does not seem to help.

"That's a lot of Catholic people, Grandpa."

"Yes, Alex, a large percentage of the population of the island is of the Catholic faith."

"Do they go to church like we go to temple, Grandpa?"

"I would like to think so, Haleigh."

"I like to go to temple, Grandpa."

"I enjoy going to temple too, especially when you're with me."

"Do Uncle Jon and Aunt Belynda go to temple, Grandpa?"

"Yes, Alex, Jon is also involved in his temple."

Belynda converted to Judaism, and now that she is involved in the temple, she has Jon involved with it. I could not believe that!

"Why did she convert?"

"That's a good question, Alex. Belynda converted because she did not have any strong personal religious feelings and she felt very comfortable in the way the family practiced Judaism."

"Grandpa, did you take any trips with Uncle Jon like you did with our daddy?"

"Yes, Alex, I took many bonding trips with Jon."

"Tell us about a trip, Papa Larry."

"I'd love to, Rebecca."

Kathy and I went to Denver to an AAO (American Association of Orthodontists) meeting. Doug, Ronni, Alex, and Haleigh came too. Jon and Belynda were there too. We went to a great baseball game with great seats that Jon had treated us to, we had a fantastic dinner, and we also went fly fishing. The trip was sensational. We stayed in the center of Denver in a hotel. Jon and Belynda also stayed in Denver so that we could do more things together. They were great with the kids, even though they don't want children themselves.

Here is a thought for a Dutch uncle—Jon. A Dutch uncle is someone who is known as an objective adviser. My son Jon, because he is a blood relative to his nieces and nephews and not their parent, has a wonderful obligation to be a teacher, an opportunity to train and educate his nieces and nephews without the emotional involvement of being a parent. Jon has a great opportunity of life in front of him with Belynda.

"Papa Larry, I want to hear more." Rebecca begins bouncing in her seat, anxious to learn more gossip about her uncle.

In order to bond some more with family, I went fly fishing with Jon and Belynda in Colorado. The weather was impossible; it was snowing and I was almost drowning. Jon asked me, "So Dad, how do you like it?" I thought for a moment that these would be my last words. The only thing I caught was a cold, some twigs, and a branch, but I loved it. I loved being in the mountains with Belynda and him.

On another occasion, I went to Colorado and Jon and Belynda took me to a place where they have a little second home. There was some ten feet of snow, and we could hardly walk, but it was a blast!

A time of bonding was when I went fly fishing again with Jon and Doug. This time I caught lots of trout. I get the feeling that Jon paid the trout off to open their mouths for my fly. Of course, we released all the trout. We went fly fishing at 9,000 feet in Bailey, Colorado. I hooked six trout; I caught four. The largest was five pounds. I cannot tell you how tough it was to bring that one in. I was in waders, waist-deep in water, chilly sprinkles coming down, in a torrent of a brook. I was hanging on for dear life, trying not to drown and trying to pull in a five-pound trout. It was like hooking Jaws. It was exciting and exhausting, and fun because I was with my sons, Doug and Jon, who had arranged the trip.

I enjoyed a trip with my sons, Jon and Doug, who took me to the Chesapeake Bay for my birthday. It was one of the greatest weekends of my life. We went to the Eastern Shore. We rented a sailboat, smoked cigars, and had cognac under the stars. I will never forget it.

"It was like Boy Scouts with Daddy and Uncle Jon!"

"It sure was, Haleigh!"

I remember a trip to New Orleans with Jon and Belynda. Jon and Belynda went to a medical meeting in New Orleans and I went to an orthodontic meeting in the same town. Because I was so proud and haughty about being an orthodontist, I invited Jon and Belynda to our famous fish party. The organization had fried sole, fried lobster, and fried shrimp. Jon did not say a word. Finally, he said, "Hey Dad, would you maybe like to spend a moment at our medical party?" I said, "Sure."

We went over to his party. My mouth opened with incredulousness as I had fresh lobster, fresh Alaskan crab claws, and fresh shrimp—and as much as I could eat. The final dessert was Bananas Foster. I had six of them. Remember, I never eat desserts. Jon to this day has been gracious enough never to say a word. He doesn't have to.

A short while ago, Jon, Belynda, and Mesa were hiking in Colorado along a river. Mesa got too close to the swirling current of the rapids and fell in. She was trying to swim against the swift current and was in deep trouble. Jon jumped into the rapids to try to save their dog. For a while, Belynda thought she was going to lose both of them. With a lot of effort, they miraculously reached the bank. When Belynda came running up to them, she found Jon and Mesa on land. Jon was nursing his scratches and Mesa was licking her hero, Jon. A dog's love for her master. That night, Mesa jumped into bed next to Jon and slept by his side. Belynda, with tears in her eyes, was so grateful that the family was together again, with the love of a special dog and a special husband.

"I'm so happy Uncle Jon and Mesa are safe!" Rebecca exclaims as she places her hands over her heart.

"Me too!" Alex and Haleigh proclaim in unison.

Jon and Belynda continue to travel all over the world—Laos, Bhutan, India, and other God-forsaken places. It is their style; it is their way. I love them for doing that, and I love their wonderful golden retriever, Mesa.

"I love Mesa!" Haleigh shouts as she cuddles her arms together as if she were giving Mesa a big hug.

"I do too!" Rebecca mimics Haleigh's gestures.

A chorus of voices calling for our appearance spills out into the yard. As we brush ourselves off to enjoy another night of Passover, we look at each other with a sentimental grin and prepare to enter the home. One by one, we grab each other's hands, entering as a grandfather bonded with his grandchildren.

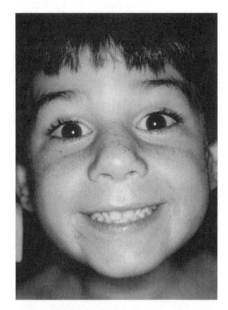

*Jonathan at four
years old*

*Alex Harte (left) mastering his origami plane-making skills, with his
Uncle Jon (center) and Aunt Belynda, 2007*

Hiking to a nearby fishing spot in Colorado, (left to right) me, Jon, and Douglas, 2004

Members of the "House of Harte" skiing in Colorado, (left to right) Ronni, Doug, Belynda, Jonathan, and Helaine, 2006

Just caught a five-pound trout, fly fishing in Colorado, 2006

Jon and Belynda, Sweden, 2006

My House as a Zoo

Baby animals can be as loving as any child.
—*Lawrence S. Harte*

It is a warm summer day of excitement and adventure as Alex, Haleigh, and Rebecca embark on a trip to Turtle Back Zoo in New Jersey with their grandfather. As the echo of howls, grunts, snorts, and various other sounds of wildlife beckons us during our walk toward the ticket booth to purchase our entrance, I couldn't help but think about how I experienced the zoo for most of my life for free.

"Did you guys know that when I was a kid, my house was a zoo?"

"You lived in a zoo? I thought you grew up in Brooklyn," Haleigh comments as she looks around, investigating which exhibit interests her more.

"It's a different kind of zoo."

"Did you live with monkeys, Papa Larry? I love monkeys."

"No, we didn't live with monkeys, Rebecca."

My mother worked all day and was separated from my father,

who cared for his mother most of the time. So my house wasn't very neat and everything was all over the place. Six days a week, I was in a zoo. When I settled down with Judi, she was very involved with animals. Since I had grown up in a zoo, it was just like never having left home, except now there were animals too. My friends used to say, "How can you let your wife take all these animals into the house and care for them?" I said, "Just the inhabitants have changed." It was kind of nice, like being home when I was a kid.

"Why did Grandma have so many animals in the house, Grandpa?"

"Your grandmother, Alex, was a wildlife rehabilitator."

"What did she do as a wildlife rehabilitator?"

"She took all kinds of wild animals into the house."

"Did she take in birds, Papa Larry?"

"Yes, Rebecca, she did, and many other types of animals. She brought in all kinds of birds; if they broke their wing, she would try to fix the wing and let them fly back into the open. Or if there were little squirrels that were left by their mother, she would feed them, let them grow up, and let them go out. Her wish was to try to let animals enjoy a whole life."

Our house had a lived-in quality; it was not supposed to be a showcase for people to come in and see everything spotless. I have cleaned the bottoms of animals more than I have ever changed the diapers of my kids. My only regret is that we did not charge admission, because people kept coming to the house to see the different animals. People kept saying, "What kind of people ARE these people? They're like animals!" And in some ways, we were. The animals were very special, even though they were wild. They just wanted to be loved, cared for, and nurtured.

"What was the first animal you and Grandma had in your home?"

"Prior to having children, Alex, we had one dog, a springer spaniel, when we lived in Rochester."

"What other animals did you have at home, Papa Larry?"

"When the children were very young, Rebecca, we had the typical dogs, rabbits, and many birds."

"I love rabbits," Rebecca exclaims. "They are fuzzy and soft."

"I love rabbits too," Haleigh agrees.

The kids grew up in a house with animals. They just didn't know any different. The house became a rehab center when the kids were much older. Even though all the kids love animals, none of them have been as fervent in wanting to rehabilitate wildlife to this day.

"What did you do with them when you went on family trips?"

"When we went on trips, Alex, we kept the animals in cages with plenty of food and water and had an animal sitter."

The raccoons, squirrels, and groundhogs lived in cages right outside the house. Each day we would open the cage, free them, give them food and water, and play with them. When they were mature enough to leave, we would open the cage and let them go to enjoy the life that was meant for them. At one time in our house, we had one dog, twenty birds, four squirrels, two groundhogs, two raccoons, and a fox.

"Did the animals bite anyone?" Rebecca questions as she looks at an alligator in its habitat yawning with its sharp, intimidating teeth.

"Unfortunately, we had one animal bite your mommy."

"Was Mommy okay?"

"Yes, she was okay."

We had bundles and bundles of baby raccoons, which were fed to adulthood and then let go. One of the raccoons, which we had named Tribble, bit Helaine, and we had to chase it and bring it to a pathology lab to make sure she didn't have rabies. Tribble had to be sacrificed. Fortunately, she did not have rabies. Helaine was fine and it really didn't make her like raccoons any less.

"What other animals did you have, Grandpa?"

"We had groundhogs that we named Amos and Andy, Haleigh."

The little babies were left on our doorstep by other people who found them. One of them eventually became the New Jersey groundhog. It was our pet for many years—that was Amos. To this day whenever I go around the world and I see a groundhog, I say this must be Amos or Amos's children or Amos's grandchildren. Amos was almost human. He would play with our dog Schooner in the house. At one time Amos was very ill. Schooner would not leave his side. He licked her and brought food and water to her. It's amazing the love that animals can have for each other. They were plain friends.

"Tell us more about the animals, Papa Larry."

"There were many animals, Rebecca."

We had a possum and a fox. We had a deer that Judi tried to take care of and bring back into the open. Judi rehabbed a rabbit that we gave to a woman who worked in my Sparta office. There was a robin that came from a small nest where the mother left it. The robin became so tame that we would feed her; she would fly away to a tree and come back to your finger. She did this for many, many weeks. We really had a robin that was like a house pet.

We had snakes. Not only did we have boa constrictors, which Judi used to take around to schools, but also an eastern ringneck snake, which we found in the Catskills and brought back in a large container.

One day the container was knocked over and, when we moved, we always wondered if the new tenants ever found that snake.

We also had a kestrel, a falcon. You had to wear gloves with it because the talons were so sharp that they could really stick you in the skin. We had little owls that we used to keep in cages, and we had bats.

Our parakeet, Paco, lived with us until he died of old age. We got Paco from a pet store. The only reason I kept Paco is I thought we would invent a new way of fertilizing men's hair for those who were going bald. He used to poop on my head and Judi would tell me that guano fertilizer would make my hair grow. Maybe I should have listened to her.

"You're silly, Grandpa," Haleigh exclaims as she heads toward the petting zoo with Rebecca. As they arrive at the petting zoo, a goat moves toward Alex and nudges him.

"I bet you didn't have a goat, Grandpa."

"Actually, Alex, we even had a goat with diarrhea that Judi brought home from the zoo for a few days."

Then there was Petey the sun conure parrot, who we donated to the Mini Zoo at the Newark Museum. Petey was donated because she was too noisy and had high shrills; she was driving us and the rest of the animals crazy. We once visited Petey at the zoo to see how she was doing. She was still shrieking and very noisy. To make a bad pun, her big mouth made other birds in the area cow tow to her. Other temporary residents were a baby fawn, a blind fox, raccoons, birds, a baby skunk, and so many more I can't remember. Most of them were released or sent to other rehabbers.

After seeing the petting zoo, we follow the path to the penguin exhibit, and Rebecca says, "I bet you didn't have penguins, Papa Larry?"

Holding in my laugh, I smile and reply, "You're right, Rebecca.

We didn't have penguins, but if your grandmother had found one, we would have had a penguin too."

"Grandpa, did you only have one dog?"

"No, Haleigh, we had many dogs too."

As for dogs, in 1960 we got a puppy, a springer spaniel we named Kim. The apartment was small; it was the first place that Judi and I lived when we got married. It was a one-bedroom apartment on the fourth floor of a walk-up, about a thousand square feet but with only one entrance and exit. God forbid we had a fire. It would've been a four-story jump. It was wrong for Kim to be in such a small place—when we took him to the fields, he would run up and down a hundred yards without stopping. We had to give him to one of Judi's students when we realized we weren't home enough to give the dog the attention it needed. Fortunately, the student lived on a farm in Fairport. We gave Kim away to the family and knew he would be happier on the farm.

When we moved to New Jersey, we had a highland terrier, another kind of terrier, and four bichons. The bichons were called Plato, Gatsby, Schooner, and Sloopy. Plato got hit by a car and died. Gatsby died of congenital kidney failure shortly before his second birthday. Judi still hasn't gotten over Gatsby. Schooner lived fifteen years and died of liver cancer. And we got Sloopy as a companion to Schooner. She died at the age of eight from a brain aneurism. There is now another dog named Simba.

The bichons were adorable. We didn't train any of them though—*they* trained *us*, and they all had physical and mental problems. They all needed psychiatrists, and when we got finished with them, *we* needed a psychiatrist!

Talking about dogs, I have to mention our cat named Fluffy that

I swear acted like a dog. You called it and it came. It purred. We had to get rid of it because Douglas was allergic to it. That cat was nearly a dog. It was terrific. Fluffy went to Judi's brother and sister-in-law, Richard and Susan. Fluffy was also the cause of Doug's asthma.

"You really did live in a zoo, Grandpa!"

"It may not be like this zoo, Haleigh, but it was a zoo."

Once, our Tudor house was chosen for a set for a Super bowl commercial with VISA and Emmet Smith, the football Hall of Famer. The advertising company came in with some twenty-five people to set up different rooms for the television shots. They gave us a lot of money and some notoriety. Our only problem was where to put all the animals for one day. It was amazing—we had so many of these professional New York City–type crewmembers playing with the animals. For them, it was like a day in the zoo.

"Do you miss living in a zoo, Grandpa?"

"I enjoyed living with the animals, Alex, but I don't miss it now."

The kids grew up in an atmosphere of dogs and animals, and the love of animals. I loved nature and was used to a messy home. It was a great environment for my family and me. To this day, we are all animal and nature lovers. At this time, Judi still rehabs squirrels. As for myself, I don't have any animals. And I really don't miss them. It is a chapter in my life that is finished.

As we walk through the different exhibits with animals from all over the world, many remind me of my worldly travels. The kangaroos, penguins, bears, and alligators were just some of the creatures I came across during my trips. As we take a break from the sightseeing and head to the pavilion, I begin to share some memories of a few of my vacations.

Judi Harte, wildlife rehabilitator, visits with a macaw.
The majority of macaws in the wild are now
endangered. 1962

Around the World

Tomorrow is but a myth in the imagination of man's mind.
Live today.

—Lawrence S. Harte

Before I share this great journey with you, I must remind you that, as an only child, I was an avid stamp collector. My grandfather gave stamps to my dad, who gave them to me. I dreamed that someday I would visit the countries on the stamps. I tried to read all about the countries. Because of this experience, I had a great lust for adventure and travel. When I was older, you could not hold me back. I wanted to see the world. One of my dreams in life was to travel around the world. To date, I have visited over 135 countries. I started traveling in college, and I've been traveling ever since. When I got married and had my children, I had the same dream for them. I wanted my children to see the world. I wanted them to experience different languages and cultures. So we traveled to places throughout the seven continents. They say that travel can be the enemy of bigotry.

"What does that mean, Grandpa?"

"Well, Haleigh, it means that if you travel the world, you gain a better understanding of people and their cultures and traditions. Bigotry is a form of discrimination, and those who travel and gain this understanding are less prone to discriminate."

"Pickle juice!"

"Where was the first place you visited with the whole family, Grandpa?"

"One of the first vacations, Alex, and we took many of them with the kids, was to St. Croix when the kids were very young."

"Did you stay for a long time?"

"No, Rebecca, we didn't stay long. In fact, we had to come back the next day because they didn't have any milk for Helaine, who was one year old at the time."

So back we came. This was our family adventure—silly, spontaneous, and my God, what a waste of money! But that was the beginning of a world-wide travel experience for the boys and Helaine.

"Did you have fun on all the trips, Grandpa?"

"Some trips, Haleigh, were more adventures rather than entertaining."

"I don't understand."

"I'll give you an example. Have you ever found yourself in a situation where everything was going wrong, hoping that it might be, at worst, a bad dream?"

"I'm not sure."

"Well, I did! This unhoped-for bad dream was transferred into the reality of a nightmare on a charter trip to Cancun, Mexico."

Our premonition of bad tidings began at Kennedy Airport, when we arrived at eight a.m., two hours before flight time. We left two hours AFTER our scheduled flight time. We arrived in Cancun two and one-half hours late.

"Why were you so late?" Alex counts the time difference.

"You see, our plane, in keeping with the late theme of the trip, delivered us an additional half hour late."

Our arrival at Cancun was the continuation of an unusual experience. Two planes holding over 500 passengers arrived at Mexican customs control at the same time. There were, would you believe, only two officials to accommodate this onslaught of humanity.

"Does that mean it took long, Grandpa?"

"It sure does, Haleigh. After clearing customs, we then had the opportunity of waiting an additional hour and a half for our luggage."

Alas, off to our recently completed deluxe luxury hotel. What happened to us until that point was just cheesecake, compared to the horror of what was yet to come.

"What happened?"

"We arrived at the hotel and found ourselves very fortunate, Rebecca."

"We were able to get a room. Unbelievably, there were guests who were denied a room, even though they had prepaid their trip."

"That's not fair."

"No, it wasn't fair, Haleigh. But after everything else that happened, I don't know how fortunate we were."

"Why was the trip so bad, Grandpa?"

"We began by being invited to a welcoming cocktail party."

"That doesn't sound bad."

"This 'welcome party' of two drinks and three cokes cost us $24."

"Is that a lot?"

"At that time, it sure was. We asked why they charged for the drinks, and their reason was that a piña colada was not a cocktail. They never did tell us what else you would call a piña colada."

"What's a cocktail, Grandpa?"

"A cocktail is an alcoholic beverage."

"Pickle juice!"

We then attempted lunch, which was inedible. After signing the check, we went up to our room, which, at six p.m., was still not ready. We weren't in our unmade room fifteen minutes when the waiter came and told us that the hotel had lost our lunch check. We signed a second check for the same lunch. Would you believe that when we checked out, they had both checks for the same lunch on our bill?

"Did you complain, Grandpa?"

"Yes, Alex, I did."

"How was the room?"

"In our unmade room, we were astounded to see three beds for five people."

We complained, but they told us we were lucky to HAVE three beds. Thus, for one week, two of our kids slept on the floor. Oh yes, by then we were tired and grungy after a long day of traveling. You guessed it—no towels and no shower head.

"No towels or shower head, how horrible," Haleigh shows a face of disgust as she imagines having to take a shower in the room.

"It was horrible."

Here is where I made one of my many mistakes—I called up for service. They told me I would be taken care of in ten minutes. These ten Mexican minutes translated into American time as "sometime this year."

"Did they ever give you service?"

"Yes, they did, Alex. The engineer finally came up with one four-inch screw driver!"

"Did he take care of the problems?"

"No, not really. Here I made another mistake by permitting him to take off the bath plumbing. Would you believe we now had no shower and no bath?"

"No shower!" Rebecca and Haleigh screech at the same time.

"Yes, no shower, but the best is yet to come."

"How could it get worse then not having a shower, Grandpa?"

"Well, Haleigh, there were so many problems with this hotel that the shower seemed like almost nothing next to everything else."

The elevator didn't work most of the time. However, if you were unfortunate enough to be on one of the elevators when it DID work, your misfortune would increase when it would get stuck between floors. The food was, at best, inedible, the service was nonexistent, and the kitchen had dirty dishes literally piled up to the ceiling. Remember, this was a luxury hotel! Oh yes, they padded our bill, increased the cost of items, or gave us the wrong change—but always with a smile!

"At least they smiled, Grandpa!"

"They were smiling their way to the bank, Alex, because they literally stole our money."

Some other tidbits—the weather was always windy during the day, and the water was cold. I had to wear sneakers on the beach because of the dampness. The nights were downright cold, and being without the proper clothing, we caught the flu. Since most everything was higher priced in Cancun than in Bloomingdale's, the only item we flew back with was the flu, which we managed to obtain "flu" of charge.

"You're funny, Grandpa. 'Flu' of charge." Haleigh laughs as she repeats the play on words.

"Would you like to hear about our gala New Year's Eve party?"

"I do!" Rebecca springs from her seat, almost dropping her ice cream scoop from the cone.

"Good."

"Grandpa, was this the same trip?"

"Yes, Alex, this is the same trip."

It all started when our reservation for five was noted as two. This problem was quickly and graciously resolved by the exchange of five American dollars from my hand to the maitre d's pocket. The liquor prices at the table started with scotch at $100, going up to champagne at $200 a bottle. The service, as usual, was slow. Our lobster appetizer turned out to be inedible hard shrimp, and our hot soup was not quite defrosted when served. The turkey tasted like cardboard. The baked Alaska oozed and tasted like camel meat in heat. The coffee was never served. There was a group playing Mexican-tempo music. This means that the band played for five minutes and was off for twenty-five minutes. Come to think of it, the musicians were "off" even when they were on. The nicest part of the evening was the price. It was "only" $150 for Judi, our three kids, and me.

"It should've been free, Grandpa. It wasn't good."

"Yes, Haleigh, you're right, but it wasn't free. The biggest bargain was that we didn't get sick that night. In fact, if we had, it would not have been from the food, but rather from starvation."

On our trip to Cancun I rented a car for the family. I parked the car close to a restaurant. There was a person standing by there looking at the car. I said, "If you mind my car, I will give you a dollar when I get back." The guy graciously said, "Gracias, señor." I came back three hours later and I gave the guy a dollar. As he ran away, I noticed all four of the wheel covers were gone.

"He's a thief!" Haleigh exclaims with a tone of annoyance.

"Could you imagine—I gave the guy a buck to steal four wheel covers!"

We ended our trip by hanging around the Cancun airport for two extra hours. We then boarded a plane where the seat numbers did not correspond to our ticket reservation. This little tidbit ended in mass confusion and chaos. And that was our trip to Cancun.

"I bet you were happy to be home."

"You're right, Rebecca. We were very tired, hungry, and happy to be home."

"What was one of the first trips you and Grandma took, Grandpa?'

"After Judi and I were first married, Alex, we went on our first orthodontic trip to Mexico City that was sponsored by the Southern Association of Orthodontics."

"Mexico again!"

"Yes, Haleigh, but this was not to Cancun, and it happened much earlier in life than the Cancun trip."

"Pickle juice!"

Here I was, the kid from Brooklyn, associating with orthodontists and their wives from several cities around the world. The orthodontists were so cordial and their wives so charming that I truly felt I was back in time with *Gone with the Wind*. I said to myself, "Wow, I am so lucky to be in a profession with such wonderful and gracious people." They made us feel so at ease and so at home.

Another time, Judi and I went to Acapulco on a charter trip. When we got to Mexico City, there were no rooms in the hotel. This was after traveling for some ten hours. Everybody was screaming at the hotel manager. He finally got cots and put them in the lobby of the hotel to sleep in. Fortunately, I was low-key, possibly too shy to yell, and they gave us a penthouse in an apartment across the street. Sometimes it pays not to open your mouth and to be a gentleman or a lady; in fact, most of the time it pays to be a gentleman or a lady.

"I'm a young lady." Haleigh smiles and bats her eyes.

"Yes you are, Haleigh."

We also visited Tijuana, Mexico. In those days Tijuana was a city where anything went—drugs, gambling, and prostitution. It was like an 1800s Western town from the movies as far as gun toters were concerned, except this wasn't a movie set; this was the real thing.

"Mexico really doesn't sound like a great place to visit."

"It wasn't the best place to visit, Alex, but it was an adventure nonetheless. What makes life exciting are experiences and adventures. You have to live life and try to enjoy everything, even if it doesn't go the way you thought it would."

"Tell us about other places."

"Have you ever heard the expression 'You get what you pay for,' Haleigh?"

"I've heard Daddy and Mommy say it."

"Well, if you're lucky, you get what you pay for."

I must've had too much scotch because I bought cheap insurance for a family trip to Martinique. On this trip, the airline company went bankrupt when we got there. There was no way to get us back into the States. My cheap insurance did not cover this fiasco. Judi, with Helaine and Jon, took three days to get home. I took my son Doug on a travel tour of the islands of the Caribbean to get home.

"Papa Larry, it sounds like it cost a lot of money."

"Again, Rebecca, you're right. I cannot tell you what this bargain charter trip to Martinique cost."

I remember taking the family three times to Israel. We went to Masada in 1969 to see where Jews of the past decided to kill themselves rather than convert from being Jews. We were there when the jets flew over in what were called maneuvers to bomb areas of Lebanon. We were in Lebanon when shells were being fired. In 1975, we went to Hebron, a town in the mountains of Judah, where there was rock throwing. We went to Jerusalem, where there was stone throwing by very religious Jews.

"Why did they throw stones at you?"

"Because, Haleigh, we came there on a Saturday. Saturday is the holiest day of the week for Jews."

They were throwing rocks because we were not abiding by Sabbath rules and we were driving on the Sabbath. Israel is in so many ways the insurance of the Jews all over the world. The world is a difficult place because of what you stand for as a Jew. There is a tremendous amount of anti-Semitism all over the world. It is not easy being a Jew.

"Especially if you drive in on a Saturday and have rocks thrown at you," Alex offers with a hint of sarcasm.

Unfortunately there is a religious war between the Arabs and the Jews. More unfortunately, there is an increasing number of ultra-Orthodox Jews who do not work, go into the military, or contribute positively to society.

On another trip to Israel in 1982, we went to the Gaza Strip in Jordan. In Gaza there was strife and shootings. As we went through the gates of Jerusalem and I was in a taxicab with Helaine, I asked the Arab taxicab driver to go to Jaffa Gate. I said to him, "Jaffa Gate, please." And with that, he took off and it seemed like we were going on and on. I kept saying "Jaffa Gate," and he kept saying some other word, "Cotel." I reached forward. I literally and physically almost strangled him to death. Helaine started crying and said, "Stop it— you're going to kill the guy!" I was about ready to strangle and kill the man and have an Arab war. Subsequently, we arrived at my interpretation of the Jaffa Gate. He just had a different word for it. Rule: try to learn two words for the sites you want to see in different lands.

"Poor man; you almost killed him."

"He was okay, Haleigh, and fortunately, so were we." I stand up from our table and lead the children toward the South America exhibit. As we look in awe of the flightless bird, the rhea, which can weigh more than sixty pounds, Rebecca begins to tug on my pants.

"Papa Larry, did you go to South America?"

"Yes, Rebecca, we visited various countries such as Chile, Argentina, Uruguay, and Brazil."

"What was Chile like, Grandpa?"

"Chile is a country with a future, Alex, and the Andes Mountains are gorgeous."

Chile has a strong middle class. Santiago, located in the country's center valley, is a cosmopolitan city and the capital of Chile. Santiago is known as one of the most modern metropolitan cities of Latin America and has some of the most modern transportation infrastructure of Latin America as well. We visited Los Ríos and the wine country route besides the city of Santiago and Valparaíso. In the wine country route, we passed through Casablanca Valley, which is known for the best white wines, and Colchagua Valley, which is known for the best red wines, as well as some others that can all be seen on a day's trip from Santiago. Valparaíso is protected by the UNESCO World Heritage and was named Chile's cultural capital by the Chilean congress. The city is built on steep hillsides that overlook the Pacific Ocean.

"Tell us more!"

"We had some great adventures in South America, Rebecca."

Our visit to Argentina was to the capital, Buenos Aires, which is highly cosmopolitan with a large Jewish population. From the capital, we took a private plane that went sideways, more than it went forward or backward, to Patagonia, which comprises the southernmost portion of the Andes and is located in Argentina and Chile. We went to the villas in Patagonia, where the winds and dust were frequently high. We stayed in Patagonia a few days. It was an awesome experience. I felt that we were on a different planet. The winds were fierce; the dust was always in your eyes. It was inconceivable to believe that people lived in this area. It was so windy that they canceled all the flights. We had to drive in a blinding dust storm.

"It sounds scary!"

"It was Haleigh. We couldn't see, we couldn't breathe, and it was an exhilarating experience."

"Pickle juice!"

We also went to the Pampas, the cattle country. The Argentineans are very sophisticated Old World country people. They dress beautifully and are very knowledgeable about the arts and education. We also visited the southernmost city in the world, Ushuaia, which is in Argentina and a gateway to the Antarctic. The homes in that town reminded me of homes on the water in New England in a foggy and cold atmosphere.

In 1980, we went to Montevideo, Uruguay, because I wanted to see the area where the German armored pocket battleship, the *Admiral Graf Spee*, had sunk. The *Admiral Graf Spee* was a warship of WWII launched in April 1934, with a displacement of 10,000 tons. The warship was armed with six 11-inch and eight 6-inch guns, eight 37 mm anti-aircraft guns, ten 20 mm anti-aircraft guns and eight 21-inch torpedo tubes. It was powered by eight sets of diesel engines, had a top speed of twenty-eight knots, and carried a crew of 1,150 men.

"That sounds like a big ship, Grandpa."

"It was a big ship, Alex."

"Why did you want to see the ship?"

"I guess I wanted to see it because I had heard about it since I was a kid."

The *Admiral Graf Spee* was scuttled by her crew off Montevideo, Uruguay, to avoid capture after engaging three British cruisers (HMS *Ajax*, HMS *Achilles*, and HMS *Exeter*) and incurring severe damage in the Battle of the River Plate in December 1939. I remember listening to the radio as a child about the scuttling of the *Admiral Graf Spee* at the Montevideo harbor before WWII, and it was eerie.

We also traveled to Ecuador in 1980. We were on the equator. There were many beautiful sites. In Ecuador you can see a lot of signs saying "La Mitad del Mundo" (Middle of the World).

"You were in the middle of the world?"

"Yes, Haleigh, Ecuador is on the equator, which is the middle of the world."

"I want to go to the middle of world."

"One day you will."

"Don't stop, Grandpa, I want to hear more about the middle of the world."

Quito was a beautiful city high up in the mountains with a large Jewish population like Argentina. Quito was on the equator yet still had a moderate climate because of its elevation. We bought beautiful multi-colored handmade sweaters that we have to this day.

"I know which sweater. It's the one with all the pretty colors."

"Yes it is, Rebecca."

The Ecuadorians, although not wealthy or educated, were very warm and hospitable. We traveled down to Guayaquil, which is on the water and the nation's main port. The heat and humidity were unbearable. At Guayaquil, which is the most populous and largest city of Ecuador, we did a study in which we found that many of the children there were born with cleft lips and also developed cancers in the mouth as they got older.

"How sad!"

"It is sad, Haleigh."

"Why were the children born that way, Grandpa?"

"I'm not too sure, Alex, but a study in New Jersey stated that there was a special kind of tobacco that caused cancer if it was chewed, and it referred to the inhabitants of some regions, such as the Ecuadorian population. In Guayaquil, cleft palates, especially hemifacial microsomia, apparently appear more in Ecuador than any place in the world."

"Tobacco is not good to smoke or chew."

"I agree, Haleigh."

While in Ecuador, we took a trip over to the Galapagos Islands. The wildlife was abundant and colorful. There were iguanas that are up to four feet long, and their skin was various shades of yellow, red, and brown. You also saw birds such as the blue-footed booby, which breeds prolifically and is pale brown with darker brown wings and bright blue feet; the masked booby bird, which is mostly white with black on the wingtips and rear edges of the wings; and the red-footed booby bird, which is gray-brown or occasionally white, with red feet. I remember swimming with the penguins and seeing nature's possibly last territory where the animals were truly not afraid of people. We walked close to the eggs and close to the ugliest critters in the world, but you know, they were kind of friendly.

On one vacation, the boys were studying in the university, so Judi and I decided to visit South America with Helaine. We went to Venezuela and decided to hire a small private plane for four. We decided to visit a little place in the Amazon. The pilot of the plane suggested we go there. The plane had room for the pilot and four other people. I was chatting with the pilot before we got on the plane. My daughter looked at the plane and said, "I hope your will is made up, but I am staying on land." Helaine decided not to go because even at that age, she was smarter than us.

"Where did Mommy stay?"

"She stayed back at Margarita Island, where we were staying at that time, Rebecca."

Off we went over the jungle and, as we were flying at 5,000 feet, the pilot said to me in broken Spanish, "Since you told me you were in the Air Force, could you help me with the navigation? You see, I can't see without my glasses." He gave me a map, and I had no idea what it is. He then got an asthma attack and gave me the plane to navigate.

"Did you fly planes, Grandpa?"

"I rode in planes in the Air Force, Alex, but I didn't fly them."

We flew toward what they call Angel Falls, which is the biggest waterfall in the world. Angel Falls is located in Canaima National Park in the Gran Sabana region of Bolivar State, Venezuela. It starts at an elevation of 3,212 feet and drops 2,647 feet.

"Did you fly into Angel Falls?"

"It seemed like we were going right into it, Haleigh, and the pilot was trying to tell me how to pull up the plane."

"Were you scared?"

"Yes! I felt like we were going to end up like the water of the falls—since the falls are of such great height, before the water gets anywhere near the ground, it is atomized by the strong winds and turned into mist."

We got out of this hair-raising experience, and we came down to a small landing field. The pilot eventually got over his asthma attack, and we landed the plane together. I had to hold his glasses, which were broken, when we came in for a landing. Fortunately, we did not stay overnight. If we did, the bugs, the natives, and the piranhas would have eaten us. We were met by some people dressed in Indian regalia. We went up the river into a small trading post, and there was a sign as big as you can see—WE ACCEPT VISA.

"Visa is accepted all over the world, Grandpa."

"Apparently it is, Alex."

I took the family to Rio de Janeiro in Brazil. We wanted to take our family trip to Rio de Janeiro to visit the Corcovado Mountain to see the statue of Christ the Redeemer. I asked the taxi driver how much it would cost. He said, "Meta, meta." I said, "No, don't play with me, I am an American and a very good businessman and you can't fool me. Give me a price." He kept saying, "Meta, meta." I said, "No, no, give me a price." So he gave me a price of $30. My family and I came back from our visit to Corcovado. The meter, known as "meta" in Portuguese, said $10. Rule: don't try to outsmart yourself in a foreign land. We also visited places such as the Lake de Freitas (Lagoa), Sugarloaf Mountains, Ipanema, and Copacabana. We were there at the beginning of Carnival, and what a mass of humanity it was. We left right before it got crazy.

"Did you like Rio, Grandpa?"

"My impression of Rio, Haleigh, was that the very poor lived in slums right next to the rich. I could not believe that there was not a revolution of the poor."

"Where else did you go besides South America?"

"We also traveled to Central America, Alex."

"Did you go to other places besides Mexico?"

"Yes, we did.

On one of our trips to Central America, we went to San José, Costa Rica, and rented a car to go up in the mountains to see the volcanoes. The roads were bad; in fact, the roads were holes with pieces of macadam in between. They were toll roads. I was shocked. A toll road in Costa Rica was where a native sat on a mule with a gun. If you went on part of his road, you paid him. It was like toll roads in the sixteenth century in England. It was eerie.

We visited Panama, where many Americans have begun to retire. The country has great warm winter weather, no hurricanes or earthquakes, and is an excellent tax haven. I met a Panamanian Orthodox Jew of Syrian origin there. She mentioned that she had three mixed marriages in her family: one child married a Reform Jew, one a Conservative Jew, and one an Ashkenazi Orthodox Jew.

"Did you visit places outside of South or Central America?"

"Yes, Alex. We also toured Europe."

Now, England was a place we took the kids many times. One of the trips led us to Stonehenge. My God, what a con job! Years ago, someone put stones all over the place and said this was a special place where gods came.

"Why did the gods go there?"

"Good question, Rebecca. The creation of Stonehenge is based on many theories. Some theories believe Stonehenge to be a place for burial, for astronomical observation, or for religious purposes. Some even think it may have been created for some supernatural or symbolic reason."

"What do you think, Grandpa?"

"I think, Alex, it's the gods' symbol of how to do good business because of the number of tourists from around the world who pay to come see it. The "mystery" of Stonehenge seems to be their marketing tactic."

"Grandpa, did you have any bad stuff happen in England, like in Mexico?"

"Not really, Haleigh. Funny thing though, with all the trips to England, we once rented a car and couldn't find our way back to the airport. I had to pay a taxicab driver to follow to the rental car place at the airport. He thought we were crazy Americans."

Talking about airports, on a trip to Malaga, Spain, Helaine and I were at the airport and the crowds were huge. We didn't know how to get on the plane. We saw a guy in a wheelchair, so I went up to the front, grabbed the wheelchair with Helaine and her guitar in tow, and went on first with the guy in the wheelchair. We left the guy on the tarmac, went into the plane, and got our seats, with Helaine sticking her guitar into peoples' stomachs, in case they wanted to take their seats. The flight from Malaga was taking us to Madrid for our trip back to the United States. In Malaga we visited Mallorca and Gibraltar, and in Madrid we visited Toledo and Madrid.

"Where else did you go?"

"We traveled to many places in Europe, Rebecca."

In Paris we also saw bombings that were apparently due to the Algerian terrorism. Paris is such a beautiful city. The French people were not quite as beautiful. They were distant compared to people in other countries. Speaking the language certainly does help. In Paris, we stayed at a hotel where the kids opened bottles of Coke that were in the bar. When I saw the price, they quickly put water into them to fill them up so that, hopefully, the hotel people wouldn't find out that we had opened them. I don't think they ever did. In France we visited Paris and Versailles and Lyons.

On another trip to the south of France near Mont Blanc with Jon, I decided to go down a luge hill and invited him to join me. Jon, who was almost as silly as I, said, "Sure thing, Dad!" So Judi and Belynda watched while Jon and I went down the luge hill without helmets. I cannot believe the silliness of it all.

"You and Uncle Jon are silly! Was it fun?"

"The experience of coming down on a luge was exhilarating at best, but ridiculous looking back. We could've been killed."

In Italy we went to Naples, Florence, Rome, Venice, and Milan and up and down the Amalfi Coast. Italians are just beautiful people, and what a beautiful country. I'd like to keep going back because they are so nice. However, I must say the Italian food is not as good as the French food. In fact, the French food is just plain darn good. We visited many places throughout Italy, like the leaning tower of Pisa in Pisa and the museum that holds *The Last Supper* in Milan. We went to Rome, but I never got an audience with the Pope.

During 9/11, Helaine, Belynda (Jon's wife), Judi, and I were in Sicily. I remember our bus driver telling us that a great calamity had struck the United States. We were speechless. We cried and prayed. The world was shut down. We went from Sicily to Sardinia to Frankfurt to Toronto to Newark. It took us over four days to return to the States. It felt like a journey of a lifetime. At the Newark airport, we were waiting in the customs line and a little girl was holding the American flag. She said, "Are we home yet, Daddy?" And the customs official said, "Welcome home!" We all cried.

We took the kids to the Grecian Islands. We took a cruise around the islands. On Santorini, Jon, Helaine, and I came down from the top of a mountain on mules. It was maybe a one-mile ride down. We all could have committed suicide by falling into the sea. We were only three feet away from the edge of the mountain. Jon and Helaine just went along, following their old man on the mule. It's amazing what kids will do.

"That sounds like fun, Papa Larry."

"It was a bit frightening, Rebecca, but it was fun riding the mules down the mountain. It took us about an hour to come down by mule."

"Where were Grandma and Daddy?"

"Your daddy and Grandma were on the ship, Haleigh."

"Was the cruise fun, Grandpa?"

"It was for the most part, Alex."

They say the Mediterranean Sea is a sea of glass. When we were on the cruise ship, it was a sea of BROKEN glass because the seas were very rough. When we got on the dance floor as the ship went from port to starboard, we literally went from one part of the dance floor to the other. I never knew I could dance so fast and so smooth.

"Where else did you go, Grandpa?"

"We also visited countries like Japan, Thailand, and many more."

On one of our trips to Japan, Jon and Doug were in first class getting high, at the ages of ten and twelve, without my knowledge. When we got to Tokyo, we went to a fish restaurant. There was a big fish tank. Doug could not eat any fish and kept saying, "How can you eat Bambi?"

"Bambi was a doe," Alex objects.

"Exactly!"

In Japan we visited Tokyo, Osaka, Kyoto, and Kamakura. The kids loved the trip because the Japanese lifestyle was so different from our lifestyle in the United States. They were also very impressed by the very good manners the Japanese people showed toward us.

We also visited Chiang Mai, which is the chief city of northern Thailand and part of the Golden Triangle. This is where Thailand, Burma, and Laos meet. It is beautiful jungles and an undeveloped area. I got on an elephant and it wouldn't stop. I guess it wanted to see its brother in Burma. They had to run after the elephant because he didn't want to let me off. It's like horses—they don't let me off either.

"They love you!"

"I'm not sure it's love, Rebecca."

The island of Komodo in the Republic of Indonesia was amazing. There are komodo dragons throughout the island. These are the largest living species of lizards in the world; they can grow to eight feet and weigh 150 pounds.

"Are they like the lizards in our yard?"

"Not quite, Haleigh. They are very quiet, but they can attack you and literally eat you."

"Pickle juice!"

The day before we visited the dragons, one person, a native, was playing with them. He tripped and was eaten by the dragons. They are absolutely ugly. I remember trying to get very close to them, and people thought I was crazy because I was trying to get a great picture. I could still be there as part of the bones. That time I was plain lucky.

"Did you go to South Africa?" Alex asked.

"Yes, we did." We continue to walk through the recreated South African coastline, looking at the African penguins.

On our trip to South Africa, we took what they call "The Blue Train" from Johannesburg to Cape Town. On the train I met a salesman who was trying to sell me alphabet trinkets made of pure gold. If I had had any guts, I would have bought them. I just was not in the mood to take a chance. Judi said, "Are you crazy?" Looking back, I should have been crazy.

On the same train, we met a person who worked with Nelson Mandela. He lived two houses down from Mandela. We spoke about apartheid and South Africa from the 1900s on. When we got to Cape Town, he invited us to his house. We became rather good acquaintances. He showed me Mandela's house a few houses away. He mentioned how the white people had ruled South Africa and how they were afraid to let go of their rule, because once they lost the majority, they could lose their land and their businesses. He was right, but that's the way life is. There were more blacks, and they just took over. Many of the whites left to go to the United States and Germany, and many Jews went to Israel.

"What's apartheid Grandpa?"

"Apartheid, Alex, is when the government separates, or segregates, people by racial groups by force."

"That's not right. That's mean."

"It is mean, Haleigh."

We were at Durban, a city on the Indian Ocean. One night I saw a display of lightning and thunder over the ocean, where there was a freighter being pushed around like a little piece of cardboard in a bathtub. This display was as good as the Macy's fireworks display in New York. It was sensational, it was chilling, and it was scary. It was as if the world were falling apart. The fascinating lightning streaks across the sky, the thunder, the winds, and the rolling ocean made it seem like you truly were on a different planet.

"That sounds beautiful," Rebecca looks up to the sky trying to picture the scene.

"It was!"

The family went on so many adventures. It was so much fun. When we went to the Arctic, I went to visit the birth place of Jack London.

"Who is he?"

"He was a famous author, Rebecca."

I read *The Call of the Wild* when I was a kid, and I wanted to see the Arctic and the small towns. It was like time had passed this region by. We went to national parks to see the white, brown, and black polar bears. We took a helicopter ride onto an icy fiord to see the golden eagles. It truly was an eventful trip, finished by sailing down the coast and seeing whales spouting water from far and up close.

Our trip to Alaska was as much fun as the Arctic. People of Alaska were kind of neat. We went on an Alaskan sled, and let me tell you that it is plain dangerous, whether on snow or the warm lands of summer. We saw the Alaskan pipeline and the thaw. We visited Nome, Alaska. We saw where the oil came from and went to.

We saw all the people—the natives, the people who had come to keep a way of life, and those who had come to get away from a life that they had left behind. We went to Antarctica; we saw ice, ice penguins, and seals. We saw raging winds and austere beauty and experienced truly frigid cold.

"What is the Alaskan pipeline?"

"The pipeline, Alex, runs about 800 miles and was built after the 1973 oil crisis in the United States. It runs oil from the Prudhoe Bay oil field to the city of Valdez."

We went with Jon and Belynda out into the ice floes outside of Nova Scotia. A helicopter dropped us off to see the new pup seals. We were all dressed in orange so the helicopter could see us when it came back for us. It was spooky because the ice floe kept moving around. If the helicopter hadn't seen us, we would probably be in England by now. It was truly exciting and adventurous.

"Grandpa, I want to hear about your trips in the United States."

"Our country is such a beautiful country, Haleigh."

Our travels within North America ranged all over. In 1975 we visited Williamsburg, Virginia. During this visit, Doug had asthma and we had to go to a hospital in Charlottesville, Virginia. Doug fortunately only had to stay a few hours in the hospital. Then, while we were eating at an English restaurant in Williamsburg, one of the waiters said, "Pardon my hands," as he served lunch to us. To this day, the kids still remember that.

The next year, we decided to take a trip to Amish country. So, we went to Amish country in Pennsylvania to celebrate the winter activities. While we were there, I once was waiting in the lobby for the family and, when I saw them, I waved my hand to greet them. I almost became the owner of the hotel, because they had an auction going on. We saw the Amish people on horse and buggy going to work. They were dressed modestly and spoke modestly. When they spoke to you they were like any other people, but it just felt more spiritual when they looked at you.

"What are Amish?"

"The Amish, Rebecca, are a group of people of a Christian religion who keep to a tradition of simple living, plain dress, not adopting the many modern conveniences of life."

"Do they watch TV, Grandpa?"

"No, they don't watch TV, Haleigh."

"Pickle juice!"

On another journey in 1984, we went to New Mexico to visit some Indian trading posts. We went to Santa Fe, Albuquerque, and Taos. Judi and I trekked through the desert, up back roads, dusty trails, and torrential rain to an Indian post. I walked around and looked at the stuff, knowing from what people had told me that the Indians, or the Native Americans, are always ready to bargain. I looked at a piece of metal, *chazerai*. I said to the person who owned the place, "Very nice, but can you give me a good buy?" With that, he looked at the *chazerai*, looked at me, put his hand out, and said, "Goodbye."

One time when we were in the Florida Keys, we were swimming and I noticed a bunch of lilies. I swam under the water lilies and Doug swam underneath them, and we both got stung by man o' war jellyfish. I got stung so much that they not only had to shave my chest, but a doctor gave me a shot of bourbon to drink and a shot of bourbon to put on the stings. That's the first time I ever used a credit card in a doctor's office. Doug lovingly followed me. To this day, I have a huge bare mark on my chest where hair does not grow.

On another trip to Florida, we got cajoled by a local fisherman to go fishing for a special kind of fish that only comes out at night. We got in his little skiff, and quietly we went through the swamps. We were the bait. The insects enjoyed us immensely. And every once in a while, he would say, "I think I have it on my line. I lost it. I think I have it. I lost it." I think we were taken. Three hours later, full of bug bites and with three empty wallets, I was happy to give in.

"Sounds like you should stay out of the water in Florida."

"I've had some bad luck Haleigh, but I still enjoy visiting Florida waters."

"Pickle juice!"

In Churchill, Canada, one of the Canadian cities closest to the North Pole, bears run the town. The bears walk through the town and you get out of the way. We would go out through the tundra and you would see bears all over the place. We had tires that were literally ten feet high, and when the bears stretched, they literally went over the tires. It was cold, it was bitter, and we were truly in bear town, where the hometown rules.

"I love bears!"

"I don't think these are the kind of bears you are thinking about, Rebecca. They aren't the cuddly, soft kind you can put on your bed."

Another time in Canada, Judi and I went heli-hiking, where a helicopter landed you on the top of a mountain ridge and you hiked through the forest and the foliage and truly vibrant nature. You had to be careful because if you missed by three feet, you went down 5,000 feet. Heli-hiking was truly adventurous.

On one trip to Washington, D.C. with the family, we went to Arlington National Cemetery. We saw all crosses and then we saw that John F. Kennedy's grave had a cross. Jon said, "Daddy, I didn't know John F. Kennedy wasn't Jewish."

"Who's John F. Kennedy?"

"John F. Kennedy, Haleigh, was the thirty-fifth president of the United States."

"Pickle juice!"

The family traveled all over the world. Sometimes it wasn't a five-star trip; it was more like a seven-demerit trip. But as a family, we enjoyed the beauty of the world and the company of each other.

"What about your trips with Kathy, Grandpa?"

"In the past few years, I've enjoyed traveling with my children, as well as with Kathy."

One memorable experience was the "almost dinner from hell" with Kathy in Lisbon, Portugal. We went to a fancy hotel there that had a restaurant on the eighth floor with a panoramic view. We walked in and no one came up to us, yet the place was empty except for one couple. I now know why. President Sarkozy from France was coming in, and they wanted to get rid of us.

Finally, a manager pushed the hostess toward us, and she said, "Table for two?" And I said, "Yes."

"And do you have a reservation?"

I said, "No."

And she said, "No reservation?"

And here we were in an empty restaurant. She gave us a table. Fine. We sat down, we waited, we waited, and we waited, and we noticed that there was nobody in the restaurant except this one couple. There were possibly ten or twelve managers, waiters, and busboys. Finally we asked someone to come over. They gave us a menu.

I said, "Do you have a wine menu?"

We waited, we waited, finally my menu came, and I said to them, "Could you share with me which of the red wines is drier?" The guy walked away; a few minutes later someone else came back.

I said, "Pardon me, could you share with us which of the red wines is drier?"

Finally, he said, "Well, these two."

I said, "Which of the two?"

And he said, "I don't know; whichever you like, you take." So, we took one. Now they gave us a menu.

On the menu there were different foods from Portugal and I said, "Can we please have some water?" The waiter walked away.

I said, "Could we please have it without gas?" He looked at me. Nobody was smiling. Nobody was even speaking. Finally, they came back with water, and we began to order.

Kathy said she would like a salad and asked if the swordfish had bones in it.

The waiter literally said, obsequiously, "The swordfish is very fit."

She said again, "Pardon me, but does it have bones in it?"

Again he said, "The swordfish is very fit."

So I said, "Pardon me, sir, does the swordfish have bones in it?"

He said, "No." So we ordered the little swordfish appetizer.

She ordered the salad and then we had to decide on the main dish, so I said, "Can I have a few moments?" The waiter walked away. Finally, he came back and again, nobody is smiling. It is really frigid cold.

"Could you share with me the difference between this green fish and the lamb cutlet? And is a lamb cutlet the same as a lamb chop?"

The waiter said, "It is a lamb cutlet."

"Thank you, but is it a lamb CHOP?"

He said, "It is a lamb cutlet."

"Pardon me, but is a lamb cutlet the same as a lamb chop?"

He said, "It is a lamb cutlet."

Finally, I said to him, "Well, how do you usually recommend ordering it?"

"Whatever you like. I'm not eating it. You are, and that's your problem."

I said, "What is the usual order the chef likes to make?"

He said, "Whatever you like." With that, we stood up and walked out. It was the first time I had ever walked out of a restaurant in my life.

He said to me, "What shall I do with the wine you ordered?"

I said, "It's yours because we are not taking it and we are not drinking it, and we are not paying for it."

Besides Portugal, Kathy and I also visited the capital city of Riga in Latvia. In the city of Riga, we went to a Jewish museum, where communicating was difficult because the primary language of Latvia is Latvian. The secondary language is Russian. Both of these are not on the top of my linguist list. In the Jewish museum, we met an elderly woman who gave us a little booklet in Latvian and Hebrew. She mentioned that there are only 2,000 Jews left in Latvia, down from a quarter of a million. During World War II, 90 percent of the Jewish population of Latvia disappeared. We went to a temple in the Old City because the Old City was the poorer part of the city, and the Jews who lived in Latvia years ago were very poor. We noticed that there was a Latvian brain-drain. Many of the young people are leaving the country for greater opportunities in the West.

The city of Riga is on the Daugava River. It is a beautiful river. Riga has a very interesting skyline. During the Russian occupation, during and after World War II, a great many of the intellectuals were taken in the morning to the gulag, in Siberia, because the Russians wanted to get rid of the middle class and the intelligentsia. Only one percent of the people who ever went to Siberia survived. The country of Latvia has been overrun by Poland, Germany, Sweden, and Russia through the years. It has a large system of welfare. But it is still, in many ways, an Eastern country.

"Where else did you go?"

"We went to many places, Rebecca."

We traveled to the capital city of Vilnius in Lithuania from Latvia. People who come from Lithuania are called Litvaks. It's an interesting country, having been dominated by Nazi and Russian rule. We went to the National Museum, which describes the exile of many Lithuanians to Siberian gulags. This was carried out by Stalin and his successors after Moscow invaded and turned independent Lithuania into a vassal Soviet republic. We saw the Museum of Genocide Victims. It was a former prison where the Soviet secret police once imprisoned, tortured, and killed Lithuanian nationalists and others. The cells are intact and you can still walk through them. We went to the former site of the Jewish Quarter, and you can still see Hebrew writings on the wall. We saw the restored synagogue on Pylimo Street.

After visiting the city's holocaust museum, we just sat back. We realized how barbaric the times were. We were told that before the Nazis came into Lithuania, Lithuanian citizens took the Jews and shot them and then confiscated their property. This was before the Nazis ever came in. One person once asked one of the people who were shooting the Jews, "What do you have against the Jews?" He said, "I don't have anything against the Jews, except that I know that the Jewish commissars in Russia made our country hate them and we are very poor." Ninety percent of the Jews were exterminated out of an original population of a quarter of a million people.

I had the opportunity of getting a Bible in Hebrew and in Russian from one of the people at the synagogue in the Old City. We were very fortunate to get into the holocaust museum. It was closed on Friday and Saturday, but a woman was kind enough to let us in. We read a letter that will always be with me forever. It was from a mother, saying the following:

> My dear family, I am in a concentration camp. All of our family has been sent to die. I will die today. Please say Kaddish for me. I love you. Please be strong. Please be happy.

"What's a *Kaddish*, Grandpa?"

"A *Kaddish*, Rebecca, is a prayer that sons and daughters say for their departed loved ones. It is a way of respect and remembrance from generation to generation."

"That is sad, Grandpa."

"It *was* very sad, Haleigh…On a different note, Haleigh, did you know that the design of the zoo in Denmark was based on the nursery rhymes of Hans Christian Anderson and other children's stories?"

"Who is Hans Christian Anderson, Grandpa?"

"He's a Danish author and poet, Alex, mostly known for his children's stories."

"Do we know any of his stories?"

"Yes, he wrote many popular stories like 'The Ugly Duckling' and 'The Little Mermaid.'"

"I love 'The Little Mermaid'; Ariel is very pretty," Haleigh blurts out.

"I was lucky enough to meet Hans Christian Anderson on one of my trips."

In 2006 we went to Denmark and met a man who came up to us and asked, "Would you like to take a trip down memory lane?" At first we thought he was crazy, but we soon realized we had the opportunity to meet the writer Hans Christian Anderson. My kids and many people think I am quite old. Well, in Copenhagen, Denmark, I met someone who was almost as old as me, possibly a little older. Hans Christian Anderson was an interesting person, and he shared with me a story about his life.

As a child, he was very gangly, high-strung, and rather effeminate. He avoided school because the kids laughed at him, so he spent his time in a fantasy world full of books and plays. When his father died, he was on his own and he was forced into manual labor. He moved to Copenhagen, where I met him. He worked as a boy soprano for the Royal Theater. When his voice changed, the director encouraged him to return to school. He went to the university and, after graduation, toured Europe. He made many trips. He began to publish. His first published work was about a young man who was poor, who came into his own while traveling in Italy. Hans told me he met many people during his life—Charles Dickens, Victor Hugo, Franz Liszt, Richard Wagner, and Henrik Ibsen.

"Who are they?"

"They are all famous writers, Haleigh."

Anderson wrote plays and travel literature, but it was his fairy tales that made him famous in Denmark and abroad. These include "The Ugly Duckling," "The Emperor's New Clothes," "The Princess and the Pea," "The Little Mermaid," and "The Red Shoes." They made him Denmark's best-known author. He was the Danish Charles Dickens. His tales were interesting because he was kind of smart. He wrote fairy tales for adults so they, in turn, could read them to their children. They appealed to children and adults alike.

Hans took us around Copenhagen. He showed us Tivoli Gardens, which is Copenhagen's classic amusement park with so many rides and food. It was good for children and adults. We went to the Rosenborg Castle and Royal Treasury, which were Renaissance castles with a statue of the larger-than-life warrior King Christian IV. We looked at Christiania, which is a colorful, counter-culture squatter's colony. We went to Christiansburg Palace, with its royal reception rooms and dazzling tapestries.

On this tour, we visited many museums, such as the National Museum, which displays a history of Danish civilization with nineteenth-century pictorial apartments. Our guide also led us to the Museum of Danish Resistance, which chronicles Denmark's struggle against the Nazis. We went to the Thorvaldsen Museum, which has works by a Danish neoclassical sculptor. We went to the Danish Museum. This exhibited tracings of the 400-year history of Danish Jews. It was a unique building that was built or designed by the American architect Daniel Libeskind. At first, the Danish king invited Jews from Portugal when they were Sephardic some 400 years ago, then Jews came from Germany to settle in Denmark. We went to the Rosenborg Gardens, which is a park surrounded by the castle; the National Art Museum, where they have really neat Danish and Impressionist collections; and the Our Savior's Church, which is a spiral, spired church with a bright Baroque interior.

As we were ending the tour, Hans Christian Anderson said to me, "I hope you enjoyed the tour. My name is Richard Karpen. I am a Jewish boy from the Bronx who came to Copenhagen many years ago. I fell in love with the city and one of its women, and now I lead these tours every day in the summertime. The rest of the year I go to Buenos Aires, where I dance the tango." Richard Karpen said his family moved to Milford, New Jersey, and he went to Kean College. As we parted from each other for the last time, he shook my hands, gave me a small hug, looked me in the eye and said, "*Shalom*" (he was Jewish).

"Where was Hans Christian Anderson?"

"He was born and died in the 1800s; this man was acting as him, Haleigh."

"Pickle juice!"

"Tell us more, tell us more." Rebecca bounces up and down.

"Don't stop, Papa Larry."

In 2007, we traveled to St. Petersburg, Russia. Peterhof Palace was one of the places we visited. Peterhof became known as the most brilliant of all the summer residences of the Russian czars. The wish of Peter the Great was to have a palace and gardens even more impressive than Versailles. During World War II the invading German forces destroyed nearly all the buildings, but before the buildings were destroyed, half of the treasures were either buried or sent to Siberia. Peterhof Palace was shelled during World War II, but the Germans never invaded it. Many of the treasures were sent to the Urals for hiding and to the basement of a church in Leningrad. The palace was constructed in 1734 with a huge fountain. There is a scene that shows Russia's victory over the Swedes in 1709. It is now in the process of a complete restoration.

While in Russia, I noticed that it was ten minutes after ten p.m. in St. Petersburg, and it was daylight, as if it were twelve or one o'clock in the afternoon. It was unreal. All through Russia there are great monuments of kings and czars and generals, but where is the monument for the little person, the soldiers and civilians who died in the millions, who sacrificed their lives, their bodies, their homelands? Where is the statue, where is the prayer for the little man, the little guy, the little woman?

In St. Petersburg I had the experience of being able to shoot two Russian weapons, the Makarov, which is a pistol, and the Kalashnikov, which is an AK-47 machine gun. It was very exciting, because this was live ammunition. Let me tell you what happened. There were some sixteen people shooting Makarovs where I shot five shots from the pistol. I hit the target two times at twenty-five meters. For the Kalashnikov, they placed the target at fifty meters, and we had to wear ear protection at all times. We first had five shots and then ten continuous shots, like from a machine gun. I think I hit the target once.

I must tell you that Kathy was the big winner among all the sixteen people. There were people there who were ex-Marines and ex-Air Force people. She did not miss a target on any of her fifteen shots and won the first prize. It was exciting—it was like going back into the military! The owner thought Kathy was a former CIA agent. To rub it in, Kathy wore her sunglasses in a dark, dreary basement.

We also visited The State Hermitage Museum, which is the largest art museum in Russia. It ranks among the most prestigious and fantastic museums in the world. It has a great collection of Western European art that is truly second to none. It was founded by Catherine the Great in 1764 as a private court museum. I saw the works of Leonardo Da Vinci, Raphael, and Titian. There are Dutch and Flemish collections, including Rembrandt, Rubens, and Anthony van Dyck. There is a collection of Spanish art, including a collection of Picasso that is second only to Madrid's Prado. The French art collection is the largest outside of France. It consisted of works of Degas, Renoir, Monet, Cezanne, Gauguin, and Matisse. I visited the Gold Room, which was an unusual opportunity. Gold pieces from 5,000 years ago until today are displayed there.

We also traveled over to Stockholm, Sweden. I was exhausted. The Swedes are such exercise freaks. I was walking through the Old City and was absolutely exhausted. I got lost; I went to a taxicab driver. He said to me, "You don't want me to take you; it's a short walk." A short walk with them is four miles. We kept walking and I wanted to stop; I was exhausted. It was hot, then it rained, then it was hot, and then it rained again.

It's a beautiful city, but it was so congested because they had all the people from all over the world coming to see the large sailboats. They were having a race from Stockholm to Poland. We visited the great synagogue in Stockholm. Unfortunately, it was closed, though we did take a picture. Stockholm has different thoughts on life, compared to the United States.

"How is that, Grandpa?"

"As an example, Alex, walking through the middle of the city, they have open and closed-door urinals, where people can go for a minute just standing up. You do what you have to do and you just close the door, without a lock, in the middle of a large thoroughfare."

"That is different."

I had an opportunity to visit the Nobel Museum in Stockholm and see the awards of some people I knew. One was Polykarp Kusch, who was my physics teacher at Columbia and won the Nobel Prize in Physics in 1955. Not only was he a brilliant physicist, but a great teacher, and he spoke English like no one else had spoken it before. He once signed a research paper of mine on simple harmonic motion,

"I'm glad someone understands this concept. My congratulations."

I also saw the Nobel Prize award for the winner in physics in 1988, Melvin Schwartz. We were classmates and good friends who lived next door to each other at Columbia. He was a brilliant man as well. I even saw the chemistry prize that was won by Linus Pauling, who was the author of my chemistry textbook at Columbia. I only had a limited opportunity to meet him there because by the time I did meet him, he just didn't want to teach chemistry to the lower college classes. However, his book taught for itself.

In mid-2008, we went sightseeing in Greece. I got a chance to relive my college studies of Western Civilization from 2000 B.C. to the present. It's exciting to relive Herodotus, Aristotle, Plato, Socrates, Euripides, all the great authors, and all the great plays. It's like coming back home again after some fifty-five years. On our first day, we went to the Acropolis and the Parthenon. We also went to the Jewish museum and the Jewish synagogue. We found out that some 87 percent of the Jews in Greece during World War II were sent to the gas chambers. Our driver, who was a very learned person, said that most of the Greek Jews went to the U.S. before the Nazi invasion and were not annihilated by the Germans.

While in Greece, they had strong forest fires in the northern part of Greece, near Delphi. Our driver said that the CIA burned the trees because Greece had signed a pact with Russia for gas. I must have asked twenty other people, and they all said the fires were set by farmers. No one said anything about the CIA. Our guide also told us a World War II joke: A person had a thousand Jews with him and he went to the United States. They said, "We can't take them because we have a quota system." They went to England and they said, "We can't take them because we are at war." They went to a German widow living in Germany and she said, "Oh, that's too many Jews—I only have a little oven." Unfortunately, our guide represents the attitude of some other people in the world.

"What is the Acropolis?"

"The Acropolis means the top of the town, Rebecca, and Athens has this acropolis, which is a sheer limestone rock standing some 300 feet over the city. It is the key to the city."

"What is the Parthenon?"

"The Parthenon is the glory of the Acropolis, and probably the most famous building in the whole world."

The Parthenon is a Doric temple, constructed between 447 and 432 B.C. by Iktinos and Kallikrates. It was supervised by Patides, who was the Michelangelo of the Periclean Age. There are no straight lines in this temple. It was designed to hold a statue of Athena. It is a magnificent place, and although broken down, it is a sight to be seen.

The city of Olympia was also a stop in Greece. This was the original home of the Olympics, which started in 676 B.C. At that time there was only one winner, and the events consisted of chariot racing, wrestling, and running. They happened every four years. The first international Olympic competition began in 1896 in Athens. We went to Delphi and saw the site of the Delphic Oracle, which was a considerable influence throughout the Greek world.

"Wow! You traveled a lot," Alex commented.

"I guess so."

There are so many other places we visited, like Turkey. We went to Sardes, a Jewish community formed in the fifth century by the Lycidiums, which was later transformed into a synagogue. Now there are mosaics on the floor. On the road to Sardes, which is outside of Ismar by about an hour's drive, there are many factories on the road.

There are cement, perfume, and dye factories. We passed minarets. There are a lot of condos near Sardes. Another stop was Ephesus, which was built in the second century A.D. This city is famed for the Temple of Artemis, one of the Seven Wonders of the Ancient World, and it contains the largest collection of Roman ruins in the Mediterranean.

In September of 2009 our travels led us to Venice, Italy, on the *Crystal Serenity*. In Venice we visited the shop that sold me my ill-fated sailboat that I never received. It was out of business. Since this was a bust, we went on to the Jewish Quarter, the historical Jewish ghetto in Venice. Established in 1516, it is the oldest ghetto in the world and houses four synagogues—three Ashkenazi and one Sephardic. There were many statues and churches, as well as a Jewish museum, and it was like a city within a city in the Cannaregio district of Venice. From there we visited the Palazzo Ducale (a UNESCO World Heritage Site), the Ponte de Sapri, the Basilica de San Marco, and the Venetian glass factories.

"Some day I want to see the Venice ghetto," Haleigh murmured.

The tour went from Venice through the Adriatic Sea into the Ionian Sea to Katakolo, a seaside port town in West Greece, the site of ancient Olympia, where the Olympics first originated. The weather was superbly hot. In Olympia, which goes back to 456 B.C., the Temple of Zeus was old, yet the Temple of Hera was even older, dating back to 600 B.C.

From there, we set sail to Mykonos, a Greek island in the Aegean Sea. This island was made famous by Jackie Onassis, and has become one of the most sophisticated and cosmopolitan island resorts in the Aegean. The Greek island offers graceful windmills and inviting beaches. It has domed churches and whitewashed houses accented in red and blue. It is said that the islanders, in order to show their distaste for the Nazis in World War II, painted all of their houses white.

"You searched for windmills, Grandpa!"

"And I found them, Alex."

Near Mykonos, we visited the island of Delos. We saw the Agora and the Temple of the Delians. The original lion statues, which were made of granite, were put into a museum inside because the acidity of the atmosphere was literally turning the marble to chalk. What will be left for future generations to see if we do not do something about the climate now?

It is said that in ancient times, the island of Delos was a very prosperous trading center. It was attacked by the Romans, and half the people of the island were killed and the other half sold into slavery on the auction block. It is said that the people of Delos who were sold into slavery took their gold and put it into bags and stuffed it into little holes in the walls in hopes that they would return. But they never returned. In the year 31 B.C., this Greek island was incorporated into the Roman Empire, which changed the island of Delos forever. It is no longer a place for people to live, only a place for people to have their bones buried. It is a place of archaeological ruins of the past. This island is literally a museum today.

From there, we moved through the Bosphorus (also known as the Istanbul Strait) and the Dardanelles to the Black Sea. Our tour took us to Constanta, the oldest living city in Romania, and Odessa, the fourth-largest city in Ukraine and a major seaport.

From Odessa, our tour took us to Yalta, a city in southern Ukraine that is set on the site of an ancient Greek colony. This is a very famous place. In February 1945, Great Britain's Prime Minister Winston Churchill, U.S. President Franklin Roosevelt, and Soviet Premier Joseph Stalin met to make decisions for the future of postwar Europe. They established the founding conference for the

United Nations.

The Yalta Conference gave the ship away to the Soviet Union by securing the Soviet Union's aggressive agreement to end the war against Japan. There was an ultimate restructuring of postwar Europe into Eastern and Western blocs. When the terrible guns were finally stilled, it took many, many years before the Eastern Bloc was able to come out of the throes of the Soviet Bloc and communism. These were very dark times in the history of the world. Roosevelt was very ill at that meeting and died two months later. He was too weak physically and mentally to stand up to the challenges of Stalin.

Russia also got back some of the islands that it had lost in the Russo-Japanese war of the early 1900s. Russia eventually declared war on Japan, but Japan succumbed possibly three or four weeks after this declaration of war.

"I remember seeing a picture of the Yalta Conference in school," Alex said.

After Yalta, we visited Sinop, a city located in the most northern side of the Turkish part of the Black Sea. In Sinop, we toured a Muslim mosque, the Alaettin Mosque. The outside has a water fountain for what they call physical absolution. That's where you wash your hands and clean yourself. The purpose is just to wash your outside body to feel that you, personally, are clean. It's not what somebody else thinks about your cleanliness. That's the physical part. When you go into the mosque, the pulpit where the iman preaches usually faces east. There, they read from the Qur'an and people usually take their shoes off because they don't want to soil the carpet, and then you face east.

You don't have to go to mosques to pray. Sometimes these people pray five times a day, because the prayer is between you and the Holy

One. It's spiritual, and it's what you feel and what you do that is important; it does not have to be done in a mosque. Most people do not go to a mosque to pray. Sometimes when you look at the carpets, they will have a design and an arrow pointing to where the east or a mosque is. East, of course, is toward Mecca. The iman, who preaches, reads the Qur'an in Arabic. There are many countries of the world that do not understand Arabic, so the preacher interprets the Qur'an into the language of the country. In this place it is Turkish.

During the 1850s, the Russians came from Sebastopol and conquered Sinop. They were very smart, because the Black Sea has a left storm region and a right storm region, and in the middle is a small area where you can sail without worrying about storms. On a foggy night they came to this area, attacked Sinop, and destroyed it because the Russians wanted an outlet from the Dardanelles to Bosphorus, to Sinop, to the Black Sea. When Sinop was attacked, Britain and France came to the aid of the Turks; thus began the Crimean War, which the Russians lost. To this day, Russia always seeks and wants to maintain outlets to the Mediterranean through the Black Sea. The order of seas through Venice is the Adriatic Sea, the Ionian Sea, the Aegean Sea, the Dardanelles, the Sea of Marmara, the Bosphorus Sea, and the Black Sea.

"The Russians were pretty smart," Rebecca said.

At the end of the tour, we ended up in Istanbul, the largest city (a megacity) in Turkey located on the Bosphorus Strait.

In some fifty-five years, I have traveled around the world to the seven continents. Some things stay vivid in my mind, such as the time I was a young Air Force officer going to a hotel in Hong Kong for some R and R (rest and recuperation). Sitting in the hotel lobby, I saw an elderly man and woman, she with thick glasses, he with a large cane. Each of them was saying to the other, "What a beautiful view!" They couldn't walk, and they couldn't see. They had saved throughout their life to see the world and now they were seeing it through the walls of the lobby in a Hong Kong hotel. I made a pact with myself—this was not going to happen to me. I was going to see the world, even if it was on seven-demerit rather than five-star trips, while I was still young and vibrant.

Now that I return some fifty-five years later to travel the seven continents once more, I have a tear in my eye because of things remembered. At the same time, I have a worrisome heart because of what I see in my travels nowadays. The ice of the Arctic and Antarctica has disappeared into the water. The marble of Greece and Turkey, because of the acidity in the atmosphere, is literally turning to chalk. When will our civilization begin to realize that what once was, may never be again?

Future generations may have to see history through movies, photos, and computers, rather than seeing what we have done over centuries and generations through the artifacts of man. I have hope, but change will require tremendous leadership around the world at a very fast pace.

I remember being in Delos, where the citizens would vie for public office, but would only have a tenure of two years because the taxpayers did not want them to be corrupt with their money. Maybe they had the right idea—maybe we need people with gumption, with power, and with leadership who might save this world for the future.

I have traveled by myself, with my family, and now with Kathy, and I have experienced the world. I continue to experience the world and travel to this day and look forward to the many more adventures to come with Kathy and my family. My dream is a reality. Now I can look at my stamp collection and say, "I've been there!" And, if I haven't been there, I can say, "I'm going there! I've visited 135 countries, and there's always more."

"I think I want to collect stamps too."

"I'd love to share mine with you, Alex."

"I'm going to travel the world like you some day, Grandpa."

"I hope you do!"

"Grandpa, you learn so much history traveling too. I want to learn more. I didn't know all of those things happened to the Jews."

"History is fascinating, and you can experience it just like me. In fact, you are making history now, Alex."

"What do you mean, Grandpa?"

"Well, I'm living history for you, like you will be for your grandchildren in the future. Everything you live now will be history for them."

"I'm living history too."

"Yes, Alex, you are."

"Grandpa, can you tell me your living history?"

"I want to know history too!" Rebecca shouts and skips around as we finish our day at the zoo.

"Me too!" Haleigh shrieks.

As we exit the zoo and make our way home, I realize that I am like a history scholar, sharing my life and my memories with a young generation that is making its own history. The most I can hope for is that they learn from the past and help form a world with more compassion, love, and understanding for all.

Pulling up my biggest catch of all, a sailfish, during a deep-sea fishing adventure in Acapulco, Mexico. Sailfish, highly prized game fish, resemble swordfish and marlin. They live in warmer oceans and are known for their incredible jumps. Sailfish grow up to ten feet and can weigh up to 200 pounds. 1990

Resting for a spell in Egypt to take a puff from the hookah, an instrument used for smoking tobacco in which the smoke is cooled and filtered by passing through water, 1989

Showing my musical talents on the marimba, in Costa Rica. The marimba has tubular resonators under the bars and is pitched an octave lower than the zylophone. 2001

Rappelling along the ravines, canyon walls, waterfalls, and bridges, Costa Rica, 1996

Petting a harp seal in Nova Scotia, Canada. Millions of harp seals feed in the cold winter months in the rich waters of Newfoundland and the Gulf of St. Lawrence. One of the most spectacular wildlife events in North America can be seen as spring approaches and one-third of the harp seals give birth on ice floes to an estimated 500,000 seal pups. 1991

Enjoying one of my many hobbies, planes, at the annual EAA AirVenture Oshkosh aviation celebration, Oshkosh, Wisconsin, 1990

During a visit to Salt Lake City, Utah, I was able to experience the thrill of speed and 4G force in the Men's Luge, Bobsled and Skeleton track run at Utah Olympic Park. The luge is a one- or two-person sled on which the riders face up and feet first. 2002

Making friends with a falcon in Greenbriar, West Virginia. Falcons are reknowned for their exceptional vision. Some have a visual acuity 2.6 times that of humans. 1988

Sharpshooter Kathlyn (Kathy) Phillips takes out the competition with a Kalashnikov (AK-47) in St. Petersburg, Russia. The AK-47 was first developed in the Soviet Union in the 1940s. It is a selective fire, gas-operated 7.62 mm assault rifle, the most popular assault rifle in the world. 2007

Kathy (back) and I take a break from rappelling over the jungles of Costa Rica to stroll over a hanging bridge. Costa Rica was named the "greenest" country in the world by the New Economics Foundation. 2006

Living History

The world is full of people who will document.
The world desperately needs people who will document,
but also change behavior.

—*Lawrence S. Harte*

"How do you know so much about history, Grandpa?"

"I guess because I lived a lot of it, Haleigh, and as a kid, I was a voracious reader. I just absolutely LOVED history."

"Did you always like to read about history?"

"Yes, I did. I probably got that from my Uncle Louie."

I tried to understand history by looking at the economic, social, political, and military aspect of each period. I used to feel that I was living in that period when I read about it. Some of the books that I read as a kid still stand out for me. The book *How to Win Friends and Influence People*, by Dale Carnegie, had a great effect on my life. I read it. And I read it. And I read it. Yet I would always think, "How can you be tough and rough, and yet be friendly and influence people?"

Another author and gentleman of many trades was Benjamin Franklin. I enjoyed reading his *Poor Richard's Almanack* and his autobiography. He was so practical, and I try to be a practical person.

I was extremely fond of the essays by the French writer and philosopher Michel de Montaigne that deal with education and bringing up children. I also used to read Rudyard Kipling because I was so excited about India and Kipling's poetry. I loved *Gunga Din*. I said to myself that someday I would visit India.

I was keen on reading about Alexander Hamilton as well. I just felt good about his kind of democracy, even though it was a Hamiltonian democracy. I'm not saying it was the right thing, but it certainly was an interesting thing. How funny though—as much as I loved to read about history when I was a kid, little did I realize how much history I was living through. Go figure!

"What history did you live through, Grandpa?"

"Where do I start, Alex? There are so many things in history that happened when I was growing up, I'm not sure I even remember it all."

In 1939 Hitler was named Man of the Year. They finally discovered the insecticidal properties of DDT (Dichloro-Diphenyl-Trichloroethane), which is a well-known synthetic pesticide that in the second half of World War II aided in warding off mosquitoes and lice and reducing diseases caused by these insects. It was also the year that Einstein wrote the first letter to President Franklin D. Roosevelt about nuclear energy. That letter is said to have launched the arms race. What's more, Winston Churchill became prime minister of the United Kingdom, and the Bolshevik revolutionary and Marxist theorist Leon Trotsky, who was one of the Russian leaders of the October Revolution, second to Lenin, was assassinated in Mexico by a soviet agent.

"What's the 'arms race,' Grandpa?" Haleigh asks in a confused tone while she looks out of the window of the car.

"It's when two or more parties, or groups, compete to have more weapons and a stronger military. They are fighting to have larger numbers of weapons and a greater military and to be superior in military technology."

"Pickle juice!"

In 1940 the polls showed that 85 percent of Americans wanted to keep out of the conflict called World War II. Wow! France, one of our allies, had more trained men and more guns, and better tanks and bombers, but the German blitzkrieg took them by surprise. The Germans beat the French under cover of dark, with soldiers and tanks. During this time, Washington finally leased fifty U.S. destroyers to London, and Henry Kaiser persuaded President Roosevelt that he could make ships much faster through mass production. He did it much quicker than the four years that the regular people wanted to do it in. This saved our country in many ways.

"What is mass production, Papa Larry?"

"Well, Rebecca, mass production is when a large number of products are made, especially using an assembly line."

"What's an assembly line?"

"An assembly line is when the parts of a product are planned in a sequential or organized way and put together quicker going down a line than by one person doing it all by hand."

"Huh?"

"Basically, it's a way to make products quicker, like dolls or ships or cars."

"Oh! I get it."

"What else happened in history, Grandpa?"

"A lot happened, Alex."

An American journalist and New York editor, Varian Fry, volunteered to help intellectuals and artists escape from Marseilles, France. Marseilles was bombed by the German and Italian forces and was occupied by the Germans from 1942 to 1944. Among the people that Fry helped to escape were Marc Chagall, a Jewish Russian artist known for his association with several key art movements, not to mention his unique career in just about every artistic medium; the prolific artist Max Ernst, who was one of the main pioneers for the Dada movement and Surrealism; the Cubist sculptor, Jacques Lipchitz; and the Polish harpsichordist Wanda Landowska.

"He was a nice man. He helped free all those people."

"It was a great thing to do, Haleigh. Fry helped some great artists."

While these artists were being freed, there was more history being made in the arts, such as the musical *Pal Joey* by Rodgers and Hart, which was often thought their best show. Some great songs were written, like "You are My Sunshine," "The Last Time I Saw Paris," "I Hear a Rhapsody," "When the Swallows Come Back to Capistrano," and "I'll Be with You in Apple Blossom Time." The American novelist Ernest Hemingway published one of his literary masterpieces, *For Whom the Bell Tolls*, and Thomas Wolfe's *You Can't Go Home Again* was published posthumously.

This year was the year that penicillin and sulphur were recognized as true discoveries as well. What a year! It was also the time that nylon stockings finally went on sale in the United States and the year of New York City's World's Fair, which promised to show "the World of Tomorrow." My Uncle Louie took me there. I saw many, many things of the future like the General Motors vision of 1960 of a device that measured the thickness of my hair. You could climb into the cockpit of a real airplane and witness television for the first time. I also saw the Trylon and Perisphere, which were the symbols of the fair. It was exciting! I was awakening to the wide, wide world. This was also the year when draft registration for approximately sixteen million men began in the United States.

"You saw television for the first time?"

"Yes, Rebecca, and it was different than the television from today."

"How was it different, Grandpa?"

"The first televisions, Alex, came as furniture; they were very bulky and heavy and had small screens. Television was also only in black and white."

"There was no color?"

"No, no color."

There was so much going on in the forties. From the time television made its debut at the 1939 World's Fair, commercial television with thirteen channels came out in 1947 and was available to everyone. Even computers were developed during the early forties, such as the ENIAC, a digital computer that weighed over thirty tons and stood two stories high and came out in 1945.

"That's a big computer, Grandpa. It's not like my laptop."

"No, Alex, it's not like your laptop. Laptops didn't even exist back in those days; they came out many years later."

Even though WWII was over in 1945, the time period after that was called the Cold War. The 1950s was a fearful time because paranoia regarding the threat of communism ran through many Americans. The outbreak of the Korean War also increased the Red Scare. Americans were on edge. They feared losing another Asian country to communism.

The most infamous politician of the early 1950s was Senator Joseph McCarthy. McCarthy encouraged witch hunts for communists and spies through fear and manipulation. His popularity took a plunge by the mid-1950s, and his reign of fear ended. Another popular communist-hunter, who would later resign from the presidency of the United States, was Richard Nixon. He even earned the name "Tricky Dick" because of his questionable financial integrity during his time as vice president under Eisenhower. It was a heck of a decade.

"There were witches, Papa Larry?"

"Not real witches, Rebecca. It's a figure of speech meaning that they were hunting a specific group of people."

"You can hunt people?"

"Not hunting; it's more like looking for a specific group of people, Haleigh."

"Pickle juice!"

"What's communism, Papa Larry?"

"Communism is when the government takes over and controls everything," Alex responds to Rebecca, remembering one of our past conversations.

"That's right, Alex. McCarthy began accusing people of being communists, those who believe in communism. And so, many people started acting a little crazy, thinking communists were trying to take over our government. This is when they started the witch hunt of looking for communists."

The 1950s was also a decade of change, with the introduction of rock and roll and such artists as Elvis Presley. Fashion changed from conservative to a more casual, loose look compared to the formal forties. Some big-name movie stars of this decade were Marilyn

Monroe, Gary Cooper, Bing Crosby, Bob Hope, and Frank Sinatra. The fifties also changed how people viewed teenagers: rather than being seen as children, they were viewed as consumers and upcoming voters.

"Grandpa, what do you mean by consumer?"

"A consumer, Haleigh, is a person who buys things in our economy."

"I buy things, Grandpa. Does that mean I'm a consumer?"

"Yes, Haleigh, you are a consumer."

"Was it expensive to buy things in the fifties, Grandpa?"

"Prices in the fifties were great, Alex! Can you believe that a house averaged around $10,000, gas ranged between eighteen and twenty-five cents a gallon, and a car cost around $2,000? What a deal."

This was a time when consumerism took off in a big way, and in turn jobs were created, and wealth. In 1953 I was a student at Columbia when General Eisenhower was our university president. Columbia, I believe, got him for his fundraising abilities. He was all business, not an intellectual, but a manager. I remember him once saying at a student council meeting, "Unless I hear anything objectionable, the resolution is carried." I still remember his technique years later. Dwight D. Eisenhower went on that same year to serve as president of the United States.

"Was he a good president?"

"He was just an okay president, Rebecca."

As president of the United States, he did one interesting thing. He introduced an extensive highway system across the United States in case there was a problem with the Russian menace. The pluses are that we have a great highway system; the minuses are that we increased the number of our cars, increased our gas consumption, increased our environmental problems, and decreased our mass transit.

Then, in 1955, I had the great privilege of meeting the Hungarian-born Jewish conductor and violinist, Eugene Ormandy. When I was at dental school in Philadelphia, he was the conductor of the Philadelphia Symphony. The guy was unbelievably involved in being not good, but great. Good was not a word in his vocabulary.

"Just like you, Grandpa?"

"What do you mean, Haleigh?"

"Good is not in your vocabulary, Grandpa. You always say, 'Good isn't enough; it has to be great.'"

"Yes, I guess you're right, we are a bit alike," I reply with a muffled chuckle. It's incredible what a child remembers.

The year 1955 was also when I bought my first car, that 1940 Plymouth Coupe, for $250. The car was "air conditioned" all year round. It had no heat, but it was great for taking out dates that were always cold. When I said, "Fill 'er up!" I meant oil, not gas.

The late fifties and early sixties were dominated by the civil rights movement. Since black men joined the armed forces and fought for their country, social equality was an issue for this group. The movement met with widespread resistance in the South. It was a violent time.

"How sad, Grandpa, that blacks weren't liked just like the Jews."

"It was a very bad time, Haleigh. The blacks suffered a lot, but eventually they were treated equally in this country."

This was the time of the famous march on Washington, D.C., in August 1963, when Martin Luther King made his "I Have A Dream" speech. Soon after, the Civil Rights Act of 1964 was signed by President Johnson, prohibiting discrimination based on race, color, religion, sex, and national origin. Feminism also took front-and-center stage in the early 1960s. The traditional role of the woman's place at home was challenged. Social movements weren't the only thing arising in the sixties. The invention of the laser, the first human spaceflight to orbit the Earth, the invention of the first computer video game, the first humans to leave Earth's gravity (Apollo 8), and the first humans to walk on the moon (Apollo 11) are some of the fascinating occurrences of the sixties.

"There were a lot of things going on in the sixties, Grandpa."

"It was such a wonderful experience, Alex. Today, I look at the video games and technology with NASA, and it's neat how technology has changed throughout the years. It just exploded!"

In 1957, I went into the Air Force as an officer. I celebrated by buying a Bel Air Chevrolet white convertible with red interior for $5,000 cash. I was in seventh heaven. I never got a speeding ticket as long as I wore my uniform. I took the car down south to Florida and up to northern Canada to go skiing. I had the most fun in this car. By 1962, the car had no heat and the convertible covering was torn. This, along with my wife's pregnancy, convinced me to buy a Mercury Comet.

"Did you ever get in a car accident, Grandpa?"

"I had my first accident in 1967, Haleigh. It was a head-on collision. I hit a Fiat that had turned into my lane."

"Was anyone hurt?"

"Fortunately, nobody was hurt. I remember calling home from the police station and your grandmother was complaining that the dinner on the table was cold. It kind of hurt my feelings."

"Grandpa, did you meet any famous people?"

"Yes I did, Alex."

I met Ted Williams in Florida in 1960, the year he retired from baseball. He was considered one of the greatest hitters in Major League baseball. I can't believe that he became a manager for the Texas Rangers in 1968. He was such a good hitter. Even when he was a manager, I really felt that he could hit better than anyone else that he ever managed. The guy was the consummate ball player. He was disciplined and a brilliant hitter. I have an autographed baseball from him.

The sixties was the first time I met Yogi Berra, too. I met him in Florida in 1965, and I met him at a little bagel place in Verona, New Jersey, in 2009. Yogi was always the same. I once mentioned to him, "You know, I was a Brooklyn fan, Yogi, and we used to come in second." Yogi said, "Yeah, but better to come in first!"

"Who was Yogi Berra?"

"He was one of the great baseball players of his time, Alex, and he played for the New York Yankees for most of his career. He was elected to the Baseball Hall of Fame and may be the greatest catcher of all time."

The fifties and sixties were also the time that New York City had a three-term mayor, Robert Ferdinand Wagner, Jr. The New York Mets were born during his term in 1957. I met the mayor in 1962.

"Did you like him, Papa Larry?"

"I thought he was a good mayor, Rebecca."

His terms allowed him to develop the city by building public housing and schools and creating the City University of New York system. Under his administration, he saw the building of Shea Stadium and the Lincoln Center. I believe Mayor Wagner really wanted to live in the footsteps of his father, who was in the national spotlight as a U.S. Senator.

In the mid-sixties I was introduced to Doc Severinsen. He was the band leader for Johnny Carson, and I met him a few times because he brought his kids to our office. His wife once said to me, "This child needs braces!" I said, "Why? The teeth look good." She said, "Take a picture." So I took a picture and saw one little rotation. It shows you that a photograph is better than the eye.

On one of Doc Severinsen's gigs in Las Vegas, I met him afterwards and he introduced me to Johnny Carson, Carol Burnett, and Danny Kaye, who was getting on in years. Johnny Carson, I found, was a very quiet person, very humble. This guy could prepare like no one could prepare. Carol Burnett was a lovely butterfly, smiling, vivacious, happy, running around on tiptoes. This was my second time seeing Danny Kaye. I once saw him when I was a camp counselor. I thought he was the consummate actor. This guy was as talented as talented could be.

When we met Doc Severinsen in Las Vegas, my cousin, Dr. Steve Grussmark, was introduced by me to him and many of his celebrity friends. I think my cousin Steve, who really got around, was open-mouthed and wide-eyed, and he said, "Oh my gosh! Look at all these people that Doc Severinsen knows, and my cousin Larry treated his kids!"

In Las Vegas I sat next to Telly Savalas (a bald, famous actor) at a craps table. He was bald, I was getting bald, he was throwing chips away like crazy, and I was trying to squeeze my chips to save them. He had a big cigar, and he gave me a cigar, so I smoked too. People came over to get his autograph, and they got MY autograph. If they only knew who I was. Telly was a very nice man, soft spoken, and had a great cigar, but it stunk like heck.

"I don't know any of those people, Grandpa," Alex confesses with a dazed look on his face.

"I don't know them either, Grandpa," Haleigh seconds.

"Me too," Rebecca adds.

"They were before your time. They were all pretty famous people from their days."

"We'll take your word for it, Grandpa," Alex declares. "What happened after the sixties?"

"Much, much more!"

The seventies started out with the nation's most liberal abortion law going into effect in New York and the gay rights demonstration march by homosexuals from New York's Greenwich Village to Central Park. National Guardsmen fired into a crowd protesting the Vietnam War at Kent State University, and President Nixon sent combat units into Cambodia. Two years later President Nixon became the first U.S. president to visit China and Moscow; he ordered the biggest bombing raid on North Vietnam, signed a strategic arms limitation treaty with the Soviet foreign minister, and won a second term in the White House. The next year Nixon agreed to turn over tape recordings that dealt with the Watergate scandal and was forced to resign due to the threat of impeachment in 1974. That same year the former president Nixon was pardoned by President Gerald Ford.

Amidst the politics and world news of the seventies, science and sports did not stay behind. Astronauts from the Apollo 15 explored the moon's surface in the Lunar Rover, and the Pioneer 10 spacecraft was sent off to Jupiter, where it sent detailed photos of the planet and moons. Joe Frazier took the heavyweight championship from Muhammad Ali. Then Ali reclaimed his title when he knocked out George Foreman, and in 1978 Leon Spinks took the title from Ali in Las Vegas. Toward the end of the seventies, Italy legalized abortion, against the Vatican's insistence that it was homicide, and the pope, Pope John Paul II, traveled to the United States, which was the first time a pope set foot on American soil.

"What's the Vatican, Papa Larry? Who's the pope?" Rebecca blurts out, hopelessly trying to understand everything.

"The Vatican, or Vatican City, is the smallest city in the world and is located within Rome, the capital city of Italy. It is a sovereign state, meaning it rules itself, and it is ruled by the bishop of Rome—the Pope. The Pope is the worldwide leader of the Catholic Church."

"Is there a worldwide rabbi, Grandpa?"

"That's a good question, Haleigh. No, there isn't a worldwide rabbi like the Pope."

"Pickle juice!"

The seventies was an eventful decade. During this time, I met various famous people. I remember meeting Abraham "Abe" David Beame in his third year of his term as mayor of New York City. He was a plain city guy, a glad-hander—the consummate politician. A person once went up to him and said, "Mayor, we'd like to give you a contribution and we'd like your ear when you get elected." Mayor Beame said, "When I get elected, you can have BOTH of my ears!"

I met the former New York City mayor, Edward Koch, who was also a congressman. Mayor Koch was a feisty, honest person, with strong values and strong beliefs on social issues. It was a pleasure to listen to him. He was a no-nonsense guy and lots of fun to be with.

I also met Governor Nelson Aldrich Rockefeller in 1973. I really felt that, with his heritage and his pristine background, he really ought to become president of the United States. He went from Democrat to Republican, but he couldn't quite make it to the presidency. He had to be happy with being the forty-first vice president of the United States. I think that, in his heart, he really wanted to be president and lead our country.

As a kid, the New York Knicks were my favorite basketball team.

Later, the great team of 1973 NBA Champions with Dave Debusschere, Earl Monroe, Walt Frazier, Willis Reed, Bill Bradley, and Jerry Lucas were my heroes. Through the years I happened to meet each of them for a short while. Bill Bradley was the consummate team player; he was a gifted athlete at Princeton and eventually became a senator from New Jersey. I was hoping that he would run for president, but I guess his plans were different. To this day, I regret it.

Dave Debusschere—God, he was so good! He was a great team man and a great organizer, and later on he became an executive in basketball. The guy had talent and leadership. Vernon Earl Monroe came from Washington, and to this day, I think that this guy's fakes and gives were absolutely outrageous. He was a fantastic basketball player.

If you had one man to go to, or one game, I would give it to Walt Frazier. The guy was Mr. Cool, and he was just extraordinary. Willis Reed's basketball career was cut short due to injuries, but not without his earning the acknowledgment of being one of the greatest Knicks next to Walt Frazier and Patrick Ewing. He was a giant of a man, a team man, and a great leader. And there was Jerry Lucas. I used to be astounded by his memory. The guy was a genius. This was an unusual basketball team managed by a great manager, Red Holtzman, who only wanted to win. And win he did.

Besides members of the Knicks, I met the 1972 Olympic gold medalist wrestler Dan Gable. I've met him a few times through the years. This guy was the greatest wrestler that America had. He almost never lost. I think he did lose once, and he was an Olympic champion. You could see his determination in his eyes, his will to win, his stamina, his athleticism. Am I glad I never wrestled HIM! He would have rolled me around like a wheelbarrow.

When I was forty, I wanted to improve my tennis skills, so I enrolled in the world-famous tennis camp of Nick Bollettieri on the west coast of Florida. It was hell! Marine boot camp had to be easier. After one week of hitting tennis balls literally forever, getting motivational psychology, and living in barracks-type hotels, I came home with my Tennis Scar.

"What's a 'Tennis Scar,' Grandpa?"

"A Tennis Scar, Alex, is a swollen ganglion on my left wrist that I have as a memento to this day."

"What's ganglion, Grandpa?"

"It's a cyst, Haleigh, which is a swelling on or around tendons and joints that usually occurs around the wrist or on the fingers."

"Pickle juice!"

Andre Agassi, who was at this same academy at about the same time, wrote an autobiography mentioning the relentless pressure and cutthroat competition there. At least he made money on the place. The only thing I have to show is my permanent ganglion swelling.

"Who is Andre Agassi, Papa Larry?"

"Agassi, Rebecca, is a former world number one professional American tennis player."

I also had the opportunity of meeting two great Australian tennis stars at Mount Washington in New Hampshire, Rod Laver and Roy Emerson. I happened to be in the Pro Am, where Roy Emerson was my partner, and Rod Laver had some other partner. I remember Emerson saying to me, "Larry, just keep the racket in front of you. Don't reach for it—I'll take care of the rest of the court." Emerson took care of the rest of the court and we won. These guys were fantastic athletes; they were perfect gentlemen and could drink like heck. Both Emerson and Laver won championships at Wimbleton and around the world.

Sam Snead was one of the greatest golfers of all time. I happened to see him at Greenbriar giving a lesson. He had a big straw hat on and was sitting on a chair, looking at this klutz and schlep who was paying him big bucks to teach him. I looked at Sam Snead's face, and he seemed to be saying, "I'll take the money, but this guy should take up a different sport." Sam Snead was not only a great golfer, but also a great teacher. It was wasted on me. He looked at me and wanted to say, "Son, where did you spend your youth, because it sure wasn't hitting a golf ball!"

Golf wasn't the only thing I wasn't too good at—ask anyone who rode in a car with me and they'll tell you about my driving. All three grandchildren nod their heads in unison, agreeing with my statement as they hold on for dear life in the car, waiting to reach our destination.

"How many cars did you have, Grandpa?"

"I had a few cars up through the seventies, Alex."

I went through two cars in the seventies. In 1971 I changed from my Mercury Comet to a Buick LeSabre. The family called it "Old Betsy." This car had a facility for going through snow. It never let us down. I was once stopped by a police officer who wanted to give me a speeding ticket. He had compassion for me. He said, "How can I give you a ticket with a car that looks like a piece of crap?" In this same car, I was caught going the wrong way on a one-way street. A police car met me bumper-to-bumper. I told the officer that since there were no cars on the street, I did not realize it was a one-way. Luckily, no ticket!

Well, Old Betsy gave us a good six years until I traded her in for an Oldsmobile 88 in 1977. The family was moving up to a yellow car. This car was neat. The problem was with getting stopped. I once ran a red light and was stopped by a police officer. The officer said, "Didn't you see the light?" I told him, "I saw the light, I just didn't see you, officer."

From the 1980s to the present, the first woman on the Supreme Court, Sandra Day O'Connor, was seated; Indian Prime Minister Indira Ghandi was assassinated; the space shuttle *Challenger* exploded, killing all seven aboard; AIDS increased in Africa and other developing countries; the World Wide Web and the personal computer (PC) became fixtures in our lives; cloning, stem cell research, and genetic engineering all increased; Microsoft grew; the mobile phone was invented; the Hubble Space Telescope was launched; the first African-American president of the United States, Barack Obama, took office; and so much more occurred.

I even met Herb Brooks in the late 1980s. He was the coach of the United States Hockey Team that won the gold medal against overwhelming odds after being trounced by the Russians in a preliminary game. The United States Hockey Team defeated Russia in the semifinals and Finland in the finals.

Brooks's eyes to me were piercing and extraordinarily focused. His handshake left imprints on my hand that remain to this day. I asked Brooks, "If the U.S. played the Russians ten times, how many games would the U.S. win?" I will always remember his answer, "If you have faith in a cause and work as a team, you can carry the day. The team believes in themselves and in their country." Herb Brooks was the consummate motivator.

"I'm living history with you too, Grandpa. I use my mommy and daddy's PC. I know how to use the Internet and I like to talk on Mommy's mobile phone!"

"You are living history with me, Haleigh."

"How many more cars did you go through since the seventies, Grandpa?"

"I went through a good number of cars, Alex."

The Oldsmobile '88 was upgraded to a diesel Cadillac in 1982. The car would not run in the cold. I wrote to Cadillac, "The Cadi lacks class." I am still waiting for an answer. So five years later we purchased a Triumph TR7 sports car. I knew there was a problem when one day at a diner, a truck driver told me to buy an extra TR7, one for parts and one to drive. He was right! Well, two years later in 1989, I upgraded to a BMW 525. What a great-looking sports car. The problem was the transmission. The car looked beautiful; it just didn't go fast.

In 1992, I became the proud owner of my best sports car, the BMW 529. I took this car to a Connecticut race track and it did 117 mph. What a ride! Then, in 1997, I decided to go with the Lexus make. I purchased a Lexus SC400. What a beautiful car. Too bad it didn't last long. It was stolen from the driveway and found in Newark. It was stripped down; what a professional job! So, I went with a Lexus RX 330, my first four-wheel drive, that drove great through the snow. I always went out in the worst weather to test the car. Now, I drive a Lexus convertible hardtop. I purchased this car in 2000, and it is the car of cars. The only problems are that it has no extra tire, no cargo space, and no back seat, and it does not go in the snow. But it is beautiful!

"Tell us more about famous people you've met, Grandpa."

"Throughout these years, Alex, not only have I had my share of unique cars, I've also had the opportunity to meet many interesting and famous people."

In 1980, I met Red Auerbach, who was the coach of the Boston Celtics. He was born in Brooklyn like me and is of Russian-Jewish decent. I had the opportunity of listening to him speak one day and then talking to him afterward for about a half hour. His philosophy was that if you gave him the best athletes and the best team people, he would give you a great winning team. And he did.

I met Jimmy Connors and John McEnroe in 1982 when they were just plain young, at the West Orange Tennis Club. They would play board hockey. They were enthusiastic smart-aleck types, and fantastically talented.

I met President George Bush, Sr., in 1991 when he came to New Jersey to campaign for Thomas Kean. Kean was campaigning for the governor's office. I found President Bush, Sr., to be the prototype of what is America—he had a CIA and military background, was a Yale alumnus, an athlete, and an all-American guy. He was a fine man, a gentle man, and a fair president, and you couldn't find a nicer person with better credentials.

In 1996, I met President Clinton at an affair in Washington, D.C. There were some 150 people there, and he came up to me and said, "Hi, my name is Bill Clinton. What is your name?" I said, "Larry Harte." He shook my hand and said, "Larry Harte. How do you spell Larry?" And I said, "L-A-R-R-Y." "And Harte, how do you spell Harte?" I said, "H-A-R-T-E." He said, "Larry Harte—that is a nice name. It's so nice to see you, and thank you for coming here and supporting me." About an hour and a half later, he came up to me and said, "Larry Harte, it's so good to see you, and thank you again for supporting me." I forgot my name, but he remembered. The guy was an unbelievable politician, with a great technique for memory. It's a shame that he had the Monica Lewinsky situation. He spent so much time of his presidency fighting an impeachment that he had little opportunity to really do what he might have done for the country, because the man had intellect, charisma, and energy.

That same year I met Pete Sampras at Flushing, New York. He was, in some ways, the most accomplished American tennis player, as far as winning tournaments goes. He was soft-spoken and quiet. I got the feeling that he was almost bored by tennis. I was also at Wimbledon, where Pete Sampras won the men's competition and Lindsay Davenport won the women's competition. It was a rare all-American, Yankee Doodle double. I remember being in the stands after traveling all night, sitting at Wimbledon at night in ninety-degree weather amidst ladies with large, long cocktail dresses and men with blue blazers and blue and white flannel suits.

I ate strawberry whipped cream pie at the fancy club. There I was in dungarees and unshaven. I remember Jimmy Connors and John McEnroe yelling and screaming, "Let's go, U.S.A!" Even I began, "Let's go, U.S.A!" The gentleman next to me, an Englishman, said, "I say, old chap, you have a bit of nationalistic spirit in you." I said, "I'm sorry, sir, but when it gets to my heart, it gets to my lungs, and it gets to my tears."

Then, in 2006, I met President George W. Bush, Jr. at an affair in Washington. He seemed like an easy-going, nice guy, but he really shouldn't have been president. I would say that he did more good things for the state of Texas when he was governor than he did for the country as president. I think his vice president had a lot to do with his changing his mind and attitude not only in politics, but also regarding the military and even conservatism.

That same year I also met the former mayor of New York City, Rudolph William Louis "Rudy" Giuliani. Mayor Giuliani had a high level of accountability in government, and he really was tough on crime. He was a no-nonsense guy and he really wanted the city to go to a higher level.

The next year, on January 31, 2007, I had the opportunity of talking to Henry Kissinger, former secretary of state under President Nixon, in an Acela train from Washington, D.C. to New York. I also have a picture of the two of us. He said (my interpretation) that the world has changed and will never really be the same. He said that it is important that we not only try military options, but that we are going to need complete diplomatic options, and we are going to have to talk to Syria, Iran, Russia, and China, who have different means of getting their ways done.

Kissinger supported using troops, even though he was not sure it would work completely, but he felt that he didn't want to leave one stone unturned. He also felt that this could give us more time to try diplomatic channels with Iran and Syria and to include Europe as part of the effort. America has lost its basic leadership in that, at one time, we were the leader in not only being creative, but also in putting our walk where our talk was.

I understood him to say that regarding the environment, if we hiked the price of a gallon of gasoline a considerable amount higher, we could then use the extra money for research and development in creating an alternative energy that would save us money in the long term. The problem is that we do not have any leaders who want to lead because they would not be elected if they did, and unfortunately, our country is not one to sacrifice.

People have changed—it's ME, ME, ME, ME. It's "What can I do today?" not "What can I do for my children?" There's an attitude of criticizing rather than being constructive. The United States is going to need a new way of living, of feeling, of saying, "How can we work together?" When Congress was under Republican leadership, the

Republicans didn't talk to the Democrats. Now that the Democrats are in, they don't talk to the Republicans. Things have changed—how can you negotiate with a person you do not talk to?

With respect to where our country is going, if we cannot compete with blouses, the only place we CAN compete is in the service industry and in the sciences, using our creativity. And again, as Newt Gingrich said, "We only graduate 70,000 engineers each year. China graduates 300,000; India graduates 400,000." If we can't compete with blouses and we can't compete with our brains, where ARE we going to compete? I had the privilege of meeting Newt Gingrich at a conference in Washington, D.C., in 2006. He is a smart man who can conceivably come back as the leader of the country and bring the Republican Party back with his good marketing and political prowess.

"You've met a lot of athletes and politicians, Grandpa."

In 2010, I had the opportunity of meeting with Tony Blair, who served as prime minister of Great Britain and Northern Ireland, and is now the Middle East envoy. He said that to have peace, the world has to find a way of giving real education to the Middle Eastern people. Under today's circumstances, I got the feeling that if the Palestinians laid down their arms, there would be peace. If the Israelis laid down their arms, there would be genocide.

I asked Blair, "What about the immigration policies and the current failure of the majority of Muslims in England to integrate? What will this do to the future of England?" He seemed to bite his tongue and said, "England has always had an open policy toward people coming from all over the world to England. Looking back, I believe that it has to be redirected and redefined."

I asked him, "What is the foreseeable outcome of the exploding

Muslim population of Western Europe?" He mentioned that they have more kids than others, and it's difficult sometimes for some of them to integrate into Western society. Blair felt that there is going to have to be a basic education pattern and that Europe may have to redefine its law of immigration and integration. His answers were quite political, but he is a politician.

Blair was also quite the comedian. He mentioned to me that he was the only sitting prime minister of England in over 150 years to have had a baby while in office. He wondered what the other prime ministers were doing at home. In the same conversation, he almost comically mentioned that he didn't understand why the United States wants to copy Great Britain's model of a health care system. He said, "We've got so many problems! Why don't' you find new problems instead of copying ours?" On a more serious note, Blair stated that the United States, despite having bigots on the left and the right, does not encourage the genteel anti-Semitism that is woven into the English academic and literary world. That's a shocker!

In 2009, I spent some time with Hank Aaron, the homerun leader in baseball, on a Crystal Cruise. Aaron had strong feelings that drugs of any kind should not be used as an enhancement to increase one's talent. He felt it was not fair to the people who played by the rules. In many ways, even though he did not directly say it, he felt that those athletes who did use enhancing drugs should not receive the same accolades and honors as others who played the right way.

As an orthodontist in Livingston, New Jersey, for many years, I had the opportunity of meeting some really neat Livingston graduates. Harlan Coben, a world-famous author, was my patient. I remember when he had a book signing in Denver, Colorado. My son

Jon asked him for an autograph. Harlan mentioned to Jon that I straightened his teeth, and he bit an indentation of his teeth into Jon's book—his personal autograph! He has become a *New York Times* best-selling author.

Both Coben and Chris Cristie, the present governor of New Jersey, were classmates of my son Doug at Livingston High School. I remember Christie's time in Livingston. He was enthusiastic, verbose, full of energy, and president of his class. He later became involved in law and became a prosecuting attorney for the State of New Jersey. I knew this kid was going to go into politics. He just had the charisma to be involved in it. Christie, now—in 2010—has a great deal of difficulty working with the state budget, and he is going to try to go against the labor unions for teachers, firemen, and the police. He feels that this type of union bureaucracy has to be modified. He said, "Why should they get all the benefits and the public that is not in government have to pay taxes for them? There has to be, somehow or other, a quid pro quo." It is a difficult question with a more difficult answer.

Jason Alexander was also a Livingston High School graduate. He played George on the *Seinfeld* comedy. I spent some time with Jason reliving the old times in Livingston and his growing up in the town. He is now a world-famous star; however, he still has that wonderful homegrown feeling for where he grew up. It's nice to see a hometown kid make the big time. In high school, Alexander was involved in the theater. He was a funny person, and he always made fun of himself. As George in the long-running television comedy series *Seinfeld*, he still made fun of himself, but he was being paid big bucks for this opportunity. It shows you what you can do with lemons—make lemonade out of them.

The Jewish Community Center, the JCC, was my home away

from home. After my travels around the world, I ended up in Livingston, New Jersey, to set up a practice. I really didn't know anybody, so I joined the JCC. Even though most of the guys didn't come from Brooklyn, they came from the Newark area, which, in many ways, was similar to Brooklyn. These middle-class guys worked hard, and eventually achieved some recognition in different fields.

I would go to the JCC in the morning to work out, and there was Michael cooking and serving pancakes, cereal, juice, and coffee. Michael was a Russian immigrant who washed our towels. His granddaughter graduated from John Hopkins and is now a urologist. Only in America! I'd come there at the end of the day and on Sunday mornings. John was our chef who cooked hamburgers and steaks and, on Sundays, he served all kinds of bagels with lox, cream cheese, and pickled herring. Throughout all these adventures in the morning, in the evening, and on Sundays, the guys would work out and then we would talk. It was like just being around the corner candy store when you were a kid, except now we were grown adults.

We had great people at the JCC. Leon Mandelbaum, who became an entrepreneur of modest retail shops called Mandee, which are known throughout the whole Northeast. We had Leon Levy, who was head of Shoe Town. Again, he has stores all over the Northeast and in many of the southern states. We had Pechter, New Jersey's best Jewish bakery, and Leon Cooperman, a senior vice president at Goldman Sachs. People thought I was so smart. If they only knew I got all my information from him.

We had all kinds of lawyers, businessmen, accountants, doctors, and laborers who hung around this corner store to shoot the bull and gamble on football and baseball games. We would fight hard with each other on the racquetball court, the basketball court, and the volleyball court. Later, we would swim with each other. After that we'd schmooze and eat. It was a fraternity of love. I looked forward to it. It was something special in my life. It was like going home to Brooklyn, but as an adult.

Like everything else, nothing stays forever. The JCC decided that we didn't need a men's or women's health club. They just wanted to take it away and put in more apparatuses, more machines, and more lockers. Yes, they put more machines in and they put more lockers in. But in doing so, they took the heart and soul out of the JCC. A time of love and passion, where you could work like heck, fight like heck, and eat and drink like heck came to an end. Those were days gone by, but days to always remember. Out of this maelstrom, there came a rainbow. The rainbow was a group of guys that got together every month to maintain their friendship with a repast of food, wine, and laughter.

"Yes, Alex, I have met many athletes and politicians, but despite the famous people I have met, the most noteworthy people I have ever met were the common men who I traveled all over the world with."

I seemed to relate better with the common men; their happiness, their sadness, their fears, their ambitions. They were just so sincere that I loved to be with them, and I always felt that I truly had a more common bond with the common man, because in so many ways, I am that common man. Many times when I would meet famous people, they seemed so full of themselves that I think if you had put a pin to them, they would have burst.

It was the common man that made me feel so good, and to whom I felt that I gave more than to these famous people. It was a joy to meet with them and be with them. If there was a small way that I could make their lives happier, I tried, because I noticed that when I tried to make their lives happier, they gave of themselves with laughter and warmth and friendliness. It was a win-win situation. Maybe they got something out of it, but I got much more. I felt that I was giving them a bit of joy, a little bit of laughter in life, when I interacted with them.

"You always give me joy and laughter, Grandpa!" Haleigh starts unbuckling her car seat as we pull up to the house.

"You make me laugh a lot, Papa Larry. You're silly!" Rebecca throws in as she shakes her legs, eager to get out of the vehicle and run around.

"I suppose I am a bit silly. I love to laugh and make others laugh too."

As the car brakes and settles into its spot, Alex helps Rebecca and Haleigh out of their chairs. They open the car door and jump out giggling and skipping as Alex looks at me and just gives a quiet smirk.

"Grandpa?"

"Yes, Alex?"

"We made history today with you."

"We did make history today, and it's the best history I can remember."

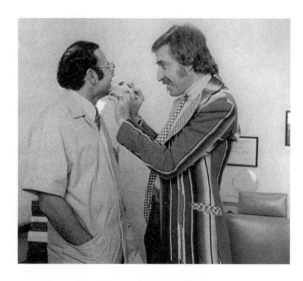

Doc Severinsen (left) giving me a "dental exam" in my office during his 1980 visit

All-time tennis great Roy Emerson (left) and me in a Pro-Am tennis tournament, at Mount Washington, New Hampshire, 1991

George Bush, Sr. (right) and me (left, front) at a campaign for Governor Kean, New Jersey, 1991

Henry Kissinger (right) and me, passengers in an Acela train from Washington, D.C. to New York, 2007

Enjoying my passion for tennis as a spectator at the Wimbledon competition, 1999

*With Newt
Gingrich (left),
in Washington,
D.C., 2007*

(Left to right) Kathlyn, comedian/actor Jason Alexander, and me

Shaking hands with Tony Blair (left), Washington, D.C., 2010

Successful Practice

I used to tell patients that when I was young, I was 6'5", and
now I am 5'5". Life just beat the beans out of me!
—*Lawrence S. Harte*

As my grandchildren and I take one of our traditional walks in
the park, Mesa finds the spot where we found a robin that had fallen
out of its nest. I can only think of how I was like that robin, trying to
fly from my nest, to soar high in the skies and experience life. Now, it
is my grandchildren who are those robins and who will eventually
find their way in life.

"Grandpa, how did you become successful?" Alex asks as he
places his hands in his pocket and keeps the same stride as mine
down the wide concrete path.

"It took hard work and a little bit of ingenuity."

There is no better place to visit than a practice that is dedicated
to the total health and happiness of every patient. Our staff treats
patients as if they were part of our family. It's the people and what

they do that make our staff so special. In fact, our team is our greatest feature. We have an office philosophy, "Good is the evil of great. It doesn't only have to be good; it has to be great."

When we first talk with a patient, we say we have two rules: the first rule is that as long as you are a lady/gentleman, you can say anything you want to us at any time, and the second rule is the only thing we ask is that you be the very best that you can be for yourself. We are fortunate to have the opportunity of changing peoples' lives. My ultimate goal is to have every patient leave our office with renewed confidence, a feeling of self-esteem from a great experience, and, of course, an incredible smile—and if possible, a straight head.

"Where did you open your office?" Alex questions as he continues to walk by my side. Haleigh and Rebecca twirl around Mesa in front of us.

"I opened a practice in Sparta, New Jersey, when I started out as an orthodontist."

"Why did you go to Sparta, Grandpa?"

"Why did I go to Sparta? I had a classmate who I knew in the Air Force, Haleigh, who lived in Sparta, and he said to me, 'Why don't you come up to Sparta? There are no orthodontists up here.' So I did."

The first time I visited, it was a culture shock. My classmate was accurate; there were no orthodontists, but there were also very few people and lots of animals. In one day, I saw more bears, dear, and birds than I saw in my whole life. I went fishing for fish like trout and hooked a fish that to me was as big as a shark compared to the sunnies I used to catch. I hoped the animals had buck teeth, since there were so many more of them than people. I did learn certain things about Sparta.

The fall foliage was the best there was in the world. In the summertime on the lake, people water-skied, motor boated, and just picnicked around the lake. In the wintertime, there was a place to go skiing, in addition to ice fishing. The spring was short, but had a full blossoming of the flowers. What made Sparta especially nice is that when people shook hands, that was a contract. It was laid back, like a Swiss village. It was so beautiful. So my mind was made up, and one of my practices was set up there. I have never regretted it; it has added years to my professional and emotional life.

"What about the office in Livingston?"

"Yes, the other practice I opened was in Livingston, New Jersey, Haleigh. While we were residents in Rochester, New York, we met someone who said there were lots of kids in Livingston."

I drove with my father-in-law at that time to visit the town of Livingston. He said, "You'll never make it here; there are too many wild animals." I did make it in Livingston. I did make it in Sparta. There is a saying, "If you can do it in New York, you can do it anywhere." I came from Brooklyn; I knew I could do it.

"What kind of fun stuff do you do at your office, Papa Larry?" Rebecca stops twirling and begins skipping in circles.

"We do a lot of fun things throughout the year with our patients, and we give a lot too."

One of the fun things our office does at the end of our young patients' treatment, when their braces are taken off, is to hold a special ceremony. We have the patients write a thank-you card to their parents. Our office also gives the patients a diploma and a button that says, "I got my smile the DR. HARTE way." Also, the patients receive a complimentary professional portrait with their new smile, flowers for their parents, a bag of candy, and balloons. Last of all, they are given some philosophical words, written on a plastic card to hopefully keep in their possession forever, called "The Art of Living," which I compiled.

Years ago, we also had the Harte Mobile. The Harte Mobile came from my idea of having a taxi service with a big heart on it. It went around picking up the eighth through twelfth graders at school. We gave them cookies (not good for teeth) when they left the office. We were the first ever to have our own taxi service. My office paid for everything as a community service to the township of Sparta.

Through the years, we have supported some 200 boys' and girls' athletic teams. We have had roller skating parties, annual Halloween parties, and other events that we literally have each month of the year. We have given scholarships, and for the last forty years, we have lectured and given health goodies to approximately fifteen schools a year. We have tried to educate and provide some fun at the same time for well over 100,000 students.

"You do a lot of community service, Grandpa," Alex exclaims, "just like Daddy."

"I believe in giving back to the community. One part of achieving a successful practice is making sure that you are an active member of the community and an active participant in your profession who is up-to-date on the latest findings."

"How do you stay active in your profession?"

"I am involved in various organizations and keep up with all the new findings in my field, Alex. Being involved helped me be one of the pioneers in the treatment of patients in a caring and professional manner in orthodontics."

My experiences include having lectured internationally, and having written numerous scientific articles in a variety of professional publications; being a leader in the American Association of Orthodontics and a past president of the New Jersey Association of Orthodontics; and, currently representing orthodontics in Washington, D.C., as a member of the Council on Governmental Affairs. I've served as chairman of the Public Health Council of New Jersey, a prestigious position that deals with the health of all citizens of the state. Also, one of my endeavors was founding the Facial and Cosmetic Enhancement Center of New Jersey.

In 2007, I had the opportunity of representing the Middle Atlantic Association of Orthodontists in Washington, D.C., on the Council on Governmental Affairs. The purpose of the council was to interact with Congress and explain the purpose of the American Association of Orthodontics. I was fortunate in being nominated, and then elected, to represent orthodontics in Washington, D.C., on two committees, the Political Action Committee and the Governmental Affairs Committee.

"What is the Political Action Committee?"

"The Political Action Committee, Alex, gave money to different congresspeople and senators."

My philosophy was that it did not make any difference whether you were a Republican or a Democrat. What was important was just that you helped the interest of patients, orthodontics and the profession.

"What's the other committee?"

"The Government Affairs Committee, Rebecca, dealt with the philosophy of what was good for the patients and the profession."

Quite honestly, being a moderate Republican in the beginning, I was outvoted five, six, or seven to one. But I still stuck to my ideals in a style that, in my opinion, was not only the best for orthodontics, but the best for our country. And as the year went by, the committee members, although they may not have agreed with me, began to understand that there was another opinion and that that opinion should be taken into account, because we are all orthodontists and we really want what is best for our patients.

Rebecca comments, "Papa Larry, you sure do talk a lot!"

"Yes, I'm afraid I do," I answered.

The tendency is that a good part of the country has a strong conservative feeling when it comes to domestic affairs, and I respect that. My philosophy has been that although I am a conservative person, I still want to try to make the little guy into a little bit bigger guy. Sometimes we, who have been fortunate to have had abundant education and monetary gain, have to give a little more out of pocket for those who have not been as fortunate or have not tried that hard. It is not easy to do that sometimes because we keep saying, "Well, they're not working hard at it. Maybe it's their culture; maybe it's their physical or mental background." But we have to give a little bit more if we are going to help give them the opportunity of being middle class.

"I want to help," Rebecca blurts out.

"That's great!"

"Grandpa, what kind of stuff have you done with the different organizations?"

"Luckily, Alex, I've been able to be a part of a lot of initiatives. As a member and former chairperson of the Public Health Council of New Jersey, I've been involved in many public health agendas."

Many of the Public Health Council agendas have covered issues such as AIDS and HIV infections; the use and abuse of tobacco, alcohol, and other drugs; bioterrorism; salmonella epidemics; the bird flu; the rabies problem; and high cancer rates in Toms River of

New Jersey. We worked on optimum health for people under Health Maintenance Organizations (HMOs) and the benefits for the physicians who work under the HMOs. We pushed for vaccinations for different diseases and we now note that with the advent of bottled water, there is an apparent increase in decay, because there isn't fluoride in most bottled water. The council also supported a bill that made it mandatory for imported fruits and vegetables to have a label of the country of origin.

"What else does the council do?" Haleigh asked.

At one time, we became the laughingstock of the world and our country. We supported a bill that would prevent people from using raw eggs on a Caesar salad because of the threat of *E-coli*. Even Johnny Carson, one of the great television personalities of the time, made fun of us. We finally had to rescind the bill because of public opinion. "You can't win them all!" These were the words of Carson's bandleader, Doc Severinsen, whose kids were patients of mine.

Having the opportunity of being appointed to the Public Health Council by Thomas Kean in the 1980s was a great honor. At that time, the council was probably the most powerful council in the whole country. The Public Health Council of New Jersey had as much, or more, power than any council in the United States. The governor and the legislature literally had to come to us so that we could work with them on the future of the health of the citizens of New Jersey. They dealt with all areas of health for the individual and the public.

By 2006, the function of the Council had eroded to an advisory nature. This was unfortunate because years ago, in the 1980s and '90s, there were people on it who represented different areas and were powerful in their expertise. They had an influence not only in the state, but in Congress.

"People like you, Papa Larry?"

"Rebecca, I always tried to learn as much as I could and to share what I'd learned with others."

"Was it easy for you to be successful?"

"There were some ups and downs, Alex. They say that, unless you are prepared to lose, you will never win."

Although my life has been successful, there have been losses. Once, I invested in a beautiful Holiday Inn in the Midwest. It was destined to be a great success. This motel seemed like a sound investment, except for the sinkhole it was built on. Unfortunately, the first floor became the basement. Since the hotel industry was a bust, my next move was to go with energy. Since, in my opinion, energy is the future of the country and the world, I invested in oil in Texas.

"Why in oil?"

"Since the former commissioner of the IRS invested in it, Haleigh, and two senior vice presidents of large marketing firms invested in it, I figured they knew what they were doing. Obviously, I had to follow them because I just didn't know anything."

The bottom line is it was a sham; we lost our money. I called up the other important people in this investment and they said, "Can't win 'em all!" But it bothered me. I had a friend who was a classmate, an attorney in Dallas. I went down there for depositions, and I found out that there were nine attorneys on the other side and just myself, my attorney, and an associate on my side, and I said, "Something is wrong. Let's go after them."

"What happened?" Rebecca asked.

At the steps of the federal courthouse, we settled. I got my money back. My attorney made his money and, as he was driving me to the airport, he said, "Larry, if you want to make money in this world, let me give you some advice. One, stick to your own profession; two, nothing good has ever left the state of Texas."

Well, after this I decided to venture out into a coal mining operation in West Virginia. Again, it didn't work out. They were a little corrupt. We had some of the general partners come and talk to us, and they said they would give us ten cents on the dollar. All the rest of the investors said, "Okay, we'll take it." I said, "No, I'd rather visit you in jail for ten cents on the dollar." We finally renegotiated for seventy-five cents on the dollar; they still went to jail.

"Did you invest more after this, Grandpa?"

"Yes, Alex, I did. I wasn't done taking risks."

Another one of my investments was in the cable television industry, since I thought it was the future of our country. So I invested in cable television in Utah, a fantastically growing area. It went broke; it didn't work out. Well, I thought gambling was the future of our country too; as you can guess, it didn't work out. I personally don't believe in gambling, but I invested in Indian casino gambling in Florida. It went broke, again.

When my orthodontic practice in Sparta had just started, I invested as a limited partner in a movie theater in a small town in New Jersey. Little did I know it was showing pornographic films. Two weeks later, there was an article on the front page of the *Star Ledger* newspaper saying that they were going to expose all of the participants in this movie theater. I could just see it—my practice going up in smoke; my career going down the tubes. What was I going to do for a living? Fortunately for me, they did not bring the story up again because a bigger headline that was more newsworthy came up; otherwise, God knows what I would be doing today.

An investment I missed out on was gold. One of the grooms at my wedding pleaded with me to buy gold at $35 an ounce. I wouldn't listen to him. Today, gold is over $1,000 an ounce. Shame on me! I even invested in Prefab plastic housing. The company went broke.

"Did you always lose, Papa Larry?"

"Not always, Rebecca."

Those were some of the losses, but I had to make some wins. My advice to all is real estate. What a fantastic investment! Especially if you know what you are doing. My own practice, my own business, was wonderful. And I invested and learned a great deal about bank stocks. Those were the three where I was able to do well—real estate, my own business, and bank stocks.

"Grandpa, I take risks in sports," Alex declares.

"You do?"

"Yes, Grandpa. I always try; even if I don't do great, I tried."

"That's the most important thing, Alex, to always try. Remember, unless you are prepared to lose, you will never win."

I look back at the wonderful places in Sparta and Livingston. In Sparta, we had Krogh's Restaurant and the Lake Mohawk area, which were built in the early 1930's. There was a world-class state fair in Branchville every August. I loved the rivalry of the annual football games between Sparta and Pope John XIII high schools.

Livingston had its old-time spots—the Ritz Diner, Livingston Bagel, and Eppes Essen. The town had its all-purpose store called Silvermans, where I used to buy the newspaper and listen to the town gossip. We had the yearly Kiwanis Carnival and the Short Hills Mall for shopping. At the Livingston High School (Lancers) football games, the crowd would scream, "Yay, Lancers!" When they saw the back of my bald head, they would sometimes yell, "Yay, Chrome Dome!"

Celebrating with a patient (left) after removal of braces, Livingston office, 1990

Honored at Brooklyn Tech for donating $60,000 for a science room, (left to right) Douglas, Ronni, me, and Helaine

Accomplishments

Most of us live our life on a ladder—reaching with one
hand for the rung in front of us, and holding on with one
foot to kick the other guy on the rung below us.
                                        —*Lawrence S. Harte*

The smell of the fresh air and the sunlit sky lead us on a scenic
tour of the park. As we come up to a set of benches, Alex and I take
a seat with Mesa by our feet. Haleigh and Rebecca begin to run back
and forth after each other.

"Grandpa?"

"Yes, Alex?"

"You are always doing things in the community."

"Yes, I am."

"Why do you do so much?"

"I guess I consider myself very fortunate, Alex, and it's important
to help others."

"I'm glad you help others, Grandpa. Daddy helps others too, and
when I get older I am going to help too."

"I'm glad to hear that Alex. Knowing you feel that way makes everything I've done worthwhile."

Throughout the years I have become extremely active in civic and professional events. One of my philosophies in life is that we should work toward the betterment of our community through economic participation, public service, volunteer work, and other means to improve life for all. Professionally, I felt that one should try to be a leader, a pioneer in one's field to be the best that one can be and help change the lives of others. For this reason, I am still an active participant in many activities, events, and organizations. I have been the longest-acting member serving under governors and acting governors over some twenty-six years in the Public Health Council of New Jersey.

"When did you start being active in the community, Grandpa?"

"I started when I was young, Alex."

As a young man, my pace was set toward being a leader and pioneer. As president of the Youth Employment Service in 1970, I believed that it was important for all students to have the opportunity to work and understand the importance of learning what life was really about. The organization stressed the importance of all students being involved with volunteer civic and religious activities. This same year, I organized dental study groups, where dental staffs had a continuing relationship with other dental staffs.

Later on, we jumped on new web-based technology and adopted the philosophy of internet and Facebook marketing, professionally asking patients for referrals, and organizing a yearly plan of going to some forty schools every year. In the referral area, this marketing technique was and still is fantastic.

I gave course lectures all over the world on the philosophy of

PMA (Positive Mental Attitude) and, in 1969, introduced the concept of dental and medical supply companies subsidizing lectures at dental and medical meetings in hospitals. In those days, it was blasphemy; today it is an accepted way of life. Being a pioneer and leader for the expanded use of dental auxiliaries was neat.

"How did that help?" Alex bends over and pets Mesa on the back.

"This plan has helped keep the fee of orthodontists at a relatively low level compared to the inflation increase in the economy, providing the opportunity of serving more patients with the highest-quality care."

"That's great, Grandpa. What else did you do?"

"I lectured to dentists around the country, Alex, on the problems with health maintenance organizations (HMO) in dentistry."

"What did you lecture on?"

"I shared with them the fact that the only industry that gains in HMOs is the insurance industry. The patients may not get good care, and the dentist will make less money."

"Is that true?"

"Yes, it is. Fortunately, the orthodontic profession stuck together, unlike medicine, which gave in to the HMOs. That changed the profession of medicine forever."

"Daddy told me you started new things like FACE. What were they?"

"There were a few, Alex."

In the early eighties, my innovativeness led me to found FACE (the Face and Cosmetic Enhancement Center—a group consisting of orthodontists, plastic surgeons, ENTs, nutritionists, and psychologists) to offer patients a multifaceted group to help patients. I was its first CEO. I also created the Mid-Atlantic Sports Dentistry Center. It is a place where children can learn safety habits in sports, including proper diet, exercise, and using mouth-guard protection. Furthermore, I was one of the first in the nation to have a center dedicated to the management of pain, the New Jersey Center for Cranial Face Pain. The group consisted of an orthodontist, dentist, oral surgeon, ENT, and psychiatrist to help patients in this different area of medicine.

During this time, my commitment to the community led me to become a member of the temple board of education. Being a member of the board allowed me to stress the importance of the philosophy that the subjects taught in schools might have nothing to do with someone's future vocation; the discipline of learning, thinking, and taking responsibility was more important than the subject matter of each course. And I helped initiate a new venture with the New Jersey Orthodontic Association, marketing orthodontist by orthodontist. The marketing technique was to have patients go to an orthodontist first.

The American Association of Orthodontists, or AAO, some thirty years later has come around to this method. They felt that the few dentists who did orthodontics would not refer and that the majority of dentists would still refer to orthodontists.

I was chosen to help lead the orthodontists of the country in forging an ongoing relationship with pediatricians for diagnosing early orthodontic problems. I was also strongly involved in changing the laws of tobacco use in New Jersey, while I was its Public Health Council chair, by stressing the importance of exercise, diet, and lowering tobacco and drug use.

Since that time until the present, my involvement in various public health issues has included lobbying in New Jersey and Washington, D.C. I was also instrumental in seeing that 330 acres of our farm land were sold to the state rather than to developers to build homes and shopping centers.

Through the Council on Government Affairs, I helped advise Congress to maintain laws that helped orthodontists offer the best possible care to their patients, I worked hard to maintain laws that supported good medicine and against the passage of law that would be a detriment to the profession and the community it served, and I helped lead the way in getting orthodontists from all over the country to support the political action of the AAO in Washington, D.C. Those efforts helped educate Congress on the importance of orthodontics to the American people. I was involved with speaking to the leading powers of both parties.

"You really have done a lot, Grandpa!"

"These accomplishments were possible because I forged through life wanting to succeed and to give back to my community. We all have a social and professional responsibility to help those around us in need in order to give them the opportunity to succeed in life as well."

"Grandpa, you searched for your Impossible Dream and found it!"

"Yes, Alex, I searched the world for windmills, and in doing so, I hope I helped the world along the way."

"I'm going to search the world for windmills too!"

The sun begins to slowly descend. Alex and I rise from the benches and head toward the girls to end our day at the park. We walk in sync, our feet thumping a rhythmic tune—my beat of many paths taken, theirs of many paths to take toward their search for windmills. Suddenly, Mesa barks, looking up toward the trees. As we look up curiously, a red robin flies onto a tree branch, chirping a joyful melody. All I could do was smile.

The New Jersey Association of Orthodontics
presents their most prestigious

Gerald A. Devlin Award to

Dr. Lawrence S. Harte

In recognition of your outstanding contributions to
the profession of orthodontics - as a clinician, a
leader, and a mentor to many orthodontists in
New Jersey and elsewhere. Your dedication,
abilities and energies are appreciated by all those
who have served with you, those of us who have
benefited from your efforts and those of us who
admire your character, wisdom, and skills.
The award goes to an outstanding orthodontist
who has made an extraordinary impact as a
visionary in education and service to patients, the
profession, and the country.

Paul F. Batastini, D.M.D
President

April 17, 2002

New Jersey Association of Orthodontics, Gerald A. Devlin Award, 2002

Sailing Into the Sunset

When Doug, Jon, and Helaine were Rebecca's, Alex's, and Haleigh's age, we used to take them sailing on Lake Hopatcong in New Jersey in a sailboat called *Harte's Delight*. It was a great family exercise and adventure. We went out, going wherever it was we were meant to go. We sailed and we raced.

Sometimes the winds were so mild that we literally had to paddle back to the dock. Other times the winds were intense, and we had to take the sails down. Whether it was heavy weather, or heavy water, or light weather, we, as a family and as a team, worked the sailboat in the wind, in the sun, and in the rain. It was fun. We were a family. The feel of the waters beneath our bodies caressing the hull with its guiding waves and the sun coming up to high noon in its glorifying tone, then retiring at the end of day, leaving only the luminescent rays of the moon as our escort—these were the backdrops to our many voyages. Sailing bestowed upon us a tremendous feeling of togetherness, of being with nature.

In anticipation of the day when I take all three of my

grandchildren on this great sail into the sunset, I crave the taste of the open waters leading us, my grandchildren and children, where the winds of time stay forever, blowing through our hair, tightening our skin, and chilling our bodies as we work together as a family, a unit, a group, a team, for sailing is a team effort. Just as my children set sail first on Lake Hopatcong and then in other parts of the world, my grandchildren, too, will set sail, first on a small lake and then on adventures all around the world.

In Greek mythology, the Sphinx blocked the path of travelers, requiring them to solve a riddle in order to be allowed to pass: what moves on four legs in the morning, two legs at noon, and three legs in the evening? The solution was that man as an infant crawls on all fours, as an adult walks on two legs, and in old age relies on a walking stick. With this correct answer, the obstructing Sphinx vanishes, allowing the travelers to continue their journey. And so we, removing through our togetherness any impediments to our journey, embark on our adventure.

We leave early one morning as the sun rises. Three generations feel the cool breezes coming from the shore onto the water. We sway gingerly like the myrtle in the morning, elated by the presence of a new day. Like children, we crawl on all fours as we begin our search together. We test ourselves; we experience movement, put up the sails, and begin to sail away. The mainsail embraces the mast and boom as the jib accepts its place, propelling the vessel and its trailblazers aboard.

Under the overhead sun of high noon, we strut from bow to stern on two feet while wrestling with the day, sailing into and against the wind, tacking back and forth. The jubilant waves briskly hit our faces, while the perspiration drawn by the sun falls into our eyes, concocting a mixture of zest. This sensation mingles with the currents of air whipping our flesh, causing us to feel a profound euphoria that is navigated only by our dreams and desires.

As the afternoon sun initiates its descent leading to twilight, I begin to tire, and Mesa, like other dogs in the past, sits at the bow. Orange, red, and yellow paint strokes adorn the sky as we sail into the sunset. My grandchildren and children gaze into the twilight, hunting for our dock. It is not the dock, but the journey, the exhilaration of going back and forth, thinking outside the box and working inside the box for a lifetime of love and caring with my family, that gifts us with the maturity of a lifetime. As in *Peter Pan*, always have a twinkle in your eye, and never, ever completely grow up.

So to my grandchildren I say:

"Haleigh, pull the jib in!"

"Alex, point more!"

"Rebecca, hike out!"

Set sail on your adventures. Let the winds guide you, tack where you have to, go where you want to, and enjoy the adventures and thrills of nature. Try different paths, be true to yourself, but enjoy each day as a voyage, and always remember that it is quite often not the end, but the journey that is valuable. It is the journey—feeling the crosswinds blowing across your face, fleeing through your hair, and at times sending chills up and down your spine as you lose track of the shoreline and have only the lure of our *Harte's Delight* and the heavens above.

As we reach and search for adventure, we may eventually come to a dock or a buoy, but it is the journey that makes it all worthwhile, that makes it all happen, that is and that always will be "With Harte."

Bon voyage.

God bless you and God bless America.

With my sailboat at Lake Hopatcong, 1990

My ceramic painting of the boat, 1997

Little Bay

The rising tide in the morn of day
Breaking its surf on Little Bay

A gentle breeze wafted on a finch's song
In harmony with nature's shrill, it knew it did belong.

The setting sun on the ending day
Slipping past the horizon with its
final ray

Others may say
He gave it away
To come to Little Bay

But as night is to day
He did it his way
And has come to stay

—*Lawrence S. Harte*
December 1986

Essays

A CALL TO ARMS
ATLANTA, GEORGIA, 1985

When I left orthodontic training, my wife and I took our first vacation at a Southern Society meeting in Mexico City. The ladies wore white gowns, the men white sports jackets and pink carnations. That hospitality was warm and caring — perhaps even to a Northerner. I had the feeling of magnolia blossoms and mint juleps. It was like being in *Gone with the Wind*.

As my kids keep saying to me, and my staff and patients constantly remind me, those days are also gone with the wind. The world has changed. If we listen to two people we can easily get many opinions as to what we should do or not do in our profession.

We hear comments such as:
- Batten down the hatches.
- Dream of the past.
- Close your eyes.
- React.
- Act.
- Have a computer model.

Try to analyze potential problems and then try to anticipate answers before the problems have become chronic. We should rather not try to fix our problems on the fly with a Band-Aid.

There is a problem, but there is also a solution. The problem is not the changing winds, but rather how we set our sails to where we want to go. Success comes from leadership and vision.

COLUMBIA ESSAY
COLUMBIA COLLEGE, NY, 2003

Professor Polykarp Kusch, the Nobel Prize Physicist, encouraged us to "look and see, listen and hear, think and have the courage to act." I have tried to live my life with these words as my guide.

After Columbia, I went on to the University of Pennsylvania Dental School, where I did research in growth and development. A stint as Air Force Captain followed, where I traveled to faraway places between filling teeth. Learning quickly that I didn't like taking orders without question led me to take an orthodontic residency at Eastman at the University of Rochester.

In addition to my private orthodontic practice, I was chairman of the Department of Dentistry at the St. Barnabas Medical Center and have lectured internationally. I founded the Face and Cosmetic Enhancement Center and have published numerous booklets. My favorite is "Oh My Aching Head," better known as: "We straighten your head, the braces are free!"

As chairman of the New Jersey Public Health Council, I have been involved in Anti-tobacco, Bioterrorism, and Children's Health and have recently been elected to represent orthodontics in Washington, D.C. as a PAC Representative.

My hobbies include racing sailboats, sculpture, poetry and travel to over 75 countries. Along with my wife, Judi, some of our highlights include heli-hiking in the Canadian Rockies, tracking polar bears in northern Canada, crawling on my belly on arctic ice floes to get a glimpse of newborn harp seals, and getting too close to the man-eating Komodo Dragon.

Our greatest joys are our three children: Douglas, my partner in orthodontics; Jonathan, a physician specializing in infectious diseases; and Helaine, marketing executive; our two daughters-in-law, Belynda and Ronni; and our grandson, Alex, whose major achievement is giving delicious hugs.

I am grateful for my Columbia education and look forward to seeing my classmates once again.

Dr. Larry Hurte

THE EDUCATION OF CHILDREN
NEW YORK CITY, NY, 2004

As a young student at Columbia, I had an opportunity of reading Montaigne on the education of children. He instilled in me the philosophy of education that I was going to give my children. I said to my children, "I offer you what I believe, not what is to be believed." I said, "I speak the mind of others, only to speak my own mind better." I would rather make of a child an able person than a learned person, but more particularly, character, understanding, and learning, is what a person should have in going about his job. I would say to my children, "Let him not be asked for an account really of the words of his lesson, but of its sense of substance. And let him judge the profit he has made, not by the testimony of his memory, but of his life."

Work hardens one against pain. Silence and modesty are very good qualities for social intercourse. A man may be wiser without ostentation, without arousing envy. By taking stock of the graces and manners of others, he or she will create in himself desire of the good ones, and contempt for the bad. Put into a child's head an honest curiosity to inquire into all things. Whatever is unusual around him, he will see; a building, a fountain.

It is not a mind, it is not body that is being trained. It is a man and woman and these parts must not be separated. At a young age keep your mind and body strong and intertwined. Sleep well, eat well, exercise well. Plan ahead. Give it your best and at the end, say, "What did I do well and what could do better?" Have a reason for doing things, and have two reasons for UNdoing things. Have a positive mental attitude, and believe that there is nothing in this world that you cannot do if you put the time in, you work hard, and you stay in good health. Money may be gained or lost, but education is yours forever. He who memorizes is bound to forget, but he who understands, it is with their soul forever.

I have not changed my philosophy of educating children. I now talk about educating grandchildren. The first lesson— enjoy and give thanks for your grandchild's milestones, whatever they are, how small or large they are. Think about them and give thanks for these things here. Feel pride for what they feel pride.

Lesson two to my grandchildren— Don't teach your grandchildren to be perfectionists— nor should you expect perfection from them— try and teach them to assess each thing they do accurately and always try to catch your child doing something right.

Try and teach your grandchildren to embrace their strengths

and understand and accept their weaknesses. You can teach them that, even if they don't do their best, they can always find fun in trying something new. Teach them to strive for excellence and not perfection. Teach them to enjoy the journey and not just the end. Teach them that love is every day and every minute of our life. So, I have changed from teaching of my own children to the teaching of my grandchildren.

THE FUTURE OF ORTHODONTICS
NEW JERSEY ASSOCIATION OF ORTHODONTISTS (NJAO), 1992

The questionnaire that the vast majority was gracious to fill out will hopefully form a basis for Society action for years to come.

Shall we consider the following important to the Society's future in offering the very best service and quality of care to the patients we serve.

1. Offer a continued education program that can provide the following:
   a. Up-to-date information on areas of technical concern
   b. An arena for discussing state issues
   c. An opportunity for orthodontists under 40 to learn management skills
   d. An arena for orthodontists over 40 to be acquainted in areas of a mature practice
2. Setting up an education program for obtaining and maintaining a skilled staff in technical and management areas.

   I would like to offer just three of fifteen brand expectation techniques that P&G offers to their staff.
   a. You are the owner of your projects. With responsibility comes accountability. I'll give you the latitude you need but in turn you must not let things "slip through the cracks." Execute with excellence. Make sure I'm involved up front to insure common goals and objectives.

      b.   Deliver agreed on results within agreed timing. If something unexpected causes a delay, let me know as early as possible. Don't wait until the deadline to let me know you won't make it.

      c.   Prioritize to make the most important things happen first. If unsure of the priority, ask up front to minimize down time and maximize output.

3.   Market the orthodontist as a specialist with one slogan saying, "Every child should be seen by their orthodontist specialist by age 7."

    We have to educate the public about the positive differences between the orthodontic specialist and others who straighten teeth. We should increase our working relationship with the general practitioner and other specialists including the pediatricians, so as to offer the patient the best possible service.

4.   Managed Care – Managed Cost Syndrome.

    Prepare a program that positions the orthodontist professionally and economically to handle present and future problems. Yes, it is important to educate the orthodontist to the latest information so that the doctor can make the best informed decision. It is even more important that the orthodontist understand the changing dynamics of increasing quality and decreasing cost.

    If patients perceive that they will get the same quality from specialists as from someone else that straightens teeth, then shame on us.

5.   Establish a public health program involving the orthodontist and (a) staying in shape, (b) mouth guard protection and (c) smoking prevention.

Public health involvement offers a stronger relationship between the participating orthodontist and the orthodontic population.

I ask each of you to "raise your arms" so that together, we can take back our profession.

                         Dr. Larry Harte
                         NJAO President-elect

Poems

Poetry

Poetry helps me problem solve.

Poetry is a succinct way to say universal truths.
How do I know who I am?
Until I see what I say?

August 1950

Searching for Life

I wake up in the rise of dawn on all four
In the heat of noon, I stand erect on two
By the setting sun, the days slowly gone,
I find myself on three.

The winding road toward the rising sun has
    many forks to choose.

October 1951

Oh Give Me

Oh give me the chance of the open road.
Oh give me the chance to smell the roses, too.
Oh give me the strength to climb every mountain,
And act every dream out.

Oh give me the time to run through the air
And play with the ghosts,
To stop time, to get on the horse
And ride through the trails.

To sail my boat over waves of hope
And promise to smell the roses
While the petal has its bloom.

Give me the strength to take my pen to paper,
My tongue to the ear,
My swirling feet to the floor.

Hold the leaves so they don't fall
And take my breath away.
Fly me to the land of royal smiles,
Lead me to the people of loving hearts.

Stop the music, let me play the tune,
Let me find someone to love,
Let me find someone to share my interests,
My dreams, my aspirations, my roses.

To love with people in strange and unstructured places,
To get up each morning,
To share the early light,
And the late laughter.

To drive the countryside
Gently by the stream,
Oh give me the chance to smell the roses, too.

March 1953

To a Sure Thing

I saw the brook under nature's cover of cold
Waiting for the opening of the buds of the maple
Waiting for the spring song of the robin.

I saw the little girl tossing in the snow
Gleefully playing with her speckled collie
Openly flirting with her mother's call for obedience.

I saw the postman come,
    his leather bag held firm with hemp of manila

Slowly, gingerly, maintaining his balance over the walk
Covered by the evening freeze with a glaze of ice.

I saw the postman fall, and with it,
    the intended to be delivered correspondence,
Some daring the heavens with their flight upward,
    others coming to rest in the friendly fallen virgin snow,
Their addresses veiled by a blast of eternity.

I saw a letter come to rest at my feet,
    addressed to my appointed name.
I gazed, I read, "To a Sure Thing."
                          August 1957

Time

The days span the nights
Hours winding themselves into weeks
Months moving out into years
As the setting sun in the horizon abuts the beginning moon
                            March 1958

Fragile

I am as fragile as a Lim without a rick
Stone without a henge
Pied without a piper
Semper without a fidelis
Pumper without a nickel
Frank without a furter
Scare without a crow
Scotch without water

I am as fragile as a Lonely light
As a Hollow site
As a Wisp of silk
One drop left of milk

February 1961

The Cloud

The gentle mist of a summer morn
Saying hello of a child unborn

The basking sun in the clouds dispersed
Scattering its rays into parts unrehearsed

The fickle wind twisting its shape into never ending forms
From places to things to nature's storms

The human eye and its picture
Of particles hot and cold

Transmits its vision to the heart
To have and to hold.

September 1961

Ode to a Shopping Spree

If you can price and decipher the labels
While others around you are licking theirs

If you can smell fresh fruit from stale
While others around you are drinking ale

If you can pick the cheese with the holes
While others around you are losing their francs

If you can stand the pace, the roar of the crowd, the clatter
of the cash register

Then, then, you, too, can feel free
To eternally go on...a shopping spree.

February 1968

I Looked

The growing trees that hide the clouds
The blooming buds spring eternal hope
Into leaves of green
And smell and look of amber

April 1968

Why

A skirt of gray – tell me why
A blouse of beige – tell me why
A gleam in the eye – I know now why

December 1969

The Golden Rose

May I have the golden chance to let others,
With whom I have the good fortune to come in contact,
Smell the roses, too.

December 1969

Give Me

Give me the song of the open road
Give me the melody of the winding trails
Give me the best of the chirping birds
Give me the breath of lasting rales.

December 1969

The Day

The sun spans the nights.
Hours unwinding themselves to weeks
Months playing out into years
As the sun lowers its horizon in the beginning moon.

May 1970

Family and Country

We go all over the world,
We see beautiful scenery, lovely mountains,
Serene lakes, exotic people.
But when it is all said and done,
 we come home to our
 country and our family.

June 1973

A Rose

A rose has beautiful color, great fragrance,
and majestic beauty.

June 1973

Lawrence

L ay me down by the side

A fter the flow of the ebbing tide

W ait for me under the moon

R egaling in a happy tune

E njoy each wave as a beat of my heart

N earing the sand neither sweet nor tart

C over me with the thrill of the tide

E re lie me down by my side

April 1975

Ode to an Autumn Day

The leaves of golden red
    set in the sunlit ray,
Held by veins of greenish hue
    on the branch of an autumn day

The air in a sky of ozone blue
    layered in crispness, sharp and true.
The sparkling soul of a Libra of eleven,
    of a joy and scent that was made in heaven
September 1975

Time Stays Forever

Time stays forever, only man moves on
As it mimics the flower form
Of a violet once strong and true
Majestic as a sea lord
Wavering over beds as a willow in the wind
Sprouting out its seed as the bee suckles its maple
Time stays forever with the memory of the color,
Smell and vitality of the once majestic violet.
February 1977

Ode to Happiness

Happy Easter
Oh what is by light of day on all of four
As a bursting ray through the sky ready for its tour
Oh what stands straight in the midday heat on two
Reaching for the sky and its eternal blue
Oh what has a tear of joy at dusk with three
Dreaming of days past, of you and me
April 1978

Shopping Spree

Would you like to shop right
Or have prices go right out of sight
Today, a full one, soon to venture
On my frolic adventure

And, alas, now free to go on a shopping spree

Orange juice and corn flakes
Milk and coffee cakes
Bananas and sugar sweet
Will get you on your feet

Off to Bloomingdale's
For one of those so-called sales
Tables stained with wicker chairs
Large enough for household wares

Matching set of silver trays
To keep in step with my wandering ways
The stomach calls, the soul does weaken
My midriff stands out as a beacon
Lunch time special – tuna pot pie
Quiche Lorraine will make you sigh

Enough of food, enough of rest
Off to Saks at my bequest

A chandelier with an adoring light
Armoire base – what a regal sight!
An Oriental rug with flowered tiles
Lovely décor, to make all smiles
Dinner time with Dubonnet
Quiche broiled of scallops bay

Potatoes fried with melted cheese
Baked Alaska – what a tease

A day was spent on shopping and feed
A day was spent on a woman freed
A day was spent on a whirling spree
A day has come to take care of me.

April 1982

Limericks

A young man arrived for his date
Not knowing his future or fate
He grasped for her hand
Not knowing her stand
As she gently gave him the gate.

There was a patient with loose braces
Who claimed it was cutting her faces
Her excuse was hard candy
Because it tasted dandy
And now it cost her ten aces.

There was an ole biddy from Kent
Who found that her life was all spent
Though she powdered her face
And now the finest of lace
Nothing helped wherever she went.

There was a young virgin from Belle Hobber
Who was accosted by an itinerant robber
She tried as she could
But it was for no good
For once she began, you couldn't stobber.

There was a magician from Peking
Who could never find what he was seeking
He tried a water pipe
That was laden with tripe
Also, to find it was quite leaking.

A young lady was accosted in bed
Under the light of the book she had read
She cried as she could
But it did her no good
By now she had hoped she'd be wed.

A model ran out of gas
What a frightful event for a lass
She waved down a fish truck
Who helped her get unstuck
As he filled her quite up, not with bass.

There was an uncle named Sam
Who, due to events, was on the lam
His forte was safe cracking
But with business still lacking
His occupation was not worth a damn.

There were two drivers from Mars
Who loved to frequent the bars
They drank of wine and gin
As they drove themselves to sin
And now they ran out of cars.

Helen was a woman of Troy
Of whom many a man could not sleep
She shaked her hips
Like two Grecian ships
Now her ancestors call her a black sheep.

There was a young lady named Hope
Who just could never say nope
Her try at being fickle
Always ended up in a pickle
Alas, there was no hope from the Pope.

There were two hands on a clock
That stopped working when hit by a rock
They tried to unwind

But fate was unkind
And now time stopped, what a crock.

One night Sammy met Mable
And found that he just wasn't able
He tried pills and grass
On his pretty, pert lass
And the only thing that worked was sable.

There was a young son named Doug
Who fashioned he had quite the mug
With a thousand lira
He bought a large mirror
Only to have it shatter over the rug.

There was a young daughter, Helaine
Who had habits of raising Cain
Chatting was her strength
Which she did well at length
Until there was no refrain.

There was a lad named Jon
Who fancied himself a skier
Who swooped down the terrain with abandon and aplomb
Waiting in anticipation to see his new hon.

There was a young lady named Trudy
Whose family thought she was moody
She knitted and smoked
While the rest of us choked
But was forgiven because of her delicious foody.

A football star named Bert
Played his days in the dirt
He tackled and blocked
Until he got rocked
And now his life is one hurt.

July 1983

Sunset at Marina Cay

The whistling wind on a run for the cay,
Fickly changing its direction to a beat in May,
The fluttering sounds of the swaying mast
Staying strong to the wind and its Nordic past.
The shimmering waves against the glistening hull
Used as a port for the swooping gull
The U-shaped rainbow in brilliant array
Stopping for time and the sunset at Marina Cay.

May 1984

Violet

Time stays forever, only man moves
As it mimics the flower form
Of a violet once strong and true
Majestic as a sea lord
Wavering over beds as a willow in the wind
Spouting out its seed as the bee suckles its nipple.

September 1989

Oh Where

Oh Where is the place where the mountains
    come out of the sea
    a sea divided by the bay of the wolf
    and the roar of the lion

Oh Where is the place where the sun
    trips through
    the glistening water and hovers in the
    clouds of the mountain top

Oh Where is the place where the natives' wealth
    is their sense of humor,
    their love of
    sport, spirit and country

Oh Where is the place where lovers
    can walk embraced
    where the sands of time will stay
    and hold their footprints forever
July 1999

The Art of Living

Assume nothing
Never go against your gut
Do not harass the opponent
Don't look back, you are never alone
Keep your options open
Never burn your bridges
Look and see
Hear and listen
Think and have the courage to act on your convictions
The greatest failure is the failure of imagination
Make each day a challenge rather than a blessing or a curse
Like and be who you are!!

Compiled by
Lawrence S. Harte,
November 2000

Publications

"Oh My Aching Head"
New Jersey Center for Cranial Face Pain, booklet, 1982

About the Author . . .

Dr. Harte received his D.D.S. degree from the University of Pennsylvania. He completed his B.A. degree at Columbia College, and his orthodontic training at the Eastman Orthodontic Center at the University of Rochester. He is currently in private practice in Livingston and Sparta, New Jersey and has been very successful in the diagnosis and treatment of patients with TMJ Dysfunction. Because of this dramatic success, Dr. Harte has opened "The N.J. Center for Cranial-Facial Pain" where he and medical specialists treat both the physical and psychological aspects of TMJ.

In addition to serving on the staff of the St. Barnabas Medical Center in New Jersey, Dr. Harte is also the Chairman of Dental Education there, sharing his knowledge and experience with new dentists entering the profession. He was formerly Director of Dentistry at St. Barnabas and has served as its Co-Director of Orthodontics and Cleft Palate since 1964.

Dr. Harte is a Fellow of the American College of Dentists and is participating in research grant programs concerning genetic and environmental problems of the head and jaw.

Dr. Harte conducts educational lecturers of TMJ for members of the nursing, dental and medical professions. He has also taught at New York University and has accepted guest invitations throughout the country and abroad to discuss TMJ problems. He has been adjunct Assistant Professor at the University of Medicine and Dentistry of New Jersey.

The doctors who are most likely to succeed in the treatment of patients with pain are those with compassion, concern and a desire to search for new knowledge. A doctor should treat the patient as a whole person and as a real human being.

"Patients should be looked at through their eyes, heard through their ears, and felt through their hearts."

Anon.

NEW JERSEY CENTER
CRANIAL • FACIAL PAIN
LIVINGSTON • SPARTA, N.J.
201-992-7558 • 201-729-5277

ALL ABOUT TMJ

TMJ
The Problem and the Expense

Pain is big business. Americans spend over one billion dollars a year on over-the-counter pain relievers alone. Millions more are spent on doctors visits, medical procedures and prescription drugs in the search for lasting relief of pain.

In recent years, a jaw disorder called temporo-mandibular joint (TMJ) Dysfunction has come to be recognized as a frequent contributor to head and neck pain — two of the most common forms of chronic pain in this country. Unfortunately, medical specialists are not always able to diagnose and treat a TMJ Dysfunction properly because the problem is a dental as well as a medical one.

Too many patients are misdiagnosed repeatedly. They are then improperly treated for medical conditions whose symptoms closely resemble those of a TMJ Dysfunction. Frequently, the medical advice forthcoming from a battery of complicated tests consist of "You'll just have to learn to live with the pain."

A far better alternative does exist. For many head and neck pain patients, proper treatment of a TMJ Dysfunction can lead to a pain-free, drug-free life.

In this booklet, you'll find out what TMJ Dysfunction is and how it develops. We'll tell you how a TMJ specialist can provide the proper diagnosis and treatment which can relieve symptoms quickly.

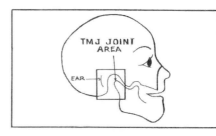

PAIN IS BIG BUSINESS

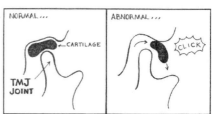

TMJ Dsyfunction: What is it?

The temporo-mandibular joint is the joint of the jaw which allows the jaw to open, close, or move in any direction. A TMJ Dysfunction often occurs when the joint is slightly misaligned or out of balance so that it can't move normally when you eat or speak. The muscles surrounding the joint must strain continuously to maintain the function of the jaw as well as to try and return it to a natural position.

After extended periods of overwork, the jaw muscles will begin to lose their resiliency. Rather than being able to guide the jaw smoothly back into its resting position after it opens, the stretched muscles will move the jaw back unevenly, often resulting in the telltale click of the TMJ Dysfunction.

Finally, when the jaw muscles have been strained to the point of exhaustion, they will contract into a tight, painful spasm which will make normal use of the jaw uncomfortable. The patient will find that opening the mouth or biting down is painful. If the spasm in the jaw joint isn't treated, the muscles in the neck and shoulders will begin to compensate for the overworked jaw muscles. Eventually, they too, will go into spasm, and pain and stiffness will spread to the neck and shoulders.

TMJ Dysfunction Symptoms: The Great Imposter

TMJ Dysfunction has been called The Great Imposter because its patterns of symptoms mimic so many other medical problems. One reason for this vast array of symptoms is the great number of nerves and blood vessels in the head and neck area which can be affected by muscle spasms radiating from the jaw joint to the neck and shoulders. The cramped muscles can entrap blood vessels and nerves which serve the head and upper body, and cause them to become irritated or to function improperly.

For example, one of the most common misdiagnoses is migraine headaches often caused when the muscles in spasm in the neck and shoulders tighten around blood vessels leading to the head and irritate them. The resultant throbbing headache closely resembles a migraine, but migraine treatments won't alleviate the headaches.

Most TMJ Dysfunction symptoms tend to be more severe on one side of the body. A list of the hallmark symptoms would include:
- Headache
- Dizziness
- Ringing, fullness or buzzing in the ears
- Clicking noise when mouth opens wide
- Pain while chewing
- Pain when opening or closing mouth
- Inability to open mouth fully
- Pain behind the eye
- Locking of the jaw
- Aching in the neck, face or shoulder area

A "CLICKING" NOISE AND PAIN WHILE CHEWING ARE MAJOR SYMPTOMS.

What causes TMJ Dysfunction?

Many factors may contribute to the development of a TMJ Dysfunction, but the major contributors are:

Trauma • Genetics • Stress

Trauma is the most obvious, but not the most common cause of TMJ Dysfunction. Any sudden impact, such as a blow to the jaw caused by a fall from a bicycle or an automobile accident, might set off a TMJ problem caused by a spasm of the muscles of the jaw mechanisms.

More commonly, TMJ problems begin as a result of inherited dental traits — an abnormal bite, for instance, where the upper and lower teeth don't mesh properly. Since the position of the teeth dictate the position of the jaw, an abnormal bite could force the jaw out of its normal position and lead to a TMJ Dysfunction.

TMJ problems also may be provoked by wearing upper and lower dentures which may place unusual stress on the jaw joint.

Stress: the most common cause

All of the above factors may play a part in TMJ Dysfunctions, but stress seems to be the major influence on the severity of the problem. A majority of TMJ patients have developed habits of clenching, gnashing or grinding their teeth as an outlet for daily stress, such as pressure at the office, trouble with the car, or arguments with a spouse. The muscular effort required for constant clenching, gnashing or grinding teeth eventually will cause a spasm around the temporo-mandibular joints and lead to a TMJ Dysfunction.

TMJ Dysfunctions caused by stress are often the most complicated problems to treat since a true cure for the disorder requires that the patient learn new ways of coping with stress to prevent the clenching, grinding and gnashing that provoked the initial TMJ problem. Most TMJ specialists have developed comprehensive programs which not only relieve immediate symptoms of stress-related TMJ Dysfunctions, but attempt to prevent future TMJ problems by instructing patients in stress management.

While the majority of patients fall between the ages of 20-50, we are beginning to see many more young and elderly patients as the stresses of daily life increasingly affect the young and old.

TMJ Dysfunction: Who has it?

While no profile of a TMJ Dysfunction sufferer exists, a common history does become apparent after speaking to many patients:

The typical TMJ Dysfunction patient has visited a variety of doctors and specialists concerning numerous symptoms that have accumulated over a period of years. Most often, a neurologist is visited to rule out migraine headaches or a nervous disorder in the neck. When the clicking in the jaw or the inability to open the mouth becomes annoying, a patient might visit an ear, nose and throat specialist to find an answer to the problem. After a series of physical exams and laboratory tests showing no disease or medically recognizable ailment, the specialists may refer the patient to a psychiatrist to overcome what is presumed to be a psychosomatic problem. Their days center around filling drug prescriptions, laboratory tests and doctor appointments.

Do you have a TMJ Dysfunction?

Take this self-assessment quiz to find out if you are suffering from a TMJ problem. If you answer yes to one or more of the questions below, your symptoms may be caused by a TMJ imbalance:

1. Do you have frequent headaches?

2. Do you take medication to relieve headache pain?

3. Do you hear noises (perhaps a "click") from your jaw or in your ears when opening and closing your mouth, or when chewing?

4. Are you unable to open your mouth to full capacity?

5. Do you experience a high level of stress in your everyday life?

6. Do you often feel tired? Irritable? Dizzy?

7. Do you have pain in the neck, shoulder, face or teeth during the day? More severely when you awaken?

"Varied Symptoms Hide Common Jaw Ailment"

The New York Times (this page and next), approximately 1982

Varied symptoms hide common jaw ailment

By LISA PETERSON

Susan is 30 years old and does not understand the headaches she has been having. They get increasingly worse and her eyes hurt and are bloodshot in the morning. Susan even hears roaring noises in her left ear that are so loud she can't hear sounds in the street. When she gets up to go to work, a dizziness causes her to hold onto the wall until the room stops spinning.

According to Dr. Lawrence S. Harte, chief of dentistry at St. Barnabas Medical Center in Livingston, Susan (a pseudonym) represents a composite patient that is among half of those people in the United States who go to their physician complaining of head pains.

"These people would never think of going to a dentist," Harte said, "though some 80 per cent of these problems can be involved with the jaws and the bite."

Harte said, "the patient usually goes to the dentist last and goes to the eye doctor first, saying, 'My ears are ringing.'"

* * *

This type of pain, which includes headaches, facial pain and muscle spasms, is called Tempro Mandibular Joint (TMJ) syndrome and is being treated now at St. Barnabas' Pain Control Center.

Harte said what he prefers to call "mild facial syndrome," can appear in adolescents and adults, though it is most common in females more than 25 years old.

In addition to muscle spasms and headaches, patients often experience symptoms such as jaw clicking and pain in opening and closing of the mouth that impair normal involvement in everyday activities.

"The causes are varied," Harte said. "Some of the problem can occur from a poor bite, a stress situation or a grinding habit."

Harte added that 50 per cent of all patients at an early age have clicking and jaw problems and 85 per cent have noise in their jaws (a clicking sound when the mouth is opened or closed) which can be symptoms of TMJ.

* * *

Harte said, "The average individual is under-exercised and overstressed." In people who live in urban areas, the lack of exercise and overstimulation can result in physical and emotional diseases which cause "tension states," he said.

At St. Barnabas a team of specialists, trained to treat a variety of individual TMJ symptoms, are available for group discussion in the dental area of the hospital each Thursday.

Harte said, "About 10 specialists are there at one time so that patients can be examined by and ask questions of all the specialists in each session. Times for meetings can be obtained by calling St. Barnabas.

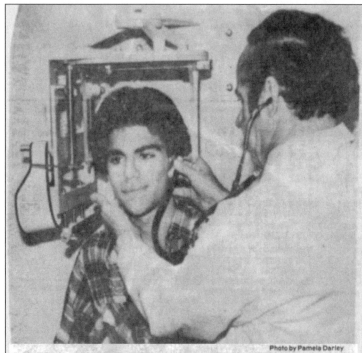

Photo by Pamela Darley

Dr. Lawrence Harte, head of orthodontics and the Pain Control Center at St. Barnabas Medical Center, examines his son, Doug, during a demonstration of the cephalometer machine which takes pictures of the side of the head to check for abnormalities

"The Free Orthodontic Forecast for the Two-Year-Old"
Booklet, Office of Lawrence S. Harte, D.D.S., 1987

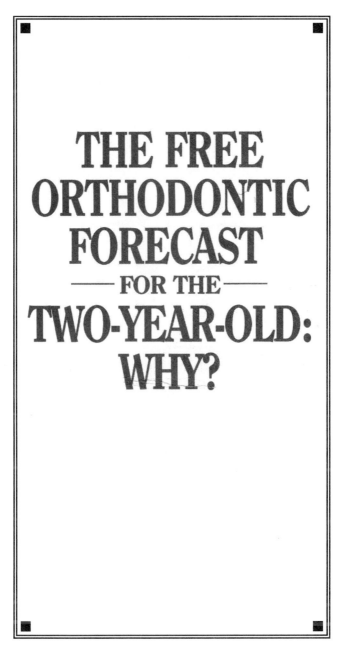

THE PARENTS' GUIDE TO
ORTHODONTIC
HEALTH AND DEVELOPMENT

Birth-1 year	■ follow the fluoride therapy recommended by your child's doctor. ■ begin oral hygiene as soon as teeth emerge.
1-2 years	■ discontinue bottle use, especially at night, in consultation with your child's doctor.
2 years	■ ask for **our complimentary orthodontic forecast** of your child's oral and facial development now, in order to enhance present growth and possibly prevent future problems, particularly if you or your child's doctor notice: consistent thumbsucking, tongue-thrusting, difficulty in chewing or swallowing, difficulty in breathing, irregular growth in mouth or jaw area, unusual patterns in tooth eruption inhibited speech development, tooth grinding, teeth that have darkened after an accident, a need for behavior modification to encourage tooth brushing and oral hygiene, hereditary problems or any other conditions that concern you. ■ begin regular dental check-ups.
3-4 years	■ evaluate recontouring of teeth to prevent permanent jaw problems, in consultation with your orthodontist. ■ adjust form of dosage of fluoride, in consultation with your child's doctor. ■ evaluate primary molars for sealants, in consultation with your dentist.
5-6 years	■ evaluate early orthodontic treatment, if needed, and consult with your orthodontist about the feasibility of instituting preventive measures now. ■ seal permanent first molars, on the advice of your dentist.
7-9 years	■ consider a protective mouthguard, custom fitted by your orthodontist, to prevent mouth and jaw injuries, if your child becomes active in sports.

10-11 years	■ begin any needed corrective orthodontic treatment now, if earlier measures were not necessary. ■ seal all premolars, on the advice of your dentist.
12 years	■ begin any needed corrective orthodontic treatment now, if earlier measures were not necessary. ■ seal permanent second molars, on the advice of your dentist. ■ discontinue fluoride therapy when recommended by your child's doctor.
13-16 years	■ continue orthodontic treatment and follow-up as long as needed to achieve optimal oral and facial growth. ■ continue regular dental check-ups during and after orthodontic treatment. ■ check for oral hygiene habits during and after orthodontic care.
17 and older	■ continue orthodontic retainer use if needed. ■ maintain dental check-up schedule. ■ anticipate eruption of permanent third molars (wisdom teeth) and consult with orthodontist or oral surgeon if necessary.

This guide has been prepared for you as a patient education service by:

LAWRENCE S. HARTE, DDS

100 W. Mt. Pleasant Ave.
Livingston NJ, 07039
(201)992-7558

83 Woodport Road
Sparta NJ, 07871
(201)729-5277

*The American Association of Orthodontists — mandates extended educational requirements and rigorous standards for members.

* Member
American Association of
Orthodontists

"Orthodontist Visits Galapagos"
West Essex Tribune, 1990

Dr. Larry Harte, Livingston orthodontist, had the opportunity to visit the Galapagos Islands with a naturalist and other doctors during his recent research trip on growth and development of the face.

The Galapagos Archipelago (archipelago means "a sea with many islands") lies on the equator 600 miles west of South America, or 1,000 miles from Central America. The Galapagos' land masses total 3,000 square miles, but are dispersed over 40,000 square miles of sea. There are 13 to 15 major islands as well as about 50 small, less significant ones. Made of lava, the islands themselves are the tops of gigantic volcanoes, most of which rise from 10,000 feet above the ocean floor.

Dr. Harte enjoyed the fact the population was richly international in flavor. Five thousand people of more than a dozen nationalities are settled in clusters on just five islands. He and his naturalist friend found the wildlife abundant and colorful. The land iguana, pictured here, is up to four feet and is found in Santa Cruz, and other off-lying islands. Its skin is made up of various shades of yellow, red, and brown.

The blue-footed booby bird, shown here with Dr. Harte, is found in three species and breeds prolifically. It is pale brown with darker brown wings and bright blue feet. There is the masked booby (white with wing-tip and a rear edge of black wings) and the red-footed booby (grey-brown or occasionally white with red feet).

A frequent speaker on growth and development of the child and orthodontics, and world-wide traveler as well, Dr. Harte has addressed professional groups throughout the U.S. and around the world. After graduating from Columbia College and the University of Pennsylvania Dental School, Dr. Harte received orthodontic training at the Eastman Dental Center at the University of Rochester and has taken additional training in behavior modification, TMJ head pain and speech therapy.

A fellow of the American College of Dentists and international College of Dentists, he has served as adjunct assistant professor of orthodontics at the University of New Jersey, chief of the Department of Dentistry at Saint Barnabas Medical Center and president of the Tri-County Dental Society of New Jersey.

"Red Barber" Editorial
Letter to the Editor, 1992

To the Editor:

The passing of Red Barber brought back memories of a carefree youth when a kid could run home from school, put his ear to the wooden notched radio and listen to the voice of the Brooklyn Dodgers. We would listen to the baseball game, try to do our homework and fantasize of growing up with dreams and hope for the future.

Red Barber was not only the voice of the Brooklyn Dodgers, but he stood for a time when a kid could listen to the radio and visualize what was happening on the playing field. We had a chance to dream that was stopped only by the end of the game or the call of our mothers.

I fear for children today that, with all the good parts of television, they have never had the opportunity to close their eyes and dream. The heights of our fantasy were only limited by our creativity.

We may have given our children an opportunity for learning and seeing more, but we have taken away from them the chance of being kids, playing box ball, punch ball, stick ball and, above all, listening to the Brooklyn Dodgers, the Boys of Summer, voice of summer, Red Barber.

During the hot summer night, the voice of the old red head was heard above the chatter of the kids playing ball under dimmed street lights and kids eating ices on the stoops of the buildings.

Each year, whether the players were Dolph Camilli, Dixie Walker, Pete Reiser or Pee Wee Reese, Jackie Robinson or the Duke, the voice of the old red head transcended time. Red Barber had the unique facility of being fair in his reporting and enthusiastic in his presentation. He had the gift of keeping our hopes up and saying, "wait till next year," when the Dodgers did not win the pennant. He had a lyrical quality of saying the present was good but there was hope for a better time and, hopefully, a championship.

A part of the Brooklyn Dodgers was in each kid. Their hope for a better year instilled in us a hope for a greater future.

Red Barber is gone. The Brooklyn Dodgers have gone west. Radio has lost some of its dream. To those of us who had the opportunity of listening to the wooden radio, the memories of our youth still linger as we also, the boys of summer, fade into autumn.

Lawrence S. Harte, D.D.S.,
Livingston, N.J.

"Twice-Told Tale"
The New York Times, Letter to the Editor, Sports Sunday, June 11, 1995

To the sports editor:

The New Jersey Devils, in so many ways, remind one of the Brooklyn Dodgers of 1952–53, immortalized by Roger Kahn in "The Boys of Summer."

The Dodgers, despite great fan support and a great team, were led away to "greener pastures" by their owner, Walter O'Malley.

For years, the Devils have played second fiddle to the Rangers. The Rangers have corporate backing, a lucrative television deal, numerous luxury boxes and high-tech marketing. The Devils do not have the same television deals' corporate sponsorship or number of luxury boxes.

The irony of this situation is that, with proper marketing techniques, the Devils could do even better in this very strong drawing area compared to other areas in the country. The National Hockey League, the Devils organization and the New Jersey Sports Authority have some obligations to the fans who have supported them through the lean years, especially the children.

Lawrence S. Harte
Livingston, NJ

"New Jersey Devils"
Sparta Independent, Letter to the Editor, Thursday, June 15, 1995

New Jersey Devils
Dear Editor:

This year the New Jersey Devils, in so many ways, remind one of the Brooklyn Dodgers who were immortalized in the book "The Boys of Summer," by Roger Kahn.

The Brooklyn Dodgers, with great fan support and a great team, were led away by Walter O'Malley for "greener pastures."

As the Dodgers related with the New York Yankees, the New Jersey Devils for years have played second fiddle to the New York Rangers. The Rangers with corporate backing and spending, a lucrative TV deal, numerous luxury boxes and high tech marketing were able to obtain the personnel to win a Stanley Cup.

The Devils, on the other hand, even though they have the fourth best attendance, do not have the same TV deals, corporate sponsorship and extra luxury boxes. The Devils at times do not even have the support of the league.

The irony of this situation is that with proper marketing techniques, the Devils could do even better in a very strong drawing area compared to other areas in the country.

The NHL, the Devils organization and the New Jersey Sports Authority have some obligation to the fans who have supported them through those lean years, especially the children.

Let not THE BOYS OF WINTER (The New Jersey Devils) uproot and leave as THE BOYS OF SUMMER did, to so called greener pastures.

It is hoped that our children will not have their dreams of the likes of Martin Brodeur, Scott Stevens and John MacLean taken away from them as my generations' dreams of the likes of Duke Snyder, Jackie Robinson, and Pee Wee Reese were taken away from us!

Sincerely,
Lawrence S. Harte, DDS, PA

"Independence Day"
Sparta Independent, Letter to the Editor, July 4, 1995

Dear Editor:

I am writing this article in response to what I feel was a lack of editorial coverage of the United States Independence Day.

I am sitting in front of the television, watching the July 4th celebrations in Washington, Boston, and the Macy fireworks in New York.

It is a very special thrill to see people, hear music and feel the joy of this special day of our independence.

This day stands as a lasting symbol for all of our days. A symbol that our country is a country of immigrants. Our strength has come from each new wave that comes to our shores. They have come to be free with the hope of a better life for themselves and their children. Hopefully, the new waves of immigrants will bring a work and moral ethic to continue to re-energize our people and our land, and that our country will continue to be a beacon of freedom and morality for the world.

Yes, our nation can learn about savings, education, family values, spending less, and business relationships. But we can still show the world a sense of humor, a glass of water that is half full, and a feeling that our Constitution has withstood the test of time.

The blessings of freedom are not free, but one cannot put a price on being free. We should criticize our shortcomings and continuously work to make it better. But can we remember that this is OUR country. The United States' greatest strength is that it gives all people the opportunity of a lifetime — the opportunity of joining in our history, music, and culture. By taking advantage of this opportunity, each person will have a greater fulfillment that will last with them forever.

Lawrence S. Harte, D.D.S.
Livingston, New Jersey

Guest Commentary

An Independence Day recollection of 60 years ago

By DR. LARRY HARTE

In 1936, I was a little boy of five years of age and on that Independence Day, I was waving my little American flag and they were singing what my Mom told me was God Bless America. In the parade marching down the street was a very small group of elderly men. I was told that they represented the last of the Grand Army of the Republic of the Civil War in our country between the North and South. I stood by the side as the band played and in the middle of the street was an elderly man and next to him a younger man, his son, and next to both of these men was a fair-haired girl, the granddaughter, and all three had an American flag that they waved as they walked down the street. The band was playing God Bless America.

It's hard to remember back so many years, some sixty years if we really have to, of that day when the people in our town in Brooklyn stood by the side while the band played on. Now, some sixty years later at our town in New Jersey, I stood by the side as the band played and in the middle of the street was an elderly man and next to him a younger man, his son, and next to both of these men was a fair-haired girl, the granddaughter and all three had an American flag that they waved as they walked down the street. The band again was playing the same song, God Bless America.

For a fleeting moment in these three people, the grandfather, the father and the grandchild, I saw my past. I was seeing my present and hopefully, I was seeing my future and more important our country's future.

'They taught me to remember the past, respect parents, work hard for the present and reach for the future...'

When I graduated from Officer's training school in Montgomery, Alabama in 1957, a Captain Roberts at our graduating ceremony mentioned that this would be the last time that we as a group would be together and from that day on we would serve our country in various capacities all over the world. We would travel to all the parts of the world and we would see beautiful scenery and majestic mountains, lively streams and the finest of sunsets. When it was all said and done, we would come home to our country and we would look around at our mountains, at our streams, at our sunsets and at our physical and our inner beauty, because this was our country. This is America. This is where our heart is.

This Captain Roberts mentioned something that brought back an inkling of when I graduated high school from Brooklyn Tech in 1949 and the guest speaker at our graduation ceremony, whom I don't remember at this time, told us a story of the great tribe that lived on the Great Plains. The braves were very strong and the squaws were very beautiful. They all worked extremely hard so that they could nourish themselves, clothe themselves, house themselves but more important take care of their little children and teach their children to be brave and honorable, compassionate and giving. They taught them to remember their past, respect their parents, work hard for the present and reach for the future so that their generations would be stronger, more beautiful, more compassionate, more loving, more caring, if that was possible.

One day, the rains came and came and came and the land was flooded and the great chief gathered the tribe and said, "The waters of the Gods have come and we cannot live here any longer, and we must separate and go to higher plains and other places so that we can exist and begin again." "But fear not the Chief said, because even though we do leave we will never leave each other's soul." We will never leave each other's life, even if we are taken to the corners of the world, we will recognize each other in centuries to come by our strength and character and by our braveness, our beauty, our compassion and our caring towards each other in tomorrow's tomorrow.

And so it is on this Independence Day, 1996, some sixty years after I saw my first parade, saw my last person of the Grand Army of the Republic and heard for the first time God Bless America. For we are blessed. We are Americans but there is a great obligation to never be satisfied with what we are, but to become strong in our right so that we can give to others who are not as fortunate, who are not as strong and pick them up so that they too can have the opportunity to live a happy and meaningful life, so they too can join us in singing God Bless America.

"Advice to Study"
The New York Times, Letter to the Editor, Sunday, August 22, 1999

THE NEW YORK TIMES, SUNDAY, AUGUST 22, 1999

Advice to Study

To the Sports Editor:

The passing of Harold (Pee Wee) Reese, team captain of the "Boys of Summer" Brooklyn Dodgers, brings back memories of a time when life seemed a bit more idyllic. My first meeting with Reese was when I was playing high school baseball. (In those days, many high school teams played at Ebbets Field.) Pee Wee came up to me, graciously signed his name on a ball, and said, "Son, what are you going to do when you grow up?"

I went home and asked my mother what Reese meant. My mother put her arms around me and said, "Son, study because it is not going to be baseball."

The years have passed, but the memories of the special person of the Boys of Summer linger.

LAWRENCE S. HARTE
Livingston, N.J.

(The writer grew up to be an orthodontist and chairman of the Public Health Council of New Jersey.)

"Remember Ted Williams"
West Essex Tribune, July 12, 2002

To the editor:

The passing of Ted Williams reminds me of a hot day in 1941, listening to the radio interview with the great hitter (we didn't have any TV or air conditioners in those days).

The interviewer asked Williams what he thought of getting four hits in four at-bats. He said, "Pretty good, but how can I make it better?" Ted Williams did not only relate his achievement to someone else's standards or societies, but also to his own bar.

Wouldn't it be nice, if each of us, from time to time could, after doing something pretty good, say, "How can I make it better?"

Dr. Lawrence Harte
100 West Mt. Pleasant Avenue,
Livingston, N.J.

Sayings

- It is said that he who lives with the classes works with the masses, and he who works with the classes lives with the masses.

- When people confront you and push you around, if at all possible, take a stand. Tell them your feelings, emotionally and physically. Odds are they will never do it again, and they will respect you.

- Most people who exercise their body and their brain are happier, mentally and physically.

- If you have lemons, make lemonade out of them. It gives you the feeling of having a great PMA (positive mental attitude). It will win the day.

- Success comes from constant, positive focus.

- Look and see, hear and listen. Think and have the courage to act on your convictions. The greatest failure is the failure of imagination. Make each day a challenge, rather than a curse. Like and be who you are.

- People who go on a merry-go-round are not venturesome people. When they come off, they are still in the same place. On a roller coaster ride, there are highs and lows, but when it stops you are still in the same place.

- I was always working double and triple overtime when I was a kid. My father said, "You only have one set of gears— once they wear out, so do you."

- If one does not leave time to smell the roses, people will smell the roses over you.

- Working five years less of your life for the same amount of money: If we did things today rather than waiting for tomorrow, we would save one day each week, so that's fifty days a year, times forty years. That's two thousand days, which comes out to about five years. We could retire early—five years.

- Have a little personal notebook, and write down something every day that you improved on. Never miss a day and never show it to anyone.

- People's views are an echo chamber—they talk, but the only thing they hear is the echo of themselves. You must get them out of the threshold so that, when they talk, they can hear someone else besides themselves and their echo.

- Our democracy depends on checks and balances, but we should also consider checking or balancing our checkbook.

- If you are a true leader, you will not be pulled down by others. Sometimes you must step on toes to get the feet going.

- Truth is a matter of opinion. Of whose opinion?

- My next excuse will be my first one.

- We have two choices—we can either watch the train of life go by us or get on the train. We can either watch the news or make the news.

- The vulture does best when there are a lot of carcasses on the ground.

- Never give a false reason or excuse for not doing something. It may come back to bite you some day.

- As Gertrude Stein once said, "There are no answers, there ain't no answers, and that will BE the answer."

- He who plays with fire may need someone else's hands to handle the fire.

- You may be right, but the car is usually left.

- An employee does not have the same interest as the boss because they don't have equity.

- Most people talk about nothing because it doesn't require much thought.

- It is not the meal; it is the company. What happens when we go out with another couple or two? Do we talk about the comments and suggestions? The laughing? No, we talk about the soup and salad and the dessert. Hmmm!

- Make a nice day, because if you *make* a nice day, then you can *have* a nice day.

- As in *Kiss Me Kate*, if George Bernard Shaw wanted you to change a line, he would change the line himself. Stick to the script; that's what scripts are for.

- In facing up to our problems today, we sow the oats of the joys of tomorrow, for in waiting, tomorrow is but a myth in the imagination of man's mind.

- We are all a tapestry of our past, but we can throw it out and try to start a new one.

- The world is full of people who will document. The world desperately needs people who will document, but also change behavior.

- In a basketball game with five seconds left and the game on the line, one player wants the ball more, because he or she believes that he or she can produce. It's self confidence, it's practice, it's a way of life.

- The grand essentials of happiness are: something to do, something to love, something to hope for.

- The door to happiness opens outwards.

- The only thing better than your children achieving your dreams, is to do it yourself.

- Be a systems person. Look at both the whole and each individual part. Real changes require a moving of the mind AND of the body.

- Focus on real solutions, not thoughtless problems.

- There is never a problem, only an opportunity. Concentrate, in business, on marketing rather than selling. The process of marketing is listening to your audience's needs and using your skills to fulfill their needs. Selling is convincing people to think they need what you are offering.

- Think outside the box. Practice inside the box.

- Prevent ankylosis of the mind and the body. This happens when your tooth attaches to the bone and doesn't move, and when your body attaches to the ground and doesn't move. Keep your mind and your body moving.

- There are ways of retiring—it requires an open mind, planning, and a passion for doing something besides waiting for the early-bird dinner.

- Be an upbeat tank with lots of fuel. Keep going in a happy, persistent, persevering, tenacious, relentless way.

- Work is the definition of movement, so if someone says, "I work hard all day," do they also move?

- It is okay to say no. If you don't take care of yourself, you can't take care of others. It is not being selfish; it is being healthy in a happy way. You will gain, and the world will gain.

- People who are full of themselves have no time, or no room, for love or for God.

- In order to cut down strength, we must create doubt.

- Too much logic gets in the way of joy.

- Whether in cancer or people, we must get rid of all of the cancer to achieve happiness.

- You get what you pay for, if you are lucky.

- Unless you ask the right question, you will not get the right answer.

- There is rarely an excuse for GIVING an excuse.

- We either get you now, or we get you later. You either work now, or you work later.

- With women, a man is going to lose. It's better to lose fast and graciously; it then becomes a win in the long run.

- People create their own reality.

- When to retire: when one does not need work to define oneself.

- In negotiation, he who speaks first loses.

- In negotiation, when you negotiate with yourself, you lose.

- A friendship that is challenged is a true friendship.

- Man and woman were not put on this earth to be spectators, but to be participants and give greater fruit and greater seed than were given to them.

- Democracy is not for everybody; in fact democracy is for very few. In order for democracy to survive, one needs a strong middle class.

- There are three choices when you are the underdog—run like hell, fight like hell, or own the bat and the ball.

- If someone writes to you, write them back. If someone speaks to you, call them back. If someone socks it to you, you have choices.

- Wars are won not by brilliant strategy, but by those who make fewer mistakes.

- A great author with ten things to say will say them in logical order. A great publisher with ten things to say will say them in ten different books to make the money.

- Whenever you misplace something, look where you are at the present.

- Weather. It is drop-dead gorgeous in Florida, it is said. In the north, it is drop-dead cold—if it were any colder, we would be dead.

- An event may be possible, but is it probable?

- When I was young, I ran around like crazy; now, at my age, if I run around, I AM crazy.

- I would rather take risk over uncertainty any time. With risk there is a probability that you can calculate; with uncertainty it's a complete guess.

- In making a point to people, anything more than three things is irrelevant.

- Forgive yourself; guilt does not go well with happiness.

- One's greatest enemy is not a person who is open to change, but someone who does not want change.

- Most workout places are so far from where you are that it's a workout to get to the workout.

- If I'm doing something wrong, let me do it by myself. I do not need your help; I know I'm doing it wrong.

- Years ago, I was on top of things. Now I am one of those things.

- He is the bundle of irrelevancy.

- I didn't do a damned thing today, but I sure am tired from doing it!

- Did you ever hear someone say, "Honestly speaking" or "Truthfully speaking"? What comes to your mind?

- The difference between insanity and genius is a thin line, which most people go over.

- I like myself more than you like yourself.

- A clown judge is called a mime reader.

- Logic only wins in the minds of the vanquished.

- People who are into themselves find it difficult to give themselves to others.

- A complicated mind is full of intellectual manure. An uncomplicated mind is full of random diarrhea.

- Like in ice cream, good humor is better than bad humor. Good humor tickles your fancy; bad humor tickles not a fancy.

- The word "try" is not a word. The word "good" is not a word. "I will" and "great" are words.

- People hurt people because they want to hurt people the way THEY hurt. It is only when we understand why people hurt that we begin to learn how the hurt can be lessened and the world can be safer.

- If you come to a fork in the road, take the least traveled.

- The smile of a child is a universal language.

- Signs of old age: When you get up at 6 o'clock in the morning fully dressed to go work out and you can't get out of bed. The mind is willing, but that's it.

- I was a Boy Scout until I was fifteen, and then I turned Girl Scout.

- To admit being wrong is to admit being enlightened.

- You can't lose them all, but you sure can try.

- You can take the kid out of Brooklyn, but you will never take the Brooklyn out of the kid.

- Listen equals silence.

- In life, losing unfortunately is not as important as loyalty even if, in the end, everybody loses.

- People tend to think that things that can be easily visualized are more likely to happen.

- I swim at the pool, and there is a rule that, if you are lapped twice, you have to move over one lane. If I get lapped once more, I am going to be in the shower.

- Practice makes perfect. One hundred percent wrong. Good practice, focused disciplined, makes perfect.

- Treat people as you would like to be treated. One hundred percent wrong. Most people don't know how to be treated. That's why it's hard for them to treat other people well. That's why it is so important to try to make people feel good about themselves.

- You certainly get more with a carrot than with a stick, but you always need a stick.

- There's no such thing as playing with the house money. When it is your pocket, it is your money. Be careful. If you go to a casino, and you begin losing in the beginning, take a deep breath, suck it up, and walk away. It usually doesn't start getting better.

- I find that the main advantage of exercising in the early morning is that it beats the crap out of you. And, after that, nothing can faze you for the rest of the day.

- How to read a book for content: Before you begin each page, ask what you want to look for on that page. At the end of the page, ask yourself, "What did I get out of it?" You'll find that, by doing this, you will remember more and sustain more.

- A superior student is not someone who generally has a high IQ, but someone who is disciplined, who is focused in a positive way, who wants to do better, and who is helped by family in a positive area.

- It is easier to become rich by using your brains and other peoples' hands.

- Some people say I am the devil's advocate. Some people say I am an advocate, and some people say I am the devil. I think I just like to question.

- There is an expression that he who talks first loses in negotiation and romance.

- The reason people double-space is so that they can read between the lines.

- Attitude—the sun is always out; once in a while the clouds are in the way.

- Success comes in many ways, from writing things down to sharing your feelings with others, and following through.

- It is not how smart you are; it is what you can do with your smarts.

- What is obvious to one can be oblivious to others.

- When I was a kid, I had an idyllic life. I didn't expect anything, I didn't want anything, and I didn't get anything.

- "You can take a horse to water, but you can't make it drink." One hundred percent wrong. You can salt the oats.

- If you want people to like you, ask them to do you a favor that is do-able.

- If you are presented with an opportunity today and you think you might do it tomorrow, do it immediately. The odds are tomorrow will never come.

- Men may have common sense; women have common sense and uncommon scents.

- Better to say it twice than miss it once.

- Common cents make uncommon dollars.

- Paranoia, a definition: when you are out to get yourself.

- The best part about life is to grow old and, of course, be healthy physically and mentally. To be in a rocking chair and say, "I climbed every mountain; I skinned my knees, I bloodied my nose, but I tried." On the other hand, the alternative is to say "If only...."

- Some people want to make it happen, others like to watch it happen, and others wonder what the heck has happened.

- By constantly rehashing the past, we will never get the opportunity to enjoy the present.

- If you leave butter out, after a while it melts and becomes rancid—the meaning being that, when you have an opportunity, you only have a certain amount of time to take advantage of that opportunity. Otherwise, it becomes the rancid butter story.

- When communicating with people, whether it's one-on-one or in an audience, speak slowly; speak into their eyes; speak in short, simple sentences; repeat the same message in different ways; and keep the alternatives down to a minimum.

- Any time you have a fifty-fifty chance of getting it right, there is a 90 percent chance of getting it wrong.

- A person that comes on to you in a hurry leaves you in a bigger hurry.

- If the shoe fits, get another shoe.

- The things that come to those who wait will be the things left by those who got there first.

- A military option prepares one battle in advance. A diplomatic option prepares years in advance.

- The way that you eat when you are young is the way you eat when you are old.

- The habits that you have when you are young, for better or for worse, stay with you when you are old.

- Change should be incentive-polled, not punishment-driven. The stick is important, but the carrot is more important, and goes longer.

- If you are in a burning seventy-story tower in a swirling ocean, dive into the water. At least you'll have a chance at being saved. We have to take chances.

- Saying I love you every day to the people who count offers the greatest dividend through the years.

- Sometimes it takes brains, sometimes it takes wealth, but the big words are: consistency, tenaciousness, perseverance. Those are the words that are going to carry the day.

- There are always home rules, and home teams always get their last lick.

- It just goes to show you that if you hang on long enough, with a little bit of luck and a little bit of love, dreams can come true.

- Education is a life-long search to know yourself and reveal yourself to other people. Only by listening, striving, having consistent goals, and modifying those goals can you truly continue to educate yourself and those around you.

- For those who are given an opportunity for a good education, there is an additional responsibility to acquire a taste to continue this education. Not only to improve themselves, but their families, their country, and the world.

- I think I must be colorblind. It's amazing how I made it in life, the way I dress.

- I think it happens when you get to a certain age and you speak your mind. Your colleagues are too kind to ask you to clam up.

- I was once in a third-world country where I saw a clinic in action. One of the people said to me, "We pretend to work, and our boss pretends to pay us."

- Some people are born with a silver spoon; I was born with a plastic fork.

- Our vital life forces are being drawn when the lower jaw is not open well. We are operating at half-mast or half-staff.

- Health is the fastest-growing failing industry in the U.S.— the only sickness that is doing so well.

- Germs do not cause disease, but they contribute to disease if they land on the right ground.

- The diet that is good for one part of your body is good for all parts of your body.

- If you want to understand other people, you must see them with their eyes, hear them with their ears, and feel them with your heart.

- Let us examine some of the types of patients who come into our office. We know that HOW a patient perceives his pain is HOW he will predict his future.

- Listen to what patients are saying. It doesn't necessarily mean that they believe what they say. As examples:

  – "I should" means they have good intentions, but will not do it. "I will try" (half-hearted) means they feel they will have no chance at success. "I'm gonna do it." OK. We got it here. "It's a habit" means I'm not really going to change. "I'm confused" means don't pin me down, or you will confuse me more. You know that by treating pain patients in a positive manner, we can do the plastic surgeons one better, by giving patients a non-surgical face lift.

  – We can ask patients what they think their chances are of getting rid of pain. If they say 50–50, it means,

"I'm not going to tell you because I don't know myself." If we push them by asking if the chances are 51–49, they will usually tell you.

– If it doesn't work in sixty days, we will gladly refund your misery.

– Changing people and habits: you can't make a tortoise into a racehorse.

– You should NOT point out the direction or the speed, but only the consequences of one's actions.

– Sense of good feeling is a combination of selfishness and altruism.

– Deniers deny everything; you can't help them.

– Paranoid: the world is against him and you will be too.

– If a husband out of work worries about expenses, you won't be paid EITHER, and you'll have a poor result.

– In listening to patients who have an opinion, we must not try to convince them to change their minds. For example, if they say the number two and we say ten, the tendency is to compromise at six, with no one satisfied. Rather, we should try to understand what the reasons and what the motivations are for saying the number two. As an example, a patient tells us that he eats too many sweets. Instead of telling him to eliminate sweets or possibly cut down, we ought to consider the reasons for the sweets consumption. Is it organic, hormonal, stress, or loneliness?

– Many of the TMJ people that come into our office are lonely. Quite often, we notice that the loneliest people are divorcees and teenagers. The loneliest day is Sunday, because it is so unstructured; the loneliest season is winter. As a whole, active people are least lonely at any age, young or old.

– We find that the best patient is the one that recognizes the problem and is motivated to do something about it. The doctors who are most likely to succeed in the treatment of patients with pain are those with compassion, concern, and a desire to search for new knowledge. As psychiatrist Adler once said, "We must see patients through their eyes, hear patients through their ears, and feel patients through their hearts."

- A fact is more important than potential.

- We are the crossroads of our destiny. We can either stay where we think we are today and try to react to our present and future problems or we can fight the fight by being active and diligent in shaping our tomorrow, today.

- It is obvious what not to do; it is NOT obvious what TO do.

- The Rolex watch—it may not tell the right time, but it tells who you are.

- Have you ever been in an argument when you know you are right and you want to prevail, and everything falls apart, including the relationship? If it's nothing important, let the other person prevail. In the long run, it's worth the happiness and it's worth the relationship.

- An employee does not have the same interest as a boss because employees don't have equity. So what do we do?

We give them a pleasant environment to work in. Have them enjoy where they are working. Make them feel that they are important and have a future in your office.

- I would rather be a person who has errors of commission rather than omission. I would rather make an incorrect decision than make none at all. How many times do we watch the trains go by — but how many times do we take a chance and get on a train? It may be the wrong stop, may be the wrong station, but boy that is where our future is.

- Most people talk about nothing because it doesn't require much thought. Have you ever listened to a conversation where, if you took out the weather, what food people ate, or the movies they saw, there would be complete, utter silence?

- Most family gatherings are boring because Uncle Max tells the same joke ten years in a row. The irony of Uncle Max's joke is that you have a family to go to and to love and be comforted by, and that is the price we pay for love, compassion, family, and loyalty—Uncle Max's ten-year-old jokes.

- People who are flexible are happier. People who are rigid are most unhappy with themselves. Try to relax and not sweat the little things. Look forward to five years from now, saying of all these things—may they be little or large and, if large, flexible.

- People who climb the highest mountains begin by planning for the smallest steps. Like anything in life, we want to look at the big picture, but we have to decide how we are to get there by design, and the design begins with little steps before we begin to make big steps. By looking only at the big steps, we never begin to use the little steps, and our dreams stay in our mind and not on our plate or in our hearts to enjoy.

- You can get further with a kind word and a gun than just with a kind word.

- After going on so many archaeological digs, which I absolutely enjoy, I said out loud, "I love this crap, but I'm crapped out."

- The nature of man has always been the same; it's how civilly we take our nature that makes us different.

- The art of buying: In negotiations the first man who talks loses. If someone quotes you a price keep asking, "What's the best you can do?" And, when they've gone down as far as they can, negotiate for half of what they've offered. Tell them you do not want the tourist price.

- I arranged to do a lecture in Turkey and I signed a contract. The day that I was to leave, I received a fax saying they would honor only two-thirds of the contract. I went to Turkey. In the morning I gave a lecture on certain problems and the causes of the problems. I asked them if they'd like to know how to take care of them, and if they did, it would be an additional third in advance.

- To the person who's selling something, it's food, but to you, it's dessert. You can always walk away from dessert.

- In politics, like everything else, you need basics, and the basics are that you have to block and you tackle. Those are the fundamentals for obtaining and staying in office. An expression: if people hate your guts, don't agitate them any further.

- If you really want to speed, keep your brights on, blink them back and forth, and get behind a speeding ambulance.

- The United States' greatest strength is that it gives all people the opportunity of a lifetime, the opportunity of joining in our history, music, and culture. By taking advantage of this opportunity, each person will have a greater fulfillment that will last with him or her forever.

- Try to analyze potential problems and then try to anticipate answers before the problems have become chronic. We should not try to fix our problems on the fly with a Band-Aid.

- There is a problem, but there is also a solution. The problem is not in the changing winds, but rather how we set our sails to where we want to go. Success comes from leadership and vision.

- Anybody anywhere should have the opportunity of expressing him- or herself, no matter what he or she feels others might do or might say. We need these little pebbles in the waves of history.

- Let us all join and let us do it so someday when we look back, we can say we climbed every mountain; we skinned our knees, we bloodied our noses, but we tried for our patients for orthodontics and for our future.

- Unless you are prepared to lose, you will never win.

- There is nothing in this world that you cannot do if you are willing to pay the price. The price is not necessarily brains, but having brains helps. The price is not necessarily wealth, but having wealth helps. But the most important thing is to be tenacious, persevering, and diligent, and the world will be yours always.

- The FIRST responsibility of a leader is to define reality. The LAST is to say thank you.

- People look but do not see, hear but do not listen, think but do not act.
- On meeting people: begin with a smile and follow with a question about the other person, and they are yours forever.

- Maintaining a pleasant, positive conversation: When other people say something, repeat the last few words they said and go on to what you want to say. This way they think that you are still talking about them.

- Success and failure: most of us live our life on a ladder—reaching with one hand for the rung in front of us, and holding on with one foot to kick the other guy on the rung below us.

- Compound interest of the mind: if you could try to learn one thing a day, you would be astounded at what you have learned after many years.

- A way of life: we have two choices—we can either watch the trains of life go by or we can get on a train.

- A woman can change her mind, but can a man change his direction?

- There are very few windows of opportunity. We must see the window, but we must also seize the opportunity. People see, but don't look. People hear, but don't listen. People think, but do not have the courage of their convictions.

- Compound interest of a *mensch* (a real person). If you could try to do one good deed a day throughout your life, after many years, your life would be overly filled with the abundance of joy and happiness that you have given to your fellow human being, which is so compounded. This is the greatest blessing of compound interest.

- If one thinks about a present subject too long, it becomes past tense.

- In the *schmatte* (rag) industry, you make your profit on the buy, not on the sell.

- Break fast: the best meal of the day to get you invigorated mentally and physically.

- At a meeting of importance, the other person may make jokes. You can laugh and smile, but do not tell jokes back.

- There are two ways to win at gambling:
  1. Never gamble.
  2. Own the casino.

- I never use medicine for my athlete's foot, because if I did, I would be taking away the only place I am an athlete.

- A best-seller needs a good author and a great marketer.

- Concentrate on marketing instead of selling. Marketing is listening to your audience's needs and utilizing your skills to fill their needs. Selling is convincing people to think that they need what you are offering. Marketing always works.

- If education is expensive, what is the cost of ignorance?

- As a toilet paper salesman says, "It may be crap to you, but it is bread to me!"

- Salutatory neglect: the basis for losing a friendship is that if you do not keep in touch, you lose touch.

- People will more easily die for an emotional principal than reason for peace.

- God gave people one mouth to speak and two ears to listen.

- If you treat me as I ought to be, I will be.
- The opposite of love is not hate, but rather indifference.

- When you memorize, you are bound to forget. When you understand, knowledge is yours forever.

- People are time starved, but not food starved.

- People have a choice: they can be part of the problem, or part of the solution.

- Control your energy. If you start every day with a sprint, you may finish each day with a crawl. Every person has a little bottle of energy. If you use it all in the morning, there's nothing left at night.

- We, the fortunate, have to give to the unfortunate, even if we think they are not trying as hard as we like. Otherwise, there will be a violent revolution.

- The difference between an amateur and a pro is that the amateur repeats the same mistakes every day, while the pro makes new mistakes every day.

- A person with no sense of urgency to do something gets few things done, and few of those are done right.

- In retirement, the body can suffer and the mind can decay.

- When you have dreams, you have love and a future.

- If the other person is better, he or she may beat you; but never beat yourself.

- The value of education: people can take your money and your clothes, but they can't take your mind.

- Tight clothes come from a hot dryer or too many doughnuts.

- Tomorrow is but a myth in the imagination of man's mind. Live today.

- Anybody over fifty who shovels snow should have excellent life and health insurance.

- Some people have role models. I have a bagel model.

- People are more concerned with what others can do for them than with what they can do for themselves.

- It is not the politics of the person, but rather the value of their politics.

- Politicians pontificate left and right, but when the bell rings, do they stand on the side of what is good for the people, or do they stand just to stretch their legs?

- Most people when they sneeze once, sneeze twice. So, say, "God bless you" twice on the first sneeze.

- People fire themselves.

- The first thing that goes when you are old is the energy you thought you had when you were young.

- If you can keep your head while others around you are losing theirs, you will live longer.

- In times of shock and despair, keep your eye on the mark.

- Some people are oblivious to their external environment. They live in their own internal environment.

- Better a person be abled than learned.

- Less is better than more in communication and presentation.

- A true statesman requires the ability to lead the masses, even when they are half-cocked.

- Act on the grandchildren's future, even if the grandparents are thinking of their present needs.

- When I was a kid, time was forever. Now that I'm an adult, there is never enough time.

- As a kid, I did handstands. As an adult, I do foot stands.

- Being spoon-fed at an early age does not sharpen one's teeth.

- If you want to teach children, have THEM look up the facts, rather than you.

- By the age of nine, children have developed most of their character traits.

- Teach children music, art, and good habits before they can say the word no, no, no.

- People who never get their feet wet never get their head straight.

- The correlation between a want and a need: I want a Mercedes, but do I need it?

- A great salesperson is someone who can have buyer accept both a want and a need.

- We honor our veterans, but should we not sacrifice for them?

- It is not the school; it is the student.

- A facilitator is a person who can encourage people to do the very things they said they couldn't or wouldn't do previously.

- Health reform:
  Some people order the drug.
  Some people use the drug.
  And the rest of us pay for the drug!

- In business people buy; you do not sell.

- If everything is important, nothing is important.

- In speaking to people or audiences, speak not only to the yesses but also to the maybe's and no's.

- Most people come into a meeting without an open mind.

- Questions are our friends.

- I want to share with you, rather than tell you something.

- If people trust you, they will take your recommendation.

- Facts and figures do not convey; human experiences convey.

- People usually do not change their mind after they make up their mind. That takes about five minutes.

- You are never so different from your competitors; it can be a difference of a human experience.
- In speaking to an audience or a patient, it's not what you say to them; it's what it means to them.

- If you ask a question, you are engaging a person—you may not like his or her answer, but there is room for dialogue.

- Give people examples of how great they are; never just say they are great.

- IMP = Inspiration + Motivation + Perspiration

Speeches

Education

Sometimes I hear that education is a means of solving problems. Sometimes we are too concerned with solving the problem that 4 + 4 = 8 and that is the only answer; we forget that what might be more important is creating and understanding opportunities. There are many times for understanding opportunities and having the guts to take advantage of them at that time. Education is a base for thinking outside the box. People who succeed quite often think outside the box and then bring their ideas back into the box. A child with a dream and hope can have both come to fruition. My son at an early age had no idea what he wanted to be when he grew up. As a kid he dreamed and played the guitar. He is now a physician.

New Jersey Society of Orthodontics
Presidential Acceptance Speech (1996) *(excerpted)*

...I remember the story of my mother, who used to live in a nursing home in Florida. My mother used to ring the bell and nobody would come, nobody would come, and finally one day my mother called 911 and you know what happened? From that day on, when my mom rang the bell, they came.

Anybody anywhere should have the opportunity of expressing themselves no matter what they feel others might do or might say. We need these little pebbles in the waves of history.

I'd like to share with you a story of the Bedouin and the swallow in the desert. And the Bedouin looked at the swallow, a little bird, and said why are you holding up your wings, and the swallow said so that the sky will not fall down, and the Bedouin said but you are only one bird, and the swallow said, yes, but one does what one can.

We must begin to understand that everybody has the right to say what they want and have the opportunity of listening as long as it is in a professional way. Your Orthodontics Society, through a relationship of family of staff and of doctors, will try and bring to you programs that will help bring our family together. It is only by working and understanding that we as a family can make our patients' lives, our professional life, and the people that look at us better than it is by offering the very best, especially to the patients who we serve.

I accept with the ability and enthusiasm the presidency of our orthodontic family. I would like to quote and rephrase an old song: Give me some family who are stout-hearted family, and I'll soon give you ten thousand strong. Shoulder-to-shoulder and boulder-to-boulder we grow as we go to the fore. And then there's nothing in the world that can halt or bar our plan when the stout-hearted family sticks together family-to-family.

Acceptance Speech on Receiving the Prestigious Gerald A. Devlin Award from the New Jersey Association of Orthodontics (1998)

President-Elect, Dr. Irene So; Dental Staff Chairperson, Dr. Fred Steritt; Distinguished Devlin Recipient, Dr. Frank Krause; Distinguished Devlin Recipient, Governor Christine Todd Whitman (accepting for the Governor, Dr. Leah Ziskin, Deputy Commissioner of Public Health of the State of New Jersey); Board of Trustees; Alumnae; Speakers; Colleagues; Staff; friends; and family.

It is with deference, humility, and respect that I graciously accept this award FROM you and FOR you, my colleagues and staff of the New Jersey Association of Orthodontists.

Some years ago, I was in a small town in Italy. I was impressed by the hotel staff. They were sensitive, knowledgeable, professional, and caring. I said to myself, "They are so great, I'm going to take them home and fire my staff." I then met a man shorter than I and with less hair than I. He said he was their leader. I said, "Leader? Don't you mean boss?" He said, "No, leader." And he went on to say, "A boss drives people. A leader coaches them. A boss gives orders. A leader makes suggestions. A boss pushes people. A leader persuades them." As soon as he finished with me, I felt like firing MYSELF and bringing him back to the States to be with our staff.

It is a rare opportunity when a person gets the occasion to introduce their family. That is a little different, to say the least—in fact, a little flaky.

From California, a physician, mountain climber, skydiver and Alpine skier, my son Jon and his friend, Belynda.

The next one left home at age sixteen to become a congressional page and senate intern in Washington. She has spent time going to school in the States, France, England, and China. If it wasn't for her dirty laundry, she would probably never come home. Our vagabond adventure queen from Beijing, China, Helaine.

The next one is a wildlife conservationist whose repertoire includes bear, deer, raccoons, the New Jersey groundhog, and snakes—their mom, Judi.

Finally, within reason, the more levelheaded, except when he is sail racing and being thrown into the water at 30 knot winds, my son, Dr. Doug, and his fiancée, Ronni.

While I was visiting my Uncle Lou in Florida, I stopped at a not-so-fancy hotel that used to be called the Raleigh, but for $100 more per night, they changed it to the Rally. To me, it will always be the Raleigh. At any rate, when I got up to the room, I unpacked and, when I went to the bathroom, there was a buzzing sound. I couldn't figure it out, and it was quite late at night, so I called the front desk and they said, "Oh, it's probably the sanitation system. Don't worry about it; they'll take care of it."

Half an hour later, it's still buzzing, and still nothing is going. Finally, I had two people come up there and they said, "It's probably the air conditioning, don't be concerned, we'll take care of it." Another half an hour later, the same noise is still going on, and I said to them, "Look, I can't sleep, give me another room." They said that they didn't have any other rooms. The only other room is a Presidential Suite. So the guy says, "Let me come up." The guy comes up, goes into the bathroom, and on the side of the john is my electric toothbrush, which had dropped to the floor and was on. He picked it up and said, "Señor ..."

My Uncle Louie used to say, "Lawrence, stop trying to be a perfectionist. You are giving everybody a headache, including yourself."

My first patient was a third-time consultation. The first time, he brought in his wife and his kid. The second time, he brought in his mother-in-law, and the third time he brought in himself. After I finished my presentation, he said, "Doc, I want a second opinion." I felt, for one time in my life, I would like to have been a psychiatrist, because then I could have said to him, "I think you're crazy, but if you want a second opinion, you're ugly, too!"

We had a monthly staff meeting and after an hour, my staff said to me, "How come you didn't talk?" I said, "I didn't want to interrupt." The afternoon was a beauty. The two P.M. patients didn't come in. The threes came in at four, the fours came in at four, and the five o'clock patients came in at four.

At the end of the day, I was so exhausted, so wound up, I said, "Larry, you better go and exercise." I did that, went home, sat down and my wife said, "Larry, can you please take me to Nordstrom's?" I looked at her and said to myself, "You're kidding!" I was going to give her a piece of my mind. Five minutes later, I was driving to Nordstrom's.

A patient came in and said they were shopping. I asked them, could you share with me what you are shopping for? Is it service, results, money? I then told her that I also was shopping. Our office was shopping for patients and for parents that want the best, will work for the best, are happy people who want to be in a happy atmosphere. People look but do not see, please hear but do not listen, people think but do not act.

You think you've got it right—guess again! My fellow colleagues and friends, I would like to share with you a story of what happened in our office some two years ago. We had a case study by two members of the Columbia and Harvard Business School staffs. Really, they were students at that time. They were conducted by my daughter, whom I call, "Little Shot," (after working my tail off to send her to the finest finishing school, she became "Big Shot") and her husband at the time, "Hot Shot." Before they came to the office, I had the office super-cleaned. I talked to the staff about training and retraining. I bought the fanciest equipment. Had a computer that sang, rang, and really whistled.

My daughter, "Big Shot," and her husband, "Hot Shot," came into the office and, a week later, they came back with their review. My daughter, Helaine, said, "Dad, I want to share with you some things about your office. If we had you as a company, we would sell you as a tax deduction. Dad, you think that, because you've been doing so many things right for so many years that it's going to work today. That, Dad, is another definition of insanity. Your profession must retool, and you must retool and begin to re-energize yourself and your staff. You need to begin to retrain yourself and your staff for the demands and exigencies of today. You and your staff must understand that things are different today. Just look at the newspapers with news about continuing layoffs and what they call "downsizing."

You must begin to work with your staff as a family, with each of you committed to each other technically and spiritually.

To our staff, to all of us—let us join and let us do it so that some day, when we look back, we can say we climbed every mountain, we skinned our knees, we bloodied our noses, but we tried for our patients, for orthodontia, and for our future.

Middle Atlantic Society of Orthodontics Speech on Focusing (2001)

I'm not enthralled with some of the antics of the NBA basketball players, but there is one word that I hear when they are interviewed. In fact, it is the ONLY word that I could almost understand, and that is focus. They focus and, for whatever reason, whatever mood I was in or not in, I was looking but I was not seeing.

So that night, after a tofu soup, tofu dinner, and tofu dessert, my wife says to me: "Larry, do you mind going out to the 7-11 and picking up five items, maybe you even ought to get something for yourself." I came home from the 7-11, and the items that I bought for myself were: Tylenol, a nice chocolate fudge cake, some past-dated milk, and the wrong bread. "What happened?" Aside from my mood, I heard, but I did not listen. And that's what focusing is about. Focusing is about looking and also seeing, and focusing is not only about hearing but also listening.

New Jersey Association of Orthodontics
Speech on Marketing (2001)

Your orthodontic society can have, with your help, an innovative and creative agenda. Orthodontic Health Month is usually in October.

Let us spread it out from August to November. Children's Dental Health Month is usually in February.

Let's run it from January to March.

Let us add a relationship with non-smoking for the children of New Jersey.

This would be a public health coup. Mother's and Father's Day in May and June, where we can emphasize adult orthodontics.

Middle Atlantic Society of Orthodontists
Speech on Communication (2002)

How many people have heard of the law of physics Action and Reaction: In action, we do something. A dental assistant may take out a wire, but the reaction to the action, what is the doctor going to do? If the phone rings and the receptionist answers the phone, "Good afternoon, orthodontist's office, Sally speaking." That's her action, but the reaction is what is the person on the other side of the phone hearing, and what are they going to do? When we have an action, we quite often internalize and say, well, okay, we've finished this action, but we have to go one step more. The next step we have to take is, from the action we have to say, what will be the reaction to what we have done with this action? Then we have completed the circle of the communication.

New Jersey Association of Orthodontists
Speech on Customer Service (2003)

A while back, the family went out to a fast-food restaurant. I had my grilled chicken and French fried potatoes because I was on a diet, and my wife ordered a medium hamburger. Do you know the first time the hamburger came—what do you think it was? That's right, rare. My wife said, "No, I don't want a rare hamburger. It's got bacteria. I don't want that." We sent it back, and I'm eating my chicken. I'm now on my French fries when the hamburger comes back again and NOW guess what the hamburger is? You bet, very, very well done—tougher than rubber. She sends it back; she doesn't give up. I probably would have put it on the side or underneath the table. Now, we wait and I'm cutting my French fries into eighths, I'm spreading ketchup on my plate like Picasso, I've made my ketchup of fifty-seven varieties into sixty-six, and finally, the burger came back just the way she wanted it, half an hour later. At that time, with the new hamburger, came a young man, possibly eighteen or nineteen, who was the manager, who said, "When a client is unhappy, I'm so sorry for the inconvenience, how can we make it right?"

New Jersey Association of Orthodontists
Speech on Damage Control (2004)

How do you take care of a problem before it becomes a problem? This is called damage control, and we have damage control in our life or work area, too. There are two parts to damage control. If there is a problem, can we recognize it? Many of us sometimes get so involved in what we are saying that we are not listening to what other people are saying. The first part of solving a potential problem is recognizing the problem, and the second part is taking care of the problem. The problem has a life span where we can do damage control, where we can say, "How can we make it right?" Because if that problem goes home, and that mother tells her friend, and her husband, and we get back to them the next day and we show them how it really was okay—do you think she is going to go back on what she says to her friend or husband? No, the damage is done. Why? Because one, possibly we didn't recognize the problem, and two, we didn't want to take care of the problem by saying, if nothing else, "How can we make it right?"

American Association of Orthodontists Speech on the Interest of Time (2005)

Has anybody ever heard of compound interest? There's a law of 72, it's a number. What it means is that, if we take what we think to be the interest on our investment every year, and let us say that these days the stock market has been extraordinarily good, let us say 12 percent—and we divide 12 percent into 72, we get what number? Six, which means that our money would double every six years. It also means that if someone was able to have or borrow $1,000 at the age of twenty-one, by the time they were in their sixties, they would have $100,000 for that $1,000. That is the powerful thrust of compounded interest. But there's another interest called the "negative" interest or "positive" interest of time. If we can save thirty minutes a day by not goofing up, we could have greater production, more fun, higher salaries, and the orthodontist could retire two years earlier at the same salary.

When did you stop dreaming? It has been said that there are three bones, a wishbone to dream, a backbone to back-up and fight for our dreams, and a funny bone to laugh at ourselves when we goof up.

Council on Governmental Affairs Speech on the Future (2007)

We will need better managed systems in our profession on a day-to-day and week-to-week basis. Those who do it will have less stress and more enjoyment, and will enjoy greater practice productivity. The ONLY DIFFERENCE between us and General Motors and Proctor and Gamble is that we are the President, the Vice President, and the Head of Marketing, and we also make the cans.

Council on Governmental Affairs
Speech on Leadership (2007)

A society that reaches heights of excellence may already be caught in the rigidities that will bring it down. An institution may hold itself up to the highest standards and yet already be in trouble by the complacency that foreshadows decline.

There is the Titanic Ship Syndrome, where some of our members in other parts of the country are on the high side and do not see, or do not want to see, some of their other colleagues on the low side touching the water. The responsibility of a leader is to FIRST define reality. The LAST is to say thank you. Coach John Wooden said, "Failure is not the crime, low aim is."

Brooklyn Technical High School Lecture

Many years ago there was an Indian tribe who lived on the waters of the Minnetonka. They had beautiful squaws and handsome heroic braves. The children idolized their parents and did as they were told. The hard-working tribe tilled the land, hunted the land, and fished the waters. They made garments, grew food, and sold or traded beads. They were a very industrious people. They taught their children the importance of hard work, their ethnic cultural values, and their evolving skills. As any parent, they wanted through education and family that their children would have a better life.

One day, the clouds loomed heavily, the sun did not shine, and the rains came in a torrent. The lands were flooded. They could no longer fish, hunt, or till the soil. Their habitat became mud. The leader of the tribe came to his people and said, "We can no longer live here. Nature has changed our way of life. We must leave this land of our fathers and our forefathers. We must go to other parts of the world to live and procreate. It is a bad time, but also a good time. We will know that no matter where we end up in generations to come, we will know each other. We will be in a new place but have the same fathers and forefathers, the same culture and the same genes; we will recognize each other always."

So it is with Brooklyn Tech: although we leave this high school where four years of our youth was spent never to return, we will go to the far ends of the earth to live and have families. In generations to come, people will meet and by their grace, their charm, work ethic, their way of life, and their love for the common man, will speak of their fathers and forefathers coming from Brooklyn Tech. They will know that even though Tech was a history of four years, it transmits through the generations. The seeds have spread and, yes, we were also members of a clan, of Brooklyn Tech forever!

The Purpose of Studying

The purpose of studying is not really to do well in school, and it's not really to get a good job; it's not really to please your parents. Yes, they probably are good reasons, but the purpose of studying is to discipline your mind as a basis for your thoughts and actions through your life.

Take geometry. Many students complain that they will never use geometry in life. So why learn it? The truth is, geometry is a discipline.

By disciplining your mind and yourself, you can learn to discipline others.

"Taking the Braces Off"
Graduation Speech to My Patients

You have come a very long way and we are very proud of you. What is more important is that you be proud of yourself. You did a spectacular job helping to straighten your teeth. I would like to share with you some thoughts. One, unless you are prepared to lose, you will never win. Two, never take criticism personally; as an example, a teacher may give you a poor grade because you did not study, but she still likes you as a human being. Be proud of yourself, your family, and your country. There is nothing in this world that you cannot do if you are willing to pay the price. The price is not necessarily brains, but it helps. The price is not necessarily wealth, but it helps. But the most important thing is to be tenacious, persevering, diligent, and the world will be yours always. The very best always.

Tidbits

At Age 40

A person who must have stimulated me in my professional life was Dr. Haus Krauss, a world-famous physiatrist. Physiatry treats musculoskeletal disease and injury, including various types of pain. A physiatrist is a medical doctor who uses an aggressive, nonsurgical approach in the specialization of physical and pain medication, and rehabilitation. Dr. Krauss was a doctor who specialized in nutrition, muscle therapy, kinesiology (assessing imbalances in the body), stress, a positive mental attitude, and exercise therapy. I came to him with severe back spasms. It was difficult to go to work, to play, to be involved in sports. He told me one leg was slightly longer than the other. I had a wedge put into one of my shoes. He went through my diet and prescribed vitamins, herbs, attitude change, and exercise therapy. He told me at age forty to go to a psychologist to talk about stress in my home life. I listened and did everything he said, except getting rid of the stress in my home life. To this day, I exercise, watch my diet, have a positive mental attitude, and I finally have learned about reducing stress. I finally found the "Fountain of Youth." Don't sweat the little things. I have begun to enjoy my grandchildren. I love being with them; it is plain fun.

Bald Tires

One day I took my car for a tire check. The garage owner said, "Larry, looking at your car, it looks like it was in a demolition derby. You should wear a crash helmet when you drive. Your tires look like the top of your head—bald!"

Characteristics of a Leader

Attitude, a positive faith in one's own ability to accomplish goals which are honorable. Good leaders have the following:
- A leader that accepts power and shares it
- Guidance, wisdom, and security

Communication

I remember lecturing in Paris and deciding to lecture in French on a very serious topic of growth and development. The harder I tried, the more seriously I tried, the more I had them in hysterics. They thought I was Maurice Chevalier. I learned that it's quite often not what you say, it's how you say it. Never again would I try to be as silly to come out so funny.

Courses I Have Taken Throughout the Years

Throughout the years, I have dabbled in interests that are too many too count. The following are a few of the courses I can remember. I started all of the ones listed, but I don't recall how many I finished:

Accordion
Acting
Ballroom Dancing
Bartending
Blackjack
Boating
Bowling
Bridge
Caricatures
Cartooning
Computers
Cooking (how to make salads and hors d'oevres, design fruit and vgetables, and make soup)
Cultures of the World
Etiquette
Fly-fishing
Flying
French
Gardening
Glassblowing
Golf
Hebrew
Humanities (over 23 courses throughout the years)
Ice-skating
Improv
Italian
Jewish
Juggling
Magic
Marketing
Meditation
Memory
Mime
Oil Painting
Opera
Personal Trainer
Photography Workshop
Piano
Poetry
Poker
Public Speaking
Russian
Sailing
Salesmanship
Scuba Diving
Sculpting
Shooting Pool
Short-Story Writing
Singing
Skeet Shooting
Skiing
Spanish
Tai-Chi
Tennis
Traveling (I have visited 7 continents and 135 countries.)
Watercolor
Weather
Yoga

Democracy

It is not for everybody. In fact, it is for very few. Most sustainable democratic countries have:
1. A strong middle class
2. Enlightened leadership
3. Civilian control of government
4. Military under control of civilians
5. Equal vote for each person

Future of the World

The future of the world depends upon:
- Immediately conserving energy
- Finding a new form of energy that does not affect the climate
- Stopping the warming of the world caused by increased use of carbon dioxide
- Drastically slowing down the removal of rainforests

Can you imagine if there was a viable, clean alternative source of energy? The world would not be hostage to countries, groups, or corporations that have those energy sources. I hope that someday we can put a pill in water and—poof!—clean energy, peace, and understanding. Understand that the Islamic mind can be based more on emotion and honor, rather than the Western mind of reason.

How the South Won the American Revolutionary War Against Britain

At the Battle of Guilford, South Carolina, Major General Nathaniel Green encountered the troops of Cornwallis. There was a large, difficult fight over rugged terrain. The Southerners were very, very smart—they knew the territory, and they lured the British into an area of swampland that was full of copperheads, two types of poisonous spiders that caused death, ticks that caused Rocky Mountain Spotted Fever and Lyme disease, and these events contributed to the carnage of battle. The troops under Cornwallis retired to Yorktown to try to take care of their wounds; thus they were in very poor condition to battle. The Battle of Yorktown was actually prefaced by the Battle of Guilford, which wore out the British and in turn changed the tide for the colonies.

Kalike

Kalike is a Jewish word for *cripple* or *misfit*. It is said in jest about some people who are clumsy or slowing down in life. Many years ago, while swimming in a pool at the YMCA, I saw a guy walking in the lane next to me chatting with his friends. I called him a *kalike* and mentioned to him after I finished my sprint, "The only thing you are exercising is your mouth." This person happened to be a well-known author. He said to me, "Larry, wait and someday you too will have slowed down to join us." I recently called up this person, who has since retired and moved to Florida. I asked him for some advice on writing a book. He could not stop laughing and said, "Larry, you have finally slowed down to join us in the walking lane. Welcome!"

Languages

I've always tried to learn a little bit of the language of the country that I was going to. Since I went to so many countries, I've tried to learn many languages. What I have learned is how to say "Hello," "You are very nice," "How much does it cost?" "Can you make it cheaper?" and "Thank you."

Letter to My Children,
December 7, 2009

Dear Doug, Jon and Helaine,

Many years ago, I was listening to a football game on a Sunday afternoon. The program was interrupted to tell the American people that the Japanese had bombed Pearl Harbor. The announcer on the PA at the game said that all military and civilian personnel should leave, and immediately report to their base. The United States was at war.

I did not even know where Pearl Harbor was. But the results of the bombing came quickly to 131 Sterling Street in Brooklyn where I lived. A mother on the fourth floor of our building was notified that her sailor son John was killed at Pearl Harbor. The mother could not stop crying. I hugged her and I began to cry for her, for her son, and for our country.

Love,
Dad

Letter to My Children,
December 11, 2009

Dear Doug, Jon and Helaine,

In 1909, my dad Joe ran against Walter Hoving for President of the class in grade school. Hoving's friends asked my dad to step out of the running. In doing so, Walter Hoving became President. When my dad shared this story with me, I became enraged. I vowed that this would never happen to me. When I had the opportunity of running for president in grade school, I left no stone unturned to make sure that I would be elected Class President, and I was.

In 1949, I met Thomas Hoving, Walter's son. I was at Columbia and he was at Princeton. Tom shared the story that his dad told him about this nice guy Joey, my dad, who stepped aside so his dad could become class president. I told Tom how I handled running for class president after my dad's experience. He laughed.

Walter Hoving eventually became president of Bonwit Teller and chairman of Tiffany and Company. Thomas Hoving eventually became director of the Metropolitan Museum of Art. Thomas Hoving passed away on December 10, 2009.

Love,
Dad

Maxwell's Plum

One time many years ago, we could not get into Maxwell's Plum, a very famous restaurant. The line was around the block. A person went up to the maitre d' and said, "I bet you twenty bucks you can get us in within ten minutes." The maitre d' said, "You lose!"

Overbooked

How to get into a hotel that is overbooked: One can say to the booking person, "I know that there are 500 people who have bookings in this hotel, and you and I know that there is going to be at least one cancellation. What can you and I do that in the event that there is a cancellation, you will give it to me?"

Retirement

People who retire completely into doing nothing lose the following:
1. A sense of identity of who they are
2. The perks that come with their job
3. Their annual income
4. A chance to do something every day that makes them get up early in the morning
5. A chance to be vital and have some discipline as far as work and, of course, as exercise.

Talking About Nothing

There were two guys on the Brooklyn subway. One said to the other, "Hey Rufus, would you like to talk about atomic energy?"

And Rufus said, "Wait a second, before you talk about atomic energy, let me ask you some questions. Have you ever seen horse manure in a barn?"

The man said, "Uh-uh."

"Have you ever seen cow dirt in the meadows?"
The man said, "Uh-uh."
"Tell me, have you ever seen sheep flop down in the pasture?"
The man said, "Uh-uh."
Rufus said, "Man, you want to talk about atomic energy when you don't know from BLIP?"

The Message to Garcia

During the Spanish–American War, the president of the United States asked a Lieutenant Nolan to carry an important message to Garcia, a rebel guerilla in the mountains of Cuba. He said, "Lieutenant, this is very important that you get this message to Garcia. The fate of the war and the future of our country depend upon it." Lieutenant Nolan said, "Yes, sir." The president did not say what Garcia looked like, what he dressed like, or where he was, but Nolan understood what he had to do and he did it. This is called "The Message to Garcia."

The Runs

I was with three kids, ages seven, nine, and eleven. So we went to this place, and they said, "No reservations." And so we hung around, and all of a sudden a maitre d' said, "Cohen, Cohen." I finally said, "That's me. I'm Cohen." I took the place of Cohen because I thought I was shrewd. Now I know why Cohen never showed up. All of us got sick that night—we got the runs. Cohen was smarter than Harte!

What Makes a Real Jew?

There is the story of Rabbi Akiba. As he was being burned at the stake by the Romans, the last words out of his mouth were, "Hear, O Israel, the Lord our God, the Lord is one." Then there is the story of Abraham, who was prepared to sacrifice his only child to God. When God said it was okay not to carry out the sacrifice,

Abraham came down from the mountains. He had to negotiate a burial place for his beloved wife. He had to own up to being the father of the Children of Israel and the father of his own family.

People say, "Who was the better Jew?" Rabbi Akiba to his dying day prayed to God. Abraham tried to be a *mensch* every day of his life, in business and social dealings with people.

I think Abraham was the better Jew because he faced reality and tried to say that he was going to continue on and give more to this world. Rabbi Akiba was a symbol for the millions of Jews who were in the Holocaust. They tried to be good, they tried to be real people, but in the end, they were burned at the stake.

Tears of Aging

When I was fifty, I had a plebhoplasty done on my eyes. The doctor intended to remove the wrinkles around the eyes so I could look younger. I asked him, "How will I look in ten years?" He said, "You won't have any wrinkles, but your eyes might tear a little." He was half right—my eyes tear a lot.

Curriculum Vitae

NAME:
Lawrence S. Harte

PLACE OF BIRTH:
Brooklyn, New York

HIGH SCHOOL EDUCATION:
Brooklyn Technical High School

UNDERGRADUATE EDUCATION:
B.A., Columbia College

PROFESSIONAL EDUCATION:
D.D.S., University of Pennsylvania

POSTDOCTORAL EDUCATION:
Orthodontics, Eastman Dental Center, University of Rochester

MILITARY SERVICE:
Captain, United States Air Force

HOSPITAL SERVICE:
St. Barnabas Medical Center—Orthodontic, cleft palate, T.M.J.
Newton Memorial Hospital

PUBLICATIONS (Booklets, Articles, and Books):
"Positive Translucencies" – Angle Orthodontics – 4/64 – with Cleall
"Oh, My Aching Head" – West Orange Press, booklet – 1982
"The Dentist in a T.M.J. Environment" – Illinois State Journal – 1988
"Orthodontics Future" – New Jersey Association of Orthodontics – 1990
"See Your Orthodontist at the Age of Two" – Booklet 1980
"Advice to Study" – *The New York Times*, letter to the editor – 8/22/99
"An Independence Day Recollection of 60 Years Ago" –
    Sparta Independent, guest commentary – 7/4/96
"Case Collection" – Orthodontic Products – 5/05
"New Jersey Devils" – *Sparta Independent*, letter to the editor – 6/15/95
"The Free Orthodontic Forecast for the Two-Year-Old: Why?" – Booklet – 1987
"The T.M.J. Center: Filling a Gap in Chronic Pain Treatment" –
    New Mexico Dental Journal – 2/1985

Journey with Grandchildren, A Life Story – 2011
Born with a Plastic Fork: An Autobiography – 2011
Brooklyn-ese Proverbs & Cartoons – 2011

AWARDS:
Fellow – American College of Dentists
Fellow – International College of Dentists
President's Plaque – Tri-County Dental Society, New Jersey
President's Plaque – Alpha Omega Society, New Jersey
Nominee – Man of the Year – Jaycees, New Jersey
U.S.A.F. Speakers Award – Toastmasters International
Rome Sculpture Award – Air Force
Scholarship Award – Eastman Dental Center, University of Rochester
Philadelphia Growth Center – Dr. Krogman and Dr. Sassouni
Associate Fellow – American Academy of Stress and Pain
President's Plaque – New Jersey Association of Orthodontics
Chairman Plaque – New Jersey Public Health Council
Devlin Award – New Jersey Association of Orthodontics
Speaking and Debating – Toastmaster International Award

FUNDRAISING:
Major donor and fundraiser for
    Political parties, charities, and alumni
    Governor Kean and Governor Whitman campaigns
    AAOF
    AAOPAC
    New Jersey Dental Association PAC
    State senate co-majority leader (fundraising chairman)
    United Fund (dental chairman)

COMMUNICATIONS AND INNOVATIONS:
Interviewed on all major TV networks
Leader and pioneer involvement in NJAO marketing model for country
Orthodontics by Orthodontists – NJAO-led marketing campaign
Founder and director, Mid-Atlantic Center for Sports Dentistry
Founder and director, New Jersey Center for Cranial Facial Pain
Founder and director, Face & Cosmetic Enhancement Center

LEADERSHIP:
President, New Jersey Association of Orthodontics
President, New Jersey Tri-County Dental Association
Chairman, Department of St. Barnabas Medical Center
Chairman, MASO Education and Research Committee
Presenter: full-day seminar, ADA National Meeting – Miami, 1985
Presenter: full-day seminar, Philadelphia Dental Society – 1986
Major speaker: National AAO Meeting – Hawaii, May 2003
Captain, United States Air Force (Ret.)
Chair, Public Health Council of New Jersey – brought vaccinations
    to the children of New Jersey
Pioneer and innovator in examining children at the age of five, and in
    bringing a dental practice act to New Jersey

THE POLITICAL PROCESS:
Chairman of The New Jersey Public Health Council, Involved with:
    Anthrax and bioterrorism
    Anti-tobacco legislation
    Health insurance
    Program on diet and physical exercise for children
    Medical privacy
    Children's dental health
MASO representative to Washington, Government Affairs Committee
    and Political Action Committee
AAO contact person for former Senator Lautenberg, Senator Bradley,
    and Congressman Franks
Legislative liaison to state assembly and state senator
Dialogue with former Governors Kean (R), Florio (D), Whitman (R),
    and McGreevey (D)
Key person to co-majority leader of New Jersey senate
Orthodontic liaison to five governors for October Orthodontic
    Health Month
Blue-ribbon committee on insurance with Governor Whitman

LECTURES AND CLINICS:
New Jersey School of Medicine & Dentistry, Hygienists,
    Orthodontics, T.M.J.
Livingston Adult School – T.M.J.
Greater New York dental meeting
Dental group – St. Barnabas Medical Center – Cleft palate
Pediatric group – St. Barnabas Medical Center – T.M.J., Cleft palate
Eastman Dental Orthodontic School – Biannual meeting,
    Rochester – T.M.J.
Speech and hearing – St. Barnabas Medical Center –
    T.M.J., cleft palate
Sussex County School – Nurses' Association – Cleft palate
Lectures in all parts of the country and overseas, University of
    Rochester, University of Tel-Aviv
Orthodontic Study Group, Paris, France
New Jersey Speech and Hearing Association
New Jersey Parent Cleft Palate Association
Clinic Presentations – American Association of Orthodontics,0
    Denver, Dallas, Philadelphia, Montreal, San Diego
Northeastern Orthodontic Society
American Association of Orthodontics
Eastman Orthodontic School – San Juan, Puerto Rico
American Dental Association
American Dental Association – Annual meeting, Miami Beach – 1985
    "The Fabrication and Use of the T.M.J. Splint" – All-day seminar
    "The Successful Management of the T.M.J. Patient"
Greater Philadelphia Dental Society – All-day seminar – 1986
Major speaker at AAO Meeting – Hawaii – 2003
    "Communication in the Orthodontic Office"
International AAO Meeting – Seattle, Washington

SOCIETIES:
A.D.A. – Member
 N.J.D.A. – State delegate
Tri-County Society – President
American Association of Orthodontics
Middle Atlantic Society of Orthodontics – President
American Academy of Stress and Pain
Pankey Society

Academy for Sports Dentistry Fellow
Cleft Palate Association

COMMUNITY:
Jaycees – Director
Youth Employment Service, New Jersey – President – 1968–1972
Board of Education – Secretary – 1974–1976
District Boy Scout commissioner – 1966–1970
State dental chairman, Kean for Governor – 1982
Temple Men's Club – Secretary – 1966
Dental Health Week – Chairman – 1970–1974
United Fund dental chairman – 1982
University of Pennsylvania Secondary School Committee
Columbia College Secondary School Committee
Brooklyn Tech – Major Donor Committee – 1994
New Jersey State Public Health Council – 1989
John Jay Associate – Columbia College – 1984
Benjamin Franklin Associate – University of Pennsylvania – 1985
Eastman Dental Society – University of Rochester – 1985
Republican Party – Congressional and governor liaison
Columbia College – Donation of yearly scholarship award

LICENSES:
New Jersey
New York
Pennsylvania
Connecticut

ACADEMIC APPOINTMENTS:
Adjunct Assistant Professor – NJ School of Medicine and Dentistry – 1981
Instructor – New York University – 1960

PAPERS:
"The Hospital in a Suburban Environment"
"Anatomy of a Successful Practice"
"T.M.J. Philosophy for Success and Failure"
Article published in *The New York Times*
The New York Times, article on the author and T.M.J.
Articles in various United States journals

ADMINISTRATIVE APPOINTMENTS:
Chief and Director of Dentistry – St. Barnabas Medical Center
Co-Orthodontic Cleft Palate Director – State of New Jersey
Attending Dental Education – St. Barnabas Medical Center

HOSPITAL APPOINTMENTS:
Credentials Committee
Public Information Committee
Graduate Education Committee

RESEARCH INTERESTS:
Major participant in Philadelphia Growth Center research
    on growth development
Major participant in $80,000 annual renewable grant concerned
    with cranial facial problems (cleft palate, surgical ortho,
    myofacial pain)

PROFESSIONAL:
Instructor – New York University
President – University Study Club
Minority report – New Jersey Dental Auxiliary Act
New Jersey Dental Association, State delegate
Chairman – Assembly Senate Liaison
Attending in Orthodontics – St. Barnabas Medical Center
Chairman of dental health program – Tri-County
Tri-County insurance representative – Tri-County
Chairman of Ethics Committee – Tri-County
Public relations dental representative – Committee of New Jersey State
Dental representative – Committee of nomination – St. Barnabas
    Medical Center
President – Tri-County Dental Society
Preview editor – American Cleft Palate Association
State Council Public Affairs
Chief – Department of Dentistry – St. Barnabas Medical Center
Chairman of Dental Education – Clinical coordinator of cleft palate
    program (State of New Jersey) – St. Barnabas Medical Center
Director and founder – New Jersey Center of Cranial Facial Pain
Adjunct Assistant Professor – New Jersey School of Medicine
    and Dentistry

Academy of Sports Dentistry

Director and founder – FACE Center and Face Cosmetic
Enhancement Center

Governmental Affairs Committee – American Cleft Palate Association

Review editor – American Academy of General Dentistry

Chairman and director – Mid-Atlantic Center for Sports Dentistry

Co-Chairman – Department of Orthodontics – St. Barnabas
Medical Center, Livingston, New Jersey – 1988

Governmental Affairs Committee – American Association
of Orthodontics – 1992

Ethics lecturer – New Jersey School of Medicine and Dentistry – 1994

President – New Jersey Association of Orthodontics – 1997

Chairman – Research and Education Committee – Middle Atlantic
Society of Orthodontics – 1998

Chairman – New Jersey Public Health Council – 1998

PRESENTATIONS:

Produced and directed shows on TV

Founder and director of Sparta Labs

Founder and director of New Jersey Center of Cranial Facial Pain

State dental chairman – Governor Thomas Kean

Appeared on all major T.V. networks

Front page of *Daily News*

Front page of Sunday Magazine section of *The New York Times*

Lectured to over 500 civic, professional, and social groups around
the world. The groups include the following:

Jaycees

Chamber of Commerce

Newcomer's Club

Kiwanis

Lions

YMCA

YMHA

Junior League

Health clubs

Attorneys

Physicians

Stock brokers

Engineers

Insurance companies
Industrial companies
Colleges and universities
Women's groups
Councils
Hospitals
Radio
TV
The subject matter included:
Stress in Suburbia: The New Epidemic
How to Avoid Stress in Business
The Modern Student with the Modern Stress
Take the Headache out of Headaches
Strong of Mind and Sound of Body
The World is What You Want it to Be
Smell the Roses
Get Paid for Working
How to Let Your Spouse Let You Enjoy Life
My Way
Born to be Free
PMA+PMI+HD
Cosmetic Reshaping
The Resculpture of Your Face
The Harmony of Your Face and Life
How to Read People
How to Have People Read You
Body Language in Practice
Cartooning in Real Life

HOBBIES AND INTERESTS:
National Geographic exploring
Yacht racing
Sculpting
Poetry
Aviation
Writing (sayings, poems, short stories, memoirs)
Cartooning
Magic
Swimming

Genealogy

DESCENDANTS OF AARON GRUSSMARK

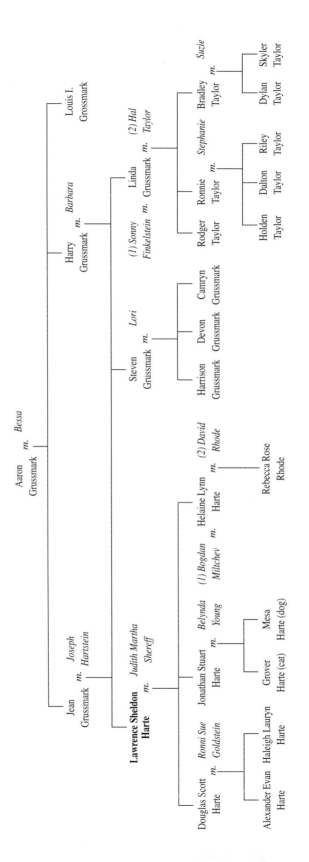

DESCENDANTS OF DAVID HARTSTEIN

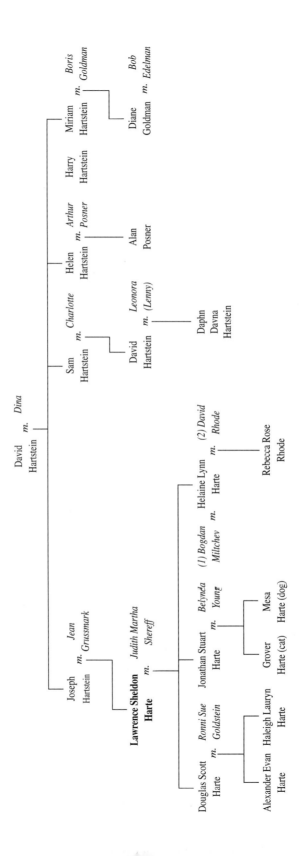

DESCENDANTS OF SAM SIGMUND KLEIN

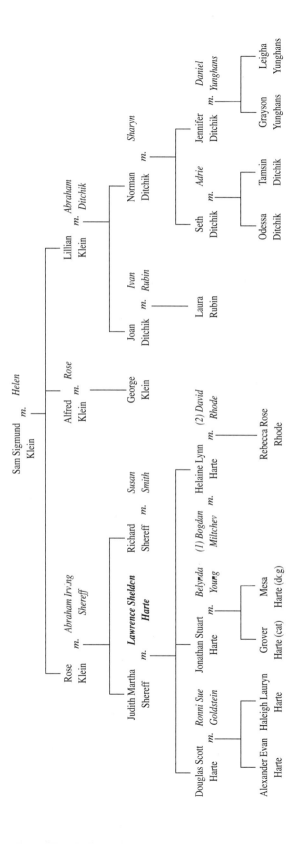

DESCENDANTS OF SOLOMAN SHERESHEVSKY

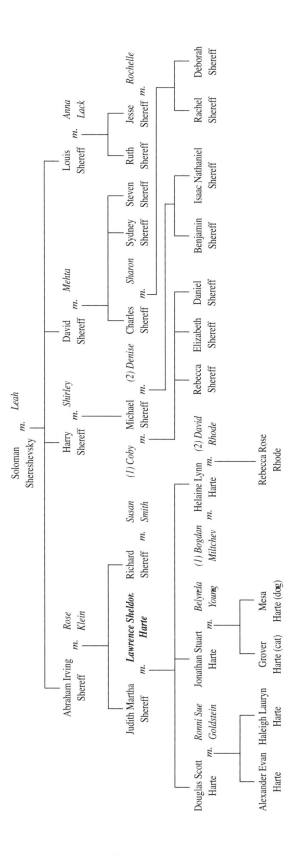